Lecture Notes in Computer Science 11408

Commenced Publication in 1973
Founding and Former Series Editors:
Gerhard Goos, Juris Hartmanis, and Jan van Leeuwen

More information about this series at http://www.springer.com/series/7407

Fred Mesnard · Peter J. Stuckey (Eds.)

Logic-Based Program Synthesis and Transformation

28th International Symposium, LOPSTR 2018
Frankfurt/Main, Germany, September 4–6, 2018
Revised Selected Papers

Springer

Editors
Fred Mesnard
University of Reunion Island
Sainte-Clotilde, France

Peter J. Stuckey
Monash University
Melbourne, VIC, Australia

ISSN 0302-9743 ISSN 1611-3349 (electronic)
Lecture Notes in Computer Science
ISBN 978-3-030-13837-0 ISBN 978-3-030-13838-7 (eBook)
https://doi.org/10.1007/978-3-030-13838-7

Library of Congress Control Number: 2019932012

LNCS Sublibrary: SL1 – Theoretical Computer Science and General Issues

This Springer imprint is published by the registered company Springer Nature Switzerland AG
The registered company address is: Gewerbestrasse 11, 6330 Cham, Switzerland

Preface

This volume contains a selection of the papers presented at LOPSTR 2018, the 28th International Symposium on Logic-Based Program Synthesis and Transformation held during September 4–6, 2018 at the the Goethe University Frankfurt am Main, Germany. It was co-located with PPDP 2018, the 20th International ACM SIGPLAN Symposium on Principles and Practice of Declarative Programming, and WFLP 2018, the 26th International Workshop on Functional and Logic Programming. The co-location of these related conferences has occurred several times and has been stimulating and cross-fertilizing.

Previous LOPSTR symposia were held in Namur (2017), Edinburgh (2016), Siena (2015), Canterbury (2014), Madrid (2013 and 2002), Leuven (2012 and 1997), Odense (2011), Hagenberg (2010), Coimbra (2009), Valencia (2008), Lyngby (2007), Venice (2006 and 1999), London (2005 and 2000), Verona (2004), Uppsala (2003), Paphos (2001), Manchester (1998, 1992, and 1991), Stockholm (1996), Arnhem (1995), Pisa (1994), and Louvain-la-Neuve (1993). More information about the symposium can be found at: http://ppdp-lopstr-18.cs.uni-frankfurt.de/lopstr18.html.

The aim of the LOPSTR series is to stimulate and promote international research and collaboration on logic-based program development. LOPSTR is open to contributions on all aspects of logic-based program development, all stages of the software life cycle, and issues of both programming-in-the-small and programming-in-the-large. LOPSTR traditionally solicits contributions, in any language paradigm, in the areas of synthesis, specification, transformation, analysis and verification, specialization, testing and certification, composition, program/model manipulation, optimization, transformational techniques in software engineering, inversion, applications, and tools. LOPSTR has a reputation for being a lively, friendly forum that allows for the presentation and discussion of both finished work and work in progress. Formal proceedings are produced only after the symposium so that authors can incorporate the feedback from the conference presentation and discussion.

In response to the calls for papers, 29 contributions were submitted from ten countries. The Program Committee accepted seven full papers for immediate inclusion in the formal proceedings, and four more papers presented at the symposium were accepted after a revision and another round of reviewing. Each submission was reviewed by at least three Program Committee members or external referees. The paper "Proving Program Properties as First-Order Satisfiability" by Salvador Lucas won the best paper award, sponsored by Springer. In addition to the 11 contributed papers, this volume includes the abstracts of the invited talks by three outstanding speakers: Philippa Gardner (Imperial College London, UK) and Jorge A. Navas (SRI International, USA), whose talks were shared with PPDP, and Laure Gonnord (University of Lyon 1, France), whose talk was shared with WFLP. We also had two invited tutorials: Fabio Fioravanti (University of Chieti-Pescara, Italy) presented "The VeriMAP System for Program Transformation and Verification" and Manuel Hermenegildo (IMDEA Software Institute and Technical University of Madrid, Spain) summarized "25 Years of Ciao."

We want to thank the Program Committee members, who worked diligently to produce high-quality reviews for the submitted papers, as well as all the external reviewers involved in the paper selection. We are very grateful to the local organizer, David Sabel, and his team for the great job they did in managing the symposium. Many thanks also to Peter Thiemann, the Program Committee chair of PPDP, and Josep Silva, the Program Committee chair of WFLP, with whom we interacted for coordinating the events. We would also like to thank Andrei Voronkov for his excellent EasyChair system that automates many of the tasks involved in chairing a conference.

Special thanks go to the invited speakers and to all the authors who submitted and presented their papers at LOPSTR 2018. We also thank our sponsors, the Goethe University Frankfurt am Main, the Deutsche Forschungsgemeinschaft (DFG, German Research Foundation), and Springer for their cooperation and support in the organization of the symposium.

January 2019

Fred Mesnard
Peter J. Stuckey

Organization

Program Committee

Elvira Albert	Universidad Complutense de Madrid, Spain
Sandrine Blazy	University of Rennes 1 - IRISA, France
Mats Carlsson	SICS, Sweden
Agostino Dovier	Università degli Studi di Udine, Italy
Wlodek Drabent	IPI PAN Warszawa, Poland
Gregory Duck	National University of Singapore, Singapore
Maurizio Gabbrielli	University of Bologna, Italy
Juergen Giesl	RWTH Aachen University, Germany
Michael Hanus	CAU Kiel, Germany
Salvador Lucas	Universitat Politècnica de València, Spain
Fred Mesnard	Université de La Réunion, France
Etienne Payet	Université de La Réunion, France
Alberto Pettorossi	Università di Roma Tor Vergata, Italy
Vitor Santos Costa	University of Porto, Portugal
Tom Schrijvers	Katholieke Universiteit Leuven, Belgium
Julien Signoles	CEA LIST, France
Harald Sondergaard	The University of Melbourne, Australia
Fausto Spoto	University of Verona, Italy
Peter Stuckey	The University of Melbourne, Australia
Markus Triska	Vienna University of Technology, Austria
Wim Vanhoof	University of Namur, Belgium
German Vidal	Universitat Politècnica de València, Spain

Additional Reviewers

Gomez-Zamalloa, Miguel
Gordillo, Pablo
Maurica, Fonenantsoa
Schubert, Aleksy
Villanueva, Alicia
Yamada, Akihisa
Yoshimizu, Akira

Abstracts of Invited Talks

Formal Methods for JavaScript

Philippa Gardner

Imperial College London, UK
pg@doc.ic.ac.uk

Abstract. We present a novel, unified approach to the development of compositional symbolic execution tools, which bridges the gap between traditional symbolic execution and compositional program reasoning based on separation logic. We apply our approach to JavaScript, providing support for full verification, whole-program symbolic testing, and automatic compositional testing based on bi-abduction.

Constrained Horn Clauses for Verification

Jorge Navas

SRI International, USA
Jorge.Navas@sri.com

Abstract. Developing scalable software verification tools is a very difficult task. First, due to the undecidability of the verification problem, these tools, must be highly tuned and engineered to provide reasonable efficiency and precision trade-offs. Second, different programming languages come with very diverse assortments of syntactic and semantic features. Third, the diverse encoding of the verification problem makes the integration with other powerful solvers and verifiers difficult. This talk presents SeaHorn – an open source automated Constrained Horn clause-based reasoning framework. SeaHorn combines advanced automated solving techniques based on Satisfiability Modulo Theory (SMT) and Abstract Interpretation. SeaHorn is built on top of LLVM using its front-end(s) to deal with the idiosyncrasies of the syntax and it highly benefits from LLVM optimizations to reduce the verification effort. SeaHorn uses Constrained Horn clauses (CHC) which are a uniform way to formally represent a broad variety of transition systems while allowing many encoding styles of verification conditions. Moreover, the recent popularity of CHC as an intermediate language for verification engines makes it possible to interface SeaHorn with a variety of new and emerging tools. All of these features make SeaHorn a versatile and highly customizable tool which allows researchers to easily build or experiment with new verification techniques.

Experiences in Designing Scalable Static Analyses

Laure Gonnord

University of Lyon 1, France
Laure.Gonnord@univ-lyon1.fr

Abstract. Proving the absence of bugs in a given software (problem which has been known to be intrinsically hard since Turing and Cook) is not the only challenge in software development. Indeed, the ever growing complexity of software increases the need for more trustable optimisations. Solving these two problems (reliability, optimisation) implies the development of safe (without false negative answers) and efficient (wrt memory and time) analyses, yet precise enough (with few false positive answers). In this talk I will present some experiences in the design of scalable static analyses inside compilers, and try to make a synthesis about the general framework we, together with my coauthors, used to develop them. I will also show some experimental evidence of the impact of this work on real-world compilers, as well as future perspective for this area of research.

Abstracts of Invited Tutorials

The VeriMAP System for Program Transformation and Verification

Fabio Fioravanti

University of Chieti-Pescara, Italy
fioravanti@unich.it

Abstract. Constrained Horn Clauses (CHC) are becoming very popular for representing programs and verification problems, and several tools have been developed for checking their satisfiability. In this tutorial we will survey recent work on satisfiability-preserving transformation techniques for CHC and we will show how the VeriMAP system can be used effectively to (i) generate CHC verification conditions from the programming language semantics, (ii) prove safety properties of imperative programs manipulating integers and arrays, (iii) prove relational program properties, such as program equivalence and non-interference, (iv) check the satisfiability of CHC with inductively-defined data structures (e.g. lists and trees), (v) prove safety and controllability properties of time-aware business processes.

25 Years of Ciao

Manuel Hermenegildo

IMDEA Software Institute and Technical University of Madrid, Spain
herme@fi.upm.es

Abstract. Ciao is a logic-based, multi-paradigm programming language which has pioneered over the years many interesting language- and programming environment-related concepts. An example is the notion of programming languages as modular language-building tools rather than closed designs. Another is the idea of dynamic languages that can optionally and gradually offer formal guarantees, which is also a solution for the classic dichotomy between dynamic and static typing: Ciao has many dynamic features (e.g., dynamically typed, dynamic program modification) but includes an assertion language for (optionally) declaring program properties and powerful tools for static inference and static/dynamic checking of such assertions, testing, documentation, etc. We will provide a hands-on overview of these features, concentrating on the novel aspects, the motivations behind their design and implementation, their evolution over time, and, specially, their use. In particular, we will show how the system can be used not only as a programming tool and as a language design tool, but also as a general-purpose program analysis and verification tool, based on the technique of translating program semantics (ranging from source to bytecode, LLVM, or assembly) into Horn-clause representation, and idea which Ciao also introduced early on. Finally, we will present some recent work in areas such as scalability, incrementality, or static vs. dynamic costs, as well as some future plans and ideas.

Contents

Analysis of Term Rewriting

Proving Program Properties as First-Order Satisfiability

Salvador Lucas(✉)

DSIC, Universitat Politècnica de València, Valencia, Spain
slucas@dsic.upv.es
http://slucas.webs.upv.es/

Abstract. Program semantics can often be expressed as a (many-sorted) first-order theory $\mathcal{S}$, and program properties as sentences φ which are intended to hold in the *canonical model* of such a theory, which is often incomputable. Recently, we have shown that properties φ expressed as the existential closure of a boolean combination of atoms can be *disproved* by just finding a model of $\mathcal{S}$ and the *negation* $\neg\varphi$ of φ. Furthermore, this idea works quite well in practice due to the existence of powerful tools for the automatic generation of models for (many-sorted) first-order theories. In this paper we extend our previous results to *arbitrary* properties, expressed as sentences without any special restriction. Consequently, one can prove a program property φ by just *finding a model* of an appropriate theory (including $\mathcal{S}$ and possibly something else) and an appropriate first-order formula related to φ. Beyond its possible theoretical interest, we show that our results can also be of practical use in several respects.

Keywords: First-order logic · Logical models · Program analysis

1 Introduction

Given a first-order theory $\mathcal{S}$ and a sentence φ, finding a model $\mathcal{A}$ of $\mathcal{S}\cup\{\neg\varphi\}$, i.e., such that $\mathcal{A}\models\mathcal{S}\cup\{\neg\varphi\}$ holds, shows indeed that φ is *not* a logical consequence of $\mathcal{S}$: there is at least one model of $\mathcal{S}$ (e.g., $\mathcal{A}$) which does not satisfy φ (as it satisfies $\neg\varphi$). Provability of φ in $\mathcal{S}$, i.e., $\mathcal{S}\vdash\varphi$, implies (by correctness of the proof calculus) that φ is a logical consequence of $\mathcal{S}$ (written $\mathcal{S}\models\varphi$). Thus, $\mathcal{A}\models\mathcal{S}\cup\{\neg\varphi\}$ *disproves* φ regarding $\mathcal{S}$; this can be written $\neg(\mathcal{S}\vdash\varphi)$ by using some metalevel notation. In general, this does not allow us to conclude that $\neg\varphi$ is proved, i.e., $\mathcal{S}\vdash\neg\varphi$, or is a logical consequence of $\mathcal{S}$, i.e., $\mathcal{S}\models\neg\varphi$. What can be concluded about $\neg\varphi$ regarding $\mathcal{S}$ from the fact that $\mathcal{A}\models\mathcal{S}\cup\{\neg\varphi\}$ holds? Can this be advantageously used in a 'logic-based' approach to program analysis?

In [14], some answers to these questions are given: a sentence φ which is an *Existentially Closed Boolean Combination of Atoms* (ECBCA for short) does *not*

Partially supported by the EU (FEDER), projects TIN2015-69175-C4-1-R, and GV PROMETEOII/2015/013.

F. Mesnard and P. J. Stuckey (Eds.): LOPSTR 2018, LNCS 11408, pp. 3–21, 2019.
https://doi.org/10.1007/978-3-030-13838-7_1

hold in the initial model $\mathcal{I}_{\mathcal{S}}$ of a theory $\mathcal{S}$ consisting of a set of ground atoms if we find a model $\mathcal{A}$ of $\mathcal{S} \cup \{\neg\varphi\}$ [14, Corollary 2]. This is useful in program analysis when considering programs P that are given a theory $\overline{P}$ representing its operational semantics so that the execution of P is described as a set $\mathcal{I}_P$ of (ground) atoms A which can be proved from $\overline{P}$ (i.e., $\mathcal{I}_P$ is the *initial* model of $\overline{P}$ in the usual first-order sense; in the following, we often refer to it as its *canonical* model [11, Sect. 1.5]). Actually, rather than being logical consequences of $\overline{P}$, the intended meaning of first-order sentences φ that represent properties of P is that they hold in the *initial model* of $\overline{P}$, see [4, Chap. 4], for instance.

In [14,16] we applied this approach to prove computational properties of rewriting-based systems in practice. This includes Term Rewriting Systems (TRSs [1]) and more general rewriting-based formalisms [3,9,18,19].

Example 1. Consider the following TRS $\mathcal{R}$ with the well-known rules defining the addition and product of natural numbers in Peano's notation:

$$\mathsf{add}(\mathsf{0}, x) \to x \tag{1}$$
$$\mathsf{add}(\mathsf{s}(x), y) \to \mathsf{s}(\mathsf{add}(x, y)) \tag{2}$$

$$\mathsf{mul}(\mathsf{0}, x) \to \mathsf{0} \tag{3}$$
$$\mathsf{mul}(\mathsf{s}(x), y) \to \mathsf{add}(y, \mathsf{mul}(x, y)) \tag{4}$$

The associated theory $\overline{\mathcal{R}}$ is the following:

$$\begin{array}{rcl}
(\forall x)\; x \to^* x & & \\
(\forall x, y, z)\; x \to y \wedge y \to^* z \Rightarrow x \to^* z & & \\
(\forall x, y)\; x \to y \Rightarrow \mathsf{s}(x) & \to & \mathsf{s}(y) \\
(\forall x, y, z)\; x \to y \Rightarrow \mathsf{add}(x, z) & \to & \mathsf{add}(y, z) \\
(\forall x, y, z)\; x \to y \Rightarrow \mathsf{add}(z, x) & \to & \mathsf{add}(z, y) \\
(\forall x, y, z)\; x \to y \Rightarrow \mathsf{mul}(x, z) & \to & \mathsf{mul}(y, z) \\
(\forall x, y, z)\; x \to y \Rightarrow \mathsf{mul}(z, x) & \to & \mathsf{mul}(z, y)
\end{array}$$

$$\begin{array}{r}
(\forall x)\; \mathsf{add}(\mathsf{0}, x) \to x \\
(\forall x, y)\; \mathsf{add}(\mathsf{s}(x), y) \to \mathsf{s}(\mathsf{add}(x, y)) \\
(\forall x)\; \mathsf{mul}(\mathsf{0}, x) \to \mathsf{0} \\
(\forall x, y)\; \mathsf{mul}(\mathsf{s}(x), y) \to \mathsf{add}(y, \mathsf{mul}(x, y))
\end{array}$$

The first sentence in the first column represents *reflexivity* of many-step rewriting, with predicate symbol $\to^*$; the second sentence shows how one-step rewriting, with predicate symbol $\to$, contributes to $\to^*$. The next sentences describe the *propagation* of rewriting steps to (arguments of) symbols s, add and mul. The second column describes the rules of $\mathcal{R}$. More details can be found in [14, Sect. 4]. In the initial or *least Herbrand model* $\mathcal{I}_{\mathcal{R}}$ of $\overline{\mathcal{R}}$, $\to$ and $\to^*$ are interpreted as the sets $(\to)^{\mathcal{I}_{\mathcal{R}}}$ and $(\to^*)^{\mathcal{I}_{\mathcal{R}}}$ of all pairs (s, t) of ground terms s and t such that $s \to_{\mathcal{R}} t$ and $s \to^*_{\mathcal{R}} t$, respectively. Now, we can express the property "*the double of some natural number can be an odd number*" as an ECBCA:

$$(\exists x)(\exists y)(\exists z)\; \mathsf{add}(x, x) \to^* z \wedge \mathsf{s}(\mathsf{mul}(\mathsf{s}(\mathsf{s}(\mathsf{0})), y)) \to^* z \tag{5}$$

With the automatic model generator Mace4 [17] we find a model of $\overline{\mathcal{R}} \cup \{\neg(5)\}$ with domain $\mathcal{A} = \{0, 1\}$. Function symbols are interpreted as follows: $\mathsf{0}^{\mathcal{A}} = 0$;

$\mathsf{s}^{\mathcal{A}}(x) = 1 - x$; $\mathsf{add}^{\mathcal{A}}(x, y)$ returns 0 if $x = y$ and 1 otherwise; $\mathsf{mul}^{\mathcal{A}}(x, y)$ returns 1 if $x = y = 1$ and 0 otherwise. Predicates $\rightarrow$ and $\rightarrow^*$ are both interpreted as the Aphequality. Thus, we have *proved* that (5) does *not* hold for $\mathcal{R}$.

Our approach in [14] relies on the notion of *preservation* of a formula under homomorphisms h between interpretations. Roughly speaking, a homomorphism h *preserves* a formula φ if φ is satisfied in the target interpretation of h whenever φ is satisfied in its domain interpretation [11, Sect. 2.4]. Homomorphisms preserve ECBCA [11, Theorem 2.4.3(a)]; the results in [14] rely on this fact. In this paper we *extend* [14] to deal with more general program properties. Homomorphisms preserve other first-order sentences if further requirements are imposed: (i) *positive* sentences (where connective '$\neg$' is absent) are preserved under *surjective* homomorphisms and (ii) *arbitrary* sentences are preserved under *embeddings* [11, Theorem 2.4.3]. In contrast to [14] (and [11]), here we focus on *many-sorted logic* [23] (see Sect. 2). This has an important advantage: since homomorphisms in many-sorted logic with set of sorts S are actually a *family* h_s of homomorphisms between components of sort s for each $s \in S$, the preservation requirements for h_s depend on the *specific quantification* of variables $x : s$ *for such a sort.* In Sect. 3 we provide a *unique* preservation theorem that subsumes the results in [14], and even improves [11]. Section 4 investigates how to guarantee surjectivity of homomorphisms. Section 5 shows several application examples taken from Table 1, which shows some properties of rewriting-based systems that could not be captured in [14] but we are able to handle now. Here, $t(\boldsymbol{x})$ is a term with variables $\boldsymbol{x}$ (or just t if it is *ground*), $\mathcal{C}$ (and $\mathcal{D}$) are the *constructor* (resp. *defined*) symbols in the TRS, and $\stackrel{\Lambda}{\rightarrow}$ is *topmost rewriting.* Section 6 discusses the possibility of providing more information about *disproved* properties by means of *refutation witnesses*, i.e., (counter)examples of *sentences* which are synthesized from the models that are used to disprove the property. Section 7 shows how to deal with completely general sentences by means of a simple example. Section 8 discusses some related work. Section 9 concludes.

Table 1. Some properties about rewriting-based systems

Property	φ
Ground *red*ucible	$(\forall \boldsymbol{x})\ (\exists y)\ t(\boldsymbol{x}) \rightarrow y$
*Comp*letely defined symbol f	$(\forall \boldsymbol{x})(\exists y)\ f(x_1, \ldots, x_k) \rightarrow y$
*Comp*letely defined TRS	$(\forall \boldsymbol{x})(\exists \boldsymbol{y}) \bigwedge_{f \in \mathcal{D}}\ f(x_1, \ldots, x_{ar(f)}) \rightarrow y_f$
*Prod*uctive	$(\forall x)(\exists \boldsymbol{y})\ \bigvee_{c \in \mathcal{C}} x \rightarrow^* c(y_1, \ldots, y_k)$
*Nont*erminating	$(\exists x)(\forall n \in \mathbb{N})(\exists y)\ x \rightarrow^n y$
*Inf*initely root-reducible	$(\exists x)(\forall n \in \mathbb{N})(\exists y)\ x(\rightarrow^* \circ \stackrel{\Lambda}{\rightarrow})^n y$
*Norm*alizing term	$(\exists x)\ (t \rightarrow^* x \wedge \neg(\exists y)\ x \rightarrow y)$
*Norm*alizing TRS (WN)	$(\forall x)(\exists y)\ (x \rightarrow^* y \wedge \neg(\exists z)\ y \rightarrow z)$
Locally confluent (WCR)	$(\forall x, y, z)\ x \rightarrow y \wedge x \rightarrow z \Rightarrow (\exists u)\ x \rightarrow^* u \wedge z \rightarrow^* u$
*Conf*luent (CR)	$(\forall x, y, z)\ x \rightarrow^* y \wedge x \rightarrow^* z \Rightarrow (\exists u)\ x \rightarrow^* u \wedge z \rightarrow^* u$

2 Many-Sorted First-Order Logic

Given a set of *sorts* S, a *(many-sorted) signature (with predicates)* $\Omega = (S, \Sigma, \Pi)$ consists of a set of sorts S, an $S^* \times S$-indexed family of sets $\Sigma = \{\Sigma_{w,s}\}_{(w,s)\in S^*\times S}$ containing *function symbols* $f \in \Sigma_{s_1\cdots s_k,s}$, with a rank declaration $f : s_1 \cdots s_k \to s$ (constant symbols c have rank declaration $c : \lambda \to s$, where λ denotes the *empty* sequence), and an S^+-indexed family of sets $\Pi = \{\Pi_w\}_{w\in S^+}$ of ranked predicates $P : w$. Given an S-sorted set $\mathcal{X} = \{\mathcal{X}_s \mid s \in S\}$ of *mutually disjoint* sets of variables (which are also disjoint from Σ), the set $\mathcal{T}_\Sigma(\mathcal{X})_s$ of terms of sort s is the least set such that $\mathcal{X}_s \subseteq \mathcal{T}_\Sigma(\mathcal{X})_s$ and for each $f : s_1 \dots s_k \to s$ and $t_i \in \mathcal{T}_\Sigma(\mathcal{X})_{s_i}$, $1 \le i \le k$, $f(t_1, \dots, t_k) \in \mathcal{T}_\Sigma(\mathcal{X})_s$. If $\mathcal{X} = \emptyset$, we write $\mathcal{T}_\Sigma$ rather than $\mathcal{T}_\Sigma(\emptyset)$ for the set of *ground* terms. The set $\mathcal{T}_\Sigma(\mathcal{X})$ of *many-sorted terms* is $\mathcal{T}_\Sigma(\mathcal{X}) = \bigcup_{s\in S} \mathcal{T}_\Sigma(\mathcal{X})_s$. For $w = s_1 \cdots s_n \in S^+$, we write $\mathcal{T}_\Sigma(\mathcal{X})_w$ rather than $\mathcal{T}_\Sigma(\mathcal{X})_{s_1} \times \cdots \times \mathcal{T}_\Sigma(\mathcal{X})_{s_n}$ and even write $\boldsymbol{t} \in \mathcal{T}_\Sigma(\mathcal{X})_w$ rather than $t_i \in \mathcal{T}_\Sigma(\mathcal{X})_{s_i}$ for each $1 \le i \le n$. The formulas $\varphi \in Form_\Omega$ of a signature Ω are built up from atoms $P(\boldsymbol{t})$ with $P \in \Pi_w$ and $\boldsymbol{t} \in \mathcal{T}_\Sigma(\mathcal{X})_w$, logic connectives ($\neg$, $\wedge$, and also $\vee$, $\Rightarrow$,...) and quantifiers ($\forall$ and $\exists$) in the usual way. A closed formula, i.e., one whose variables are all universally or existentially quantified, is called a *sentence*. In the following, substitutions σ are assumed to be S-sorted mappings such that for all sorts $s \in S$, we have $\sigma(x) \in \mathcal{T}_\Sigma(\mathcal{X})_s$.

An *Ω-structure* $\mathcal{A}$ consists of (i) a family $\{\mathcal{A}_s \mid s \in S\}$ of sets called the *carriers* or *domains* together with (ii) a function $f^{\mathcal{A}}_{w,s} \in \mathcal{A}_w \to \mathcal{A}_s$ for each $f \in \Sigma_{w,s}$ ($\mathcal{A}_w$ is a one point set when $w = \lambda$ and hence $\mathcal{A}_w \to \mathcal{A}_s$ is isomorphic to $\mathcal{A}_s$), and (iii) an assignment to each $P \in \Pi_w$ of a subset $P^{\mathcal{A}}_w \subseteq \mathcal{A}_w$; if the identity predicate $\_ = \_ : ss$ is in Π_{ss}, then $(=)^{\mathcal{A}}_{s\,s} = \{(a, a) \mid a \in \mathcal{A}_s\}$, i.e., $\_ = \_ : ss$ is interpreted as the identity on $\mathcal{A}_s$.

Let $\mathcal{A}$ and $\mathcal{A}'$ be Ω-structures. An *Ω-homomorphism* $h : \mathcal{A} \to \mathcal{A}'$ is an S-sorted function $h = \{h_s : \mathcal{A}_s \to \mathcal{A}'_s \mid s \in S\}$ such that for each $f \in \Sigma_{w,s}$ and $P \in \Pi_w$ with $w = s_1, \dots, s_k$, (i) $h_s(f^{\mathcal{A}}_{w,s}(a_1, \dots, a_k)) = f^{\mathcal{A}'}_{w,s}(h_{s_1}(a_1), \dots, h_{s_k}(a_k))$ and (ii) if $\boldsymbol{a} \in P^{\mathcal{A}}_w$, then $h(\boldsymbol{a}) \in P^{\mathcal{A}'}_w$. Given an S-sorted *valuation mapping* $\alpha : \mathcal{X} \to \mathcal{A}$, the evaluation mapping $[\_]^\alpha_{\mathcal{A}} : \mathcal{T}_\Sigma(\mathcal{X}) \to \mathcal{A}$ is the unique (S, Σ)-homomorphism extending α. Finally, $[\_]^\alpha_{\mathcal{A}} : Form_\Omega \to Bool$ is given by:

1. $[P(t_1, \dots, t_n)]^\alpha_{\mathcal{A}} = true$ (with $P \in \Pi_w$) if and only if $([t_1]^\alpha_{\mathcal{A}}, \dots, [t_n]^\alpha_{\mathcal{A}}) \in P^{\mathcal{A}}_w$;
2. $[\neg\varphi]^\alpha_{\mathcal{A}} = true$ if and only if $[\varphi]^\alpha_{\mathcal{A}} = false$;
3. $[\varphi \wedge \psi]^\alpha_{\mathcal{A}} = true$ if and only if $[\varphi]^\alpha_{\mathcal{A}} = true$ and $[\psi]^\alpha_{\mathcal{A}} = true$; and
4. $[(\forall x : s)\, \varphi]^\alpha_{\mathcal{A}} = true$ if and only if for all $a \in \mathcal{A}_s$, $[\varphi]^{\alpha[x\mapsto a]}_{\mathcal{A}} = true$.

A valuation $\alpha \in \mathcal{X} \to \mathcal{A}$ *satisfies* φ in $\mathcal{A}$ (written $\mathcal{A} \models \varphi\,[\alpha]$) if $[\varphi]^\alpha_{\mathcal{A}} = true$. We then say that φ is *satisfiable*. If $\mathcal{A} \models \varphi\,[\alpha]$ for *all* valuations α, we write $\mathcal{A} \models \varphi$ and say that $\mathcal{A}$ is a *model* of φ or that φ is *true* in $\mathcal{A}$. We say that $\mathcal{A}$ is *a model of a set of sentences* $\mathcal{S} \subseteq Form_\Omega$ (written $\mathcal{A} \models \mathcal{S}$) if for all $\varphi \in \mathcal{S}$, $\mathcal{A} \models \varphi$. Given a sentence φ, we write $\mathcal{S} \models \varphi$ iff $\mathcal{A} \models \varphi$ holds for *all models* $\mathcal{A}$ of $\mathcal{S}$.

3 Preservation of Many-Sorted First-Order Sentences

Every set $\mathcal{S}$ of ground atoms has an *initial model* $\mathcal{I}_{\mathcal{S}}$ (or just $\mathcal{I}$ if no confusion arises) which consists of the usual (many-sorted) *Herbrand Domain* of ground terms modulo the equivalence $\sim$ generated by the equations in $\mathcal{S}$. There is a unique homomorphism $h : \mathcal{I} \to \mathcal{A}$ from $\mathcal{I}$ to any model $\mathcal{A}$ of $\mathcal{S}$ [9, Sect. 3.2]. In the following, h refers to such a homomorphism. If $\mathcal{S}$ contains no equation, then $\mathcal{I}$ is the (many-sorted) *Least Herbrand Model* of $\mathcal{S}$ and $\mathcal{I}_s$ is $\mathcal{T}_{\Sigma s}$ for each sort $s \in S$. In the following, we consider sentences in *prenex* form as follows:

$$(Q_1 x_1 : s_1) \cdots (Q_k x_k : s_k) \bigvee_{i=1}^{m} \bigwedge_{j=1}^{n_i} L_{ij} \tag{6}$$

where (i) for all $1 \le i \le m$ and $1 \le j \le n_i$, L_{ij} are *literals*, i.e., $L_{ij} = A_{ij}$ or $L_{ij} = \neg A_{ij}$ for some atom A_{ij} (in the first case, we say that L_{ij} is *positive*; otherwise, it is *negative*), (ii) $x_1, \ldots, x_k$ for some $k \ge 0$ are the variables occurring in those literals (of sorts $s_1, \ldots, s_k$, respectively), and (iii) $Q_1, \ldots, Q_k$ are universal/existential quantifiers. A sentence φ (equivalent to) (6) is said to be *positive* if all literals are.

Theorem 1. *Let Ω be a signature, $\mathcal{S}$ be a set of ground atoms, φ be a sentence (6), and $\mathcal{A}$ be a model of $\mathcal{S}$ such that (a) for all q, $1 \le q \le k$, if $Q_q = \forall$ then h_{s_q} is surjective*[1] *and (b) for all negative literals $L_{ij} = \neg P(\boldsymbol{t})$, with $P \in \Pi_w$, and substitutions σ, if $h(\sigma(\boldsymbol{t})) \in P^{\mathcal{A}}$ then $\sigma(\boldsymbol{t}) \in P^{\mathcal{I}}$. Then, $\mathcal{I}_{\mathcal{S}} \models \varphi \Longrightarrow \mathcal{A} \models \varphi$.*

In order to achieve condition (*b*) in Theorem 1, given $P \in \Pi_w$, let $N(P) = \mathcal{I}_w - P^{\mathcal{I}}$ be the complement of the (Herbrand) interpretation of P. Let $\mathcal{N}(P) = \{\neg P(\boldsymbol{t}) \mid \boldsymbol{t} \in N(P)\}$ (cf. Reiter's *Closed World Assumption* [20]). In general, $\mathcal{N}(P)$ is infinite and incomputable. In some simple cases, though, we can provide a *finite description* of $\mathcal{N}(P)$ for the required predicates P (see Sect. 7).

Proposition 1. *Let Ω be a signature, $\mathcal{S}$ be a set of ground atoms, φ be a sentence (6), $\mathcal{A}$ be a model of $\mathcal{S}$, and $\mathcal{N} = \bigcup_{L_{ij}=\neg P(\boldsymbol{t})} \mathcal{N}(P)$ be such that $\mathcal{A} \models \mathcal{N}$. Let $L_{ij} = \neg P(\boldsymbol{t})$ be a negative literal and σ be a substitution. If $h(\sigma(\boldsymbol{t})) \in P^{\mathcal{A}}$, then $\sigma(\boldsymbol{t}) \in P^{\mathcal{I}}$.*

Consider a theory $\mathcal{S}$ and let $\mathcal{S}^{\vdash}$ be the set of ground atoms obtained as the *deductive closure* of $\mathcal{S}$, i.e., the set of *atoms* $P(t_1, \ldots, t_n)$ for each n-ary predicate symbol P and ground terms $t_1, \ldots, t_n$, such that $\mathcal{S} \vdash P(t_1, \ldots, t_n)$. The following result is the basis of the practical applications discussed in the following sections.

Corollary 1 (Semantic criterion). *Let Ω be a signature, $\mathcal{S}_0$ be a theory, $\mathcal{S} = \mathcal{S}_0^{\vdash}$, φ be a sentence (6), and $\mathcal{A}$ be a model of $\mathcal{S}_0$ such that (a) for all q, $1 \le q \le k$, if $Q_q = \forall$ then h_{s_q} is surjective and (b) for all negative literals $L_{ij} = \neg P(\boldsymbol{t})$, with $P \in \Pi_w$ and substitutions σ, if $h(\sigma(\boldsymbol{t})) \in P^{\mathcal{A}}$ then $\sigma(\boldsymbol{t}) \in P^{\mathcal{I}}$. If $\mathcal{A} \models \neg\varphi$, then $\mathcal{I}_{\mathcal{S}} \models \neg\varphi$.*

---

[1] A mapping $f : A \to B$ is *surjective* if for all $b \in B$ there is $a \in A$ such that $f(a) = b$.

In the following, we will not distinguish between theories $\mathcal{S}$ and their ground deductive closure $\mathcal{S}^{\vdash}$; we rather use $\mathcal{S}$ in both cases.

Remark 1 (Proofs by satisfiability). We can prove an arbitrary sentence φ valid in $\mathcal{I}_{\mathcal{S}}$ by *satisfiability* in some model $\mathcal{A}$ of $\mathcal{S}$. First define $\overline{\varphi}$ as the negation $\neg\varphi$ of φ. Then, find an appropriate structure $\mathcal{A}$ satisfying (a) and (b) (with regard to $\overline{\varphi}$) and such that $\mathcal{A} \models \mathcal{S} \cup \{\neg\overline{\varphi}\}$. By Corollary 1, $\mathcal{I} \models \neg\overline{\varphi}$ holds. Since $\neg\overline{\varphi}$ is equivalent to φ, $\mathcal{I} \models \varphi$ holds.

Models $\mathcal{A}$ to be used in Corollary 1 can be automatically generated from the theory $\mathcal{S}$ and sentence φ by using a tool like AGES [10] or Mace4. In the following section, we investigate how to ensure *surjectivity* when required in Corollary 1.

4 Surjective Homomorphisms

Given $\Omega = (S, \Sigma, \Pi)$, $s \in S$ and $T \subseteq \mathcal{T}_{\Sigma s}$, consider the following sentences:

$$(\forall x : s) \bigvee_{t \in T} x = t \tag{7}$$

$$\bigwedge_{t,u \in T, t \neq u} \neg(t = u) \tag{8}$$

In the following, we write $(7)_s$ to make sort s referred in (7) explicit. We do the same in similar formulas below.

Proposition 2. *Let Ω be a signature, $\mathcal{S}$ be a theory, $\mathcal{A}$ be a model of $\mathcal{S}$, $s \in S$, and $T \subseteq \mathcal{T}_{\Sigma s}$. (a) If $T \neq \emptyset$ and $\mathcal{A} \models (7)_s$, then h_s is surjective and $|\mathcal{A}_s| \leq |T|$. (b) If $\mathcal{A}_s \neq \emptyset$ and $\mathcal{A} \models (8)$, then $|\mathcal{A}_s| \geq |T|$.*

In view of Proposition 2(a), denote $(7)_s$ as $\mathsf{SuH}_s^T(\Omega)$ (or just SuH_s^T or SuH^T if no confusion arises). Whenever T is finite, Proposition 2(a) imposes that the interpretation domain $\mathcal{A}_s$ for sort s is finite. This is appropriate for tools like Mace4 which generate structures with finite domains only. However, the *choice* of T in Proposition 2, when used together with a theory $\mathcal{S}$ imposing further requirements on symbols, can be crucial for Corollary 1 to succeed. Restricting the attention to finite domains can also be a drawback. In the following, we investigate a different approach which avoids any choice of terms T and is valid for infinite structures as well. Consider the following sentence:

$$(\forall x : s)(\exists n : \mathit{Nat})\ \mathit{term}_s(x, n) \tag{9}$$

where Nat is a new sort, to be interpreted as the set $\mathbb{N}$ of natural numbers, and $\mathit{term}_s : s\ \mathit{Nat}$ is a new predicate for each $s \in S$. The intended meaning of $(9)_s$ is that, for all $x \in \mathcal{A}_s$, there is $t \in \mathcal{T}_{\Sigma s}$ of height at most n such that $x = t^{\mathcal{A}}$. We substantiate this, for each sort $s \in S$, by means of two (families of) formulas:

$$(\forall x : s)(\forall n : Nat)\ term_s(x, 0) \Rightarrow \bigvee_{c \in \Sigma_{\lambda,s}} x = c \tag{10}$$

$$(\forall x : s)(\forall n : Nat)(\exists m : Nat)\ (n > 0 \wedge term_s(x, n)) \Rightarrow$$
$$n > m \wedge \left(term_s(x, m) \vee \bigvee_{\substack{f \in \Sigma_{w,s} \\ w \in S^+}} (\exists \boldsymbol{y} : w) \left(x = f(\boldsymbol{y}) \wedge \bigwedge_{s_i \in w} terms_{s_i}(y_i, m) \right) \right) \tag{11}$$

Thus, by $(10)_s$, values x satisfying $term_s(x, 0)$ will be represented by some constant symbol c of sort s. Similarly, by $(11)_s$, values x satisfying $term_s(x, n)$ for some $n > 0$ will be represented by some ground term s of height m for some $m < n$, or by a term $t = f(t_1, \ldots, t_k)$, where f has rank $w \to s$ for some $w \in S^+$ and $t_1, \ldots, t_k$ have height m at most.

The set $K(s)$ of *s-relevant* sorts is the least set satisfying: (i) $s \in K(s)$ and (ii) if $f \in \Sigma_{s_1 \cdots s_k, s'}$ and $s' \in K(s)$, then $\{s_1, \ldots, s_n\} \subseteq K(s)$. Let $\Omega_{Nat,s} = (S_{Nat}, \Sigma_{Nat}, \Pi_{Nat,K(s)})$ be an *extension* of Ω where $S_{Nat} = S \cup \{Nat\}$, Σ_{Nat} extends Σ with a new constant $\mathsf{0} : \lambda \to Nat$, and $\Pi_{Nat,K(s)}$ extends Π with $> : Nat\ Nat$ and a predicate $term_{s'} : s'\ Nat$ for each $s' \in K(s)$. We let

$$\mathsf{SuH}_s = \{(9)_{s'}, (10)_{s'}, (11)_{s'} \mid s' \in K(s)\} \tag{12}$$

Proposition 3. *Let Ω be a signature, $\mathcal{S}$ be a theory, $s \in S$, and $\mathcal{A}$ be an $\Omega_{Nat,s}$-structure which is a model of $\mathcal{S}$. Assume that $\mathcal{A}_{Nat} = \mathbb{N}$, $\mathsf{0}^{\mathcal{A}} = 0$, and $\mathsf{m} >^{\mathcal{A}} \mathsf{n} \Leftrightarrow \mathsf{m} >_{\mathbb{N}} \mathsf{n}$ for all $\mathsf{m}, \mathsf{n} \in \mathcal{A}_{Nat}$. If $\mathcal{A} \models \mathsf{SuH}_s$, then $h_{s'}$ is surjective for all $s' \in K(s)$.*

Given an extension Ω' of a signature Ω, every Ω'-structure $\mathcal{A}'$ defines an Ω-structure $\mathcal{A}$: just take $\mathcal{A}_s = \mathcal{A}'_s$ for all $s \in S$, and then $f^{\mathcal{A}}_{w,s} = f^{\mathcal{A}'}_{w,s}$ and $P^{\mathcal{A}}_w = P^{\mathcal{A}'}_w$ for all $w \in S^*$, $s \in S$, $f \in \Sigma_{w,s}$, and $P \in \Pi_w$. Thus, Proposition 3 is used to guarantee surjectivity of $h : \mathcal{T}_{\Sigma s'} \to \mathcal{A}_{s'}$, rather than $h : \mathcal{T}_{\Sigma_{Nat}\, s'} \to \mathcal{A}_{s'}$.

5 Examples of Application with Positive Sentences

In this section we exemplify the use of Corollary 1 together with the approach in Sect. 4 to deal with *positive* sentences (6), i.e., all literals are positive.

5.1 Complete Definedness and Commutativity

Consider the following Maude specification (hopefully self-explained, but see [5]) for the arithmetic operations in Example 1 together with function head, which returns the head of a list of natural numbers:

```
mod ExAddMulHead is
  sorts N LN . *** Sorts for numbers and lists of numbers
  op Z : -> N .          op suc : N -> N .  ops add mul : N N -> N .
  op head : LN -> N .  op nil : -> LN .    op cons : N LN -> LN .
  vars x y : N .         var xs : LN .
  rl add(Z,x) => x .     rl add(suc(x),y) => suc(add(x,y)) .
  rl mul(Z,x) => Z .     rl mul(suc(x),y) => add(y,mul(x,y)) .
  rl head(cons(x,xs)) => x .
endm
```

(1) *Complete definedness.* We claim head to be completely defined as follows:

$$(\forall xs : \mathtt{LN})(\exists x : \mathtt{N})\ \mathtt{head}(xs) \to x \tag{13}$$

We *disprove* (13) by using Corollary 1. Due to the universal quantification of xs in (13), we need to ensure that $h_{\mathtt{LN}} : \mathcal{T}_{\Sigma\mathtt{LN}} \to \mathcal{A}_{\mathtt{LN}}$ is surjective for any structure $\mathcal{A}$ we may use. We use Proposition 3. Since $K(\mathtt{LN}) = \{\mathtt{N}, \mathtt{LN}\}$ due to cons, whose first argument is of sort N, $\mathsf{SuH}_{\mathtt{LN}}$ consists of the following sentences:

$$\begin{array}{lr}
(\forall x : \mathtt{N})(\exists n : Nat)\ term_{\mathtt{N}}(x, n) & (9)_{\mathtt{N}}\\
(\forall x : \mathtt{N})\ term_{\mathtt{N}}(x, 0) \Rightarrow x = \mathtt{Z} & (10)_{\mathtt{N}}\\
(\forall x : \mathtt{N})(\forall n : Nat)(\exists m : Nat)(\exists y : \mathtt{N})(\exists z : \mathtt{N})(\exists ys : \mathtt{LN}) & (11)_{\mathtt{N}}\\
\quad n > 0 \wedge term_{\mathtt{N}}(x, n) \Rightarrow n > m \wedge [term_{\mathtt{N}}(x, m) \vee & \\
\quad\quad (term_{\mathtt{N}}(y, m) \wedge term_{\mathtt{N}}(z, m) \wedge term_{\mathtt{LN}}(ys, m) \wedge & \\
\quad\quad\quad (x = \mathtt{suc}(y) \vee x = \mathtt{add}(y, z) \vee x = \mathtt{mul}(y, z) \vee x = \mathtt{head}(ys)))] & \\
(\forall xs : \mathtt{LN})(\exists n : Nat)\ term_{\mathtt{LN}}(xs, n) & (9)_{\mathtt{LN}}\\
(\forall xs : \mathtt{LN})\ term_{\mathtt{LN}}(xs, 0) \Rightarrow xs = \mathtt{nil} & (10)_{\mathtt{LN}}\\
(\forall xs : \mathtt{LN})(\forall n : Nat)(\exists m : Nat)(\exists y : \mathtt{N})(\exists ys : \mathtt{LN}) & (11)_{\mathtt{LN}}\\
\quad\quad n > 0 \wedge term_{\mathtt{N}}(x, n) \Rightarrow n > m \wedge [term_{\mathtt{N}}(x, m) \vee & \\
\quad\quad\quad (term_{\mathtt{N}}(y, m) \wedge term_{\mathtt{LN}}(ys, m) \wedge xs = \mathtt{cons}(y, ys))] &
\end{array}$$

We obtain a model $\mathcal{A}$ of $\overline{\mathtt{ExAddMulHead}} \cup \mathsf{SuH}_{\mathtt{LN}} \cup \{\neg(13)\}$ with AGES. Sorts are interpreted as follows: $\mathcal{A}_{\mathtt{N}} = \mathcal{A}_{\mathtt{LN}} = \{-1, 0\}$ and $\mathcal{A}_{Nat} = \mathbb{N}$. For function symbols:

$$\begin{array}{cccc}
\mathtt{Z}^{\mathcal{A}} = -1 & \mathtt{nil}^{\mathcal{A}} = 0 & \mathtt{suc}^{\mathcal{A}}(x) = x & \mathtt{add}^{\mathcal{A}}(x, y) = 0\\
\mathtt{mul}^{\mathcal{A}}(x, y) = 0 & \mathtt{cons}^{\mathcal{A}}(x, xs) = -1 & \mathtt{head}^{\mathcal{A}}(xs) = -xs - 1 &
\end{array}$$

For predicates, $x \to_{\mathtt{N}}^{\mathcal{A}} y \Leftrightarrow x \geq y \wedge x \geq 0$, $x \to_{\mathtt{LN}}^{\mathcal{A}} y \Leftrightarrow x = y = -1$, and both $x(\to_{\mathtt{N}}^{*})^{\mathcal{A}} y$ and $x(\to_{\mathtt{LN}}^{*})^{\mathcal{A}} y$ are *true*. We can check surjectivity of $h_s : \mathcal{T}_{\Sigma s} \to \mathcal{A}_s$ (for $s \in \{\mathtt{N}, \mathtt{LN}\}$). For instance, we have:

$$\begin{array}{rrl}
[\mathtt{Z}]_{\mathcal{A}} = -1 & [\mathtt{add}(\mathtt{Z}, \mathtt{Z})]_{\mathcal{A}} = 0 & \text{for sort } \mathtt{N}\\
[\mathtt{cons}(\mathtt{Z}, \mathtt{nil})]_{\mathcal{A}} = -1 & [\mathtt{nil}]_{\mathcal{A}} = 0 & \text{for sort } \mathtt{LN}
\end{array}$$

(2) *Commutativity.* It is well-known that both add and mul as defined by the rules of $\mathcal{R}$ in Example 1 are *commutative* on ground terms, i.e., for all ground terms s and t, $\mathsf{add}(s,t) =_{\mathcal{R}} \mathsf{add}(t,s)$ and $\mathsf{mul}(s,t) =_{\mathcal{R}} \mathsf{mul}(t,s)$, where $=_{\mathcal{R}}$ is the equational theory induced by the rules $\ell \to r$ in $\mathcal{R}$ treated as equations $\ell = r$. Actually, by using Birkhoff's theorem and the fact that $\mathcal{R}$ is *confluent*, we can rephrase commutativity of add as *joinability* as follows:

$$(\forall x)(\forall y)(\exists z)\ \mathsf{add}(x,y) \to^* z \wedge \mathsf{add}(y,x) \to^* z \tag{14}$$

Remark 2. Proving commutativity of add and mul when defined by $\mathcal{R}$ in Example 1 by using Corollary 1 is possible (see Remark 1) but unlikely. We should first define $\overline{\varphi}$ as $\neg$(14), i.e., $\overline{\varphi}$ is

$$(\exists x)(\exists y)(\forall z)\ \neg(\mathsf{add}(x,y) \to^* z) \vee \neg(\mathsf{add}(y,x) \to^* z) \tag{15}$$

Since (15) contains two negative literals, Corollary 1 requires the use of $\mathcal{N}(\to^*)$.

Since **head** is not completely defined, **add** and **mul** are *not* commutative in **ExAddMulHead**. We prove this fact by disproving the sorted version of (14), i.e.,

$$(\forall x : \mathtt{N})(\forall y : \mathtt{N})(\exists z : \mathtt{N})\ \mathtt{add}(x,y) \to^* z \wedge \mathtt{add}(y,x) \to^* z \tag{16}$$

Due to the universal quantification of x and y in (16), we need to ensure that $h_{\mathtt{N}} : \mathcal{T}_{\Sigma\mathtt{N}} \to \mathcal{A}_{\mathtt{N}}$ is surjective. Since $K(\mathtt{N}) = \{\mathtt{N}, \mathtt{LN}\}$ due to **head**, we have $\mathsf{SuH}_{\mathtt{N}} = \mathsf{SuH}_{\mathtt{LN}}$ as above. AGES obtain a model $\mathcal{A}$ of $\overline{\mathtt{ExAddMulHead}} \cup \mathsf{SuH}_{\mathtt{N}} \cup \{\neg(16)\}$ as follows: $\mathcal{A}_{\mathtt{N}} = \{0,1\}$, $\mathcal{A}_{\mathtt{LN}} = \{-1,0\}$ and $\mathcal{A}_{Nat} = \mathbb{N}$. Also,

$$\begin{array}{llll}
\mathsf{Z}^{\mathcal{A}} = 1 & \mathsf{nil}^{\mathcal{A}} = -1 & \mathtt{suc}^{\mathcal{A}}(x) = x & \mathtt{add}^{\mathcal{A}}(x,y) = y \\
\mathtt{mul}^{\mathcal{A}}(x,y) = x & \mathtt{cons}^{\mathcal{A}}(x,xs) = x - 1 & \mathtt{head}^{\mathcal{A}}(xs) = xs + 1 & \\
x \to_{\mathtt{N}}^{\mathcal{A}} y \Leftrightarrow x = y & x(\to_{\mathtt{N}}^{*})^{\mathcal{A}} y \Leftrightarrow x = y & x \to_{\mathtt{LN}}^{\mathcal{A}} y \Leftrightarrow x = y & x(\to_{\mathtt{LN}}^{*})^{\mathcal{A}} y \Leftrightarrow true
\end{array}$$

5.2 Top-Termination

A TRS $\mathcal{R}$ is *top-terminating* if no infinitary reduction sequence performs infinitely many rewrites at topmost position Λ [7]. From a computational point of view, top-termination is important in the semantic description of lazy languages as it is an important ingredient to guarantee that every initial expression has an infinite normal form [7,8]. Accordingly, given a *dummy* sort S, the *negation* of

$$(\exists x : \mathtt{S})(\forall n \in \mathbb{N})(\exists y : \mathtt{S})\ x(\to^* \circ \stackrel{\Lambda}{\to})^n y \tag{17}$$

(which claims for the existence of a term with infinitely many rewriting steps at top) captures top-termination. We introduce a new predicate $\to_{\star,\Lambda}$ for the composition $\to^* \circ \stackrel{\Lambda}{\to}$ of the many-step rewriting relation $\to^*$ (defined as usual, i.e., by the whole theory $\overline{\mathcal{R}}$ associated to $\mathcal{R}$) and topmost rewriting $\stackrel{\Lambda}{\to}$ defined by a theory $\mathcal{R}_\Lambda = \{(\forall \boldsymbol{x} : \mathtt{S})\ \ell \stackrel{\Lambda}{\to} r \mid \ell \to r \in \mathcal{R}\}$. Sequences $s \to^n_{\star,\Lambda} t$ meaning that $s \to_{\star,\Lambda}$-reduces into t in $n+1$ $\to_{\star,\Lambda}$-steps are defined as follows:

$$(\forall x, y, z : \mathtt{S})\ \ x \to^* y \wedge y \stackrel{\Lambda}{\to} z \Rightarrow x \to^0_{\star,\Lambda} z \tag{18}$$

$$(\forall x, y, z : \mathtt{S})(\forall n \in \mathbb{N})\ \ x \to^0_{\star,\Lambda} y \wedge y \to^n_{\star,\Lambda} z \Rightarrow x \to^{n+1}_{\star,\Lambda} z \tag{19}$$

Overall, the sentence φ to be disproved is:

$$(\exists x : \mathtt{S})(\forall n : Nat)(\exists y : \mathtt{S})\ x \to^n_{\star,\Lambda} y \tag{20}$$

Remark 3. We use $\mathbb{N}$ in (17) but *Nat* in (20). Indeed, (17) is *not* a valid sentence because $\mathbb{N}$ is not first-order axiomatizable, see, e.g. [11, Sect. 2.2]. This is consistent with the well-known fact that termination (or top-termination) can*not* be encoded in first-order logic [22, Sect. 5.1.4]. We can use (20) together with Corollary 1 provided that *Nat* is interpreted as $\mathbb{N}$. This is possible with AGES.

Example 2. Consider the following (nonterminating) TRS $\mathcal{R}$ [8, Sect. 9.5]:

$$\mathsf{non} \to \mathsf{f}(\mathsf{g}, \mathsf{f}(\mathsf{non}, \mathsf{g})) \tag{21}$$

$$\mathsf{g} \to \mathsf{a} \tag{22}$$

$$\mathsf{f}(\mathsf{a}, x) \to \mathsf{a} \tag{23}$$

$$\mathsf{f}(\mathsf{b}, \mathsf{b}) \to \mathsf{b} \tag{24}$$

$$\mathsf{f}(\mathsf{b}, \mathsf{a}) \to \mathsf{b} \tag{25}$$

The associated theory $\mathcal{R}_{topT}$ is $\mathcal{R}_{topT} = \overline{\mathcal{R}} \cup \mathcal{R}_\Lambda \cup \{(18), (19)\}$, where $\mathcal{R}_\Lambda$ is

$$\mathsf{non} \stackrel{\Lambda}{\to} \mathsf{f}(\mathsf{g}, \mathsf{f}(\mathsf{non}, \mathsf{g})) \tag{26}$$

$$\mathsf{g} \stackrel{\Lambda}{\to} \mathsf{a} \tag{27}$$

$$(\forall x : \mathtt{S})\ \mathsf{f}(\mathsf{b}, x) \stackrel{\Lambda}{\to} \mathsf{b} \tag{28}$$

$$\mathsf{f}(\mathsf{b}, \mathsf{b}) \stackrel{\Lambda}{\to} \mathsf{b} \tag{29}$$

$$\mathsf{f}(\mathsf{b}, \mathsf{a}) \stackrel{\Lambda}{\to} \mathsf{b} \tag{30}$$

Note that (20) only requires that the homomorphism mapping terms of sort *Nat* to $\mathbb{N}$ is surjective, which is automatically achieved by AGES. The structure $\mathcal{A}$ with $\mathcal{A}_{\mathtt{S}} = \{-1, 0, 1\}$, $\mathcal{A}_{Nat} = \mathbb{N}$, function symbols interpreted by: $\mathsf{a}^\mathcal{A} = 1$, $\mathsf{b}^\mathcal{A} = 1$, $\mathsf{g}^\mathcal{A} = 0$, $\mathsf{non}^\mathcal{A} = -1$, and $\mathsf{f}^\mathcal{A}(x) = 0$; and predicate symbols as follows:

$$x \to^\mathcal{A} y \Leftrightarrow y \geq x \wedge x + y \geq -1 \qquad x(\to^*)^\mathcal{A} y \Leftrightarrow y \geq x$$

$$x(\stackrel{\Lambda}{\to})^\mathcal{A} y \Leftrightarrow y > x \qquad x(\to^n_{\star,\Lambda})^\mathcal{A} y \Leftrightarrow y > x + n$$

is a model of $\mathcal{R}_{topT} \cup \{\neg(20)\}$ and proves top-termination of $\mathcal{R}$.

6 Refutation Witnesses

In logic, a *witness* for an existentially quantified sentence $(\exists x)\varphi(x)$ is a specific value b to be substituted by x in $\varphi(x)$ so that $\varphi(b)$ is true (see, e.g., [2, p. 81]). Similarly, we can think of a value b such that $\neg\varphi(b)$ holds as a witness of $(\exists x)\neg\varphi(x)$ or as a *refutation witness* for $(\forall x)\varphi(x)$; we can also think of b as a *counterexample* to $(\forall x)\varphi(x)$ [13, p. 284]. Note, however, that witnesses that are given as values b belonging to an *interpretation domain* $\mathcal{A}$ can be meaningless for the user who is acquainted with the first-order language Ω but not so much with abstract values from $\mathcal{A}$ (which is often automatically synthesized by using some tool). Users can be happier to deal with *terms* t which are somehow connected to witnesses b by a homomorphism, so that $t^{\mathcal{A}} = b$. Corollary 1 permits a refutation of φ by finding a model $\mathcal{A}$ of $\neg\varphi$ to conclude that $\mathcal{I} \models \neg\varphi$. We want to obtain instances of φ to better understand unsatisfiability of φ. In this section we investigate this problem.

The negation $\neg$(6) of (6), i.e., of $(Q_1x_1 : s_1)\cdots(Q_kx_k : s_k)\bigvee_{i=1}^{m}\bigwedge_{j=1}^{n_i} L_{ij}$ is

$$(\overline{Q}_1x_1 : s_1)\cdots(\overline{Q}_kx_k : s_k)\bigwedge_{i=1}^{m}\bigvee_{j=1}^{n_i}\neg L_{ij}(x_1,\ldots,x_k) \tag{31}$$

where $\overline{Q}_i$ is $\forall$ whenever Q_i is $\exists$ and $\overline{Q}_i$ is $\exists$ whenever Q_i is $\forall$. We assume $\eta \leq k$ universal quantifiers in (31) with indices $U = \{\upsilon_1,\ldots,\upsilon_\eta\} \subseteq \{1,\ldots,k\}$ and hence $k-\eta$ existential quantifiers with indices $E = \{\epsilon_1,\ldots,\epsilon_{k-\eta}\} = \{1,\ldots,k\} - U$. In the following $\overline{\eta}$ denotes $k-\eta$. For each $\epsilon \in E$, we let $U_\epsilon = \{\upsilon \in U \mid \upsilon < \epsilon\}$ be the (possibly empty) set of indices of universally quantified variables in (31) occurring before x_ϵ in the quantification prefix of (31). Let $\eta_\epsilon = |U_\epsilon|$. Note that $U_{\epsilon_1} \subseteq U_{\epsilon_2} \subseteq \cdots \subseteq U_{\epsilon_{\overline{\eta}}}$. Let $U_\exists$ be the set of indices of universally quantified variables occurring *before* some existentially quantified variable in the quantification prefix of (31). Note that $U_\exists$ is empty whenever $\upsilon_1 > \epsilon_{k-\eta}$ (no existential quantification after a universal quantification); otherwise, $U_\exists = \{\upsilon_1,\ldots,\upsilon_\exists\}$ for some $\upsilon_\exists \leq \upsilon_\eta$. Accordingly, $U_\forall = U - U_\exists = \{\epsilon_{\overline{\eta}}+1,\ldots,k\}$ is the set of indices of universally quantified variables occurring *after* all existentially quantified variables in the quantification prefix of (31). Note that $U_\forall$ is empty whenever $\epsilon_1 > \upsilon_\eta$ (no universal quantification after an existential quantification).

Most theorem provers transform sentences into universally quantified formulas by Skolemization (see, e.g., [12]). Thus, if $k > \eta$, i.e., (31) contains existential quantifiers, we need to introduce *Skolem function symbols* $sk_\epsilon : w_\epsilon \to s_\epsilon$ for each $\epsilon \in E$, where w_ϵ is the (possibly empty) sequence of η_ϵ sorts indexed by U_ϵ. Note that sk_ϵ is a *constant* if $\eta_\epsilon = 0$. The *Skolem normal form* of (31) is

$$(\forall x_{\upsilon_1} : s_{\upsilon_1})\cdots(\forall x_{\upsilon_\eta} : s_{\upsilon_\eta})\bigwedge_{i=1}^{m}\bigvee_{j=1}^{n_i}\neg L_{ij}(e_1,\ldots,e_k) \tag{32}$$

where for all $1 \leq q \leq k$, (i) $e_q \equiv x_q$ if $q \in U$ and (ii) $e_q \equiv sk_q(\boldsymbol{x}_{\eta_q})$ if $q \in E$, where $\boldsymbol{x}_{\eta_q}$ is the sequence of variables $x_{\nu_1},\ldots,x_{\nu_{\eta_q}}$. If $E \neq \emptyset$ (i.e., (31) and

(32) differ), then (32) is a sentence of an *extended* signature $\Omega^{sk} = (S, \Sigma^{sk}, \Pi)$ where Σ^{sk} extends Σ with skolem functions. Since (32) logically implies (31) [2, Sect. 19.2], every model $\mathcal{A}$ of (33) is a model of (32) as well.

Definition 1 (Set of refutation witnesses). *Using the notation developed in the previous paragraphs, let $\mathcal{A}$ be an Ω^{sk}-structure such that h_{s_q} is* surjective *for all $q \in U_\exists \cup E$. The Ω^{sk}-sentence (32) is given a* set of refutation witnesses *Φ consisting of Ω-sentences ϕ_α for each valuation α of the variables $x_{\upsilon_1}, \ldots, x_{\upsilon_\exists}$ indexed by $U_\exists$; each ϕ_α is (nondeterministically) defined as follows:*

$$(\forall x_{\epsilon_{\overline{\eta}}+1} : s_{\epsilon_{\overline{\eta}}+1}) \cdots (\forall x_k : s_k) \bigwedge_{i=1}^{m} \bigvee_{j=1}^{n_i} \neg L_{ij}(e'_1, \ldots, e'_k) \tag{33}$$

where for all $1 \leq q \leq k$, (i) $e'_q \equiv x_q$ if $q \in U_\forall$ and (ii) $e'_q \equiv t$ if $q \in U_\exists \cup E$ and $t \in \mathcal{T}_{\Sigma s_q}$ is such that $[t]_\mathcal{A} = [e_q]^\alpha_\mathcal{A}$.

Note that, in Definition 1 we could emphfail to find the necessary terms $t \in \mathcal{T}_{\Sigma s_q}$ if h_{s_q} is *not* surjective. Note also that, whenever E is empty, Φ is a singleton consisting of (33) which coincides with (32). We have the following:

Proposition 4. *For every Ω^{sk}-structure $\mathcal{A}$, $\mathcal{A} \models$ (33) if and only if $\mathcal{A} \models \Phi$.*

Refutation witnesses are built from symbols in the original signature Ω only. We can use them as more intuitive *counterexamples* to the refuted property φ.

Proposition 5. *Let Ω be a signature, $\mathcal{S}$ be a theory, φ be a sentence (6), and $\mathcal{A}$ be a model of $\mathcal{S}$ such that for all negative literals $L_{ij} = \neg P(\mathbf{t})$ with $P \in \Pi_w$ and substitutions σ, if $h(\sigma(\mathbf{t})) \in P^\mathcal{A}$ then $\sigma(\mathbf{t}) \in P^\mathcal{I}$. For all $\phi \in \Phi$, $\mathcal{I} \models \phi$.*

Corollary 2. *If (6) is positive, then for all refutation witnesses $\phi \in \Phi$, $\mathcal{I} \models \phi$.*

Example 3. Consider `ExAddMulHead` in Sect. 5. The *refutation* of (13) using AGES actually proceeds by skolemization of the negation of (13), i.e., of

$$(\exists xs : \mathtt{LN})(\forall x : \mathtt{N})\ \neg(\mathtt{head}(xs) \to x) \tag{34}$$

With regard to (34), we have $E = \{1\}$, $U_\exists = \emptyset$ and $U_\forall = \{2\}$, where 1 and 2 refer to variables xs and x, respectively. Accordingly, $\upsilon_\exists = 0$. The only sort involved in the variables indexed by $U_\exists \cup E$ is `LN`. Since variables of sort `LN` are universally quantified in (13), the application of Corollary 1 in Sect. 5 already required surjectivity of $h_{\mathtt{LN}}$. The *Skolem normal form* of (34) is:

$$(\forall x : \mathtt{N})\ \neg(\mathtt{head}(\mathsf{sk}_{xs}) \to x) \tag{35}$$

where sk_{xs} is a new constant of sort `LN`. The structure $\mathcal{A}$ computed by AGES is actually a model of $\overline{\mathcal{R}} \cup \mathsf{SuH}_{\mathtt{LN}} \cup \{(36)\}$, for $\mathsf{SuH}_{\mathtt{LN}}$ in Sect. 5. For sk_{xs}, we have $\mathsf{sk}^\mathcal{A}_{xs} = 0$. There is a single (empty) valuation α of variables indexed by $U_\exists$ (which is empty). Hence, $\Phi = \{\phi_\alpha\}$ is a singleton. According to Definition 1, since $[\mathtt{nil}]_\mathcal{A} = 0 = [\mathsf{sk}_{xs}]_\mathcal{A}$, the following sentence could be associated to the refutation witness ϕ_α: $(\forall x : \mathtt{N})\ \neg(\mathtt{head}(\mathtt{nil}) \to x)$.

Example 4. With regard to the computation of refutation witnesses for $\mathcal{R}$ in Example 2, we start with the negation of (17), i.e.,

$$(\forall x : \mathsf{S})(\exists n : Nat)(\forall y : \mathsf{S})\ \neg(x(\to^* \circ \xrightarrow{\Lambda})^n y) \tag{36}$$

We have $E = \{2\}$, $U_\exists = \{1\}$ and $U_\forall = \{3\}$. The Skolem normal form of (36) is

$$(\forall x : \mathsf{S})(\forall y : \mathsf{S})\ \neg(x(\to^* \circ \xrightarrow{\Lambda})^{\mathsf{sk}_n(x)} y) \tag{37}$$

where $\mathsf{sk}_n : \mathsf{S} \to Nat$ is a new (monadic) function symbol. Since the sorts for variables indexed by $U_\exists \cup E$ are S and Nat, we require surjectivity of h_S and h_{Nat}. This is achieved by using SuH_S and interpreting Nat as $\mathbb{N}$ as done in AGES. The structure $\mathcal{A}$ in Example 2 is a model of $\mathcal{R}_{topT} \cup \mathsf{SuH}_\mathsf{S} \cup \{(38)\}$. The interpretation obtained for sk_n is

$$\mathsf{sk}_n^{\mathcal{A}}(x) = 1 - x$$

Now we can compute refutation witnesses for (37). Since $U_\epsilon = \{1\}$ is a singleton whose index refers to a variable x of sort S and $\mathcal{A}_\mathsf{S} = \{-1, 0, 1\}$, we have to deal with three valuation functions for the only variable x to be considered:

$$\alpha_{-1}(x) = -1 \qquad \alpha_0(x) = 0 \qquad \alpha_1(x) = 1$$

We have $\Phi = \{\phi_{\alpha_{-1}}, \phi_{\alpha_0}, \phi_{\alpha_1}\}$, where $\phi_{\alpha_{-1}}$ is $(\forall y : \mathsf{S})\neg(\mathsf{non}(\to^* \circ \xrightarrow{\Lambda})^2 y)$, ϕ_{α_0} is $(\forall y : \mathsf{S})\neg(\mathsf{g}(\to^* \circ \xrightarrow{\Lambda})^1 y)$, and ϕ_{α_1} is $(\forall y : \mathsf{S})\neg(\mathsf{a}(\to^* \circ \xrightarrow{\Lambda})^0 y)$.
Note that, since $\mathsf{f}^{\mathcal{A}}(x) = 0$, we could also write ϕ_{α_0} as $(\forall y : \mathsf{S})\ \neg(\mathsf{f}(t)(\to^* \circ \xrightarrow{\Lambda})^1 y)$ for *every ground term* t. This gives additional, complementary information.

7 Example of Application with General Sentences

Consider a well-known example of a *locally confluent* but *nonconfluent* TRS $\mathcal{R}$:

$$\mathsf{b} \to \mathsf{a} \qquad \mathsf{b} \to \mathsf{c} \qquad \mathsf{c} \to \mathsf{b} \qquad \mathsf{c} \to \mathsf{d}$$

Example 5 (Local confluence of $\mathcal{R}$). Local confluence corresponds to φ_{WCR} in Table 1. As explained in Remark 1, we start with $\overline{\varphi}_{WCR} = \neg\varphi_{WCR}$ i.e.,

$$(\exists x, y, z : \mathsf{S})(\forall u : \mathsf{S})\ (x \to y \wedge x \to z \wedge \neg(x \to^* u)) \vee (x \to y \wedge x \to z \wedge \neg(z \to^* u)) \tag{38}$$

Due to the universal quantifier, $h_\mathsf{S} : \mathcal{T}_{\Sigma\mathsf{S}} \to \mathcal{A}_\mathsf{S}$ must be surjective. We can achieve this by adding the following sentence $\mathsf{SuH}_\mathsf{S}^T$ for $T = \{\mathsf{a}, \mathsf{b}, \mathsf{c}, \mathsf{d}\}$:

$$(\forall x : \mathsf{S})\ x = \mathsf{a} \vee x = \mathsf{b} \vee x = \mathsf{c} \vee x = \mathsf{d} \tag{39}$$

Due to the negative literals $\neg(x \to^* u)$ and $\neg(z \to^* u)$, we consider $\mathcal{N}$, representing the forbidden many-step rewriting steps, explicitly given by:

$$\mathcal{N} = \{\, \neg(\mathsf{a} \to^* \mathsf{b}), \neg(\mathsf{a} \to^* \mathsf{c}), \neg(\mathsf{a} \to^* \mathsf{d}), \neg(\mathsf{d} \to^* \mathsf{a}), \neg(\mathsf{d} \to^* \mathsf{b}), \neg(\mathsf{d} \to^* \mathsf{c}) \,\}$$

We apply Corollary 1 to prove that $\neg\overline{\varphi}_{WCR}$ (i.e., φ_{WCR}) holds by obtaining a model of $\overline{\mathcal{R}} \cup \mathsf{SuH}_{\mathtt{S}}^{T} \cup \mathcal{N} \cup \{\varphi_{WCR}\}$ with Mace4.[2] The structure has domain $\mathcal{A}_{\mathtt{S}} = \{0, 1, 2, 3\}$; constants are interpreted as follows: $\mathsf{a}^{\mathcal{A}} = 0$, $\mathsf{b}^{\mathcal{A}} = 1$, $\mathsf{c}^{\mathcal{A}} = 3$, and $\mathsf{d}^{\mathcal{A}} = 2$. With regard to predicate symbols, we have:

$$x \rightarrow^{\mathcal{A}} y = \{(1,0),(1,3),(3,1),(3,2)\} \qquad x(\rightarrow^*)^{\mathcal{A}} y = \{(1,x),(3,x) \mid x \in \mathcal{A}_{\mathtt{S}}\}$$

This proves $\mathcal{R}$ locally confluent.

Example 6 (Nonconfluence of $\mathcal{R}$). In order to *disprove* confluence of $\mathcal{R}$, which is represented by φ_{CR} in Table 1, we first write φ_{CR} in the form (6), i.e.,

$$(\forall x, y, z : \mathtt{S})(\exists u : \mathtt{S})\ \neg(x \rightarrow^* y) \vee \neg(x \rightarrow^* z) \vee (y \rightarrow^* u \wedge z \rightarrow^* u) \tag{40}$$

Due to the universal quantification and negative literals, we use $\mathsf{SuH}_{\mathtt{S}}^{T}$ and $\mathcal{N}$ as in Example 5. We obtain a model $\mathcal{A}$ of $\overline{\mathcal{R}} \cup \mathsf{SuH}_{\mathtt{S}}^{T} \cup \mathcal{N} \cup \{\neg\varphi_{CR}\}$ with Mace4. The domain is $\mathcal{A}_{\mathtt{S}} = \{0, 1, 2\}$ and symbols are interpreted by: $\mathsf{a}^{\mathcal{A}} = 0$, $\mathsf{b}^{\mathcal{A}} = \mathsf{c}^{\mathcal{A}} = 1$, $\mathsf{d}^{\mathcal{A}} = 2$, $x \rightarrow^{\mathcal{A}} y \Leftrightarrow x = 1$, and $x(\rightarrow^*)^{\mathcal{A}} y \Leftrightarrow x = y \vee x = 1$. This proves nonconfluence of $\mathcal{R}$. With regard to the refutation witnesses, $\neg\varphi_{CR}$ is

$$(\exists x, y, z : \mathtt{S})(\forall u : \mathtt{S})\ x \rightarrow^* y \wedge x \rightarrow^* z \wedge \neg(y \rightarrow^* u \wedge z \rightarrow^* u) \tag{41}$$

and its Skolem normal form is

$$(\forall u : \mathtt{S})\ \mathsf{sk}_x \rightarrow^* \mathsf{sk}_y \wedge \mathsf{sk}_x \rightarrow^* \mathsf{sk}_z \wedge \neg(\mathsf{sk}_y \rightarrow^* u \wedge \mathsf{sk}_z \rightarrow^* u) \tag{42}$$

Mace4 yields $\mathsf{sk}_x^{\mathcal{A}} = 1$, $\mathsf{sk}_y^{\mathcal{A}} = 0$ and $\mathsf{sk}_z^{\mathcal{A}} = 2$; Φ consists of a single sentence; e.g.,

$$(\forall u : \mathtt{S})\ \mathsf{b} \rightarrow^* \mathsf{a} \wedge \mathsf{b} \rightarrow^* \mathsf{d} \wedge \neg(\mathsf{a} \rightarrow^* u \wedge \mathsf{d} \rightarrow^* u) \tag{43}$$

but also: $(\forall u : \mathtt{S})\ \mathsf{c} \rightarrow^* \mathsf{a} \wedge \mathsf{c} \rightarrow^* \mathsf{d} \wedge \neg(\mathsf{a} \rightarrow^* u \wedge \mathsf{d} \rightarrow^* u)$. Indeed, they represent the two possible cases of nonconfluent behavior in $\mathcal{R}$.

Example 7 (Normalizing TRS). $\mathcal{R}$ is not terminating, but we can prove it *normalizing* (i.e., every term has a normal form) by *disproving* $\overline{\varphi}_{WN}$, for φ_{WN} in Table 1. Therefore, $\overline{\varphi}_{WN}$ is $(\exists x : \mathtt{S})(\forall y : \mathtt{S})(\exists z : \mathtt{S})\ (\neg(x \rightarrow^* y) \vee y \rightarrow z)$. We guarantee surjectivity by using $\mathsf{SuH}_{\mathtt{S}}^{T}$ in Example 5; we also use $\mathcal{N}$ in Example 5. Mace4 obtains a model $\mathcal{A}$ of $\overline{\mathcal{R}} \cup \mathsf{SuH}_{\mathtt{S}}^{T} \cup \mathcal{N} \cup \{\varphi_{WN}\}$ with $\mathcal{A}_{\mathtt{S}} = \{0, 1, 2\}$, $\mathsf{a}^{\mathcal{A}} = 0$, $\mathsf{b}^{\mathcal{A}} = \mathsf{c}^{\mathcal{A}} = 1$, $\mathsf{d}^{\mathcal{A}} = 2$, $x \rightarrow^{\mathcal{A}} y \Leftrightarrow x = 1$, and $x(\rightarrow^*)^{\mathcal{A}} y \Leftrightarrow x = y \vee x = 1$.

8 Related Work

In [14, Sect. 6] we already compared our approach to existing techniques and tools for the so-called First-Order Theory of Rewriting [6], which applies to restricted classes of TRSs and formulas. In [16], we show that our semantic approach is practical when applied to arbitrary (Conditional) TRSs.

---

[2] This proves $\mathcal{R}$ *ground* locally confluent, i.e., variables in φ_{WCR} refer to *ground* terms only; since $\mathcal{R}$ is a ground TRS, local confluence and ground local confluence coincide.

McCune's Prover9/Mace4 are popular automated systems for theorem proving in first-order and equational logic. Given a theory $\mathcal{S}$ and a *goal* or *statement* φ, Prover9 tries to prove that $\mathcal{S} \vdash \varphi$ holds. The generator of models Mace4 complements Prover9 as follows: "*If the statement is the denial of some conjecture, any structures found by* Mace4 *are counterexamples to the conjecture*".[3] Accordingly, the user introduces φ in the *goal* section of Mace4, but the system seeks a model of $\mathcal{S} \cup \{\neg\varphi\}$. Indeed, as discussed in Sect. 1, if $\mathcal{A} \models \mathcal{S} \cup \{\neg\varphi\}$ holds, then $\mathcal{S} \vdash \varphi$ does not hold. But, unless φ is an ECBCA, this does not necessarily mean that φ *does not hold* of a program P with $\mathcal{S} = \overline{P}$! Consider the following 'misleading' session with Mace4 that '*disproves*' commutativity of the addition.

Example 8. Consider $\mathcal{R}$ in Example 1. Mace4 obtains a model $\mathcal{A}$ of $\overline{\mathcal{R}} \cup \{\neg(14)\}$ with domain $\mathcal{A} = \{0, 1\}$, and function and predicate symbols as follows: $0^{\mathcal{A}} = 0$, $\mathsf{s}^{\mathcal{A}}(x) = x$, $\mathsf{add}^{\mathcal{A}}(x, y) = \begin{cases} 1 \text{ if } x = 0 \wedge y = 1 \\ 0 \text{ otherwise} \end{cases}$, $\mathsf{mul}^{\mathcal{A}}(x, y) = 0$, and $\to^{\mathcal{A}}$ and $(\to^*)^{\mathcal{A}}$ both interpreted as the equality. Additionally, Mace4 also displays the following: $\mathtt{c1}^{\mathcal{A}} = 0$ and $\mathtt{c2}^{\mathcal{A}} = 1$. These c1 and c2 are *new* Skolem symbols (but *unexpected* for most users!). In practice, Mace4 finds a model for the *Skolem normal form* of $\neg(14)$, which is

$$(\forall z)\ \neg(\mathsf{add}(\mathtt{c1}, \mathtt{c2}) \to^* z \wedge \mathsf{add}(\mathtt{c2}, \mathtt{c1}) \to^* z) \tag{44}$$

Indeed, $\mathcal{A}$ is a model of $\overline{\mathcal{R}} \cup \{(45)\}$. But we *should not* conclude (as suggested by the aforementioned sentences in Mace4 manual) that add is *not* commutative!

The problem in Example 8 is that $h : \mathcal{I}_{\overline{\mathcal{R}}} \to \mathcal{A}$ is *not surjective*. For instance, no ground term $t \in \mathcal{T}_\Sigma$ satisfies $t^{\mathcal{A}} = 1$; note that $\mathtt{c1}, \mathtt{c2} \notin \Sigma$. Since proving validity in $\mathcal{I}_{\mathcal{S}}$ is not the main purpose of Mace4, no warning in its documentation prevents the prospective user to give credit to the 'refutation' of (ground) commutativity for the addition computed by Mace4. We believe that our work is helpful to clarify the use of such tools, and even improve it by adding (for instance) sentences reinforcing surjectivity to avoid the problem discussed above. For instance, Mace4 obtains no model of $\overline{\mathcal{R}} \cup \mathsf{SuH}^T \cup \{(45)\}$ with, e.g., $T = \{\mathsf{0}, \mathsf{s}(\mathsf{0})\}$.

Proofs by Satisfiability vs. Theorem Proving. In order to further clarify the differences between our approach and the use of first-order theorem proving tools, consider the CTRS $\mathcal{R}$ in [14, Example 1], consisting of the rules

$$\mathsf{b} \to \mathsf{a} \tag{45}$$

$$\mathsf{a} \to \mathsf{b} \Leftarrow \mathsf{c} \to \mathsf{b} \tag{46}$$

[3] https://www.cs.unm.edu/~mccune/prover9/manual/2009-11A/mace4.html.

Its associated Horn theory $\overline{\mathcal{R}}$ is:

$$(\forall x)\, x \to^* x \tag{47}$$

$$(\forall x, y, z)\, x \to y \wedge y \to^* z \Rightarrow x \to^* z \tag{48}$$

$$\mathsf{b} \to \mathsf{a} \tag{49}$$

$$\mathsf{c} \to^* \mathsf{b} \Rightarrow \mathsf{a} \to \mathsf{b} \tag{50}$$

We consider some simple tests regarding goals $\mathsf{b} \to \mathsf{a}$ and $\mathsf{a} \to \mathsf{b}$ and their negations. We tried such four goals with the following theorem provers: Alt-Ergo,[4] Prover9/Mace4, PDL-tableau,[5] and Princess[6] (most of them with a web-interface). Besides attempting a *proof* of each goal with respect to $\overline{\mathcal{R}}$, tools Alt-Ergo, Mace4, and Princess can also generate *models* of the negation of the tested goal when the proof attempt fails. The following table summarizes the results of our test:

#	Goal		Alt-Ergo		Mace4		PDL-tableau		Princess	
	φ	$\mathcal{I}_{\mathcal{R}} \models \varphi$	$\overline{\mathcal{R}} \vdash \varphi$	$\mathcal{A} \models \neg\varphi$	$\overline{\mathcal{R}} \vdash \varphi$	$\mathcal{A} \models \neg\varphi$	$\overline{\mathcal{R}} \vdash \varphi$	$\mathcal{A} \models \neg\varphi$	$\overline{\mathcal{R}} \vdash \varphi$	$\mathcal{A} \models \neg\varphi$
1	$\mathsf{b} \to \mathsf{a}$	*true*	Y	N	Y	N	Y	–	Y	N
2	$\neg(\mathsf{b} \to \mathsf{a})$	*false*	N	Y	N	Y	N	–	N	Y
3	$\mathsf{a} \to \mathsf{b}$	*false*	N	Y	N	Y	N	–	N	Y
4	$\neg(\mathsf{a} \to \mathsf{b})$	*true*	N	Y	N	Y	N	–	N	Y

Goal $\neg(\mathsf{a} \to \mathsf{b})$ in row 4 is *not* directly proved by any tool. Indeed, since $\neg(\mathsf{a} \to \mathsf{b})$ is *not* a logical consequence of $\overline{\mathcal{R}}$ (see [14, Example 2]), $\overline{\mathcal{R}} \vdash \neg(\mathsf{a} \to \mathsf{b})$ does *not* hold. Our *satisfiability* approach can be used to formally prove that $\mathcal{R}$ cannot reduce a into b, i.e., that $\mathcal{I}_{\mathcal{R}} \models \neg(\mathsf{a} \to \mathsf{b})$ (or $\mathsf{a} \not\to_{\mathcal{R}} \mathsf{b}$) holds: from row 3 we see that $\mathcal{A} \models \neg(\mathsf{a} \to \mathsf{b})$ holds for the models $\mathcal{A}$ of $\overline{\mathcal{R}}$ computed by some of the tools. By Corollary 1, the desired conclusion $\mathsf{a} \not\to_{\mathcal{R}} \mathsf{b}$ follows. Note also that row 4 reports on the ability of some tools to obtain models of $\mathsf{a} \to \mathsf{b}$. However, Corollary 1 cannot be used to conclude that $\mathsf{a} \to_{\mathcal{R}} \mathsf{b}$ holds (which is obviously wrong): since φ in row 4 is a *negative* literal, condition (b) in Corollary 1 must be fulfilled before being able to conclude $\mathcal{I}_{\mathcal{R}} \models \mathsf{a} \to \mathsf{b}$ from $\mathcal{A} \models \mathsf{a} \to \mathsf{b}$ for some model $\mathcal{A}$ of $\overline{\mathcal{R}}$. But this is *not* the case in our test set.

Although Remark 1 explains how an arbitrary program property φ can be proved by using Corollary 1 (see also Sect. 7), from a practical point of view we better think of our approach as *complementary* to the use of first-order proof techniques and tools. Provability of φ (i.e., $\mathcal{S} \vdash \varphi$) implies that $\mathcal{I}_{\mathcal{S}} \models \varphi$ holds. Thus, as usual, a proof of φ with respect to $\mathcal{S}$ implies that a program P with $\mathcal{S} = \overline{P}$ has property φ. However, as discussed above, showing that $\mathcal{S} \vdash \varphi$ or $\mathcal{S} \vdash \neg\varphi$ holds is often impossible. We can try to prove $\mathcal{I}_{\mathcal{S}} \models \neg\varphi$ by using Corollary 1, though. For positive sentences φ, this is often affordable.

[4] https://alt-ergo.ocamlpro.com/.
[5] http://www.cs.man.ac.uk/~schmidt/pdl-tableau/.
[6] http://www.philipp.ruemmer.org/princess.shtml.

9 Conclusions and Future Work

We have shown how to prove properties φ of computational systems whose semantics can be given as a first-order theory $\mathcal{S}$. Our *proofs by satisfiability* proceed (see Remark 1) by just finding a model $\mathcal{A}$ of $\mathcal{S} \cup \mathcal{Z} \cup \{\varphi\}$ where $\mathcal{Z}$ is an *auxiliary* theory representing the requirements (a) and (b) in Corollary 1 (referred to $\neg\varphi$), so that $\mathcal{A} \models \mathcal{S} \cup \mathcal{Z} \cup \{\varphi\}$ implies $\mathcal{I}_{\mathcal{S}} \models \varphi$. Surjectivity of the interpretation homomorphisms (requirement (a) in Corollary 1) is ensured if $\mathcal{Z}$ includes the appropriate theory SuH (see Sect. 4); and requirement (b), for dealing with negative literals, is fulfilled if $\mathcal{Z}$ includes $\mathcal{N}$ in Proposition 1. Our results properly subsume the ones in [14], which concern *existentially closed boolean combinations of atoms* only. We have also introduced the notion of *refutation witness* which is useful to obtain counterexamples by using the symbols in the first-order language rather than values of the computed model.

From a theoretical point of view, the idea of *proving program properties as satisfiability* (see Remark 1) is appealing as it emphasizes the role of *abstraction* (introduced by semantic structures) in theorem proving and logic-based program analysis. However, the requirement of surjectivity of the interpretation homomorphisms and the use of theories $\mathcal{N}$ with *negative* information about some of the predicates introduce additional difficulties in the model generation process. Investigating methods for the practical implementation of our techniques, and also finding specific areas of application where our approach can be useful (as done in [16], for instance) is an interesting subject for future work.

Also, our research suggests that further investigation on the generation of models for many-sorted theories that combines the use of finite and infinite domains is necessary. For instance, [15] explains how to generate such models by interpreting the sort, function, and predicate symbols by using linear algebra techniques. This is implemented in AGES. Domains are defined as the solutions of matrix inequalities, possibly restricted to an underlying set of values (e.g., $\mathbb{Z}$); thus, finite and infinite domains can be obtained as particular cases of the same technique. Since piecewise definitions are allowed, we could eventually provide fully detailed descriptions of functions and predicates by just adding more pieces to the interpretations. However, such a flexibility is expensive. In contrast, Mace4 is based on a different principle (similar to [12]) and it is really fast, but only finite domains can be generated. This is a problem, for instance, when using Proposition 3 to guarantee surjectivity of homomorphisms $h_s : \mathcal{T}_{\Sigma s} \to \mathcal{A}_s$. Even though $\mathcal{A}_s$ is finite, we still need to be able to interpret *Nat* as $\mathbb{N}$, which is not possible with Mace4. For this reason, the examples in Sect. 5 (where the computed structures $\mathcal{A}$ have finite domains for the 'proper' sorts `N`, `LN`, and `S`, and only *Nat* is interpreted as an infinite set) could not be handled with Mace4, or with similar tools that are able to deal with sorts (e.g., SEM [24] or the work in [21]) but which generate finite domains only.

Acknowledgements. I thank the anonymous referees for their comments and suggestions. I also thank Philipp Rümmer and Mohamed Iguernlala for their clarifying remarks about the use of Princess and Alt-Ergo, respectively.

References

1. Baader, F., Nipkow, T.: Term Rewriting and All That. Cambridge University Press, New York (1998)
2. Boolos, G.S., Burgess, J.P., Jeffrey, R.C.: Computability and Logic, 4th edn. Cambridge University Press, Cambridge (2002)
3. Bruni, R., Meseguer, J.: Semantic foundations for generalized rewrite theories. Theoret. Comput. Sci. **351**(1), 386–414 (2006)
4. Clark, K.L.: Predicate logic as a computational formalism. Ph.D. thesis, Research Monograph 79/59 TOC, Department of Computing, Imperial College of Science, and Technology, University of London, December 1979
5. Clavel, M., et al.: All About Maude - A High-Performance Logical Framework. LNCS, vol. 4350. Springer, Heidelberg (2007). https://doi.org/10.1007/978-3-540-71999-1
6. Dauchet, M., Tison, S.: The theory of ground rewrite systems is decidable. In: Proceedings of LICS 1990, pp. 242–248. IEEE Press (1990)
7. Dershowitz, N., Kaplan, S., Plaisted, D.: Rewrite, rewrite, rewrite, rewrite, rewrite, ... Theoret. Comput. Sci. **83**, 71–96 (1991)
8. Endrullis, J., Hendriks, D.: Lazy productivity via termination. Theoret. Comput. Sci. **412**, 3203–3225 (2011)
9. Goguen, J.A., Meseguer, J.: Models and equality for logical programming. In: Ehrig, H., Kowalski, R., Levi, G., Montanari, U. (eds.) TAPSOFT 1987. LNCS, vol. 250, pp. 1–22. Springer, Heidelberg (1987). https://doi.org/10.1007/BFb0014969
10. Gutiérrez, R., Lucas, S., Reinoso, P.: A tool for the automatic generation of logical models of order-sorted first-order theories. In: Proceedings of PROLE 2016, pp. 215–230 (2016). Tool available at http://zenon.dsic.upv.es/ages/
11. Hodges, W.: Model Theory. Cambridge University Press, Cambridge (1993)
12. Kim, S., Zhang, H.: ModGen: theorem proving by model generation. In: Proceedings of AAAI 1994, pp. 162–167. AAAI Press/MIT Press (1994)
13. Kleene, S.C.: Mathematical Logic. Wiley, Hoboken (1967). (Dover 2002)
14. Lucas, S.: Analysis of rewriting-based systems as first-order theories. In: Fioravanti, F., Gallagher, J.P. (eds.) LOPSTR 2017. LNCS, vol. 10855, pp. 180–197. Springer, Cham (2018). https://doi.org/10.1007/978-3-319-94460-9_11
15. Lucas, S., Gutiérrez, R.: Automatic synthesis of logical models for order-sorted first-order theories. J. Autom. Reason. **60**(4), 465–501 (2018)
16. Lucas, S., Gutiérrez, R.: Use of logical models for proving infeasibility in term rewriting. Inf. Process. Lett. **136**, 90–95 (2018)
17. McCune, W.: Prover9 and Mace4 (2005–2010). http://www.cs.unm.edu/~mccune/prover9/
18. Meseguer, J.: Twenty years of rewriting logic. J. Logic Algebraic Program. **81**, 721–781 (2012)
19. Ohlebusch, E.: Advanced Topics in Term Rewriting. Springer, New York (2002). https://doi.org/10.1007/978-1-4757-3661-8
20. Reiter, R.: On closed world data bases. In: Logic and Data Bases, pp. 119–140. Plenum Press, New York (1978)
21. Reger, G., Suda, M., Voronkov, A.: Finding finite models in multi-sorted first-order logic. In: Creignou, N., Le Berre, D. (eds.) SAT 2016. LNCS, vol. 9710, pp. 323–341. Springer, Cham (2016). https://doi.org/10.1007/978-3-319-40970-2_20

22. Shapiro, S.: Foundations Without Foundationalism: A Case for Second-Order Logic. Clarendon Press, Oxford (1991)
23. Wang, H.: Logic of many-sorted theories. J. Symbolic Logic **17**(2), 105–116 (1952)
24. Zhang, J., Zhang, H.: Generating models by SEM. In: McRobbie, M.A., Slaney, J.K. (eds.) CADE 1996. LNCS, vol. 1104, pp. 308–312. Springer, New York (1996)

Guided Unfoldings for Finding Loops in Standard Term Rewriting

Étienne Payet(✉)

LIM, Université de La Réunion, Saint-Denis, France
etienne.payet@univ-reunion.fr

Abstract. In this paper, we reconsider the unfolding-based technique that we have introduced previously for detecting loops in standard term rewriting. We modify it by *guiding* the unfolding process, using disagreement pairs in rewrite rules. This results in a partial computation of the unfoldings, whereas the original technique consists of a thorough computation followed by a mechanism for eliminating some rules. We have implemented this new approach in our tool NTI and conducted successful experiments on a large set of term rewrite systems.

Keywords: Term rewrite systems · Dependency pairs · Non-termination · Loop · Unfolding

1 Introduction

In [13], we have introduced a technique for finding *loops* (a periodic, special form of non-termination) in standard term rewriting. It consists of unfolding the term rewrite system (TRS) $\mathcal{R}$ under analysis and of performing a semi-unification [10] test on the unfolded rules for detecting loops. The unfolding operator $U_{\mathcal{R}}$ which is applied processes both forwards and backwards and considers *every* subterm of the rules to unfold, including variable subterms.

Example 1. Let $\mathcal{R}$ be the TRS consisting of the following rules (x is a variable):

$$R_1 = \underbrace{\mathsf{f}(\mathsf{s}(\mathsf{0}),\mathsf{s}(\mathsf{1}),x)}_{l} \rightarrow \underbrace{\mathsf{f}(x,x,x)}_{r} \qquad R_2 = \mathsf{h} \rightarrow \mathsf{0} \qquad R_3 = \mathsf{h} \rightarrow \mathsf{1}.$$

Note that $\mathcal{R}$ is a variation of a well-known example by Toyama [18]. Unfolding the subterm $\mathsf{0}$ of l backwards with the rule R_2, we get the unfolded rule $U_1 = \mathsf{f}(\mathsf{s}(\mathsf{h}),\mathsf{s}(\mathsf{1}),x) \rightarrow \mathsf{f}(x,x,x)$. Unfolding the subterm x (a variable) of l backwards with R_2, we get $U_2 = \mathsf{f}(\mathsf{s}(\mathsf{0}),\mathsf{s}(\mathsf{1}),\mathsf{h}) \rightarrow \mathsf{f}(\mathsf{0},\mathsf{0},\mathsf{0})$. Unfolding the first (from the left) occurrence of x in r forwards with R_2, we get $U_3 = \mathsf{f}(\mathsf{s}(\mathsf{0}),\mathsf{s}(\mathsf{1}),\mathsf{h}) \rightarrow \mathsf{f}(\mathsf{0},\mathsf{h},\mathsf{h})$. We have $\{U_1, U_2, U_3\} \subseteq U_{\mathcal{R}}(\mathcal{R})$. Now, if we unfold the subterm $\mathsf{1}$ of U_1 backwards with R_3, we get $\mathsf{f}(\mathsf{s}(\mathsf{h}),\mathsf{s}(\mathsf{h}),x) \rightarrow \mathsf{f}(x,x,x)$, which is an element of $U_{\mathcal{R}}(U_{\mathcal{R}}(\mathcal{R}))$. The left-hand side l_1 of this rule semi-unifies with its right-hand side r_1 *i.e.*, $l_1\theta_1\theta_2 = r_1\theta_1$ for the substitutions $\theta_1 = \{x/\mathsf{s}(\mathsf{h})\}$ and $\theta_2 = \{\}$. Therefore,

F. Mesnard and P. J. Stuckey (Eds.): LOPSTR 2018, LNCS 11408, pp. 22–37, 2019.
https://doi.org/10.1007/978-3-030-13838-7_2

$l\theta_1 = \mathsf{f}(\mathsf{s}(\mathsf{h}), \mathsf{s}(\mathsf{h}), \mathsf{s}(\mathsf{h}))$ loops with respect to $\mathcal{R}$ because it can be rewritten to itself using the rules of $\mathcal{R}$ (the redex is underlined at each step):

$$\mathsf{f}(\mathsf{s}(\underline{\mathsf{h}}), \mathsf{s}(\mathsf{h}), \mathsf{s}(\mathsf{h})) \underset{R_2}{\rightarrow} \mathsf{f}(\mathsf{s}(0), \mathsf{s}(\underline{\mathsf{h}}), \mathsf{s}(\mathsf{h})) \underset{R_3}{\rightarrow} \underline{\mathsf{f}(\mathsf{s}(0), \mathsf{s}(1), \mathsf{s}(\mathsf{h}))} \underset{R_1}{\rightarrow} \mathsf{f}(\mathsf{s}(\mathsf{h}), \mathsf{s}(\mathsf{h}), \mathsf{s}(\mathsf{h})).$$

Iterative applications of the operator $U_{\mathcal{R}}$ result in a combinatorial explosion which significantly limits the approach. In order to reduce it, a mechanism is introduced in [13] for eliminating unfolded rules which are estimated as *useless* for detecting loops. Moreover, in practice, three analyses are run in parallel (in different threads): one with forward unfoldings only, one with backward unfoldings only and one with forward and backward unfoldings together.

So, the technique of [13] roughly consists in computing *all* the rules of $U_{\mathcal{R}}(\mathcal{R})$, $U_{\mathcal{R}}(U_{\mathcal{R}}(\mathcal{R}))$, ... and removing some useless ones, until the semi-unification test succeeds on an unfolded rule or a time limit is reached. Therefore, this approach corresponds to a breadth-first search for a loop, as the successive iterations of $U_{\mathcal{R}}$ are computed thoroughly, one after the other. However, it is not always necessary to compute all the elements of each iteration of $U_{\mathcal{R}}$. For instance, in Example 1 above, U_2 and U_3 do not lead to an unfolded rule satisfying the semi-unification criterion. This is detected by the eliminating mechanism of [13], but only *after* these two rules are generated. In order to *avoid* the generation of these useless rules, one can notice that l and r differ at the first argument of f: in l, the first argument is $\mathsf{s}(0)$ while in r it is x. We say that $\langle \mathsf{s}(0), x \rangle$ is a *disagreement pair* of l and r. Hence, one can first concentrate on resolving this disagreement, unfolding this pair only, and then, once this is resolved, apply the same process to another disagreement pair.

Example 2 (Example 1 *continued).* There are two ways to resolve the disagreement pair $\langle \mathsf{s}(0), x \rangle$ of l and r (*i.e.*, make it disappear).

The first way consists in unifying $\mathsf{s}(0)$ and x, *i.e.*, in computing $R_1\theta$ where θ is the substitution $\{x/\mathsf{s}(0)\}$, which gives $V_0 = \mathsf{f}(\mathsf{s}(0), \mathsf{s}(1), \mathsf{s}(0)) \rightarrow \mathsf{f}(\mathsf{s}(0), \mathsf{s}(0), \mathsf{s}(0))$. The left-hand side of V_0 does not semi-unify with its right-hand side.

The other way is to unfold $\mathsf{s}(0)$ or x. We decide not to unfold variable subterms, hence we select $\mathsf{s}(0)$. As it occurs in the left-hand side of R_1, we unfold it backwards. The only possibility is to use R_2, which results in

$$V_1 = \mathsf{f}(\mathsf{s}(\mathsf{h}), \mathsf{s}(1), x) \rightarrow \mathsf{f}(x, x, x).$$

Note that this approach only generates two rules (V_0 and V_1) at the first iteration of the unfolding operator. In comparison, the approach of [13] produces 14 rules (before elimination), as all the subterms of R_1 are considered for unfolding.

Hence, the disagreement pair $\langle \mathsf{s}(0), x \rangle$ has been replaced with the disagreement pair $\langle \mathsf{s}(\mathsf{h}), x \rangle$ in V_1. Unifying $\mathsf{s}(\mathsf{h})$ and x *i.e.*, computing $V_1\theta'$ where θ' is the substitution $\{x/\mathsf{s}(\mathsf{h})\}$, we get $V_1' = \mathsf{f}(\mathsf{s}(\mathsf{h}), \mathsf{s}(1), \mathsf{s}(\mathsf{h})) \rightarrow \mathsf{f}(\mathsf{s}(\mathsf{h}), \mathsf{s}(\mathsf{h}), \mathsf{s}(\mathsf{h}))$. So, the disagreement $\langle \mathsf{s}(0), x \rangle$ is solved: it has been replaced with $\langle \mathsf{s}(\mathsf{h}), \mathsf{s}(\mathsf{h}) \rangle$. Now, $\langle 1, \mathsf{h} \rangle$ is a disagreement pair in V_1' (here we mean the second occurrence of h in the right-hand side of V_1'). Unfolding 1 backwards with R_3, we get $W = \mathsf{f}(\mathsf{s}(\mathsf{h}), \mathsf{s}(\mathsf{h}), \mathsf{s}(\mathsf{h})) \rightarrow \mathsf{f}(\mathsf{s}(\mathsf{h}), \mathsf{s}(\mathsf{h}), \mathsf{s}(\mathsf{h}))$ and unfolding h forwards with

R_3, we get $W' = \mathsf{f}(\mathsf{s}(\mathsf{h}), \mathsf{s}(1), \mathsf{s}(\mathsf{h})) \rightarrow \mathsf{f}(\mathsf{s}(\mathsf{h}), \mathsf{s}(1), \mathsf{s}(\mathsf{h}))$. The semi-unification test succeeds on both rules: we get the looping terms $\mathsf{f}(\mathsf{s}(\mathsf{h}), \mathsf{s}(\mathsf{h}), \mathsf{s}(\mathsf{h}))$ and $\mathsf{f}(\mathsf{s}(\mathsf{h}), \mathsf{s}(1), \mathsf{s}(\mathsf{h}))$ from W and W', respectively.

In the approach sketched in Example 2, the iterations of $U_{\mathcal{R}}$ are not thoroughly computed because only some selected disagreement pairs are considered for unfolding, unlike in our previous approach [13] which tries to unfold all the subterms in rules. Hence, now the unfoldings are *guided* by disagreement pairs. In this paper, we formally describe the intuitions presented above (Sects. 3–5). We also report experiments on a large set of rewrite systems from the TPBD [17] (Sect. 6). The results we get in practice with the new approach are better than those obtained with the approach of [13] and we do not need to perform several analyses in parallel, nor to unfold variable subterms, unlike [13].

2 Preliminaries

If Y is an operator from a set E to itself, then for any $e \in E$ we let

$$(Y \uparrow 0)(e) = e \quad \text{and} \quad \forall n \in \mathbb{N} : (Y \uparrow n+1)(e) = Y\big((Y \uparrow n)(e)\big) \; .$$

We refer to [4] for the basics of rewriting. From now on, we fix a finite *signature* $\mathcal{F}$ together with an infinite countable set $\mathcal{V}$ of *variables* with $\mathcal{F} \cap \mathcal{V} = \emptyset$. Elements of $\mathcal{F}$ (*symbols*) are denoted by $\mathsf{f}, \mathsf{g}, \mathsf{h}, 0, 1, \ldots$ and elements of $\mathcal{V}$ by $x, y, z, \ldots$ The set of terms over $\mathcal{F} \cup \mathcal{V}$ is denoted by $\mathcal{T}(\mathcal{F}, \mathcal{V})$. For any $t \in \mathcal{T}(\mathcal{F}, \mathcal{V})$, we let $root(t)$ denote the root symbol of t: $root(t) = \mathsf{f}$ if $t = \mathsf{f}(t_1, \ldots, t_m)$ and $root(t) = \bot$ if $t \in \mathcal{V}$, where $\bot$ is a new symbol not occurring in $\mathcal{F}$ and $\mathcal{V}$. We let $Var(t)$ denote the set of variables occurring in t and $Pos(t)$ the set of positions of t. For any $p \in Pos(t)$, we write $t|_p$ to denote the subterm of t at position p and $t[p \leftarrow s]$ to denote the term obtained from t by replacing $t|_p$ with a term s. For any $p, q \in Pos(t)$, we write $p \leq q$ iff p is a prefix of q and we write $p < q$ iff $p \leq q$ and $p \neq q$. We also define the set of non-variable positions of t which either are a prefix of p or include p as a prefix:

$$NPos(t, p) = \{q \in Pos(t) \mid q \leq p \vee p \leq q,\ t|_q \notin \mathcal{V}\}.$$

A *disagreement position* of terms s and t is a position $p \in Pos(s) \cap Pos(t)$ such that $root(s|_p) \neq root(t|_p)$ and, for every $q < p$, $root(s|_q) = root(t|_q)$. The set of disagreement positions of s and t is denoted as $DPos(s, t)$. A *disagreement pair* of s and t is an ordered pair $\langle s|_p, t|_p \rangle$ where $p \in DPos(s, t)$.

Example 3. Let $s = \mathsf{f}(\mathsf{s}(0), \mathsf{s}(1), y)$, $t = \mathsf{f}(x, x, x)$, $p_1 = 1$, $p_2 = 2$ and $p_3 = 3$. Then, $\{p_1, p_2\} \subseteq DPos(s, t)$ and $\langle s|_{p_1}, t|_{p_1} \rangle = \langle \mathsf{s}(0), x \rangle$ and $\langle s|_{p_2}, t|_{p_2} \rangle = \langle \mathsf{s}(1), x \rangle$ are disagreement pairs of s and t. However, $p_3 \notin DPos(s, t)$ because $\langle s|_{p_3}, t|_{p_3} \rangle = \langle y, x \rangle$ and $root(y) = root(x) = \bot$.

We write substitutions as sets of the form $\{x_1/t_1, \ldots, x_n/t_n\}$ denoting that for each $1 \leq i \leq n$, variable x_i is mapped to term t_i (note that x_i may occur in t_i).

The empty substitution (identity) is denoted by *id*. The application of a substitution θ to a syntactic object o is denoted by $o\theta$. We let $mgu(s,t)$ denote the (up to variable renaming) most general unifier of terms s and t. We say that s *semi-unifies* with t when $s\theta_1\theta_2 = t\theta_1$ for some substitutions θ_1 and θ_2.

A *rewrite rule* (or *rule*) over $\mathcal{F} \cup \mathcal{V}$ has the form $l \to r$ with $l, r \in \mathcal{T}(\mathcal{F},\mathcal{V})$, $l \notin \mathcal{V}$ and $Var(r) \subseteq Var(l)$. A *term rewriting system* (TRS) over $\mathcal{F} \cup \mathcal{V}$ is a finite set of rewrite rules over $\mathcal{F} \cup \mathcal{V}$. Given a TRS $\mathcal{R}$ and some terms s and t, we write $s \underset{\mathcal{R}}{\to} t$ if there is a rewrite rule $l \to r$ in $\mathcal{R}$, a substitution θ and $p \in Pos(s)$ such that $s|_p = l\theta$ and $t = s[p \leftarrow r\theta]$. We let $\overset{+}{\underset{\mathcal{R}}{\to}}$ (resp. $\overset{*}{\underset{\mathcal{R}}{\to}}$) denote the transitive (resp. reflexive and transitive) closure of $\underset{\mathcal{R}}{\to}$. We say that a term t is *non-terminating* with respect to (*w.r.t.*) $\mathcal{R}$ when there exist infinitely many terms $t_1, t_2, \ldots$ such that $t \underset{\mathcal{R}}{\to} t_1 \underset{\mathcal{R}}{\to} t_2 \underset{\mathcal{R}}{\to} \cdots$. We say that $\mathcal{R}$ is *non-terminating* if there exists a non-terminating term *w.r.t.* it. A term t *loops w.r.t.* $\mathcal{R}$ when $t \overset{+}{\underset{\mathcal{R}}{\to}} C[t\theta]$ for some context C and substitution θ. Then $t \overset{+}{\underset{\mathcal{R}}{\to}} C[t\theta]$ is called a *loop* for $\mathcal{R}$. We say that $\mathcal{R}$ is *looping* when it admits a loop. If a term loops *w.r.t.* $\mathcal{R}$ then it is non-terminating *w.r.t.* $\mathcal{R}$.

The unfolding operators that we define in Sect. 3 of this paper use *narrowing*. We say that a term s narrows forwards (resp. backwards) to a term t *w.r.t.* a TRS $\mathcal{R}$ when there exists a non-variable position p of s and a rule $l \to r$ of $\mathcal{R}$ renamed with new variables not previously met such that $t = s[p \leftarrow r]\theta$ (resp. $t = s[p \leftarrow l]\theta$) where $\theta = mgu(s|_p, l)$ (resp. $\theta = mgu(s|_p, r)$).

We refer to [3] for details on dependency pairs. The *defined symbols* of a TRS $\mathcal{R}$ over $\mathcal{F} \cup \mathcal{V}$ are $\mathcal{D}_{\mathcal{R}} = \{root(l) \mid l \to r \in \mathcal{R}\}$. For every $\mathsf{f} \in \mathcal{F}$ we let $\mathsf{f}^\#$ be a fresh *tuple symbol* with the same arity as f. The set of tuple symbols is denoted as $\mathcal{F}^\#$. The notations and definitions above with terms over $\mathcal{F} \cup \mathcal{V}$ are naturally extended to terms over $(\mathcal{F} \cup \mathcal{F}^\#) \cup \mathcal{V}$. Elements of $\mathcal{F} \cup \mathcal{F}^\#$ are denoted as $f, g, \ldots$ If $t = \mathsf{f}(t_1, \ldots, t_m) \in \mathcal{T}(\mathcal{F},\mathcal{V})$, we let $t^\#$ denote the term $\mathsf{f}^\#(t_1, \ldots, t_m)$, and we call $t^\#$ an $\mathcal{F}^\#$*-term*. An $\mathcal{F}^\#$*-rule* is a rule whose left-hand and right-hand sides are $\mathcal{F}^\#$-terms. The set of *dependency pairs* of $\mathcal{R}$ is

$$\{l^\# \to t^\# \mid l \to r \in \mathcal{R},\ t \text{ is a subterm of } r,\ root(t) \in \mathcal{D}_{\mathcal{R}}\}.$$

A sequence $s_1 \to t_1, \ldots, s_n \to t_n$ of dependency pairs of $\mathcal{R}$ is an $\mathcal{R}$*-chain* if there exists a substitution σ such that $t_i\sigma \overset{*}{\underset{\mathcal{R}}{\to}} s_{i+1}\sigma$ holds for every two consecutive pairs $s_i \to t_i$ and $s_{i+1} \to t_{i+1}$ in the sequence.

Theorem 1 ([3]). *$\mathcal{R}$ is non-terminating iff there exists an infinite $\mathcal{R}$-chain.*

The *dependency graph* of $\mathcal{R}$ is the graph whose nodes are the dependency pairs of $\mathcal{R}$ and there is an arc from $s \to t$ to $u \to v$ iff $s \to t, u \to v$ is an $\mathcal{R}$-chain. This graph is not computable in general since it is undecidable whether two dependency pairs of $\mathcal{R}$ form an $\mathcal{R}$-chain. Hence, for automation, one constructs an estimated graph containing all the arcs of the real graph. This is done by computing *connectable terms*, which form a superset of those terms

s, t where $s\sigma \xrightarrow[\mathcal{R}]{*} t\sigma$ holds for some substitution σ. The approximation uses the transformations CAP and REN where, for any $t \in \mathcal{T}(\mathcal{F} \cup \mathcal{F}^{\#}, \mathcal{V})$, $\text{CAP}(t)$ (resp. $\text{REN}(t)$) results from replacing all subterms of t with defined root symbol (resp. all variable occurrences in t) by different new variables not previously met. More formally:

$$\text{CAP}(x) = x \text{ if } x \in \mathcal{V}$$

$$\text{CAP}(f(t_1, \dots, t_m)) = \begin{cases} \text{a new variable not previously met} & \text{if } f \in \mathcal{D}_{\mathcal{R}} \\ f(\text{CAP}(t_1), \dots, \text{CAP}(t_m)) & \text{if } f \notin \mathcal{D}_{\mathcal{R}} \end{cases}$$

$$\text{REN}(x) = \text{a new variable not previously met if } x \text{ is an occurrence of a variable}$$

$$\text{REN}(f(t_1, \dots, t_m)) = f(\text{REN}(t_1), \dots, \text{REN}(t_m))$$

A term s is *connectable* to a term t if $\text{REN}(\text{CAP}(s))$ unifies with t. An $\mathcal{F}^{\#}$-rule $l \to r$ is connectable to an $\mathcal{F}^{\#}$-rule $s \to t$ if r is connectable to s. The *estimated dependency graph* of $\mathcal{R}$ is denoted as $DG(\mathcal{R})$. Its nodes are the dependency pairs of $\mathcal{R}$ and there is an arc from N to N' iff N is connectable to N'. We let $SCC(\mathcal{R})$ denote the set of strongly connected components of $DG(\mathcal{R})$ that contain at least one arc. Hence, a strongly connected component consisting of a unique node is in $SCC(\mathcal{R})$ only if there is an arc from the node to itself.

Example 4. Let $\mathcal{R}$ be the TRS of Example 1. We have $SCC(\mathcal{R}) = \{\mathcal{C}\}$ where $\mathcal{C}$ consists of the node $N = \mathsf{f}^{\#}(\mathsf{s}(0), \mathsf{s}(1), x) \to \mathsf{f}^{\#}(x, x, x)$ and of the arc (N, N).

Example 5. Let $\mathcal{R}' = \{\mathsf{f}(0) \to \mathsf{f}(1),\ \mathsf{f}(2) \to \mathsf{f}(0),\ 1 \to 0\}$. We have $SCC(\mathcal{R}') = \{\mathcal{C}'\}$ where $\mathcal{C}'$ consists of the nodes $N_1 = \mathsf{f}^{\#}(0) \to \mathsf{f}^{\#}(1)$ and $N_2 = \mathsf{f}^{\#}(2) \to \mathsf{f}^{\#}(0)$ and of the arcs $\{N_1, N_2\} \times \{N_1, N_2\} \setminus \{(N_2, N_2)\}$. The strongly connected component of $DG(\mathcal{R}')$ which consists of the unique node $\mathsf{f}^{\#}(0) \to 1^{\#}$ does not belong to $SCC(\mathcal{R}')$ because it has no arc.

Finite sequences are written as $[e_1, \dots, e_n]$. We let :: denote the concatenation operator over finite sequences. A *path* in $DG(\mathcal{R})$ is a finite sequence $[N_1, N_2, \dots, N_n]$ of nodes where, for each $1 \leq i < n$, there is an arc from N_i to N_{i+1}. When there is also an arc from N_n to N_1, the path is called a *cycle*. It is called a *simple cycle* if, moreover, there is no repetition of nodes (modulo variable renaming).

3 Guided Unfoldings

In the sequel of this paper, we let $\mathcal{R}$ denote a TRS over $\mathcal{F} \cup \mathcal{V}$.

While the method sketched in Example 2 can be applied directly to the TRS $\mathcal{R}$ under analysis, we use a refinement based on the estimated dependency graph of $\mathcal{R}$. The cycles in $DG(\mathcal{R})$ are over-approximations of the infinite $\mathcal{R}$-chains *i.e.*, any infinite $\mathcal{R}$-chain corresponds to a cycle in the graph but some cycles in the graph may not correspond to any $\mathcal{R}$-chain. Moreover, by Theorem 1, if we find an infinite $\mathcal{R}$-chain then we have proved that $\mathcal{R}$ is non-terminating. Hence, we concentrate on the cycles in $DG(\mathcal{R})$. We try to *solve* them, *i.e.*, to find out if they correspond to any infinite $\mathcal{R}$-chain. This is done by iteratively unfolding the $\mathcal{F}^{\#}$-rules of the cycles. If the semi-unification test succeeds on one of the generated unfolded rules, then we have found a loop.

Definition 1 (Syntactic loop). *A* syntactic loop *in* $\mathcal{R}$ *is a finite sequence* $[N_1, \ldots, N_n]$ *of distinct (modulo variable renaming)* $\mathcal{F}^{\#}$*-rules where, for each* $1 \leq i < n$, N_i *is connectable to* N_{i+1} *and* N_n *is connectable to* N_1. *We identify syntactic loops consisting of the same (modulo variable renaming) elements, not necessarily in the same order.*

Note that the simple cycles in $DG(\mathcal{R})$ are syntactic loops. For any $\mathcal{C} \in SCC(\mathcal{R})$, we let *s-cycles*$(\mathcal{C})$ denote the set of simple cycles in $\mathcal{C}$. We also let

$$s\text{-}cycles(\mathcal{R}) = \cup_{\mathcal{C} \in SCC(\mathcal{R})}\, s\text{-}cycles(\mathcal{C})$$

be the set of simple cycles in $\mathcal{R}$. The rules of any simple cycle in $\mathcal{R}$ are assumed to be pairwise variable disjoint.

Example 6 (Examples 4 *and* 5 *continued).* We have

$$s\text{-}cycles(\mathcal{R}) = \{[N]\} \quad \text{and} \quad s\text{-}cycles(\mathcal{R}') = \{[N_1], [N_1, N_2]\}$$

with, in *s-cycles*$(\mathcal{R}')$, $[N_1, N_2] = [N_2, N_1]$.

The operators we use for unfolding an $\mathcal{F}^{\#}$-rule R at a disagreement position p are defined as follows. They are guided by a given term u and they only work on the non-variable subterms of R. They unify a subterm of R with a subterm of u, see (1) in Definitions 2–3. This corresponds to what we did in Example 2 for generating V_1' from V_1, but in the definitions below we do not only consider p, we consider all its prefixes. The operators also unfold R using narrowing, see (2) in Definitions 2–3: there, $l' \to r' \ll \mathcal{R}$ means that $l' \to r'$ is a new occurrence of a rule of $\mathcal{R}$ that contains new variables not previously met. This corresponds to what we did in Example 2 for generating V_1 from R_1. In contrast to (1), the positions that are greater than p are also considered in (2); for instance in Example 2, we unfolded the inner subterm $\mathsf{0}$ of the disagreement pair component $\mathsf{s}(\mathsf{0})$.

Definition 2 (Forward guided unfoldings). *Let* $l \to r$ *be an* $\mathcal{F}^{\#}$*-rule,* s *be an* $\mathcal{F}^{\#}$*-term and* $p \in DPos(r, s)$. *The forward unfoldings of* $l \to r$ *at position* p*, guided by* s *and w.r.t.* $\mathcal{R}$ *are*

$$F_{\mathcal{R}}(l \to r, s, p) = \left\{ U \;\middle|\; \begin{array}{l} q \in NPos(r, p),\ q \leq p \\ \theta = mgu(r|_q, s|_q),\ U = (l \to r)\theta \end{array} \right\}^{(1)} \cup \left\{ U \;\middle|\; \begin{array}{l} q \in NPos(r, p),\ l' \to r' \ll \mathcal{R} \\ \theta = mgu(r|_q, l'),\ U = (l \to r[q \leftarrow r'])\theta \end{array} \right\}^{(2)}.$$

Definition 3 (Backward guided unfoldings). *Let $s \to t$ be an $\mathcal{F}^{\#}$-rule, r be an $\mathcal{F}^{\#}$-term and $p \in DPos(r,s)$. The backward unfoldings of $s \to t$ at position p, guided by r and w.r.t. $\mathcal{R}$ are*

$$B_{\mathcal{R}}(s \to t, r, p) = \left\{ U \;\middle|\; \begin{array}{l} q \in NPos(s,p),\ q \leq p \\ \theta = mgu(r|_q, s|_q),\ U = (s \to t)\theta \end{array} \right\}^{(1)} \cup$$
$$\left\{ U \;\middle|\; \begin{array}{l} q \in NPos(s,p),\ l' \to r' \ll \mathcal{R} \\ \theta = mgu(s|_q, r'),\ U = (s[q \leftarrow l'] \to t)\theta \end{array} \right\}^{(2)}.$$

Example 7 (Examples 4 and 6 continued). $[N]$ is a simple cycle in $\mathcal{R}$ with

$$N = \underbrace{\mathsf{f}^{\#}(\mathsf{s}(\mathsf{0}), \mathsf{s}(\mathsf{1}), x)}_{s} \to \underbrace{\mathsf{f}^{\#}(x, x, x)}_{t}.$$

Let $r = t$. Then $p = 1 \in DPos(r,s)$. Moreover, $q = 1.1 \in NPos(s,p)$ because $p \leq q$ and $s|_q = \mathsf{0}$ is not a variable. Let $l' \to r' = \mathsf{h} \to \mathsf{0} \in \mathcal{R}$. We have $id = mgu(s|_q, r')$. Hence, by (2) in Definition 3, we have

$$U_1 = \underbrace{\mathsf{f}^{\#}(\mathsf{s}(\mathsf{h}), \mathsf{s}(\mathsf{1}), x)}_{s_1} \to \underbrace{\mathsf{f}^{\#}(x, x, x)}_{t_1} \in B_{\mathcal{R}}(N, r, p).$$

Let $r_1 = t_1$. Then, $p = 1 \in DPos(r_1, s_1)$. Moreover, $p \in NPos(s_1, p)$ with $s_1|_p = \mathsf{s}(\mathsf{h})$, $p \leq p$ and $r_1|_p = x$. As $\{x/\mathsf{s}(\mathsf{h})\} = mgu(r_1|_p, s_1|_p)$, by (1) in Definition 3 we have

$$U_1' = \underbrace{\mathsf{f}^{\#}(\mathsf{s}(\mathsf{h}), \mathsf{s}(\mathsf{1}), \mathsf{s}(\mathsf{h}))}_{s_1'} \to \underbrace{\mathsf{f}^{\#}(\mathsf{s}(\mathsf{h}), \mathsf{s}(\mathsf{h}), \mathsf{s}(\mathsf{h}))}_{t_1'} \in B_{\mathcal{R}}(U_1, r_1, p).$$

Let $r_1' = t_1'$. Then, $p' = 2.1 \in DPos(r_1', s_1')$ with $p' \in NPos(s_1', p')$. Let $l'' \to r'' = \mathsf{h} \to \mathsf{1} \in \mathcal{R}$. We have $id = mgu(s_1'|_{p'}, r'')$. Hence, by (2) in Definition 3, we have

$$U_1'' = \mathsf{f}^{\#}(\mathsf{s}(\mathsf{h}), \mathsf{s}(\mathsf{h}), \mathsf{s}(\mathsf{h})) \to \mathsf{f}^{\#}(\mathsf{s}(\mathsf{h}), \mathsf{s}(\mathsf{h}), \mathsf{s}(\mathsf{h})) \in B_{\mathcal{R}}(U_1', r_1', p').$$

Our approach consists of iteratively unfolding syntactic loops using the following operator.

Definition 4 (Guided unfoldings). *Let X be a set of syntactic loops of $\mathcal{R}$. The* guided unfoldings *of X w.r.t. $\mathcal{R}$ are defined as*

$$GU_{\mathcal{R}}(X) = \left\{ L :: [U] :: L' \;\middle|\; \begin{array}{l} L :: [l \to r, s \to t] :: L' \in X,\ \theta = mgu(r,s) \\ U = (l \to t)\theta,\ L :: [U] :: L' \text{ is a syntactic loop} \end{array} \right\}^{(1)} \cup$$
$$\left\{ L :: [U, s \to t] :: L' \;\middle|\; \begin{array}{l} L :: [l \to r, s \to t] :: L' \in X \\ p \in DPos(r,s),\ U \in F_{\mathcal{R}}(l \to r, s, p) \\ L :: [U, s \to t] :: L' \text{ is a syntactic loop} \end{array} \right\}^{(2)} \cup$$

$$\left\{ L::[l \to r, U]::L' \;\middle|\; \begin{array}{l} L::[l \to r, s \to t]::L' \in X \\ p \in DPos(r,s),\ U \in B_{\mathcal{R}}(s \to t, r, p) \\ L::[l \to r, U]::L' \textit{ is a syntactic loop} \end{array} \right\}^{(3)} \cup$$

$$\left\{ [U] \;\middle|\; \begin{array}{l} [l \to r] \in X,\ p \in DPos(r,l) \\ U \in F_{\mathcal{R}}(l \to r, l, p) \cup B_{\mathcal{R}}(l \to r, r, p) \\ [U] \textit{ is a syntactic loop} \end{array} \right\}^{(4)} .$$

The general idea is to *compress* the syntactic loops into singletons by iterated applications of this operator. The semi-unification criterion can then be applied to these singletons, see Theorem 2 below. Compression takes place in case (1) of Definition 4: when the right-hand side of a rule unifies with the left-hand side of its successor, then both rules are merged. When merging two successive rules is not possible yet, the operators $F_{\mathcal{R}}$ and $B_{\mathcal{R}}$ are applied to try to transform the rules into mergeable ones, see cases (2) and (3). Once a syntactic loop has been compressed to a singleton, we keep on unfolding (case (4)) to try reaching a compressed form satisfying the semi-unification criterion. Note that after an unfolding step, we might get a sequence which is not a syntactic loop: the newly generated rule U might be identical to another rule in the sequence or it might not be connectable to its predecessor or successor. So, (1)–(4) require that the generated sequence is a syntactic loop.

The guided unfolding semantics is defined as follows, in the style of [1,13].

Definition 5 (Guided unfolding semantics). *The* guided unfolding semantics *of $\mathcal{R}$ is the limit of the unfolding process described in Definition 4, starting from the simple cycles in $\mathcal{R}$: $gunf(\mathcal{R}) = \cup_{n \in \mathbb{N}} gunf(\mathcal{R}, n)$ where, for all $n \in \mathbb{N}$,*

$$gunf(\mathcal{R}, n) = (GU_{\mathcal{R}} \uparrow n)(s\text{-}cycles(\mathcal{R})).$$

This semantics is very similar to the *overlap closure* [7] of $\mathcal{R}$ (denoted by $OC(\mathcal{R})$). A difference is that for computing $gunf(\mathcal{R})$ one starts from dependency pairs of $\mathcal{R}$ ($s\text{-}cycles(\mathcal{R})$), whereas for computing $OC(\mathcal{R})$ one starts directly from the rules of $\mathcal{R}$. In case (1) of Definition 4, we merge two unfolded rules. Similarly, for computing $OC(\mathcal{R})$ one overlaps closures with closures. However, in cases (2)–(4) the operators $F_{\mathcal{R}}$ and $B_{\mathcal{R}}$ narrow an unfolded rule with a rule of $\mathcal{R}$, not with another unfolded rule, unlike in the computation of $OC(\mathcal{R})$.

Example 8. By Example 7 and (4) in Definition 4, we have $[U_1''] \in gunf(\mathcal{R}, 3)$.

Example 9. Let $\mathcal{R} = \{\mathsf{f}(0) \to \mathsf{g}(1),\ \mathsf{g}(1) \to \mathsf{f}(0)\}$. Then, $SCC(\mathcal{R}) = \{\mathcal{C}\}$ where $\mathcal{C}$ consists of the nodes $N_1 = \mathsf{f}^{\#}(0) \to \mathsf{g}^{\#}(1)$ and $N_2 = \mathsf{g}^{\#}(1) \to \mathsf{f}^{\#}(0)$ and of the arcs (N_1, N_2) and (N_2, N_1). Moreover, $s\text{-}cycles(\mathcal{R}) = \{[N_1, N_2]\}$. As $id = mgu(\mathsf{g}^{\#}(1), \mathsf{g}^{\#}(1))$ and $(\mathsf{f}^{\#}(0) \to \mathsf{f}^{\#}(0))id = \mathsf{f}^{\#}(0) \to \mathsf{f}^{\#}(0)$, by (1) in Definition 4 we have $[\mathsf{f}^{\#}(0) \to \mathsf{f}^{\#}(0)] \in gunf(\mathcal{R}, 1)$.

Proposition 1. *For any $n \in \mathbb{N}$ and $[s^{\#} \to t^{\#}] \in gunf(\mathcal{R}, n)$ there exists some context C such that $s \xrightarrow[\mathcal{R}]{+} C[t]$.*

Proof. For some context C, we have $s \to C[t] \in unf(\mathcal{R})$ where $unf(\mathcal{R})$ is the unfolding semantics defined in [13]. So, by Prop. 3.12 of [13], $s \xrightarrow[\mathcal{R}]{+} C[t]$.

4 Inferring Terms that Loop

As in [13], we use semi-unification [10] for detecting loops. Semi-unification encompasses both matching and unification, and a polynomial-time algorithm for it can be found in [8].

Theorem 2. *For any $n \in \mathbb{N}$, if there exist $[s^\# \to t^\#] \in gunf(\mathcal{R}, n)$ and some substitutions θ_1 and θ_2 such that $s\theta_1\theta_2 = t\theta_1$, then the term $s\theta_1$ loops w.r.t. $\mathcal{R}$.*

Proof. By Proposition 1, $s \xrightarrow[\mathcal{R}]{+} C[t]$ for some context C. Since $\xrightarrow[\mathcal{R}]{}$ is stable, we have

$$s\theta_1 \xrightarrow[\mathcal{R}]{+} C[t]\theta_1 \quad i.e., \quad s\theta_1 \xrightarrow[\mathcal{R}]{+} C\theta_1[t\theta_1] \quad i.e., \quad s\theta_1 \xrightarrow[\mathcal{R}]{+} C\theta_1[s\theta_1\theta_2].$$

Hence, $s\theta_1$ loops *w.r.t.* $\mathcal{R}$.

Example 10 (Example 8 continued). We have

$$\underbrace{[\mathsf{f}^\#(\mathsf{s}(\mathsf{h}), \mathsf{s}(\mathsf{h}), \mathsf{s}(\mathsf{h})) \to \mathsf{f}^\#(\mathsf{s}(\mathsf{h}), \mathsf{s}(\mathsf{h}), \mathsf{s}(\mathsf{h}))]}_{U_1''} \in gunf(\mathcal{R}, 3)$$

with $\mathsf{f}(\mathsf{s}(\mathsf{h}), \mathsf{s}(\mathsf{h}), \mathsf{s}(\mathsf{h}))\theta_1\theta_2 = \mathsf{f}(\mathsf{s}(\mathsf{h}), \mathsf{s}(\mathsf{h}), \mathsf{s}(\mathsf{h}))\theta_1$ for $\theta_1 = \theta_2 = id$. Consequently, $\mathsf{f}(\mathsf{s}(\mathsf{h}), \mathsf{s}(\mathsf{h}), \mathsf{s}(\mathsf{h}))\theta_1 = \mathsf{f}(\mathsf{s}(\mathsf{h}), \mathsf{s}(\mathsf{h}), \mathsf{s}(\mathsf{h}))$ loops *w.r.t.* $\mathcal{R}$.

Example 11 (Example 9 continued). $[\mathsf{f}^\#(\mathsf{0}) \to \mathsf{f}^\#(\mathsf{0})] \in gunf(\mathcal{R}, 1)$ with $\mathsf{f}(\mathsf{0})\theta_1\theta_2 = \mathsf{f}(\mathsf{0})\theta_1$ for $\theta_1 = \theta_2 = id$. Hence, $\mathsf{f}(\mathsf{0})\theta_1 = \mathsf{f}(\mathsf{0})$ loops *w.r.t.* $\mathcal{R}$.

The substitutions θ_1 and θ_2 that we use in the next example are more sophisticated than in Examples 10 and 11.

Example 12. Let $\mathcal{R} = \{\mathsf{f}(\mathsf{g}(x, \mathsf{0}), y) \to \mathsf{f}(\mathsf{g}(\mathsf{0}, x), \mathsf{h}(y))\}$. Then, $SCC(\mathcal{R}) = \{\mathcal{C}\}$ where $\mathcal{C}$ consists of the node $N = \mathsf{f}^\#(\mathsf{g}(x, \mathsf{0}), y) \to \mathsf{f}^\#(\mathsf{g}(\mathsf{0}, x), \mathsf{h}(y))$ and of the arc (N, N). Moreover, $s\text{-}cycles(\mathcal{R}) = \{[N]\}$ hence $[N] \in gunf(\mathcal{R}, 0)$. Therefore, as $\mathsf{f}(\mathsf{g}(x, \mathsf{0}), y)\theta_1\theta_2 = \mathsf{f}(\mathsf{g}(\mathsf{0}, x), \mathsf{h}(y))\theta_1$ for $\theta_1 = \{x/\mathsf{0}\}$ and $\theta_2 = \{y/\mathsf{h}(y)\}$, by Theorem 2 we have that $\mathsf{f}(\mathsf{g}(x, \mathsf{0}), y)\theta_1 = \mathsf{f}(\mathsf{g}(\mathsf{0}, \mathsf{0}), y)$ loops *w.r.t.* $\mathcal{R}$.

We do not have an example where semi-unification is necessary for detecting a loop. In every example that we have considered, matching or unification were enough. However, semi-unification sometimes allows us to detect loops earlier in the unfolding process than with matching and unification. This is important in practice, because the number of unfolded rules can grow rapidly from iteration to iteration.

Example 13 (Example 12 continued). Semi-unification allows us to detect a loop at iteration 0 of $GU_{\mathcal{R}}$. But a loop can also be detected at iteration 1 using matching. Indeed, we have

$$N = \underbrace{\mathsf{f}^\#(\mathsf{g}(x, \mathsf{0}), y)}_{l} \to \underbrace{\mathsf{f}^\#(\mathsf{g}(\mathsf{0}, x), \mathsf{h}(y))}_{r}$$

with $p = 1.1 \in \mathit{DPos}(r, l)$. Hence,

$$U = \underbrace{\mathsf{f}^{\#}(\mathsf{g}(0,0), y)}_{s^{\#}} \rightarrow \underbrace{\mathsf{f}^{\#}(\mathsf{g}(0,0), \mathsf{h}(y))}_{t^{\#}} \in F_{\mathcal{R}}(l \rightarrow r, l, p).$$

So, by (4) in Definition 4, we have $[U] \in \mathit{gunf}(\mathcal{R}, 1)$. Notice that $s\theta = t$ for $\theta = \{y/\mathsf{h}(y)\}$, so s matches t. Moreover, by Theorem 2, $s = \mathsf{f}(\mathsf{g}(0,0), y)$ loops *w.r.t.* $\mathcal{R}$ (take $\theta_1 = \mathit{id}$ and $\theta_2 = \theta$).

5 Further Comparisons with the Approach of [13]

The approach that we have presented in [13] relies on an unfolding operator $U_{\mathcal{R}}$ (where $\mathcal{R}$ is the TRS under analysis) which is also based on forward and backward narrowing (as $F_{\mathcal{R}}$ and $B_{\mathcal{R}}$ herein). But, unlike the technique that we have presented above, it directly unfolds the rules (not the dependency pairs) of $\mathcal{R}$ and it does not compute any SCC. Moreover, it consists of a thorough computation of the iterations of $U_{\mathcal{R}}$ followed by a mechanism for eliminating rules that cannot be further unfolded to a rule $l \rightarrow r$ where l semi-unifies with r. Such rules are said to be *root-useless*. The set of root-useless rules is an overapproximation of the set of useless rules (rules that cannot contribute to detecting a loop), hence the elimination technique of [13] may remove some rules which are actually useful for detecting a loop. Our non-termination analyser which is based on [13] uses a time limit. It stops whenever it has detected a loop within the limit (then it answers NO, standing for *No, this TRS does not terminate* as in the Termination Competition [15]) or when the limit has been reached (then it answers TIME OUT) or when no more unfolded rule could be generated at some point within the limit ($(U_{\mathcal{R}} \uparrow n)(\mathcal{R}) = \emptyset$ for some n). In the last situation, either the TRS under analysis is not looping (it is terminating or non-looping non-terminating) or it is looping but a loop for it cannot be captured by the approach (for instance, the elimination mechanism has removed all the useful rules). In such a situation, our analyser answers DON'T KNOW.

Example 14. Consider the terminating TRS $\mathcal{R} = \{0 \rightarrow 1\}$. As the left-hand (resp. right-hand) side of the rule of $\mathcal{R}$ cannot be narrowed backwards (resp. forwards) with $\mathcal{R}$ then we have $(U_{\mathcal{R}} \uparrow 1)(\mathcal{R}) = \emptyset$.

In contrast, the approach that we have presented in Sects. 3–4 above avoids the generation of some rules by only unfolding disagreement pairs. Currently, in terms of loop detection power, we do not have any theoretical comparison between this new technique and that of [13]. Our new non-termination analyser also uses a time limit and answers NO, TIME OUT or DON'T KNOW when no more unfolded rules are generated at some point ($\mathit{gunf}(\mathcal{R}, n) = \emptyset$ for some n, as in Example 14). Moreover, it allows the user to fix a *selection strategy* of disagreement pairs: in Definition 4, the conditions $p \in \mathit{DPos}(r, s)$ (cases (2)–(3)) and $p \in \mathit{DPos}(r, l)$ (case (4)) are replaced with $p \in \mathit{select}_{\mathcal{R}}(l \rightarrow r, s \rightarrow t)$ and $p \in \mathit{select}_{\mathcal{R}}(l \rightarrow r, l \rightarrow r)$ respectively, where $\mathit{select}_{\mathcal{R}}$ can be one of the following functions.

Selection of all the pairs: $select\_all_{\mathcal{R}}(l \to r, s \to t) = DPos(r, s)$.

Leftmost selection: if $DPos(r, s) = \emptyset$ then $select\_lm_{\mathcal{R}}(l \to r, s \to t) = \emptyset$, otherwise $select\_lm_{\mathcal{R}}(l \to r, s \to t) = \{p\}$ where p is the leftmost disagreement position of r and s.

Leftmost selection with non-empty unfoldings:

$$select\_lmne_{\mathcal{R}}(l \to r, s \to t) = \{p\}$$

where p is the leftmost disagreement position of r and s such that

$$F_{\mathcal{R}}(l \to r, s, p) \cup B_{\mathcal{R}}(s \to t, r, p) \neq \emptyset.$$

If such a position p does not exist then $select\_lmne_{\mathcal{R}}(l \to r, s \to t) = \emptyset$.

Example 15. Let $\mathcal{R} = \{\mathsf{f}(\mathsf{s}(0), \mathsf{s}(1), z) \to \mathsf{f}(x, y, z)\}$ and $l = \mathsf{f}^{\#}(\mathsf{s}(0), \mathsf{s}(1), z)$ and $r = \mathsf{f}^{\#}(x, y, z)$. Then, we have $select\_all_{\mathcal{R}}(l \to r, l \to r) = DPos(r, l) = \{1, 2\}$. Moreover, 1 is the leftmost disagreement position of r and l because $r|_1 = x$ occurs to the left of $r|_2 = y$ in r and $l|_1 = \mathsf{s}(0)$ occurs to the left of $l|_2 = \mathsf{s}(1)$ in l. Therefore, we have $select\_lm_{\mathcal{R}}(l \to r, l \to r) = \{1\}$.

Example 16. Let $\mathcal{R} = \{\mathsf{f}(x, x) \to \mathsf{f}(\mathsf{g}(x), \mathsf{h}(x)),\ \mathsf{h}(x) \to \mathsf{g}(x)\}$. Then, $SCC(\mathcal{R}) = \{\mathcal{C}\}$ where $\mathcal{C}$ consists of the node $N = l \to r = \mathsf{f}^{\#}(x, x) \to \mathsf{f}^{\#}(\mathsf{g}(x), \mathsf{h}(x))$ and of the arc (N, N). Then, $DPos(r, l) = \{1, 2\}$ and $select\_lm_{\mathcal{R}}(N, N) = \{1\}$. As $F_{\mathcal{R}}(N, l, 1) \cup B_{\mathcal{R}}(N, r, 1) = \emptyset$ and $F_{\mathcal{R}}(N, l, 2) \cup B_{\mathcal{R}}(N, r, 2) \neq \emptyset$ (for instance, $\mathsf{f}^{\#}(x, x) \to \mathsf{f}^{\#}(\mathsf{g}(x), \mathsf{g}(x)) \in F_{\mathcal{R}}(N, l, 2)$ is obtained from narrowing $r|_2 = \mathsf{h}(x)$ forwards with $\mathsf{h}(x) \to \mathsf{g}(x)$), then $select\_lmne_{\mathcal{R}}(N, N) = \{2\}$.

As the approach of [13], and depending on the strategy used for selecting disagreement pairs, our new technique is not complete in the sense that it may miss some loop witnesses.

Example 17 (Example 16 *continued).* We have $gunf(\mathcal{R}, 0) = s\text{-}cycles(\mathcal{R}) = \{[N]\}$. As l does not semi-unify with r, no loop is detected from $gunf(\mathcal{R}, 0)$, so we go on and compute $gunf(\mathcal{R}, 1)$. Only case (4) of Definition 4 is applicable to $[N]$. First, suppose that $select_{\mathcal{R}} = select\_lm_{\mathcal{R}}$. Then, $select_{\mathcal{R}}(N, N) = \{1\}$ and, as $F_{\mathcal{R}}(N, l, 1) \cup B_{\mathcal{R}}(N, r, 1) = \emptyset$, case (4) does not produce any rule. Consequently, we have $gunf(\mathcal{R}, 1) = \emptyset$, hence no loop is detected for $\mathcal{R}$. Now, suppose that $select_{\mathcal{R}} = select\_lmne_{\mathcal{R}}$. Then, $select_{\mathcal{R}}(N, N) = \{2\}$. Narrowing $r|_2 = \mathsf{h}(x)$ forwards with $\mathsf{h}(x) \to \mathsf{g}(x)$, we get the rule $N' = \mathsf{f}^{\#}(x, x) \to \mathsf{f}^{\#}(\mathsf{g}(x), \mathsf{g}(x))$ which is an element of $F_{\mathcal{R}}(N, l, 2)$. Hence, $[N'] \in gunf(\mathcal{R}, 1)$. As in N' we have that $\mathsf{f}(x, x)$ semi-unifies with $\mathsf{f}(\mathsf{g}(x), \mathsf{g}(x))$ (take $\theta_1 = id$ and $\theta_2 = \{x/\mathsf{g}(x)\}$), then $\mathsf{f}(x, x)$ loops *w.r.t.* $\mathcal{R}$. This loop is also detected by the approach of [13].

6 Experiments

We have implemented the technique of this paper in our analyser NTI[1] (Non-Termination Inference). For our experiments, we have extracted from the directory `TRS_Standard` of the TPBD [17] all the valid rewrite systems[2] that were

[1] http://lim.univ-reunion.fr/staff/epayet/Research/NTI/NTI.html.

[2] Surprisingly, the subdirectory `Transformed_CSR_04` contains 60 files where a pair $l \to r$ with $Var(r) \not\subseteq Var(l)$ occurs. These pairs are not valid rewrite rules.

either proved looping or unproved[3] during the Termination Competition 2017 (TC'17) [15]. Otherwise stated, we removed from `TRS_Standard` all the non-valid TRSs and all the TRSs that were proved terminating or non-looping non-terminating by a tool participating in the competition. We ended up with a set $\mathcal{S}$ of 333 rewrite systems. We let $\mathcal{L}$ (resp. $\mathcal{U}$) be the subset of $\mathcal{S}$ consisting of all the systems that were proved looping (resp. that were unproved) during TC'17. Some characteristics of $\mathcal{L}$ and $\mathcal{U}$ are reported in Table 1. Note that the complete set of simple cycles of a TRS may be really huge, hence NTI only computes a subset of it. The simple cycle characteristics given in Table 1 relate to the subsets computed by NTI.

Table 1. Some characteristics of the analysed TRSs. Sizes are in number of rules. In square brackets, we report the number of TRSs with the corresponding min or max.

$\mathcal{S} = \mathcal{L} \uplus \mathcal{U}$ (333 TRSs)	$\mathcal{L}$ (173 TRSs)			$\mathcal{U}$ (160 TRSs)		
	Min	Max	Average	Min	Max	Average
TRS size	1 [17]	104 [1]	11.08	1 [9]	837 [1]	64.78
Number of SCCs	1 [101]	12 [1]	1.95	1 [70]	130 [1]	6.14
SCC size	1 [96]	192 [1]	4.44	1 [54]	473 [1]	10.79
Number of simple cycles	1 [47]	185 [1]	8.55	2 [15]	1,176 [1]	69.02
Simple cycle size	1 [157]	9 [2]	2.23	1 [157]	9 [4]	2.21
Number of symbols	1 [4]	66 [1]	9.09	2 [7]	259 [1]	24.14
Symbol arity	0 [153]	5 [2]	1.07	0 [150]	12 [2]	1.94
Number of defined symbols	1 [28]	58 [1]	5.21	1 [15]	132 [2]	17.19
Defined symbol arity	0 [74]	5 [2]	1.38	0 [28]	12 [2]	2.27

We have run our new approach (NTI'18) and that of [13] (NTI'08) on the TRSs of $\mathcal{S}$. The results are reported in Tables 2 and 3. We used an Intel 2-core i5 at 2 GHz with 8 GB of RAM and the time limit fixed for a proof was 120 s. For every selection strategy, NTI'18 issues more successful proofs (NO) and generates less unfolded rules than NTI'08. Moreover, as it avoids the generation of some rules instead of computing all the unfolding and then eliminating some rules (as NTI'08 does), its times are better. At the bottom of the tables, we give the numbers of TRSs proved looping by both approaches and by one approach only. NTI'18 succeeds on all the TRSs of $\mathcal{L}$ on which NTI'08 succeeds, but it fails on one TRS of $\mathcal{U}$ on which NTI'08 succeeds. This is due to our simplified computation of the set of simple cycles: our algorithm does not generate the cycle that would allow NTI'18 to succeed and NTI'18 times out, trying to unfold syntactic loops from which it cannot detect anything. Another point to note is that the implementation of the new approach does not need to run several

[3] By *unproved* we mean that no tool succeeded in proving that these TRSs were terminating or non-terminating (all the tools failed on these TRSs).

analyses in parallel to achieve the results presented in Tables 2 and 3. One single thread of computation is enough. On the contrary, for the approach of [13], 3 parallel threads are necessary: one with forward unfoldings only, one with backward unfoldings only and one with forward and backward unfoldings together. The results get worse if NTI'08 only runs one thread performing forward and backward unfoldings together. In Tables 2 and 3, we report in square brackets the number of successes of NTI'08 when it only runs one thread performing both forward and backward unfoldings.

Table 2. Analysis results on the TRSs of $\mathcal{L}$.

$\mathcal{L}$ (173 TRSs)	NTI'08	NTI'18		
		select_all	*select_lm*	*select_lmne*
NO	152 [149]	157	157	158
DON'T KNOW	0	0	1	0
TIME OUT	21	16	15	15
Time	2,966 s	2,194 s	1,890 s	1,889 s
Generated rules	11,167,976	9,030,962	8,857,421	8,860,560
NO(NTI'08) ∩ NO(NTI'18)		152	151	152
NO(NTI'08) \ NO(NTI'18)		0	1	0
NO(NTI'18) \ NO(NTI'08)		5	6	6

Table 3. Analysis results on the TRSs of $\mathcal{U}$.

$\mathcal{U}$ (160 TRSs)	NTI'08	NTI'18		
		select_all	*select_lm*	*select_lmne*
NO	4 [3]	6	6	6
DON'T KNOW	0	0	1	0
TIME OUT	156	154	153	154
Time	18,742 s	18,563 s	18,414 s	18,534 s
Generated rules	64,011,002	53,134,334	61,245,705	63,300,604
NO(NTI'08) ∩ NO(NTI'18)		3	3	3
NO(NTI'08) \ NO(NTI'18)		1	1	1
NO(NTI'18) \ NO(NTI'08)		3	3	3

Four tools participated in the category *TRS Standard* of TC'17: AProVE [2,5], MU-TERM [11], NaTT [12] and WANDA [9]. The numbers of TRSs proved looping by each of them during the competition is reported in Table 4. An important point to note here is that the time limit fixed in TC'17 was 300s, whereas in our experiments with NTI'18 and NTI'08 it was 120s. Moreover, the machine we

Table 4. Number of successes (NO) on $\mathcal{L}$ and $\mathcal{U}$ obtained during TC'17 and those obtained by NTI during our experiments.

$\mathcal{S} = \mathcal{L} \uplus \mathcal{U}$ (333 TRSs)	TC'17 (time limit = 300 s)				(time limit = 120 s)	
	AProVE	MU-TERM	NaTT	WANDA	NTI'08	NTI'18 (*select_lmne*)
$\mathcal{L}$ (173 TRSs)	172	81	109	0	152	158
$\mathcal{U}$ (160 TRSs)	0	0	0	0	4	6

used (an Intel 2-core i5 at 2 GHz with 8 GB of RAM) is much less powerful than the machine used during TC'17 (the StarExec platform [14] running on an Intel Xeon E5-2609 at 2.4 GHz with 129 GB of RAM). All the tools of TC'17 failed on all the rewrite systems of $\mathcal{U}$. In contrast, NTI'18 (resp. NTI'08) finds a loop for 6 (resp. 4) of them. Regarding $\mathcal{L}$, AProVE was able to prove loopingness of 172 out of 173 TRSs. The only TRS of $\mathcal{L}$ on which AProVE failed[4] was proved looping by NaTT. In comparison, our approach succeeds on 158 systems of $\mathcal{L}$, less than AProVE but more than the other tools of TC'17. Similarly to our approach, AProVE handles the SCCs of the estimated dependency graph independently, but it first performs a termination analysis. The non-termination analysis is then only applied to those SCCs that could not be proved terminating. On the contrary, NTI only performs non-termination proofs. If an SCC is terminating, it cannot prove it and keeps on trying a non-termination proof, unnecessarily generating unfolded rules at the expense of the analysis of the other SCCs. The loop detection techniques implemented in AProVE and NTI'18 are based on the idea of searching for loops by forward and backward narrowing of dependency pairs and by using semi-unification to detect potential loops. This idea has been presented in [6] where heuristics are used to select forward or backward narrowing. Note that in constrast, the technique that we present herein does not use any heuristics and proceeds both forwards and backwards.

7 Conclusion

We have reconsidered and modified the unfolding-based technique of [13] for detecting loops in standard term rewriting. The new approach uses disagreement pairs for guiding the unfoldings, which now are only partially computed, whereas the technique of [13] consists of a thorough computation followed by a mechanism for eliminating some rules. Two theoretical questions remain open: in terms of loop detection, is an approach more powerful than the other and does semi-unification subsume matching and unification?

We have implemented the new approach in our tool NTI and compared it to [13] on a set of 333 rewrite systems. The new results are better (better times, more successful proofs, less unfolded rules). Moreover, the approach compares well to the tools that participated in TC'17. However, the number of generated

[4] `Ex6_15_AEL02_FR.xml` in the directory `TRS_Standard/Transformed_CSR_04`.

rules is still important. In an attempt to reduce it, during our experiments we added the elimination mechanism of [13] to the new approach, but the results we recorded were not satisfactory (an equivalent, slightly smaller, number of generated rules but, due to the computational overhead, bigger times and less successes); hence, we removed it. Termination analysis may help to reduce the number of unfolded rules by detecting terminating SCCs in the estimated dependency graph *i.e.*, SCCs on which it is useless to try a non-termination proof. In other words, we could use termination analysis as an elimination mechanism. Several efficient and powerful termination analysers have been implemented so far [16] and one of them could be called by NTI. A final idea to improve our approach would be to consider more sophisticated strategies for selecting disagreement pairs.

Acknowledgements. The author thanks the anonymous reviewers for their many helpful comments and constructive criticisms. He also thanks Fred Mesnard for presenting the paper at the symposium.

References

1. Alpuente, M., Falaschi, M., Moreno, G., Vidal, G.: Safe folding/unfolding with conditional narrowing. In: Hanus, M., Heering, J., Meinke, K. (eds.) ALP/HOA -1997. LNCS, vol. 1298, pp. 1–15. Springer, Heidelberg (1997). https://doi.org/10.1007/BFb0026999
2. AProVE Web site. http://aprove.informatik.rwth-aachen.de/
3. Arts, T., Giesl, J.: Termination of term rewriting using dependency pairs. Theor. Comput. Sci. **236**, 133–178 (2000)
4. Baader, F., Nipkow, T.: Term Rewriting and All That. Cambridge University Press, Cambridge (1998)
5. Giesl, J., et al.: Analyzing program termination and complexity automatically with AProVE. J. Autom. Reason. **58**(1), 3–31 (2017)
6. Giesl, J., Thiemann, R., Schneider-Kamp, P.: Proving and disproving termination of higher-order functions. In: Gramlich, B. (ed.) FroCoS 2005. LNCS (LNAI), vol. 3717, pp. 216–231. Springer, Heidelberg (2005). https://doi.org/10.1007/11559306_12
7. Guttag, J.V., Kapur, D., Musser, D.R.: On proving uniform termination and restricted termination of rewriting systems. SIAM J. Comput. **12**(1), 189–214 (1983)
8. Kapur, D., Musser, D., Narendran, P., Stillman, J.: Semi-unification. Theor. Comput. Sci. **81**(2), 169–187 (1991)
9. Kop, C.: WANDA - A higher-order termination tool. http://wandahot.sourceforge.net
10. Lankford, D.S., Musser, D.R.: A finite termination criterion. Unpublished Draft, USC Information Sciences Institute, Marina Del Rey, CA (1978)
11. MU-TERM Web site. http://zenon.dsic.upv.es/muterm/
12. NaTT - The Nagoya Termination Tool. https://www.trs.css.i.nagoya-u.ac.jp/NaTT/
13. Payet, É.: Loop detection in term rewriting using the eliminating unfoldings. Theor. Comput. Sci. **403**(2–3), 307–327 (2008)

14. StarExec - A cross-community solver execution and benchmark library service. http://www.starexec.org/
15. The Annual International Termination Competition. http://termination-portal.org/wiki/Termination_Competition
16. Termination Portal – An (incomplete) overview of existing tools for termination analysis. http://termination-portal.org/wiki/Category:Tools
17. Termination Problems Data Base. http://termination-portal.org/wiki/TPDB
18. Toyama, Y.: Counterexamples to the termination for the direct sum of term rewriting systems. Inf. Process. Lett. **25**(3), 141–143 (1987)

Homeomorphic Embedding Modulo Combinations of Associativity and Commutativity Axioms

María Alpuente[1], Angel Cuenca-Ortega[1,3], Santiago Escobar[1(✉)], and José Meseguer[2]

[1] DSIC-ELP, Universitat Politècnica de València, Valencia, Spain
{alpuente,acuenca,sescobar}@dsic.upv.es
[2] University of Illinois at Urbana-Champaign, Urbana, IL, USA
meseguer@illinois.edu
[3] Universidad de Guayaquil, Guayaquil, Ecuador
angel.cuencao@ug.edu.ec

Abstract. The Homeomorphic Embedding relation has been amply used for defining termination criteria of symbolic methods for program analysis, transformation, and verification. However, homeomorphic embedding has never been investigated in the context of order-sorted rewrite theories that support symbolic execution methods *modulo* equational axioms. This paper generalizes the symbolic homeomorphic embedding relation to order–sorted rewrite theories that may contain various combinations of associativity and/or commutativity axioms for different binary operators. We systematically measure the performance of increasingly efficient formulations of the homeomorphic embedding relation modulo associativity and commutativity axioms. From our experimental results, we conclude that our most efficient version indeed pays off in practice.

1 Introduction

Homeomorphic Embedding is a control mechanism that is commonly used to ensure termination of symbolic methods and program optimization techniques. Homeomorphic embedding is a structural preorder relation under which a term t' is greater than (i.e., it embeds) another term t represented by $t \trianglelefteq t'$ if t can be obtained from t' by deleting some symbols of t'. For instance, $v = s(0 + s(X)) * s(X + Y)$ embeds $u = s(X) * s(Y)$. The usefulness of homeomorphic embedding for ensuring termination is given by the following well-known property of well-quasi-orderings: given a finite signature, for every infinite sequence of terms

This work has been partially supported by the EU (FEDER) and the Spanish MINECO under grant TIN 2015-69175-C4-1-R, and by Generalitat Valenciana under grant PROMETEOII/2015/013. Jose Meseguer was partially supported by NRL under contract number N00173-17-1-G002. Angel Cuenca-Ortega has been supported by the SENESCYT, Ecuador (scholarship program 2013).

F. Mesnard and P. J. Stuckey (Eds.): LOPSTR 2018, LNCS 11408, pp. 38–55, 2019.
https://doi.org/10.1007/978-3-030-13838-7_3

$t_1, t_2, \ldots$, there exist $i < j$ such that $t_i \trianglelefteq t_j$. Therefore, if we iteratively compute a sequence $t_1, t_2, \ldots, t_n$, we can guarantee finiteness of the sequence by using the embedding as a whistle: whenever a new expression t_{n+1} is to be added to the sequence, we first check whether t_{n+1} embeds any of the expressions that are already in the sequence. If that is the case, the computation must be stopped because the whistle ($\trianglelefteq$) signals (potential) non-termination. Otherwise, t_{n+1} can be safely added to the sequence and the computation proceeds.

In [2], an extension of homeomorphic embedding modulo equational axioms, such as associativity and commutativity, was defined as a key component of the symbolic partial evaluator Victoria. Unfortunately, the formulation in [2] was done with a concern for simplicity in mind and degrades the tool performance because the proposed implementation of equational homeomorphic embedding did not scale well to realistic problems. This was not unexpected since other equational problems (such as equational matching, equational unification, or equational least general generalization) are typically much more involved than their corresponding "syntactic" counterparts, and achieving efficient implementations has required years of significant investigation.

Our Contribution. In this paper, we introduce four different formulations of homeomorphic embedding modulo axioms in rewrite theories that may contain sorts, subsort polymorphism, overloading, and rewriting with (conditional) rules and equations modulo a set B of equational axioms, and we compare their performance. We propose an equational homeomorphic embedding formulation $\trianglelefteq_B^{sml}$ that runs up to 5 orders of magnitude faster than the original definition of $\trianglelefteq_B$ in [2]. For this improvement in performance, we take advantage of Maude's powerful capabilities such as the efficiency of deterministic computations with equations versus non-deterministic computations with rewriting rules, or the use of non-strict definitions of the boolean operators versus more speculative standard boolean definitions [5].

Plan of the Paper. After some preliminaries in Sect. 2, Sect. 3 recalls the homeomorphic equational embedding relation of [2] that extends the "syntactically simpler" homeomorphic embedding on nonground terms to the order-sorted case *modulo* equational axioms. Section 4 provides two *goal-driven* formulations for equational homeomorphic embedding: first, a calculus for embeddability goals that directly handles the algebraic axioms in the deduction system, and then a reachability oriented characterization that cuts down the search space by taking advantage of pattern matching modulo associativity and commutativity axioms. Section 5 is concerned with an efficient meta-level formulation of equational homeomorphic embedding that relies on the classical flattening transformation that canonizes terms w.r.t. associativity and/or commutativity axioms (for instance, $1 + (2 + 3)$ gets flattened to $+(1, 2, 3)$). An improvement of the algorithm is also achieved by replacing the classical boolean operators by short-circuit, strategic versions of these operators. We provide an experimental performance evaluation of the proposed formulations showing that we can efficiently deal with realistic embedding problems modulo axioms.

2 Preliminaries

We introduce some key concepts of order-sorted rewriting logic theories, see [5] for further details.

Given an *order-sorted signature* Σ, with a finite poset of sorts $(S, \leq)$, we consider an S-sorted family $\mathcal{X} = \{\mathcal{X}_{\mathsf{s}}\}_{\mathsf{s} \in \mathsf{S}}$ of disjoint variable sets. $\mathcal{T}_{\Sigma}(\mathcal{X})_{\mathsf{s}}$ and $\mathcal{T}_{\Sigma_{\mathsf{s}}}$ denote the sets of terms and ground terms of sorts s, respectively. We also write $\mathcal{T}_{\Sigma}(\mathcal{X})$ and $\mathcal{T}_{\Sigma}$ for the corresponding term algebras. In order to simplify the presentation, we often disregard sorts when no confusion can arise. A *position* p in a term t is represented by a sequence of natural numbers (Λ denotes the empty sequence, i.e., the root position). $t|_p$ denotes the *subterm* of t at position p, and $t[u]_p$ denotes the result of *replacing the subterm* $t|_p$ by the term u. A *substitution* σ is a sorted mapping from a finite subset of $\mathcal{X}$ to $\mathcal{T}_{\Sigma}(\mathcal{X})$. The application of a substitution σ to a term t is called *an instance* of t and is denoted by $t\sigma$.

A Σ*-equation* is an unoriented pair $t = t'$, where $t, t' \in \mathcal{T}_{\Sigma}(\mathcal{X})_{\mathsf{s}}$ for some sort $\mathsf{s} \in \mathsf{S}$. Given Σ and a set E of Σ-equations, order-sorted equational logic induces a congruence relation $=_E$ on terms $t, t' \in \mathcal{T}_{\Sigma}(\mathcal{X})$ (see [4]). An *equational theory* (Σ, E) is a pair with Σ being an order-sorted signature and E a set of Σ-equations. A substitution θ is more (or equally) general than σ modulo E, denoted by $\theta \leq_E \sigma$, if there is a substitution γ such that $\sigma =_E \theta\gamma$, i.e., for all $x \in \mathcal{X}, x\sigma =_E x\theta\gamma$. A substitution σ is called a renaming if $\sigma = \{X_1 \mapsto Y_1, \ldots, X_n \mapsto Y_n\}$, the sorts of X_i and Y_i coincide, and variables $Y_1, \ldots, Y_n$ are pairwise distinct. The renaming substitution σ is a renaming for expression E if $(\mathcal{V}ar(E) - \{X, \ldots, X_n\}) \cap \{Y_1, \ldots, Y_n\} = \emptyset$.

A *rewrite theory* is a triple $\mathcal{R} = (\Sigma, E, R)$, where (Σ, E) is the equational theory modulo that we rewrite and R is a set of rewrite rules. Rules are of the form $l \to r$ where terms $l, r \in \mathcal{T}_{\Sigma}(\mathcal{X})_{\mathsf{s}}$ for some sort s are respectively called the *left-hand side* (or *lhs*) and the *right-hand side* (or *rhs*) of the rule and $\mathcal{V}ar(r) \subseteq \mathcal{V}ar(l)$. Let $\to \subseteq A \times A$ be a binary relation on a set A. We denote its transitive closure by $\to^+$, and its reflexive and transitive closure by $\to^*$. We define the relation $\to_{R,E}$ on $\mathcal{T}_{\Sigma}(\mathcal{X})$ by $t \to_{p,R,E} t'$ (or simply $t \to_{R,E} t'$) iff there is a non-variable position $p \in Pos_{\Sigma}(t)$, a rule $l \to r$ in R, and a substitution σ such that $t|_p =_E l\sigma$ and $t' = t[r\sigma]_p$.

2.1 Pure Homeomorphic Embedding

The pure (syntactic) homeomorphic embedding relation known from term algebra [10] was introduced by Dershowitz for variable-arity symbols in [6] and for fixed-arity symbols in [7]. In the following, we consider only fixed-arity symbols.

Definition 1 (Homeomorphic embedding, Dershowitz [7]). *The homeomorphic embedding relation* $\trianglelefteq$ *over* $\mathcal{T}_{\Sigma}$ *is defined as follows, with* $n \geq 0$*:*

$$\frac{\exists i \in \{1, \ldots, n\} \ : \ s \trianglelefteq t_i}{s \trianglelefteq f(t_1, \ldots, t_n)} \qquad \frac{\forall i \in \{1, \ldots, n\} \ : \ s_i \trianglelefteq t_i}{f(s_1, \ldots, s_n) \trianglelefteq f(t_1, \ldots, t_n)}$$

Roughly speaking, the left inference rule deletes subterms, while the right inference rule deletes context. We write $s \underline{\blacktriangleleft}\, t$ if s is derivable from t using the above rules. When $s \underline{\blacktriangleleft}\, t$, we say that s is (syntactically) *embedded* in t (or t syntactically *embeds* s). Note that $\equiv\, \subseteq\, \underline{\blacktriangleleft}$, where $\equiv$ denotes syntactic identity.

A well-quasi ordering $\preceq$ is a transitive and reflexive binary relation such that, for any infinite sequence of terms $t_1, t_2, \ldots$ with a finite number of operators, there exist j, k with $j < k$ and $t_j \preceq t_k$.

Theorem 1 (Tree Theorem, Kruskal [10]). *The embedding relation $\underline{\blacktriangleleft}$ is a well-quasi-ordering on $\mathscr{T}_\Sigma$.*

The derivability relation given by $\underline{\blacktriangleleft}$ is mechanized in [14] by introducing the following term rewriting system $Emb(\Sigma)$ as follows: $t \underline{\blacktriangleleft}\, t'$ if and only if $t' \rightarrow^*_{Emb(\Sigma)} t$.

Definition 2 (Homeomorphic embedding rewrite rules, Middeldorp [14]). *Let Σ be a signature. The homeomorphic embedding can be decided by a rewrite theory $Emb(\Sigma) = (\Sigma, \emptyset, R)$ such that R consists of rewrite rules of the form $f(X_1, \cdots, X_n) \rightarrow X_i$ where $f \in \Sigma$ is a function symbol of arity $n \geq 1$ and $i \in \{1, \cdots, n\}$.*

Definition 1 can be applied to terms of $\mathscr{T}_\Sigma(\mathscr{X})$ by simply regarding the variables in terms as constants. However, this definition cannot be used when existentially quantified variables are considered. The following definition from [11,15] adapts the pure (syntactic) homeomorphic embedding from [6] by adding a simple treatment of logical variables where all variables are treated as if they were identical, which is enough for many symbolic methods such as the partial evaluation of [2]. Some extensions of $\trianglelefteq$ dealing with varyadic symbols and infinite signatures are investigated in [12].

Definition 3 (Variable-extended homeomorphic embedding, Leuschel [11]). *The extended homeomorphic embedding relation $\trianglelefteq$ over $\mathscr{T}_\Sigma(\mathscr{X})$ is defined in Fig. 1, where the Variable inference rule allows dealing with free (unsorted) variables in terms, while the Diving and Coupling inference rules are equal to the pure (syntactic) homeomorphic embedding definition.*

Variable

$$\frac{}{x \trianglelefteq y}$$

Diving

$$\frac{\exists i \in \{1, \ldots, n\} : s \trianglelefteq t_i}{s \trianglelefteq f(t_1, \ldots, t_n)}$$

Coupling

$$\frac{\forall i \in \{1, \ldots, n\} : s_i \trianglelefteq t_i}{f(s_1, \ldots, s_n) \trianglelefteq f(t_1, \ldots, t_n)}$$

Fig. 1. Variable-extended homeomorphic embedding

The extended embedding relation $\trianglelefteq$ is a well-quasi-ordering on the set of terms $\mathscr{T}_\Sigma(\mathscr{X})$ [11,15]. An alternative characterization without the hassle of explicitly handling variables can be proved as follows.

Lemma 1 (Variable-less characterization of $\trianglelefteq$). *Given a signature Σ, let $\Sigma^\sharp$ be an extension of Σ with a new constant $\sharp$, and let $t^\sharp$ denote the (ground) instance of t where all variables have been replaced by $\sharp$. Given terms t_1 and t_2, $t_1 \trianglelefteq t_2$ iff $t_1^\sharp \trianglelefteq t_2^\sharp$ iff $t_1^\sharp \blacktriangleleft t_2^\sharp$.*

Moreover, Lemma 1 above allows the variable-extended relation $\trianglelefteq$ of Definition 3 to be mechanized in a way similar to the rewriting relation $\rightarrow^*_{Emb(\Sigma)}$ used in Definition 2 for the embedding $\blacktriangleleft$ of Definition 1: $t_1 \trianglelefteq t_2$ if and only if $t_2^\sharp \rightarrow^*_{Emb(\Sigma^\sharp)} t_1^\sharp$. By abuse of notation, from now on, we will indistinctly consider either terms with variables or ground terms with $\sharp$, whenever one formulation is simpler than the other.

3 Homeomorphic Embedding Modulo Equational Axioms

The following definition given in [2] extends the "syntactically simpler" homeomorphic embedding relation on nonground terms to the order-sorted case *modulo* a set of axioms B. The (order-sorted) relation $\trianglelefteq_B$ is called B–embedding (or embedding modulo B). We define $v \overset{ren}{=}_B v'$ iff there is a renaming substitution σ for v' such that $v =_B v'\sigma$.

Definition 4 ((Order-sorted) homeomorphic embedding modulo B). *We define the B–embedding relation $\trianglelefteq_B$ (or embedding modulo B) as $(\overset{ren}{=}_B).(\trianglelefteq).(\overset{ren}{=}_B)$.*

Example 1. Consider the following rewrite theory (written in Maude syntax) that defines the signature of natural numbers, with sort `Nat` and constructor operators `0`, and `suc` for sort `Nat`. We also define the associative and commutative addition operator symbol `_+_`.

```
fmod NAT is sort Nat .
  op 0 : -> Nat .
  op suc : Nat -> Nat .
  op _+_ : Nat Nat -> Nat [assoc comm] .
endfm
```

We have $+(1, X{:}Nat) \trianglelefteq_B +(Y{:}Nat, +(1, 3))$ because $+(Y{:}Nat, +(1, 3))$ is equal to $+(1, +(Y{:}Nat, 3))$ modulo AC, and $+(1, X{:}Nat) \trianglelefteq +(1, +(Y{:}Nat, 3))$.

The following result extends Kruskal's Tree Theorem for the equational theories considered in this paper. We have to restrict it to the class of finite equational theories in order to prove the result. $\mathscr{B}$ is called *class-finite* if all $\mathscr{B}$-equivalence classes are finite. This includes the class of permutative equational theories. An equational theory $\mathscr{E}$ is permutative if for all terms t, t', the fact that $t =_{\mathscr{E}} t'$ implies that the terms t and t' contain the same symbols with the same number of occurrences [9]. Permutative theories include any theory with any combination of symbols obeying any combination of associativity and commutativity axioms.

Theorem 2. *For class-finite theories, the embedding relation $\trianglelefteq_B$ is a well-quasi ordering of the set $\mathcal{T}_\Sigma(\mathcal{X})$ for finite Σ, that is, $\trianglelefteq_B$ is a quasi-order.*

Function symbols with variable arity are sometimes seen as associative operators. Let us briefly discuss the homeomorphic embedding modulo axioms $\trianglelefteq_B$ of Definition 4 in comparison to the variadic extension $\trianglelefteq^v$ of Definition 1 as given in [6]:

$$\textbf{Diving}\quad \frac{\exists i\in\{1,\ldots,n\} : s \trianglelefteq^v t_i}{s \trianglelefteq^v f(t_1,\ldots,t_n)} \qquad \textbf{Coupling}\quad \frac{\forall i\in\{1,\ldots,m\} : s_i \trianglelefteq^v t_{j_i}, \text{with } 1\leq j_1<j_2<\cdots<j_m\leq n}{f(s_1,\ldots,s_m) \trianglelefteq^v f(t_1,\ldots,t_n)}$$

Example 2. Consider a variadic version of the addition symbol $+$ of Example 1 that allows any number of natural numbers to be used as arguments; for instance, $+(1,2,3)$. On the one hand, $+(1) \trianglelefteq^v +(1,2,3)$ whereas $+(1) \ntrianglelefteq_B +(1,2,3)$, with B consisting of the associativity and commutativity axioms for the operator $+$ (actually, $+(1)$ is ill-formed). On the other hand, we have both $+(1,2) \trianglelefteq^v +(1,0,3,2)$ and $+(1,2) \trianglelefteq_B +(1,0,3,2)$. This is because any well-formed term that consists of the addition (in any order) of the constants 0, 1, 2, and 3 (for instance, $+(+(1,0),+(3,2))$ can be given a flat representation $+(1,0,2,3)$. Note that there are many other equivalent terms, e.g., $+(+(1,2),+(3,0))$ or $+(+(1,+(3,2)),0)$, all of which are represented by the flattened term $+(0,1,2,3)$. Actually, because of the associativity and commutativity of symbol $+$, flattened terms like $+(1,0,2,3)$ can be further simplified into a single[1] *canonical representative* $+(0,1,2,3)$, hence also $+(1,2) \trianglelefteq_B +(0,1,2,3)$. A more detailed explanation of flat terms can be found in Sect. 5. However, note that $+(2,1) \trianglelefteq_B +(1,0,3,2)$ but $+(2,1) \ntrianglelefteq^v +(1,0,3,2)$ because the $\trianglelefteq^v$ does not consider the commutativity of symbol $+$.

Roughly speaking, in the worst case, the homeomorphic embedding modulo axioms of Definition 4, $t \trianglelefteq_B t'$, amounts to considering all the elements in the B-equivalence classes of t and t' and then checking for standard homeomorphic embedding, $u \trianglelefteq u'$, every pair u and u' of such terms, one term from each class. According to Definition 2, checking $u \trianglelefteq u'$ essentially boils down to the reachability analysis given by $u' \rightarrow^*_{Emb(\Sigma)} u$. Unfortunately, the enumeration of all terms in a B-equivalence class is impractical, as shown in the following example.

Example 3. Consider the AC binary symbol $+$ of Example 1 and the terms $t = +(1,2)$ and $t' = +(2,+(3,1))$. The AC-equivalence class of t contains two terms whereas the AC-equivalence class of t' contains 12 terms. This implies computing 24 reachability problems $u' \rightarrow^*_{Emb(\Sigma)} u$ in order to decide $t \trianglelefteq_{AC} t'$, in the worst case. Moreover, we know a priori that half of these reachability tests will fail (those in which 1 and 2 occur in different order in u' and u; for instance $u' = +(1,+(2,3))$ and $u = +(2,1)$.

[1] Maude uses a term lexicographic order for the arguments of flattened terms [8].

A more effective rewriting characterization of $\unlhd_B$ can be achieved by lifting Definition 2 to the order-sorted and *modulo* case in a natural way. However, ill-formed terms can be produced by naïvely applying the rules $f(X_1,\ldots,X_n) \rightarrow X_i$ of Definition 2 to typed (i.e., order-sorted) terms. For example, "$(0 \leq 1)$ or true" → "0 or true".

In the order-sorted context we can overcome this drawback as follows. Assume that Σ has no ad-hoc overloading. We can extend Σ to a new signature $\Sigma^{\mathscr{U}}$ by adding a new top sort $\mathscr{U}$ that is bigger than all other sorts. For each $f : A_1,\ldots,A_n \rightarrow A$ in Σ, we add the rules $f(X_1{:}\mathscr{U},\ldots,X_n{:}\mathscr{U}) \rightarrow X_i{:}\mathscr{U}, 1 \leq i \leq n$. In this way, rewriting with $\rightarrow^*_{Emb(\Sigma^{\mathscr{U}}),B}$ becomes a relation between well-formed $\Sigma^{\mathscr{U}}$-terms, see [2].

Definition 5. ((Order-sorted) homeomorphic embedding rewrite rules modulo B **[2]).** *Let Σ be an order-sorted signature and B be a set of axioms. Let us introduce the following signature transformation $\Sigma \ni (f : \mathsf{s}_1 \ldots \mathsf{s}_n \rightarrow \mathsf{s}) \mapsto (f : \mathscr{U} \overset{n}{\ldots} \mathscr{U} \rightarrow \mathscr{U}) \in \Sigma^u$, where $\mathscr{U}$ conceptually represents a universal supersort of all sorts in Σ. Also, for any Σ-term t, t^u leaves the term t unchanged but regards all its variable as unsorted (i.e., of sort $\mathscr{U}$). We define the TRS $Emb(\Sigma)$ that consists of all rewrite rules $f(X_1{:}\mathscr{U},\ldots,X_n{:}\mathscr{U}) \rightarrow X_i{:}\mathscr{U}$ for each $f : A_1,\ldots,A_n \rightarrow A$ in Σ and $i \in \{1,\ldots,n\}$.*

In the sequel, we consider equational theories B that may contain any combination of associativity and/or commutativity axioms for any binary symbol in the signature. Also, for the sake of simplicity we often omit sorts when no confusion can arise.

Proposition 1. *Given Σ, B, and t,t' in $\mathscr{T}_\Sigma(\mathscr{X})$, $t \unlhd_B t'$ iff $(t'^u)^\sharp \rightarrow^*_{Emb((\Sigma^{\mathscr{U}})^\sharp),B} (t^u)^\sharp$.*

Example 4. Consider the order-sorted signature for natural numbers of Example 1. Let us represent by sort U in Maude the unique (top) sort of the transformed signature:

```
fmod NAT-U is sort U .
  op 0 : -> U .
  op suc : U -> U .
  op _+_ : U U -> U [assoc comm] .
endfm
```

Likewise, the terms expressed in Σ must also be transformed to be expressed as $\Sigma^{\mathscr{U}}$-terms. For instance, given the Σ-terms $t =$ X:Nat[2] and $t' =$ suc(Y:Nat), the corresponding $\Sigma^{\mathscr{U}}$-terms are $t =$ X:U and suc(Y:U), respectively.

The associated TRS $Emb(\Sigma)$ contains the following two rules: $+(X_1{:}U, X_2{:}U) \rightarrow X_1{:}U$ and $+(X_1{:}U, X_2{:}U) \rightarrow X_2{:}U$. However, since the rules of $Emb(\Sigma)$ are applied modulo the commutativity of symbol +, in practice, we can get rid of either of the two rules above since only one is required in Maude.

[2] The expression $X{:}S$ represents an explicit definition of a variable X of sort S in Maude.

Example 5. Following Example 3, instead of comparing pairwisely all terms in the equivalence classes of t and t', we choose $Emb(\Sigma)$ to contain just the rewrite rule $+(X_1{:}U, X_2{:}U) \rightarrow X_2{:}U$, we use it to prove the rewrite step $+(2, +(3,1)) \rightarrow_{Emb(\Sigma),B} +(2,1)$, and finally we check that $+(2,1) =_B +(1,2)$, with $B = \{A, C\}$. However, there are six alternative rewriting steps stemming from the initial term $+(2, +(3,1))$, all of which result from applying the very same rewrite rule above to the term (modulo AC), five of which are useless for proving the considered embedding (the selected redex is underlined):

$$
\begin{array}{ll}
+(2, \underline{+(3,1)}) \rightarrow_{Emb(\Sigma),B} +(2,1) & \underline{+(2,+(3,1))} \rightarrow_{Emb(\Sigma),B} 1 \\
+(2, \underline{+(3,1)}) \rightarrow_{Emb(\Sigma),B} +(2,3) & \underline{+(2,+(3,1))} \rightarrow_{Emb(\Sigma),B} 2 \\
\underline{+(2,+(3,1))} \rightarrow_{Emb(\Sigma),B} +(3,1) & \underline{+(2,+(3,1))} \rightarrow_{Emb(\Sigma),B} 3
\end{array}
$$

For a term with k addends, we have $(2^k) - 2$ rewriting steps. This leads to a huge combinatorial explosion when considering the complete rewrite search tree.

Moreover, there are three problems with Definition 5. First, the intrinsic non-determinism of the rules may unnecessarily produce an extremely large search space. Second, as shown in Example 5, this intrinsic non-determinism in the presence of axioms is intolerable, that is, unfeasible to handle. Third, the associated reachability problems do not scale up to complex embedding problems so that a suitable search strategy must be introduced. We address these problems stepwisely in the sequel.

4 Goal-Driven Homeomorphic Embedding Modulo *B*

The formulation of homeomorphic embedding as a reachability problem by using the rewrite rules of Definition 5 generates a blind search that does not take advantage of the actual terms t and t' being compared for embedding. In this section, we provide a more refined formulation of homeomorphic embedding modulo axioms that is *goal driven* in the sense that, given an embedding problem (or *goal*), $t \trianglelefteq_B t'$, it inductively processes the terms t and t' in a top-down manner.

First, we introduce in the following section a calculus that extends the homeomorphic embedding relation of Definition 3 to the order-sorted equational case.

4.1 An Homeomorphic Embedding Calculus Modulo *B*

Let us introduce a calculus for embeddability goals $t \trianglelefteq_B^{gd} t'$ that directly handles in the deduction system the algebraic axioms of B, with B being any combination of A and/or C axioms for the theory operators. Roughly speaking, this is achieved by specializing w.r.t. B the coupling rule of Definition 3.

Definition 6. (Goal-driven homeomorphic embedding modulo B**).** *The homeomorphic embedding relation modulo B is defined as the smallest relation that satisfies the inference rules of Definition 3 together with the new inference* *rules given in Fig. 2: (i) the three inference rules (Variable, Diving, and Coupling) of Definition 3 for any function symbol; (ii) one extra coupling rule for the case of a commutative symbol with or without associativity (Coupling$_C$); (iii) two extra coupling rules for the case of an associative symbol with or without commutativity (Coupling$_A$); and (iv) two extra coupling rules for the case of an associative-commutative symbol (Coupling$_{AC}$).*

$$\textbf{Coupling}_C \quad \frac{s_0 \trianglelefteq_B^{gd} t_1 \ \wedge\ s_1 \trianglelefteq_B^{gd} t_0}{f(s_0,s_1) \trianglelefteq_B^{gd} f(t_0,t_1)}$$

$$\textbf{Coupling}_A \quad \frac{f(s_0,s_1) \trianglelefteq_B^{gd} t_0 \ \wedge\ s_2 \trianglelefteq_B^{gd} t_1}{f(s_0,f(s_1,s_2)) \trianglelefteq_B^{gd} f(t_0,t_1)} \qquad \frac{s_0 \trianglelefteq_B^{gd} f(t_0,t_1) \ \wedge\ s_1 \trianglelefteq_B^{gd} t_2}{f(s_0,s_1) \trianglelefteq_B^{gd} f(t_0,f(t_1,t_2))}$$

$$\textbf{Coupling}_{AC} \quad \frac{f(s_0,s_1) \trianglelefteq_B^{gd} t_1 \ \wedge\ s_2 \trianglelefteq_B^{gd} t_0}{f(s_0,f(s_1,s_2)) \trianglelefteq_B^{gd} f(t_0,t_1)} \qquad \frac{s_1 \trianglelefteq_B^{gd} f(t_0,t_1) \ \wedge\ s_0 \trianglelefteq_B^{gd} t_2}{f(s_0,s_1) \trianglelefteq_B^{gd} f(t_0,f(t_1,t_2))}$$

Fig. 2. Extra coupling rules for A, C, AC symbols

Proposition 2. *Given Σ and B, for terms t and t' in $\mathcal{T}_\Sigma(\mathcal{X})$, $t \trianglelefteq_B t'$ iff $t \trianglelefteq_B^{gd} t'$.*

Example 6. Consider the binary symbol + obeying associativity and commutativity axioms, and the terms $t = +(1,2)$ and $t' = +(2,+(3,1))$ of Example 5. We can prove $t \trianglelefteq_B^{gd} t'$ by

$$\frac{\dfrac{1 \trianglelefteq_B^{gd} 1}{1 \trianglelefteq_B^{gd} +(3,1)} \qquad 2 \trianglelefteq_B^{gd} 2}{+(1,2) \trianglelefteq_B^{gd} +(2,+(3,1))}$$

We can also prove a more complex embedding goal by first using the right inference rule for AC of Fig. 2 and then the generic Coupling and Diving inference rules.

$$\frac{\dfrac{\dfrac{2 \trianglelefteq_B^{gd} 2}{2 \trianglelefteq_B^{gd} +(4,2)} \qquad 3 \trianglelefteq_B^{gd} 3}{+(2,3) \trianglelefteq_B^{gd} +(+(4,2),3)} \qquad 1 \trianglelefteq_B^{gd} 1}{+(1,+(2,3)) \trianglelefteq_B^{gd} +(+(4,2),+(3,1))}$$

It is immediate to see that, when the size of the involved terms t and t' grows, the improvement in performance of $\trianglelefteq_B^{gd}$ w.r.t. $\trianglelefteq_B$ can be significant (just compare these two embedding proofs with the corresponding search trees for $\trianglelefteq_B$).

4.2 Reachability-Based, Goal-Driven Homeomorphic Embedding Formulation

Let us provide a more operational goal-driven characterization of the homeomorphic embedding modulo B. We formalize it in the reachability style of Definition 5. The main challenge here is how to generate a suitable rewrite theory $R^{rogd}(\Sigma, B)$ that can decide embedding modulo B by running a reachability goal.

Definition 7 (Goal-driven homeomorphic embedding rewrite rules modulo B). *Given Σ and B, we define the TRS $R^{rogd}(\Sigma, B)$ as follows.*

1. *We include in $R^{rogd}(\Sigma, B)$ a rewrite rule of the form $u \trianglelefteq_B^{rogd} v \to true$ for each (particular instance of the) inference rules of the form $\frac{}{u \trianglelefteq_B^{gd} v}$ given Definition 6 (e.g., the Variable Inference Rule from Definition 3 or the Coupling Inference Rule from Definition 3, for the case of a constant symbol c).*
2. *We include in $R^{rogd}(\Sigma, B)$ a rewrite rule of the form $u \trianglelefteq_B^{rogd} v \to u_1 \trianglelefteq_B^{rogd} v_1 \wedge \cdots \wedge u_k \trianglelefteq_B^{rogd} v_k$ for each (particular instance of the) inference rules of the form $\frac{u_1 \trianglelefteq_B^{gd} v_1 \wedge \cdots \wedge u_k \trianglelefteq_B^{gd} v_k}{u \trianglelefteq_B^{gd} v}$ given in Definition 6.*

Proposition 3. *Given Σ, B, and terms t, t', $t \trianglelefteq_B^{gd} t'$ iff $(t \trianglelefteq_B^{rogd} t') \to^*_{R^{rogd}(\Sigma,B),B} true$.*

Example 7. Consider the binary symbol $+$ of Example 1. According to Definition 6, there are twelve inference rules for $\trianglelefteq_B^{gd}$:

Variable

$$\frac{}{x \trianglelefteq_B^{gd} y}$$

Diving

$$\frac{x \trianglelefteq_B^{gd} t_1}{x \trianglelefteq_B^{gd} suc(t_1)} \qquad \frac{x \trianglelefteq_B^{gd} t_1}{x \trianglelefteq_B^{gd} +(t_1,t_2)} \qquad \frac{x \trianglelefteq_B^{gd} t_2}{x \trianglelefteq_B^{gd} +(t_1,t_2)}$$

Coupling

$$\frac{}{0 \trianglelefteq_B^{gd} 0} \qquad \frac{t_1 \trianglelefteq_B^{gd} t_1'}{suc(t_1) \trianglelefteq_B^{gd} suc(t_1')} \qquad \frac{t_1 \trianglelefteq_B^{gd} t_1' \wedge t_2 \trianglelefteq_B^{gd} t_2'}{+(t_1,t_2) \trianglelefteq_B^{gd} +(t_1',t_2')}$$

Coupling$_C$

$$\frac{t_1 \trianglelefteq_B^{gd} t_2' \wedge t_2 \trianglelefteq_B^{gd} t_1'}{+(t_1,t_2) \trianglelefteq_B^{gd} +(t_1',t_2')}$$

Coupling$_A$

$$\frac{+(t_0,t_1) \trianglelefteq_B^{gd} t_1' \wedge t_2 \trianglelefteq_B^{gd} t_2'}{+(t_0,+(t_1,t_2)) \trianglelefteq_B^{gd} +(t_1',t_2')} \qquad \frac{t_1 \trianglelefteq_B^{gd} +(t_0',t_1') \wedge t_2 \trianglelefteq_B^{gd} t_2'}{+(t_1,t_2) \trianglelefteq_B^{gd} +(t_0',+(t_1',t_2'))}$$

Coupling$_{AC}$

$$\frac{+(t_0,t_1) \trianglelefteq_B^{gd} t_2' \wedge t_2 \trianglelefteq_B^{gd} t_1'}{+(t_0,+(t_1,t_2)) \trianglelefteq_B^{gd} +(t_1',t_2')} \qquad \frac{t_2 \trianglelefteq_B^{gd} +(t_0',t_1') \wedge t_1 \trianglelefteq_B^{gd} t_2'}{+(t_1,t_2) \trianglelefteq_B^{gd} +(t_0',+(t_1',t_2'))}$$

However, the corresponding TRS $R^{rogd}(\Sigma, B)$ only contains six rewrite rules because, due to pattern matching modulo associativity and commutativity in rewriting logic, the other rules are redundant:

$$\begin{array}{lrcl}
\text{(Diving)} & x \trianglelefteq_B^{rogd} suc(T_1) & \to & x \trianglelefteq_B^{rogd} T_1 \\
 & x \trianglelefteq_B^{rogd} +(T_1,T_2) & \to & x \trianglelefteq_B^{rogd} T_1 \\
\text{(Coupling)} & \sharp \trianglelefteq_B^{rogd} \sharp & \to & true \\
 & 0 \trianglelefteq_B^{rogd} 0 & \to & true \\
 & suc(T_1) \trianglelefteq_B^{rogd} suc(T_1') & \to & T_1 \trianglelefteq_B^{rogd} T_1' \\
\text{(Coupling}_{\emptyset,C,A,AC}) & +(T_1,T_2) \trianglelefteq_B^{rogd} +(T_1',T_2') & \to & T_1 \trianglelefteq_B^{rogd} T_1' \wedge T_2 \trianglelefteq_B^{rogd} T_2'
\end{array}$$

For example, the rewrite sequence proving $+(1,+(2,3)) \trianglelefteq_B^{rogd} +(+(4,2), +(3,1))$ is:

$$\begin{aligned}
&+(1,+(2,3)) \trianglelefteq_B^{rogd} +(+(4,2),+(3,1))\\
&\qquad\to_{R^{rogd}(\Sigma,B),B} +(2,3)) \trianglelefteq_B^{rogd} +(+(4,2),3) \wedge 1 \trianglelefteq_B^{rogd} 1\\
&\qquad\to_{R^{rogd}(\Sigma,B),B} 2 \trianglelefteq_B^{rogd} +(4,2) \wedge 3 \trianglelefteq_B^{rogd} 3\\
&\qquad\to_{R^{rogd}(\Sigma,B),B} 2 \trianglelefteq_B^{rogd} 2\\
&\qquad\to_{R^{rogd}(\Sigma,B),B} true
\end{aligned}$$

Although the improvement in performance achieved by using the rewriting relation $\to_{R^{rogd}(\Sigma,B),B}$ versus the rewriting relation $\to^*_{Emb(\Sigma),B}$ is important, the search space is still huge since the expression $+(1,+(2,3)) \trianglelefteq_B^{gd} +(+(4,2),+(3,1))$ matches the left-hand side $+(T_1,T_2) \trianglelefteq_B^{gd} +(T_1',T_2')$ in many different ways (e.g., $\{T_1 \mapsto 1, T_2 \mapsto +(2,3),\ldots\}$, $\{T_1 \mapsto 2, T_2 \mapsto +(1,3),\ldots\}$, $\{T_1 \mapsto 3, T_2 \mapsto +(1,2),\ldots\}$).

In the following section, we further optimize the calculus of homeomorphic embedding modulo axioms by considering equational (deterministic) normalization (thus avoiding search) and by exploiting the meta-level features of Maude (thus avoiding any theory generation).

5 Meta-Level Deterministic Goal-Driven Homeomorphic Embedding Modulo *B*

The meta-level representation of terms in Maude [5, Chapter 14] works with flattened versions of the terms that are rooted by poly-variadic versions of the associative (or associative-commutative) symbols. For instance, given an associative (or associative-commutative) symbol f with n arguments and $n \geq 2$, flattened terms rooted by f are canonical forms w.r.t. the set of rules given by the following rule schema

$$f(x_1,\ldots,f(t_1,\ldots,t_n),\ldots,x_m) \to f(x_1,\ldots,t_1,\ldots,t_n,\ldots,x_m) \quad n,m \geq 2$$

Given an associative (or associative-commutative) symbol f and a term $f(t_1,\ldots,t_n)$, we call *f-alien terms* (or simply *alien terms*) those terms among the $t_1,\ldots,t_n$ that are not rooted by f. In the following, we implicitly consider that all terms are in B-canonical form.

In the sequel, a variable x of sort s is meta-represented as $\bar{x}$ = 'x:s and a non-variable term $t = f(t_1,\ldots,t_n)$, with $n \geq 0$, is meta-represented as $\bar{t}$ = '$f[\bar{t_1},\ldots,\bar{t_n}]$.

Definition 8 (Meta-level homeomorphic embedding modulo B). *The meta-level homeomorphic embedding modulo B, $\trianglelefteq_B^{ml}$, is defined for term meta-representations by means of the equational theory E^{ml} of Fig. 3, where the auxiliary meta-level functions* **any** *and* **all** *implement the existential and universal*

$$
\begin{array}{lll}
\sharp \trianglelefteq_B^{ml} \sharp & = \textbf{true} & \\
F[TermList] \trianglelefteq_B^{ml} \sharp & = \textbf{false} & \\
T \trianglelefteq_B^{ml} F[TermList] & = \textbf{any}(T, TermList) & \text{if } root(T) \neq F \\
F[TermList1] \trianglelefteq_B^{ml} F[TermList2] & = \textbf{any}(F[TermList1], TermList2) & \\
 & \quad \textbf{or all}(TermList1, TermList2) & \\
F[U,V] \trianglelefteq_B^{ml} F[X,Y] & = \textbf{any}(F[U,V],[X,Y]) & \text{if } F \text{ is } C \\
 & \quad \textbf{or}(\ U \trianglelefteq_B^{ml} X \textbf{ and } V \trianglelefteq_B^{ml} Y\ ) & \\
 & \quad \textbf{or}\ (\ U \trianglelefteq_B^{ml} Y \textbf{ and } V \trianglelefteq_B^{ml} X\ ) & \\
F[TermList1] \trianglelefteq_B^{ml} F[TermList2] & = \textbf{any}(F[TermList1], TermList2) & \text{if } F \text{ is } A \\
 & \quad \textbf{or all\_A}(TermList1, TermList2) & \\
F[TermList1] \trianglelefteq_B^{ml} F[TermList2] & = \textbf{any}(F[TermList1], TermList2) & \text{if } F \text{ is } AC \\
 & \quad \textbf{or all\_AC}(TermList1, TermList2) &
\end{array}
$$

$$
\begin{array}{rl}
\textbf{any}(U, nil) & = \textbf{false} \\
\textbf{any}(U, V : L) & = U \trianglelefteq_B^{ml} V \textbf{ or any}(U, L)
\end{array}
$$

$$
\begin{array}{rl}
\textbf{all}(nil, nil) & = \textbf{true} \\
\textbf{all}(nil, U : L) & = \textbf{false} \\
\textbf{all}(U : L, nil) & = \textbf{false} \\
\textbf{all}(U : L1, V : L2) & = U \trianglelefteq_B^{ml} V \textbf{ and all}(L1, L2)
\end{array}
$$

$$
\begin{array}{rl}
\textbf{all\_A}(nil, L) & = \textbf{true} \\
\textbf{all\_A}(U : L, nil) & = \textbf{false} \\
\textbf{all\_A}(U : L1, V : L2) & = (U \trianglelefteq_B^{ml} V \textbf{ and all\_A}(L1, L2)) \textbf{ or all\_A}(U : L1, L2))
\end{array}
$$

$$
\begin{array}{rl}
\textbf{all\_AC}(nil, L) & = \textbf{true} \\
\textbf{all\_AC}(U : L1, L2) & = \textbf{all\_AC\_Aux}(U : L1, L2, L2) \\
\textbf{all\_AC\_Aux}(U : L1, nil, L3) & = \textbf{false} \\
\textbf{all\_AC\_Aux}(U : L1, V : L2, L3) & = (U \trianglelefteq_B^{ml} V \textbf{ and all\_AC}(L1, \text{remove}\ (V, L3))) \\
 & \quad \textbf{or all\_AC\_Aux}(U : L1, L2, L3))
\end{array}
$$

$$
\begin{array}{rl}
\textbf{remove}(U, nil) & = \text{nil} \\
\textbf{remove}(U, V : L) & = \text{if } U = V \textbf{ then } L \text{ else } V : \text{remove}\ (U, L)
\end{array}
$$

Fig. 3. Meta-level homeomorphic embedding modulo axioms

tests in the Diving and Coupling inference rules of Fig. 1, and we introduce two new meta-level functions **all_A** *and* **all_AC** *that implement existential tests that are specific to A and AC symbols. For the sake of readability, these new existential tests are also formulated (for ordinary terms instead of meta-level terms) as the inference rules* $Coupling_A$ *and* $Coupling_{AC}$ *of Fig. 4.*

$$
\textbf{Coupling}_A \ \frac{\exists j \in \{1,\ldots,m-n+1\} : s_1 \trianglelefteq_B^{ml} t_j \wedge f(s_2,\ldots,s_n) \trianglelefteq_B^{ml} f(t_{j+1},\ldots,t_m) \wedge \forall k < j : s_1 \not\trianglelefteq_B^{ml} t_k}{f(s_1,\ldots,s_n) \trianglelefteq_B^{ml} f(t_1,\ldots,t_m)}
$$

$$
\textbf{Coupling}_{AC} \ \frac{\exists j \in \{1,\ldots,m\} : s_1 \trianglelefteq_B^{ml} t_j \wedge f(s_2,\ldots,s_n) \trianglelefteq_B^{ml} f(t_1,\ldots,t_{j-1},t_{j+1},\ldots,t_m)}{f(s_1,\ldots,s_n) \trianglelefteq_B^{ml} f(t_1,\ldots,t_m)}
$$

Fig. 4. Coupling rule for associativity-commutativity functions

Example 8. Given the embedding problem for $+(1, +(2,3))$ and $+(+(4,2), +(3,1))$, the corresponding call to the meta-level homeomorphic embedding $\unlhd_B^{ml}$ of Definition 8 is $'+['1, '2, '3] \unlhd_B^{ml} '+['4, '2, '3, '1]$.

Proposition 4. *Given Σ, B, and terms t and t', $t \unlhd_B^{gd} t'$ iff $(t \unlhd_B^{ml} t')!_{E^{ml},B} =$ true.*

Finally, a further optimized version of Definition 8 can be easily defined by replacing the Boolean conjunction (*and*) and disjunction (*or*) operators with the computationally more efficient Maude Boolean operators `and-then` and `or-else` that avoid evaluating the second argument when the result of evaluating the first one suffices to compute the result.

Definition 9. (Strategic meta-level deterministic embedding modulo B). *We define $\unlhd_B^{sml}$ as the strategic version of relation $\unlhd_B^{ml}$ that is obtained by replacing the Boolean operators* `and` *and* `or` *with the* `and-then` *operator for* short-circuit *version of conjunction and the* `or-else` *operator for short-circuit disjunction [5, Chapter 9.1], respectively.*

6 Experiments

We have implemented in Maude all four equational homeomorphic embedding formulations $\unlhd_B$, $\unlhd_B^{rogd}$, $\unlhd_B^{ml}$, and $\unlhd_B^{sml}$ of previous sections. The implementation consists of approximately 250 function definitions (2.2K lines of Maude source code) and is publicly available online[3]. In this section, we provide an experimental comparison of the four equational homeomorphic embedding implementations by running a significant number of equational embedding goals. In order to compare the performance of the different implementations in the worst possible scenario, all benchmarked goals return false, which ensures that the whole search space for each goal has been completely explored, while the execution times for succeeding goals whimsically depend on the particular node of the search tree where success is found.

We tested our implementations on a 3.3 GHz Intel Xeon E5-1660 with 64 GB of RAM running Maude v2.7.1, and we considered the average of ten executions for each test. We have chosen four representative programs: (i) *KMP*, the classical KMP string pattern matcher [3]; (ii) *NatList*, a Maude implementation of lists of natural numbers; (iii) *Maze*, a non-deterministic Maude specification that defines a maze game in which multiple players must reach a given exit point by walking or jumping, where colliding players are eliminated from the game [1]; and (iv) *Dekker*, a Maude specification that models a faulty version of Dekker's protocol, one of the earliest solutions to the mutual exclusion problem that appeared in [5]. As testing benchmarks we considered a set of representative embeddability problems for the four programs that are generated during the execution of the partial evaluator Victoria [2].

[3] At http://safe-tools.dsic.upv.es/embedding/.

Table 1. Size of generated theories for naïve and goal-driven definitions vs. meta-level definitions

Benchmark	$\sharp$ Axioms				$\trianglelefteq_B$			$\trianglelefteq_B^{rogd}$			$\trianglelefteq_B^{ml}$, $\trianglelefteq_B^{sml}$		
	∅	A	C	AC	$\sharp$E	$\sharp$R	GT (ms)	$\sharp$E	$\sharp$R	GT (ms)	$\sharp$E	$\sharp$R	GT (ms)
Kmp	9	0	0	0	0	15	1	0	57	2	21	0	0
NatList	5	1	1	2	0	10	1	0	26	1	21	0	0
Maze	5	1	0	1	0	36	7	0	787	15	21	0	0
Dekker	16	1	0	2	0	59	8	0	823	18	21	0	0

Table 2. Performance of equational homeomorphic embedding implementations

Benchmark	$\sharp$ Symbols		Size		$\trianglelefteq_B$	$\trianglelefteq_B^{rogd}$	$\trianglelefteq_B^{ml}$	$\trianglelefteq_B^{sml}$
	A	AC	T1	T2	Time (ms)	Time (ms)	Time (ms)	Time (ms)
Kmp	0	0	5	5	10	6	1	1
				10	150	125	4	1
				100	TO	TO	280	95
				500	TO	TO	714	460
NatList	1	2	5	5	2508	2892	1	1
				10	840310	640540	1	1
				100	TO	TO	8	2
				500	TO	TO	60	5
Maze	1	1	5	5	40	25	1	1
				10	TO	20790	4	1
				100	TO	TO	256	2
				500	TO	TO	19808	10
Dekker	1	1	5	5	50	40	1	1
				10	111468	110517	2	1
				100	TO	TO	5	3
				500	TO	TO	20	13

Tables 1, 2, and 3 analyze different aspects of the implementation. In Table 1, we compare the size of the generated rewrite theories for the naïve and the goal-driven definitions versus the meta-level definitions. For both, $\trianglelefteq_B^{ml}$ and $\trianglelefteq_B^{sml}$, there are the same number (21) of generated equations ($\sharp$E), whereas the number of generated rules ($\sharp$R) is zero because both definitions are purely equational (deterministic) and just differ in the version of the boolean operators being used. As for the generated rewrite theories for computing $\trianglelefteq_B$ and $\trianglelefteq_B^{rogd}$, they contain no equations, while the number of generated rules increases with the complexity of the program (that heavily depends on the equational axioms that the function symbols obey). The number of generated rules is much bigger for $\trianglelefteq_B^{rogd}$

Table 3. Performance of equational homeomorphic embedding implementations w.r.t. axiom entanglement for the NatList example

T1						T2						$\trianglelefteq_B$	$\trianglelefteq_B^{rogd}$	$\trianglelefteq_B^{ml}$	$\trianglelefteq_B^{sml}$
Size		♯ Symbols				Size		♯ Symbols				Time (ms)	Time (ms)	Time (ms)	Time (ms)
OT	FT	∅	C	A	AC	OT	FT	∅	C	A	AC				
5	5	5	0	0	0	100	100	100	0	0	0	165	70	1	1
5	5	3	2	0	0	100	100	50	50	0	0	TO	38	60	35
5	2	4	0	1	0	100	2	50	0	50	0	TO	TO	108035	3
5	2	4	0	0	1	100	2	50	0	0	50	TO	TO	42800	4
5	3	8	0	1	2	100	3	50	0	25	25	TO	TO	22796	5
5	5	5	0	0	0	500	500	500	0	0	0	48339	34000	12	4
5	5	3	2	0	0	500	500	250	250	0	0	TO	2183	6350	2005
5	2	4	0	1	0	500	2	250	0	250	0	TO	TO	TO	30
5	2	4	0	0	1	500	2	250	0	0	250	TO	TO	TO	27
5	3	8	0	1	2	500	3	250	0	125	125	TO	TO	TO	50

than for $\trianglelefteq_B$ (for instance, $\trianglelefteq_B^{rogd}$ is encoded by 823 rules for the Dekker program versus the 59 rules of $\trianglelefteq_B$). Columns ∅, A, C, and AC summarize the number of free, associative, commutative, and associative-commutative symbols, respectively, for each benchmark program. The generation times (GT) are negligible for all rewrite theories.

For all benchmarks $T1 \trianglelefteq_B^{\alpha} T2$ in Table 2, we have fixed to five the size of `T1` that is measured in the depth of (the non-flattened version of) the term. As for `T2`, we have considered terms with increasing depths: five, ten, one hundred, and five hundred. The ♯ `Symbols` column records the number of A (resp. AC) symbols occurring in the benchmarked goals.

The figures in Table 2 confirm our expectations regarding $\trianglelefteq_B$ and $\trianglelefteq_B^{rogd}$ that the search space is huge and increases exponentially with the size of `T2` (discussed for $\trianglelefteq_B$ in Example 5 and for $\trianglelefteq_B^{rogd}$ in Example 6). Actually, when the size of `T2` is 100 (and beyond) a given timeout (represented by TO in the tables) is reached that is set for 3.6e+6 ms (1 h). The reader can also check that the more A, C, and AC symbols occur in the original program signature, the bigger the execution times. An odd exception is the Maze example, where the timeout is already reached for the size 10 of `T2` even if the number of equational axioms is comparable to the other programs. This is because the AC-normalized, flattened version of the terms is much smaller than the original term size for the NatList and Dekker benchmarks but not for Maze, where the flattened and original terms have similar size. On the other hand, our experiments demonstrate that both $\trianglelefteq_B^{ml}$ and $\trianglelefteq_B^{sml}$ bring impressive speedups, with $\trianglelefteq_B^{sml}$ working outstandingly well in practice even for really complex terms.

The reader may wonder how big the impact is having A, C, or AC operators. In order to compare the relevance of these symbols, in Table 3 we fix one single benchmark program (NatList) that contains all three kinds of operators: two associative operators (list concatenation ; and natural division /), a commutative (natural pairing) operator (| |), and two associative-commutative arithmetic operators (+,*). With regard to the size of the considered terms, we confront the size of the original term (OT) versus the size of its flattened version (FT); e.g., 500 versus 2 for the size of T2 in the last row.

We have included the execution times of $\trianglelefteq_B$ and $\trianglelefteq_B^{rogd}$ for completeness, but they do not reveal a dramatic improvement of $\trianglelefteq_B^{rogd}$ with respect to $\trianglelefteq_B$ for the benchmarked (false) goals, contrary to what we initially expected. This means that $\trianglelefteq_B^{rogd}$ cannot be generally used in real applications due to the risk of intolerable embedding test times, even if $\trianglelefteq_B^{rogd}$ may be far less wasteful than $\trianglelefteq_B$ for succeeding goals, as discussed in Sect. 4. For $\trianglelefteq_B^{ml}$ and $\trianglelefteq_B^{sml}$, the figures show that the more A and AC operators comparatively occur in the problem, the bigger the improvement achieved. This is due to the following: (i) these two embedding definitions manipulate flattened meta-level terms; (ii) they are equationally defined, which has a much better performance in Maude than doing search; and (iii) our definitions are highly optimized for lists (that obey associativity) and sets (that obey both associativity and commutativity).

Homeomorphic embedding has been extensively used in Prolog for different purposes, such as termination analysis and partial deduction.

In Fig. 5, we have compared on a logarithmic scale our best embedding definition, $\trianglelefteq_B^{sml}$, with a standard meta-level Prolog[4] implementation of the (syntactic) pure homeomorphic embedding $\trianglelefteq$ of Definition 3.

We chose the NatList example and terms T1 and T2 that do not contain symbols obeying equational axioms as this is the only case that can be handled by the syntactic Prolog implementation. Our experiments show that our refined deterministic formulation $\trianglelefteq_B^{sml}$ (i.e. without search) outperforms the Prolog version so no penalty is incurred when syntactic embeddability tests are run in our equational implementation.

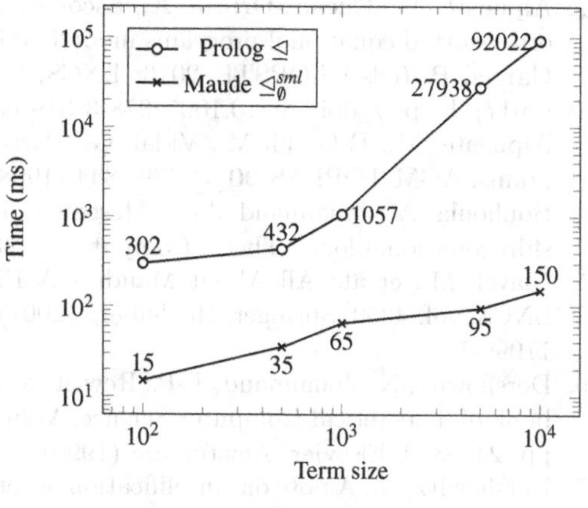

Fig. 5. Comparison of $\trianglelefteq$ vs. $\trianglelefteq_\emptyset^{sml}$ for NatList

---

[4] To avoid any bias, we took the Prolog code for the homeomorphic embedding of the ECCE system [13] that is available at https://github.com/leuschel/ecce, and we run it in SWI-Prolog 7.6.3.

7 Concluding Remarks

Homeomorphic embedding has been extensively used in Prolog but it has never been investigated in the context of expressive rule-based languages like Maude, CafeOBJ, OBJ, ASF+SDF, and ELAN that support symbolic reasoning methods modulo equational axioms. We have introduced a new equational definition of homeomorphic embedding with a remarkably good performance for theories with symbols having any combination of associativity and commutativity. We have also compared different definitions of embedding identifying some key conclusions: (i) definitions of equational homeomorphic embedding based on (non-deterministic) search in Maude perform dramatically worse than their equational counterparts and are not feasible in practice, (ii) definitions of equational homeomorphic embedding based on generated theories perform dramatically worse than meta-level definitions; and (iii) the flattened meta-representation of terms is crucial for homeomorphic embedding definitions dealing with A and AC operators to pay off in practice. As future work, we plan to extend our results to the case when the equational theory B may contain the identity axiom, which is non-trivial since B is not class-finite.

References

1. Alpuente, M., Ballis, D., Frechina, F., Sapiña, J.: Exploring conditional rewriting logic computations. J. Symbolic Comput. **69**, 3–39 (2015)
2. Alpuente, M., Cuenca-Ortega, A., Escobar, S., Meseguer, J.: Partial evaluation of order-sorted equational programs modulo axioms. In: Hermenegildo, M.V., Lopez-Garcia, P. (eds.) LOPSTR 2016. LNCS, vol. 10184, pp. 3–20. Springer, Cham (2017). https://doi.org/10.1007/978-3-319-63139-4_1
3. Alpuente, M., Falaschi, M., Vidal, G.: Partial evaluation of functional logic programs. ACM TOPLAS **20**(4), 768–844 (1998)
4. Bouhoula, A., Jouannaud, J.-P., Meseguer, J.: Specification and proof in membership equational logic. Theor. Comput. Sci. **236**(1–2), 35–132 (2000)
5. Clavel, M., et al.: All About Maude - A High-Performance Logical Framework. LNCS, vol. 4350. Springer, Heidelberg (2007). https://doi.org/10.1007/978-3-540-71999-1
6. Dershowitz, N., Jouannaud, J.-P.: Rewrite systems. In: van Leeuwen, J. (ed.) Handbook of Theoretical Computer Science. Volume B: Formal Models and Semantics, pp. 243–320. Elsevier, Amsterdam (1990)
7. Dershowitz, N.: A note on simplification orderings. Inf. Process. Lett. **9**(5), 212–215 (1979)
8. Eker, S.: Single elementary associative-commutative matching. J. Autom. Reasoning **28**(1), 35–51 (2002)
9. Bürckert, H.J., Herold, A., Schmidt-Schau, M.: On equational theories, unification, and (un)decidability. J. Symbolic Comput. **8**(1–2), 3–49 (1989)
10. Kruskal, J.B.: Well-quasi-ordering, the tree theorem, and Vazsonyi's conjecture. Trans. Am. Math. Soc. **95**, 210–225 (1960)
11. Leuschel, M.: On the power of homeomorphic embedding for online termination. In: Levi, G. (ed.) SAS 1998. LNCS, vol. 1503, pp. 230–245. Springer, Heidelberg (1998). https://doi.org/10.1007/3-540-49727-7_14

12. Leuschel, M.: Homeomorphic embedding for online termination of symbolic methods. In: Mogensen, T.Æ., Schmidt, D.A., Sudborough, I.H. (eds.) The Essence of Computation. LNCS, vol. 2566, pp. 379–403. Springer, Heidelberg (2002). https://doi.org/10.1007/3-540-36377-7_17
13. Leuschel, M., Martens, B., De Schreye, D.: Controlling generalization and polyvariance in partial deduction of normal logic programs. ACM TOPLAS **20**(1), 208–258 (1998)
14. Middeldorp, A., Gramlich, B.: Simple termination is difficult. Appl. Algebra Eng. Commun. Comput. **6**(2), 115–128 (1995)
15. Sørensen, M.H., Glück, R.: An algorithm of generalization in positive supercompilation. In: Lloyd, J.W. (ed.) Proceedings of International Symposium on Logic Programming, ILPS 1995, pp. 465–479. MIT Press, Cambridge (1995)

Logic-Based Distributed/Concurrent Programming

Multiparty Classical Choreographies

Marco Carbone[1(✉)], Luís Cruz-Filipe[2], Fabrizio Montesi[2], and Agata Murawska[1]

[1] IT University of Copenhagen, Copenhagen, Denmark
{carbonem,agmu}@itu.dk

[2] University of Southern Denmark, Odense, Denmark
{lcf,fmontesi}@imada.sdu.dk

Abstract. We present Multiparty Classical Choreographies (MCC), a language model where global descriptions of communicating systems (choreographies) implement typed multiparty sessions. Typing is achieved by generalising classical linear logic to judgements that explicitly record parallelism by means of hypersequents. Our approach unifies different lines of work on choreographies and processes with multiparty sessions, as well as their connection to linear logic. Thus, results developed in one context are carried over to the others. Key novelties of MCC include support for server invocation in choreographies, as well as logic-driven compilation of choreographies with replicated processes.

1 Introduction

Choreographic Programming [17] is a programming paradigm where programs, called *choreographies*, define the intended communication behaviour of a system based on message passing, using an "Alice and Bob" notation, rather than the behaviour of each endpoint. Choreographies are useful for several reasons: they give a succinct description, or *blueprint*, of the intended behaviour of a whole system, making the implementation less error-prone. Then, correct-by-construction distributed implementations can be synthesised automatically by means of *projection*, a compilation algorithm that generates the code for each endpoint described in the choreography [6,8]. Reversely, it is often possible to obtain a choreography from an endpoint implementation by means of *extraction*, providing a precise blueprint of a distributed system.

Choreographic programming has a deep relationship with the proof theory of linear logic [9]. Specifically, choreographic programs can be seen as terms describing the reduction steps of cut elimination in linear logic (choreographies as cut reductions). The key advantage of this result is that it provides a logical reconstruction of two useful translations, one from choreographies to processes (*projection*, or synthesis) and another from processes to choreographies (*extraction*) – this is obtained by exploiting the correspondence between intuitionistic linear logic and a variant of the π-calculus [4]. These translations can be used to keep process implementations aligned with the desired communication flows given as choreographies, whenever code changes are applied to any of the two.

F. Mesnard and P. J. Stuckey (Eds.): LOPSTR 2018, LNCS 11408, pp. 59–76, 2019.
https://doi.org/10.1007/978-3-030-13838-7_4

This kind of alignment is a desirable property in practice, e.g., it is the basis of the Testable Architecture development lifecycle for web services [14].

Unfortunately, the logical reconstruction of choreographies in [9] covers only the multiplicative-additive fragment of intuitionistic linear logic, limiting its practical applicability to simple scenarios. The aim of this paper is to push the boundaries of this approach towards more realistic scenarios with sophisticated features. In this article, we define a model, strictly related to classical linear logic, that allows for *replicated services*, and *multiparty sessions.*

Reaching our aim is challenging for both design and technical reasons. In the multiplicative-additive fragment of linear logic considered in [9], all reductions intuitively match choreographic terms explored in previous works on choreographies, i.e., communication of a channel and branch selection [8]. This is not the case for the exponential fragment, which yields *reductions never considered before in choreographies*, e.g., explicit garbage collection of services and server cloning (see kill and clone operations). To bridge this gap, we exploit the fact that these operations occur naturally in the process language and, through the logic, can be reflected to choreographic primitives for management of services as explicit resources that can be duplicated, used, or destroyed. We show that the reductions for these terms correspond to the principal cut reductions for exponentials in classical linear logic. Typing guarantees that resource management is safe, e.g., no destroyed resource is ever used again.

In [9], all sessions (protocols) have exactly two participants. This works well in intuitionistic linear logic, where sequents are two-sided: two processes can be connected if one "provides" a behaviour and the other "needs" it. This is verified by checking identity of types, respectively between a type on the right-hand side of the sequent of the first process and a type of the left-hand side of the sequent for the second. To date, it is still unclear how identity for two-sided sequents can be generalised to multiparty sessions, where a session can have multiple participants and thus we need to check compatibility of multiple types. Instead, this topic has been investigated in the setting of classical linear logic, where multiparty compatibility is captured by coherence, a generalisation of duality [10]. Therefore, our formulation of Multiparty Classical Choreographies (MCC) is based on classical linear logic. In order to bridge choreographies to multiparty sessions, we introduce a new session environment, which records the types of multiparty communications performed by a choreography as *global types* [13]. The manipulation of the session environment reveals that typing a choreography with multiparty sessions corresponds to *building the coherence proofs for typing its sessions.* Since a proof of coherence is the type compatibility check required by the multiparty version of cut in classical linear logic, our result generalises the choreographies as cut reductions approach to the multiparty case as one would expect, providing further evidence of the robustness of this idea. The final result of our efforts is an expressive calculus for programming choreographies with multiparty sessions and services, which supports both projection and extraction operations *for all typable programs.*

2 Preview

We start by introducing MCC informally, focusing on modelling a protocol inspired by OpenID [20], where a client authenticates through a third-party identity provider. MCC offers a way of specifying protocols in terms of global types. For example, our variant of OpenID can be specified by the global type G:

$$u \to rp(\mathsf{String}); u \to ip(\mathsf{String}); u \to ip(\mathsf{PWD}); ip \to rp.\mathsf{case}(\ u \to rp(\mathsf{String}); G_1,\ G_2)$$

This protocol concerns three endpoints (often called roles in literature) denoted by u (user), rp (relaying party) and ip (identity provider). The user starts by sending its login string to both rp and ip. Then, it sends its password to ip which will either confirm or reject u's authentication to rp. If the authentication is successful then the user will send an evaluation of the authentication service to rp, and then complete as the unspecified protocol G_1. Otherwise, if the password is wrong, then the protocol continues as G_2. The specification given by the global type G can be used by a programmer during an implementation. In MCC, we could give an implementation in terms of the choreography:

$$
\begin{array}{ll}
u\ \mathsf{starts}\ rp, ip; & \texttt{// } u \texttt{ starts protocol with rp and ip} \\
u(user_u) \to rp(user_{rp}); & \texttt{// } u \texttt{ sends its login to } rp \\
u(login_u) \to ip(login_{ip}); & \texttt{// } u \texttt{ sends its login to } ip \\
u(pwd_u) \to ip(pwd_{ip}); & \texttt{// } u \texttt{ authenticates with } ip \\
ip \to rp. \left\{ \begin{array}{lll}
\mathsf{inl}: & u'\ \mathsf{starts}\ s; & \texttt{// } u' \texttt{ starts protocol with } s \\
 & u'(rep_{u'}) \to s(rep_s); & \texttt{// } u' \texttt{ sends report to } s \\
 & s(ack_s) \to u'(ack_{u'}); & \texttt{// } s \texttt{ acknowledges to } u' \\
 & u(rep_u) \to rp(rep_{rp}); P, & \texttt{// } u \texttt{ sends report to } rp \\
\mathsf{inr}: & Q & \texttt{// authentication fails}
\end{array} \right\} &
\end{array}
$$

Each line is commented with an explanation of the performed action. We observe that two different protocols are started. The first line starts the OpenID protocol between u, rp and ip described above. Moreover, after branching, the choreography starts another session between the user (named u') and a server s that is used for reviewing the authentication service given by ip. In this case, the protocol used is $G' = u' \to s(\mathsf{String}); s \to u'(\mathsf{String}); G_3$, for some unspecified G_3. We leave undefined the case in which the identity provider receives a wrong password (term Q).

In this work, we show how a choreography that follows a protocol such as G can be expressed as a proof in a proof theory strictly related to classical linear logic. Moreover, thanks to proof transformations, the choreography above can be projected into a parallel composition of endpoint processes, each running a different endpoint. As an example, the endpoint process for the user would correspond to the process P_u, defined as

$$\mathsf{use}\ u; \overline{u}(user_u); \overline{u}(login_u); \overline{u}(pwd_u); \mathsf{use}\ u'; \overline{u'}(rep_{u'}); u'(ack_{u'}); \overline{u}(rep_u); R$$

which mimics the behaviour of u and u' specified in the choreography. Operator use is used to start a session, while the other two operators utilised above are for in-session communication. Similarly, we can have the endpoint processes for rp, ip and s:

$$P_{rp} = \mathsf{srv}\, rp; rp(user_{rp}); rp.\mathsf{case}(rp(rep_{rp}); R_1, Q_1)$$
$$P_{ip} = \mathsf{srv}\, ip; ip(login_{ip}); ip(pwd_{ip}); R_2 \qquad P_s = \mathsf{srv}\, s; s(rep_s); \overline{s}(ack_s); R_3$$

3 GCP with Hypersequents

In this section, we present the *action fragment* of MCC, where we only consider local actions, e.g., inputs or outputs. The action fragment is a variant of Globally-governed Classical Processes (GCP) [7] whose typing rules use hypersequents. In the remainder, we denote a vector of endpoints $x_1, \ldots, x_n$ as $\tilde{x}$ or $(x_i)_i$.

Syntax. The action fragment is a generalisation of Classical Processes [22] that supports multiparty session types. As hinted in Sect. 2, when writing a program in our language, we do not identify sessions via channel names, but rather we name sessions' *endpoints*. Each process owns a single endpoint of a session it participates in. The complete syntax is given by the following grammar:

$P ::=$	$x^A \to y$	link	$\mid\ \mathsf{use}\, x; P$	client
	$\mid\ P \mid Q$	parallel	$\mid\ \mathsf{srv}\, y; P$	server
	$\mid\ (\nu\tilde{x} : G)\, P$	restriction	$\mid\ \mathsf{kill}\, x \mid P$	server kill
	$\mid\ \overline{x}(x'); (P \mid Q)$	send	$\mid\ \mathsf{clone}\, x(x'); P$	server clone
	$\mid\ y(y'); P$	receive		
	$\mid\ \mathsf{close}[x]$	close session		
	$\mid\ \mathsf{wait}[y]; P$	receive close	$\mid\ y.\mathsf{case}(P, Q)$	branching
	$\mid\ x.\mathsf{inl}; P$	left selection	$\mid\ x.(\mathsf{inl} : P, \mathsf{inr} : Q)$	general selection
	$\mid\ x.\mathsf{inr}; Q$	right selection	$\mid\ x^{\tilde{u}}.\mathsf{case}()$	empty choice

With a few exceptions, the terms above are identical to those of GCP. *For space restriction reasons, we only discuss the key differences.* Parallel and restriction constructs form a single term $(\nu\tilde{x} : G)(P \mid Q)$ in the original GCP. The link process $x^A \to y$ is a forwarder from x to y. We further allow the general selection $x.(\mathsf{inl} : P, \mathsf{inr} : Q)$, denoting a process that non-deterministically selects a left or a right branch. For services, an endpoint x may kill all servers by executing the action $\mathsf{kill}\, x \mid P$, or duplicate them by means of $\mathsf{clone}\, x(x'); P$ – these operations were silent in the original GCP. In cloning, the new server copies are replicated at fresh endpoints, ready to engage in a session with new endpoint x'. More generally, we follow the convention of [22], denoting the result of refreshing names in Q by Q' (changing each $x \in \mathsf{fv}(Q)$ into a fresh x').

Types. Types, used to ensure proper behaviour of endpoints, are defined as:

$$
\begin{array}{lllll}
A ::= & A \otimes B \text{ output} & \mid A \mathbin{\rotatebox[origin=c]{180}{\&}} B \text{ input} \\
& \mid A \oplus B \text{ selection} & \mid A \,\&\, B \text{ choice} \\
& \mid\, !A \quad \text{server} & \mid\, ?A \quad \text{client} \\
& \mid \mathbf{1} \quad \text{close} & \mid \bot \quad \text{wait} \\
& \mid 0 \quad \text{false} & \mid \top \quad \text{empty} \\
& \mid X \quad \text{variable} & \mid X^{\bot} \quad \text{dual variable}
\end{array}
\qquad
\begin{array}{lll}
G ::= & \tilde{x} \to y(G); H & (\otimes \mathbin{\rotatebox[origin=c]{180}{\&}}) \\
& \mid x \to \tilde{y}.\mathsf{case}(G, H) & (\oplus \,\&) \\
& \mid\, !x \to \tilde{y}(G) & (!?) \\
& \mid \tilde{x} \to y & (\mathbf{1}\bot) \\
& \mid x \to \tilde{y}.\mathsf{case}() & (0\top) \\
& \mid x^{A} \to y & (\text{AXIOM})
\end{array}
$$

In the multiparty setting, types can be split into *local types* A, which specify behaviours of a single process, and *global types* G, which describe interaction within sessions (and choreography actions). Again, most global types correspond to pairs of local types, the exception being the global axiom type, describing a linking session (restricted by typing to type variables and their duals). Local type operators are based on connectives from classical linear logic – thus, $A \otimes B$ is the type of a process that outputs an endpoint of type A and continues with type B, whereas $A \mathbin{\rotatebox[origin=c]{180}{\&}} B$ is the type of a process that receives endpoints of type A and is itself ready to continue as B. The corresponding global type $\tilde{x} \to y(G); H$ types the interaction where each of the processes owning an endpoint x_i sends their new endpoint to y. Type 0 is justified by the necessity of having a type dual to $\top$, while the rule $0\top$ is essential for the definition of coherence. Type variables are used to represent concrete datatypes. It is worth noting that the logic formulas in our type system enjoy the usual notion of duality, where a formula's dual is obtained by recursively replacing each connective by the other one in the same row in the table above. For example, the dual of $!(A \otimes 0)$ is $?(A^{\bot} \mathbin{\rotatebox[origin=c]{180}{\&}} \top)$, where $A^{\bot}$ is the dual of formula A.

Typing. We type our terms in judgements of the form $\Sigma \Vdash P \,⦂\, \Psi$, where: (i) Σ is a set of session typings of the form $(x_i)_i : G$; (ii) P is a process; and, (iii) Ψ is a hypersequent, a set of classical linear logic sequents. Intuitively, $\Sigma \Vdash P \,⦂\, \Psi$ reads as "*Ψ types P under the session protocols described in Σ.*"

Given a judgment $\Sigma \Vdash P \,⦂\, \Psi \mid\, \vdash \Gamma, x : A$, checking whether x is *available* – not engaged in a session – is implicitly done by verifying that x does not occur in the domain of Σ. Note that names cannot occur more than once in Σ: each endpoint x may only belong to (at most) one session G. Hypersequents Ψ_1, Ψ_2 and sets of sessions Σ_1, Σ_2 can only be joined if their domains do not intersect. Moreover, we use indexing in different ways: $\left(\Sigma_i \Vdash P_i \,⦂\, \Psi_i\right)_i$ denotes several judgements $\Sigma_1 \Vdash P_1 \,⦂\, \Psi_1, \ldots, \Sigma_n \Vdash P_n \,⦂\, \Psi_n$; indexed pairs $(x_i : A_i)_i$ are a set of pairs $x_1 : A_1, \ldots, x_n : A_n$; and, finally, $(\vdash \Gamma_i)_i$ denotes the hypersequent $\vdash \Gamma_1 \mid \ldots \mid\, \vdash \Gamma_n$.

In order to separate restriction and parallel (reasons for this separation will be explained in Sect. 4), we split the classical linear logic Cut rule into two:

$$
\frac{\left(\Sigma_i \Vdash P_i \,⦂\, \Psi_i \mid\, \vdash \Gamma_i, x_i : A_i\right)_i \quad G \vDash (x_i : A_i)_i}{(\Sigma_i)_i, (x_i)_i : G \Vdash (P_i)_i \,⦂\, \left(\Psi_i \mid\, \vdash \Gamma_i, x_i : A_i\right)_i}\ \mathsf{Conn}
\qquad
\frac{\Sigma, (x_i)_i : G \Vdash P \,⦂\, \Psi \mid \left(\vdash \Gamma_i, x_i : A_i\right)_i}{\Sigma \Vdash (\nu \tilde{x} : G)\, P \,⦂\, \Psi \mid\, \vdash (\Gamma_i)_i}\ \mathsf{Scope}
$$

Rule Conn is used for merging proofs that provide *coherent* types (we address coherence below), but without removing them from the environment. Since such types need to remain in the conclusion of the rule, we need to use hypersequents. The sequents involved in a session get merged once a Scope rule is applied. This hypersequent presentation is similar to a classical linear logic variant of [9] with sessions explicitly remembered in a separate context Σ.

Coherence is a generalisation of duality [7] to more than two parties: when describing a multiparty session, simple duality of types does not suffice to talk about their compatibility. In Fig. 1, we report the rules defining the coherence relation $\vDash$. We do not describe these here in detail, as they remain unchanged compared to the original GCP presentation, with the exception of the axiom rule which is only applicable to atomic types in our system.

$$\frac{G \vDash (x_i : A_i)_i,\ y : C \qquad H \vDash \Gamma,\ (x_i : B_i)_i,\ y : D}{\tilde{x} \to y(G); H \quad \vDash \quad \Gamma,\ (x_i : A_i \otimes B_i)_i,\ y : C \parr D}\ \otimes\parr \qquad \frac{}{\tilde{x} \to y \vDash (x_i : \mathbf{1})_i, y : \bot}\ \mathbf{1}\bot$$

$$\frac{G_1 \vDash \Gamma, x : A, (y_i : C_i)_i \qquad G_2 \vDash \Gamma, x : B, (y_i : D_i)_i}{x \to \tilde{y}.\mathsf{case}(G_1, G_2) \vDash \Gamma, x : A \oplus B, (y_i : C_i \ \&\ D_i)_i}\ \oplus\& \qquad \frac{G \vDash x : A, (y_i : B_i)_i}{!x \to \tilde{y}(G) \vDash x : ?A, (y_i : !B_i)_i}\ !?$$

$$\frac{}{x \to \tilde{y}.\mathsf{case}() \vDash \Gamma, x : 0, (y_i : \top)_i}\ 0\top \qquad \frac{A^\top = X \text{ or } A = X^\perp}{x^A \to y \vDash x : A, y : A^\perp}\ \textsc{Axiom}$$

Fig. 1. Coherence rules.

$$\frac{A = X \text{ or } A = X^\perp}{\cdot \Vdash x^A \to y \ \mathbin{⨾}\ \vdash x : A, y : A^\perp}\ \mathsf{Ax} \qquad \frac{\Sigma_1 \Vdash P \mathbin{⨾} \Psi_1 \mid \vdash \Gamma_1, x' : A \qquad \Sigma_2 \Vdash Q \mathbin{⨾} \Psi_2 \mid \vdash \Gamma_2, x : B}{\Sigma_1, \Sigma_2 \Vdash \overline{x}(x'); (P \mid Q) \mathbin{⨾} \Psi_1 \mid \Psi_2 \mid \vdash \Gamma_1, \Gamma_2, x : A \otimes B}\ \otimes$$

$$\frac{\Sigma \Vdash P \mathbin{⨾} \Psi \mid \vdash \Gamma, y' : A, y : B}{\Sigma \Vdash y(y'); P \mathbin{⨾} \Psi \mid \vdash \Gamma, y : A \parr B}\ \parr \qquad \frac{\Sigma \Vdash P \mathbin{⨾} \Psi \mid \vdash \Gamma}{\Sigma \Vdash \mathsf{wait}[y]; P \mathbin{⨾} \Psi \mid \vdash \Gamma, y : \bot}\ \bot$$

$$\frac{}{\cdot \Vdash \mathsf{close}[x] \mathbin{⨾} \vdash x : \mathbf{1}}\ \mathbf{1} \qquad (\text{no rule for } \mathbf{0}) \qquad \frac{\mathsf{vars}(\Gamma) = \tilde{u}}{\cdot \Vdash x^{\tilde{u}}.\mathsf{case}() \mathbin{⨾} \vdash \Gamma, x : \top}\ \top$$

$$\frac{\Sigma \Vdash P \mathbin{⨾} \Psi \mid \vdash \Gamma, x : A}{\Sigma \Vdash x.\mathsf{inl}; P \mathbin{⨾} \Psi \mid \vdash \Gamma, x : A \oplus B}\ \oplus_1 \qquad \frac{\Sigma \Vdash Q \mathbin{⨾} \Psi \mid \vdash \Gamma, x : B}{\Sigma \Vdash x.\mathsf{inr}; Q \mathbin{⨾} \Psi \mid \vdash \Gamma, x : A \oplus B}\ \oplus_2$$

$$\frac{\Sigma \Vdash P \mathbin{⨾} \Psi \mid \vdash \Gamma, x : A \qquad \Sigma \Vdash Q \mathbin{⨾} \Psi \mid \vdash \Gamma, x : B}{\Sigma \Vdash x.(\mathsf{inl} : P, \mathsf{inr} : Q) \mathbin{⨾} \Psi \mid \vdash \Gamma, x : A \oplus B}\ \oplus \qquad \frac{\cdot \Vdash P \mathbin{⨾} \vdash ?\Gamma, y : A}{\cdot \Vdash \mathsf{srv}\, y; P \mathbin{⨾} \vdash ?\Gamma, y : !A}\ !$$

$$\frac{\Sigma \Vdash P \mathbin{⨾} \Psi \mid \vdash \Gamma, y : A \qquad \Sigma \Vdash Q \mathbin{⨾} \Psi \mid \vdash \Gamma, y : B}{\Sigma \Vdash y.\mathsf{case}(P, Q) \mathbin{⨾} \Psi \mid \vdash \Gamma, y : A \ \&\ B}\ \& \qquad \frac{\Sigma \Vdash P \mathbin{⨾} \Psi \mid \vdash \Gamma, x : A}{\Sigma \Vdash \mathsf{use}\, x; P \mathbin{⨾} \Psi \mid \vdash \Gamma, x : ?A}\ ?$$

$$\frac{\Sigma \Vdash P \mathbin{⨾} \Psi \mid \vdash \Gamma}{\Sigma \Vdash \mathsf{kill}\, x \mid P \mathbin{⨾} \Psi \mid \vdash \Gamma, x : ?A}\ \mathsf{Weaken} \qquad \frac{\Sigma \Vdash P \mathbin{⨾} \Psi \mid \vdash \Gamma, x : ?A, x' : ?A}{\Sigma \Vdash \mathsf{clone}\, x(x'); P \mathbin{⨾} \Psi \mid \vdash \Gamma, x : ?A}\ \mathsf{Contract}$$

Fig. 2. Rules for the action fragment.

The remaining typing rules for the action fragment, presented in Fig. 2 are identical to those of GCP with the exception that a context in GCP may be distributed among several sequents here. For example, rule $\otimes$ takes two sequents $\vdash \Gamma_1, x' : A$ and $\vdash \Gamma_2, x : B$ from two different hypersequents, and merges them into $\vdash \Gamma_1, \Gamma_2, x : A \otimes B$, as in classical linear logic. However, elements of Γ_1 and Γ_2 may be connected through Σ_1 and Σ_2 to other parts of Ψ_1 and Ψ_2 respectively (as a result of previously applied Conn). Note that the rules of this fragment work only with processes not engaged in any session, since the endpoints explicitly mentioned in proof terms cannot occur in the domain of Σ: this is an implicit check in all rules of Fig. 2. Rule $\top$ introduces a single sequent $\Gamma, x : \top$, allowing for any Γ. The proof term $x^{\tilde{u}}.\mathsf{case}()$ keeps track of the endpoints introduced in Γ: it ensures that all endpoints in the typing are mentioned in the proof term, which is useful when defining semantics. In this article, we restrict the axiom to only type variables (see Sect. 6).

Semantics. The semantics of the action fragment is almost identical to that of standard GCP. It is obtained from cases of the proof of cut elimination: the principal cases describe reductions ($\longrightarrow$), while the permutations of rule applications give rise to the rules for structural equivalence ($\equiv$), reported in Fig. 3. Note that as we are interested only in commuting conversions of typable programs, there are certain cases where the correct equivalence can be found only by looking at the typing derivation which contains information that is not part of the process term. Under $\equiv$, parallel distributes safely over case (because only the actions of one branch are going to be executed). A similar mechanism can be found in the original presentation of Classical Processes [22], and was

$$
\begin{array}{l}
(\tilde{P} \mid Q) \mid \tilde{S} \equiv \tilde{P} \mid (Q \mid \tilde{S}) \\
(\overline{x}(x'); (P \mid Q)) \mid \tilde{S} \equiv \overline{x}(x'); ((P \mid \tilde{S}) \mid Q) \\
(\overline{x}(x'); (P \mid Q)) \mid \tilde{S} \equiv \overline{x}(x'); (P \mid (Q \mid \tilde{S})) \\
y(y'); P \mid \tilde{Q} \equiv y(y'); (P \mid \tilde{Q}) \\
\mathsf{wait}[y]; P \mid \tilde{Q} \equiv \mathsf{wait}[y]; (P \mid \tilde{Q}) \\
x.\mathsf{inl}; P \mid \tilde{Q} \equiv x.\mathsf{inl}; (P \mid \tilde{Q}) \\
x.\mathsf{inr}; Q \mid \tilde{Q} \equiv x.\mathsf{inr}; (P \mid \tilde{Q}) \\
x.(\mathsf{inl} : P, \mathsf{inr} : Q) \mid \tilde{S} \equiv \\
\qquad x.(\mathsf{inl} : P \mid \tilde{S}, \mathsf{inr} : Q \mid \tilde{S}) \\
y.\mathsf{case}(P, Q) \mid \tilde{S} \equiv y.\mathsf{case}(P \mid \tilde{S}, Q \mid \tilde{S}) \\
\mathsf{use}\, x; P \mid \tilde{Q} \equiv \mathsf{use}\, x; (P \mid \tilde{Q}) \\
\mathsf{kill}\, x \mid P \mid \tilde{Q} \equiv \mathsf{kill}\, x \mid (P \mid \tilde{Q}) \\
\mathsf{clone}\, x(x'); P \mid \tilde{Q} \equiv \mathsf{clone}\, x(x'); (P \mid \tilde{Q})
\end{array}
$$

$$
\begin{array}{l}
(\boldsymbol{\nu}\tilde{x} : G)(P \mid \tilde{Q}) \equiv (\boldsymbol{\nu}\tilde{x} : G)\, P \mid \tilde{Q} \\
(\boldsymbol{\nu}\tilde{x} : G)(\boldsymbol{\nu}\tilde{y} : H)\, P \equiv (\boldsymbol{\nu}\tilde{y} : H)(\boldsymbol{\nu}\tilde{x} : G)\, P \\
(\boldsymbol{\nu}\tilde{w} : G)(\overline{x}(x'); (P \mid Q)) \equiv \\
\qquad \overline{x}(x'); ((\boldsymbol{\nu}\tilde{w} : G)\, P \mid Q) \quad (\exists i. w_i \in \mathsf{fv}(P)) \\
(\boldsymbol{\nu}\tilde{w} : G)(\overline{x}(x'); (P \mid Q)) \equiv \\
\qquad \overline{x}(x'); (P \mid (\boldsymbol{\nu}\tilde{w} : G)\, Q) \quad (\exists i. w_i \in \mathsf{fv}(Q)) \\
(\boldsymbol{\nu}\tilde{w} : G)(y(y'); P) \equiv y(y'); (\boldsymbol{\nu}\tilde{w} : G)\, P \\
(\boldsymbol{\nu}\tilde{w} : G)(x.\mathsf{inl}; P) \equiv x.\mathsf{inl}; (\boldsymbol{\nu}\tilde{w} : G)\, P \\
(\boldsymbol{\nu}\tilde{w} : G)(x.\mathsf{inr}; Q) \equiv x.\mathsf{inr}; (\boldsymbol{\nu}\tilde{w} : G)\, Q \\
(\boldsymbol{\nu}\tilde{w} : G)(x.(\mathsf{inl} : P, \mathsf{inr} : Q)) \equiv \\
\qquad x.(\mathsf{inl} : (\boldsymbol{\nu}\tilde{w} : G)\, P, \mathsf{inr} : (\boldsymbol{\nu}\tilde{w} : G)\, Q) \\
(\boldsymbol{\nu}\tilde{w} : G)(y.\mathsf{case}(P, Q)) \equiv \\
\qquad y.\mathsf{case}((\boldsymbol{\nu}\tilde{w} : G)\, P, (\boldsymbol{\nu}\tilde{w} : G)\, Q) \\
(\boldsymbol{\nu}\tilde{w} : G)(\mathsf{use}\, x; P) \equiv \mathsf{use}\, x; (\boldsymbol{\nu}\tilde{w} : G)\, P \\
(\boldsymbol{\nu}\tilde{w} : G)(\mathsf{kill}\, x \mid P) \equiv \mathsf{kill}\, x \mid (\boldsymbol{\nu}\tilde{w} : G)\, P \\
(\boldsymbol{\nu}\tilde{w} : G)(\mathsf{clone}\, x(x'); P) \equiv \mathsf{clone}\, x(x'); (\boldsymbol{\nu}\tilde{w} : G)\, P
\end{array}
$$

$$
\begin{array}{l}
(\boldsymbol{\nu}\tilde{x} : G)(\mathsf{srv}\, y; P \mid \tilde{Q}) \equiv \mathsf{srv}\, y; (\boldsymbol{\nu}\tilde{x} : G)(P \mid \tilde{Q}) \\
(\boldsymbol{\nu}\tilde{z}z : G)(x^{\tilde{u},z}.\mathsf{case}() \mid \tilde{Q}) \equiv x^{\tilde{u},\tilde{v}}.\mathsf{case}() \qquad \text{where } \tilde{v} = \mathsf{vars}(\tilde{Q}) \setminus \tilde{z}
\end{array}
$$

Fig. 3. Equivalences for commuting the action fragment with Conn and Scope. All rules assume that both sides of the equation are typable in the same context.

$$
\begin{array}{ll}
(\boldsymbol{\nu}\tilde{x}, y, \tilde{z} : \tilde{x} \to y(G); H)\,((\overline{x_i}(x_i'); (P_i \mid Q_i))_i \mid y(y'); R \mid \tilde{S}) & \\
\qquad\longrightarrow\ (\boldsymbol{\nu}\tilde{x}', y' : G\{\tilde{x}'/\tilde{x}, y'/y\})\,(\tilde{P} \mid (\boldsymbol{\nu}\tilde{x}, y, \tilde{z} : H)\,(\tilde{Q} \mid R \mid \tilde{S})) & \\
(\boldsymbol{\nu}\tilde{x}, y : \tilde{x} \to y)\,((\mathsf{close}[x_i])_i \mid \mathsf{wait}[y]; P) & \longrightarrow P \\
(\boldsymbol{\nu}x, \tilde{y}, \tilde{z} : x \to \tilde{y}.\mathsf{case}(G, H))\,(x.\mathsf{inl}; P \mid (y_i.\mathsf{case}(Q_i, R_i))_i \mid \tilde{S}) & \\
 & \longrightarrow (\boldsymbol{\nu}x, \tilde{y}, \tilde{z} : G)\,(P \mid \tilde{Q} \mid \tilde{S}) \\
(\boldsymbol{\nu}x, \tilde{y}, \tilde{z} : x \to \tilde{y}.\mathsf{case}(G, H))\,(x.\mathsf{inr}; P \mid (y_i.\mathsf{case}(Q_i, R_i))_i \mid \tilde{S}) & \\
 & \longrightarrow (\boldsymbol{\nu}x, \tilde{y}, \tilde{z} : H)\,(P \mid \tilde{R} \mid \tilde{S}) \\
(\boldsymbol{\nu}x, \tilde{y}, \tilde{z} : x \to \tilde{y}.\mathsf{case}(G, H))\,(x.(\mathsf{inl} : P, \mathsf{inr} : Q) \mid (y_i.\mathsf{case}(R_i, S_i))_i \mid \tilde{T}) & \\
 & \longrightarrow (\boldsymbol{\nu}x, \tilde{y}, \tilde{z} : G)\,(P \mid \tilde{R} \mid \tilde{T}) \\
(\boldsymbol{\nu}x, \tilde{y}, \tilde{z} : x \to \tilde{y}.\mathsf{case}(G, H))\,(x.(\mathsf{inl} : P, \mathsf{inr} : Q) \mid (y_i.\mathsf{case}(R_i, S_i))_i \mid \tilde{T}) & \\
 & \longrightarrow (\boldsymbol{\nu}x, \tilde{y}, \tilde{z} : H)\,(Q \mid \tilde{S} \mid \tilde{T}) \\
(\boldsymbol{\nu}x, \tilde{y} : !x \to \tilde{y}(G))\,(\mathsf{use}\,x; P \mid (\mathsf{srv}\,y_i; Q_i)_i) & \longrightarrow (\boldsymbol{\nu}x, \tilde{y} : G)\,(P \mid \tilde{Q}) \\
(\boldsymbol{\nu}x, \tilde{y} : !x \to \tilde{y}(G))\,(\mathsf{kill}\,x \mid P \mid (\mathsf{srv}\,y_i; Q_i)_i) & \longrightarrow (\mathsf{kill}\,u_j)_j \mid P \\
 & \qquad \text{where } \forall i.\forall v_i \in \mathsf{fv}(Q_i).v_i \neq y_i \Rightarrow \exists j.v_i = u_j \\
(\boldsymbol{\nu}x, \tilde{y} : !x \to \tilde{y}(G))\,(\mathsf{clone}\,x(x'); P \mid (\mathsf{srv}\,y_i; Q_i)_i) & \longrightarrow \\
\multicolumn{2}{l}{\left(\mathsf{clone}\,u_j(u_j')\right)_j; (\boldsymbol{\nu}x, \tilde{y} : !x \to \tilde{y}(G))\,(\boldsymbol{\nu}x', \tilde{y}' : !x' \to \tilde{y}'(G\{x'/x, \tilde{y}'/\tilde{y}\}))\,(P \mid (\mathsf{srv}\,y_i; Q_i)_i \mid (\mathsf{srv}\,y_i'; Q_i')_i)} \\
 & \qquad \text{where } \forall i.\forall v_i \in \mathsf{fv}(Q_i).v_i \neq y_i \Rightarrow \exists j.v_i = u_j \\
(\boldsymbol{\nu}x, y : x^X \to y)\,(x^X \to w \mid P) & \longrightarrow P\{w/y\} \\
(\boldsymbol{\nu}x, y : x^{X^\perp} \to y)\,(w^X \to x \mid P) & \longrightarrow P\{w/y\}
\end{array}
$$

Fig. 4. Semantics for the action fragment.

later demonstrated to correspond to a bisimulation law in [1]. The semantics of the action fragment of our calculus is presented in Fig. 4. Notice that the β-reductions are coordinated by a global type, as they correspond to multiple parties communicating.[1] The reduction rules for server killing and cloning may look strange because both kill and clone remain in the proof term after reduction. This is because of the corresponding reduction in classical linear logic, where it is necessary to use weakening and contraction (corresponding to kill and clone respectively) also after reduction. As a consequence, we get them as proof terms.

4 Extending GCP with Choreographies

In order to obtain full MCC, we extend the action fragment presented in the previous section with choreography terms (interactions).

Syntax. Unlike a process in the action fragment, a choreography, which describes a global view of the communications of a process, will own all of the endpoints of

[1] It may be surprising that some of the rules also include a restriction to a vector $\tilde{z}$, and a session using a vector of processes $\tilde{S}$, whose shape we do not inspect. This follows from the shape of coherence rules: rules such as $\otimes ⅋$, $\oplus \&$ and $0\top$ contain an additional context Γ, captured here by $\tilde{z}$.

the sessions it describes. We call the fragment of MCC with choreography terms the *interaction fragment*. Formally, MCC syntax is extended as follows:

$P ::= \ \ldots$ as in the action fragment ...		$\mid x \ \mathsf{starts}\ \tilde{y}; P$	server accept/request
$\mid z \leftarrow y^B \rightarrow x; P$	link	$\mid x \ \mathsf{kills}\ \widetilde{y(Q)}; P$	server kill
$\mid \tilde{x}(\tilde{x}') \rightarrow y(y'); P$	communication	$\mid x \ \mathsf{clones}\ \tilde{y}(x', \tilde{y}'); P$	server clone
$\mid \tilde{x} \ \mathsf{closes}\ y; P$	session close		
$\mid x \rightarrow \tilde{y}.\mathsf{inl}(P; Q_1, \ldots, Q_n)$	left selection	$\mid x \rightarrow \tilde{y}.(\mathsf{inl} : P, \mathsf{inr} : Q)$	general selection
$\mid x \rightarrow \tilde{y}.\mathsf{inr}(P_1, \ldots, P_n; Q)$	right selection		

The link term $z \leftarrow y^B \rightarrow x; P$ gives the choreographic view of an axiom connected to some other process P through endpoints x and y. A linear interaction $\tilde{x}(\tilde{x}') \rightarrow y(y'); P$ denotes a communication from endpoints $\tilde{x}$ to the endpoint y, where a new session with endpoints $\tilde{x}'$,y' is created. The choreography $\tilde{x}\ \mathsf{closes}\ y; P$ closes a session between endpoints $\tilde{x}$, y. When it comes to branching, we have two choreographic terms denoting left and right selection: $x \rightarrow \tilde{y}.\mathsf{inl}(P; Q_1, \ldots, Q_n)$ and $x \rightarrow \tilde{y}.\mathsf{inr}(P_1, \ldots, P_n; Q)$. A third term, $x \rightarrow \tilde{y}.(\mathsf{inl} : P, \mathsf{inr} : Q)$, is used for non-deterministic choice. In MCC, we can model non-linear behaviour: this is done with the terms $x\ \mathsf{starts}\ \tilde{y}; P$, $x\ \mathsf{kills}\ \widetilde{y(Q)}; P$ and $x\ \mathsf{clones}\ \tilde{y}(x', \tilde{y}'); P$. The first term features a client x starting a new session with servers $\tilde{y}$, while the second term is used by endpoint x to shut down servers $\tilde{y}$. Finally, we have a term for cloning servers so that they can be used by different clients in different sessions.

Typing. Figure 5 details the rules for typing choreography terms. Each of these rules combines two rules from the action fragment simulating their reduction, where the conclusion of a rule corresponds to the redex and the premise to the reductum. Unlike process rules, the choreography rules now also look at Σ to check that the interactions described conform to the types of the ongoing sessions. In rule $\mathsf{C}_{1\bot}$, we close a session (removed from Σ) and terminate all processes involved in it. Rule $\mathsf{C}_{\otimes ⅋}$ types the creation of a new session with protocol G, created among endpoints $\tilde{z}$ and w; this session is stored in Σ, while the process types are updated as in rules $\otimes$ and ⅋ above. The remaining rules in the linear fragment are similarly understood. Exponentials give rise to three rules, all of them combining ! with another rule. In rule C!?, process x invokes the services provided by $\tilde{y}$, creating a new session among these processes with type G. Rule $\mathsf{C}_{!\mathsf{w}}$ combines ! with Weaken: here the processes providing the service are simply removed from the context. Finally, rule $\mathsf{C}_{!\mathsf{C}}$ combines ! with Contract, allowing a service to be duplicated.

Reduction Semantics. Figure 6 gives the reductions for the interaction fragment. From a proof-theoretical perspective, these reductions correspond to proof transformations of C rules from Fig. 5 followed by a structural Scope rule; the transformation removes the C rule and pushes Scope higher up in the proof tree.

Linear Fragment:

$$\frac{\Sigma \Vdash P\{w/x\} \mathrel{{\circ}\atop{\circ}} \Psi \mid \vdash \Gamma, \underline{w:A} \quad w \notin \mathsf{vars}(\Sigma) \quad A^\perp = B \quad A = X \text{ or } A = X^\perp}{\Sigma, \boxed{(x,y):x^A \to y} \Vdash w \leftarrow y^B \to x; P \mathrel{{\circ}\atop{\circ}} \Psi \mid \vdash \Gamma, \underline{x:A} \mid \underline{\vdash w:A, y:B}}\ \mathsf{C_{Ax}}$$

$$\frac{\Sigma, \boxed{(\tilde{x}, y, \tilde{u}):H, (\tilde{x}', y'):G\{\tilde{x}'/\tilde{x}, y'/y\}} \Vdash P \mathrel{{\circ}\atop{\circ}} \Psi \mid \underline{(\vdash \Gamma_{i1}, x_i':A_i)_i \mid (\vdash \Gamma_{i2}, x_i:B_i)_i} \mid \vdash \Gamma, \underline{y':C, y:D}}{\Sigma, \boxed{(\tilde{x}, y, \tilde{u}):\tilde{x} \to y(G); H} \Vdash \tilde{x}(\tilde{x}') \to y(y'); P \mathrel{{\circ}\atop{\circ}} \Psi \mid \underline{(\vdash \Gamma_{i1}, \Gamma_{i2}, x_i:A_i \otimes B_i)_i} \mid \vdash \Gamma, \underline{y:C \parr D}}\ \mathsf{C_{\otimes\parr}}$$

$$\frac{\Sigma \Vdash P \mathrel{{\circ}\atop{\circ}} \Psi \mid \vdash \Gamma}{\Sigma, \boxed{(\tilde{x}, y):\tilde{x} \to y} \Vdash \tilde{x} \text{ closes } y; P \mathrel{{\circ}\atop{\circ}} \Psi \mid \underline{(\vdash x_i:1)_i} \mid \vdash \Gamma, \underline{y:\perp}}\ \mathsf{C_{1\perp}}$$

$$\frac{\begin{array}{c}\Sigma, (\Sigma_i)_i, \boxed{(x, \tilde{y}, \tilde{u}):G} \Vdash P \mathrel{{\circ}\atop{\circ}} \Psi \mid (\Psi_i)_i \mid \vdash \Gamma, \underline{x:A} \mid \underline{(\vdash \Gamma_i, y_i:C_i)_i} \mid (\vdash \Gamma_j, u_j:E_j)_j \\ \left(\Sigma_i \Vdash Q_i \mathrel{{\circ}\atop{\circ}} \Psi_i \mid \underline{\vdash \Gamma_i, y_i:D_i}\right)_i \qquad H \vDash x:B, (y_i:D_i)_i, (u_j:E_j)_j\end{array}}{\Sigma, (\Sigma_i)_i, \boxed{(x, \tilde{y}, \tilde{u}):x \to \tilde{y}.\mathsf{case}(G, H)} \Vdash x \to \tilde{y}.\mathsf{inl}(P; Q_1, \ldots, Q_n) \mathrel{{\circ}\atop{\circ}} \begin{array}{l}\Psi \mid (\Psi_i)_i \mid \vdash \Gamma, \underline{x:A \oplus B} \mid \\ \underline{(\vdash \Gamma_i, y_i:C_i \ \&\ D_i)_i} \mid (\vdash \Gamma_j, u_j:E_j)_j\end{array}}\ \mathsf{C^1_{\oplus\&}}$$

$$\frac{\begin{array}{c}\left(\Sigma_i \Vdash P_i \mathrel{{\circ}\atop{\circ}} \Psi_i \mid \underline{\vdash \Gamma_i, y_i:C_i}\right)_i \qquad G \vDash x:A, (y_i:C_i)_i, (u_j:E_j)_j \\ \Sigma, (\Sigma_i)_i, \boxed{(x, \tilde{y}, \tilde{u}):H} \Vdash Q \mathrel{{\circ}\atop{\circ}} \Psi \mid (\Psi_i)_i \mid \vdash \Gamma, \underline{x:B} \mid \underline{(\vdash \Gamma_i, y_i:D_i)_i} \mid (\vdash \Gamma_j, u_j:E_j)_j\end{array}}{\Sigma, (\Sigma_i)_i, \boxed{(x, \tilde{y}, \tilde{u}):x \to \tilde{y}.\mathsf{case}(G, H)} \Vdash x \to \tilde{y}.\mathsf{inr}(P_1, \ldots, P_n; Q) \mathrel{{\circ}\atop{\circ}} \begin{array}{l}\Psi \mid (\Psi_i)_i \mid \vdash \Gamma, \underline{x:A \oplus B} \mid \\ \underline{(\vdash \Gamma_i, y_i:C_i \ \&\ D_i)_i} \mid (\vdash \Gamma_j, u_j:E_j)_j\end{array}}\ \mathsf{C^2_{\oplus\&}}$$

$$\frac{\Sigma, \boxed{(x, \tilde{y}, \tilde{u}):G} \Vdash P \mathrel{{\circ}\atop{\circ}} \Psi \mid \vdash \Gamma, \underline{x:A} \mid \underline{(\vdash \Gamma_i, y_i:C_i)_i} \quad \Sigma, \boxed{(x, \tilde{y}, \tilde{u}):H} \Vdash Q \mathrel{{\circ}\atop{\circ}} \Psi \mid \vdash \Gamma, \underline{x:B} \mid \underline{(\vdash \Gamma_i, y_i:D_i)_i}}{\Sigma, \boxed{(x, \tilde{y}, \tilde{u}):x \to \tilde{y}.\mathsf{case}(G, H)} \Vdash x \to \tilde{y}.(\mathsf{inl}: P, \mathsf{inr}: Q) \mathrel{{\circ}\atop{\circ}} \Psi \mid \vdash \Gamma, \underline{x:A \oplus B} \mid \underline{(\vdash \Gamma_i, y_i:C_i \ \&\ D_i)_i}}\ \mathsf{C_{\oplus\&}}$$

Exponential Fragment:

$$\frac{\Sigma, \boxed{(x, \tilde{y}):G} \Vdash P \mathrel{{\circ}\atop{\circ}} \Psi \mid \vdash \Gamma, \underline{x:A} \mid \underline{(\vdash ?\Gamma_i, y_i:B_i)_i} \quad \forall i.\, \mathsf{vars}(?\Gamma_i) \cap \mathsf{vars}(\Sigma) = \emptyset}{\Sigma, \boxed{(x, \tilde{y}):!x \to \tilde{y}(G)} \Vdash x \text{ starts } \tilde{y}; P \mathrel{{\circ}\atop{\circ}} \Psi \mid \vdash \Gamma, \underline{x:?A} \mid \underline{(\vdash ?\Gamma_i, y_i:!B_i)_i}}\ \mathsf{C!?}$$

$$\frac{\Sigma \Vdash P \mathrel{{\circ}\atop{\circ}} \Psi \mid \vdash \Gamma \quad \left(\cdot \Vdash Q_i \mathrel{{\circ}\atop{\circ}} \underline{\vdash ?\Gamma_i, y_i:B_i}\right)_i \quad G \vDash x:A, (y_i:B_i)_i}{\Sigma, \boxed{(x, \tilde{y}):!x \to \tilde{y}(G)} \Vdash x \text{ kills } \widetilde{y(Q)}; P \mathrel{{\circ}\atop{\circ}} \Psi \mid \vdash \Gamma, \underline{x:?A} \mid \underline{(\vdash ?\Gamma_i, y_i:!B_i)_i}}\ \mathsf{C_{!w}}$$

$$\frac{\Sigma, \begin{array}{|l|}\hline (x, \tilde{y}):!x \to \tilde{y}(G), \\ \hline (x', \tilde{y}'):!x' \to \tilde{y}'(G\{x'/x, \tilde{y}'/\tilde{y}\}) \\ \hline\end{array} \Vdash P \mathrel{{\circ}\atop{\circ}} \Psi \mid \begin{array}{l}\vdash \Gamma, \underline{x:?A, x':?A} \\ \underline{(\vdash ?\Gamma_i, y_i:!B_i \mid \vdash ?\Gamma_i', y_i':!B_i)_i}\end{array} \quad \begin{array}{l}\mathsf{vars}(?\Gamma_i) \cap \mathsf{vars}(\Sigma) = \emptyset \\ \mathsf{vars}(?\Gamma_i') \cap \mathsf{vars}(\Sigma) = \emptyset\end{array}}{\Sigma, \boxed{(x, \tilde{y}):!x \to \tilde{y}(G)} \Vdash x \text{ clones } \tilde{y}(x', \tilde{y}'); P \mathrel{{\circ}\atop{\circ}} \Psi \mid \vdash \Gamma, \underline{x:?A} \mid \underline{(\vdash ?\Gamma_i, y_i:!B_i)_i}}\ \mathsf{C_{!C}}$$

Fig. 5. Rules for the interaction fragment.

Remark 1 (Server Cloning). The reduction rule for a server cloning choreography must clone all of the doubled endpoints. Looking at the typing rule $\mathsf{C_{!C}}$ on Fig. 5, cloned variables u_j are all of the endpoints mentioned in $(?\Gamma_i)_i$, and u_j' are corresponding endpoints from $(?\Gamma_i')_i$. To make the search for these variables syntactic, one could do an endpoint projection, as described in the next section, and look at the appropriate subterm of the Conn rule which connects y_i and x. The u_j are then the free variables of this subterm, excluding y_i.

Structural Equivalence. The reductions given earlier require that programs are written in the very specific form given in their left-hand side. Formally, this is achieved by closing $\longrightarrow$ under structural equivalence: if $P \equiv P'$, $P' \longrightarrow Q'$ and $Q' \equiv Q$, then $P \longrightarrow Q$. The equivalences for the interaction part are given in Fig. 7. As in the action fragment, we are only interested in commuting conversions of typable programs, and therefore rely on typing derivations for finding the correct equivalence. Besides the commuting conversions, we also have the usual structural equivalence rules where parallel composition under restriction,

$$
\begin{aligned}
(\boldsymbol{\nu} x, y : x^{X} \to y)\,(w \leftarrow y^{X^{\perp}} \to x; P) &\longrightarrow P\{w/x\} \\
(\boldsymbol{\nu} x, y : x^{X^{\perp}} \to y)\,(w \leftarrow y^{X} \to x; P) &\longrightarrow P\{w/x\} \\
(\boldsymbol{\nu} \tilde{x}, y, \tilde{z} : \tilde{x} \to y(G); H)\,\big(\tilde{x}(\tilde{x}') \to y(y'); P\big) &\longrightarrow (\boldsymbol{\nu} \tilde{x}', y' : G\{\tilde{x}'/\tilde{x}, y'/y\})\,(\boldsymbol{\nu} \tilde{x}, y, \tilde{z} : H)\,P \\
(\boldsymbol{\nu} \tilde{x}, y : \tilde{x} \to y)\,(\tilde{x} \text{ closes } y; P) &\longrightarrow P \\
(\boldsymbol{\nu} x, \tilde{y}, \tilde{z} : x \to \tilde{y}.\mathsf{case}(G, H))\,(x \to \tilde{y}.\mathsf{inl}(P; Q_1, \ldots, Q_n)) &\longrightarrow (\boldsymbol{\nu} x, \tilde{y}, \tilde{z} : G)\,P \\
(\boldsymbol{\nu} x, \tilde{y}, \tilde{z} : x \to \tilde{y}.\mathsf{case}(G, H))\,(x \to \tilde{y}.\mathsf{inr}(P_1, \ldots, P_n; Q)) &\longrightarrow (\boldsymbol{\nu} x, \tilde{y}, \tilde{z} : H)\,Q \\
(\boldsymbol{\nu} x, \tilde{y}, \tilde{z} : x \to \tilde{y}.\mathsf{case}(G, H))\,(x \to \tilde{y}.(\mathsf{inl} : P, \mathsf{inr} : Q)) &\longrightarrow (\boldsymbol{\nu} x, \tilde{y}, \tilde{z} : G)\,P \\
(\boldsymbol{\nu} x, \tilde{y}, \tilde{z} : x \to \tilde{y}.\mathsf{case}(G, H))\,(x \to \tilde{y}.(\mathsf{inl} : P, \mathsf{inr} : Q)) &\longrightarrow (\boldsymbol{\nu} x, \tilde{y}, \tilde{z} : H)\,Q \\
(\boldsymbol{\nu} x, \tilde{y} : !x \to \tilde{y}(G))\,(x \text{ starts } \tilde{y}; P) &\longrightarrow (\boldsymbol{\nu} x, \tilde{y} : G)\,P \\
(\boldsymbol{\nu} x, \tilde{y} : !x \to \tilde{y}(G))\,\big(x \text{ kills } \widetilde{y(Q)}; P\big) &\longrightarrow (\mathsf{kill}\, u_j)_j \mid P \qquad (\forall v_i \in \mathsf{fv}(Q_i).v_i \neq y_i \Rightarrow \exists j.v_i = u_j) \\
(\boldsymbol{\nu} x, \tilde{y} : !x \to \tilde{y}(G))\,(x \text{ clones } \tilde{y}(x', \tilde{y}'); P) &\longrightarrow \\
(\mathsf{clone}\, u_j\,(u_j'))_j; (\boldsymbol{\nu} x, \tilde{y} : !x \to \tilde{y}(G))\,(\boldsymbol{\nu} x', \tilde{y}' : !x' \to \tilde{y}'(G\{x'/x, \tilde{y}'/\tilde{y}\}))\,P & \qquad \text{(see Remark 1)}
\end{aligned}
$$

Fig. 6. Semantics for the interaction fragment.

$$
\begin{aligned}
& w \leftarrow y^{B} \to x; P \mid \tilde{Q} \equiv w \leftarrow y^{B} \to x; (P \mid \tilde{Q}) \\
& \tilde{x}(\tilde{x}') \to y(y'); P \mid \tilde{Q} \equiv \tilde{x}(\tilde{x}') \to y(y'); (P \mid \tilde{Q}) \\
& \tilde{x} \text{ closes } y; P \mid \tilde{Q} \equiv \tilde{x} \text{ closes } y; (P \mid \tilde{Q}) \\
& x \to \tilde{y}.\mathsf{inl}(P; Q_1, \ldots, Q_n) \mid \tilde{S} \equiv x \to \tilde{y}.\mathsf{inl}((P \mid \tilde{S}); Q_1, \ldots, Q_n) \\
& x \to \tilde{y}.\mathsf{inl}(P; Q_1, \ldots, Q_n) \mid \tilde{S} \equiv x \to \tilde{y}.\mathsf{inl}((P \mid \tilde{S}); (Q_1, \ldots, (Q_i \mid \tilde{S}), \ldots, Q_n)) \\
& x \to \tilde{y}.\mathsf{inr}(P_1, \ldots, P_n; Q) \mid \tilde{S} \equiv x \to \tilde{y}.\mathsf{inr}(P_1, \ldots, P_n; (Q \mid \tilde{S})) \\
& x \to \tilde{y}.\mathsf{inr}(P_1, \ldots, P_n; Q) \mid \tilde{S} \equiv x \to \tilde{y}.\mathsf{inr}((P_1, \ldots, (P_i \mid \tilde{S}), \ldots, P_n); (Q \mid \tilde{S})) \\
& x \text{ starts } \tilde{y}; P \mid \tilde{Q} \equiv x \text{ starts } \tilde{y}; (P \mid \tilde{Q}) \\
& x \text{ kills } \widetilde{y(Q)}; P \mid \tilde{S} \equiv x \text{ kills } \widetilde{y(Q)}; (P \mid \tilde{S}) \\
& x \text{ clones } \tilde{y}(x', \tilde{y}'); P \mid \tilde{Q} \equiv x \text{ clones } \tilde{y}(x', \tilde{y}'); (P \mid \tilde{Q}) \\
& (\boldsymbol{\nu} \tilde{w} : G)\,(\tilde{x}(\tilde{x}') \to y(y'); P) \equiv \tilde{x}(\tilde{x}') \to y(y'); (\boldsymbol{\nu} \tilde{w} : G)\,P \\
& (\boldsymbol{\nu} \tilde{w} : G)\,(\tilde{x} \text{ closes } y; P) \equiv \tilde{x} \text{ closes } y; (\boldsymbol{\nu} \tilde{w} : G)\,P \\
& (\boldsymbol{\nu} \tilde{w} : G)\,(x \to \tilde{y}.\mathsf{inl}(P; Q_1, \ldots, Q_n)) \equiv x \to \tilde{y}.\mathsf{inl}((\boldsymbol{\nu} \tilde{w} : G)\,P; Q_1, \ldots, Q_n) \\
& (\boldsymbol{\nu} \tilde{w} : G)\,(x \to \tilde{y}.\mathsf{inl}(P; Q_1, \ldots, Q_n)) \equiv x \to \tilde{y}.\mathsf{inl}((\boldsymbol{\nu} \tilde{w} : G)\,P; Q_1, \ldots, (\boldsymbol{\nu} \tilde{w} : G)\,Q_i, \ldots, Q_n) \\
& (\boldsymbol{\nu} \tilde{w} : G)\,(x \to \tilde{y}.\mathsf{inr}(P_1, \ldots, P_n; Q)) \equiv x \to \tilde{y}.\mathsf{inr}(P_1, \ldots, P_n; (\boldsymbol{\nu} \tilde{w} : G)\,Q) \\
& (\boldsymbol{\nu} \tilde{w} : G)\,(x \to \tilde{y}.\mathsf{inr}(P_1, \ldots, P_n; Q)) \equiv x \to \tilde{y}.\mathsf{inr}(P_1, \ldots, (\boldsymbol{\nu} \tilde{w} : G)\,P_i, \ldots, P_n; (\boldsymbol{\nu} \tilde{w} : G)\,Q) \\
& (\boldsymbol{\nu} \tilde{w} : G)\,(x.(\mathsf{inl} : P, \mathsf{inr} : Q)) \equiv x.(\mathsf{inl} : (\boldsymbol{\nu} \tilde{w} : G)\,P, \mathsf{inr} : (\boldsymbol{\nu} \tilde{w} : G)\,Q) \\
& (\boldsymbol{\nu} \tilde{w} : G)\,(x \text{ starts } \tilde{y}; P) \equiv x \text{ starts } \tilde{y}; (\boldsymbol{\nu} \tilde{w} : G)\,P \\
& (\boldsymbol{\nu} \tilde{w} : G)\,(x \text{ kills } \widetilde{y(Q)}; P) \equiv x \text{ kills } \widetilde{y_i(Q_i)}; (\boldsymbol{\nu} \tilde{w} : G)\,P \\
& (\boldsymbol{\nu} \tilde{w} : G)\,(x \text{ clones } \tilde{y}(x', \tilde{y}'); P) \equiv x \text{ clones } \tilde{y}(x', \tilde{y}'); (\boldsymbol{\nu} \tilde{w} : G)\,P \\
& (\boldsymbol{\nu} \tilde{z} : G)\,(x \text{ clones } \tilde{y}(x', \tilde{y}'); P \mid \tilde{Q}) \equiv x \text{ clones } \tilde{y}(x', \tilde{y}'); (\boldsymbol{\nu} \tilde{z} : G)\,(P \mid \tilde{Q})
\end{aligned}
$$

Fig. 7. Equivalences for commuting C-rules with Conn and Scope. All rules assume that both sides are typable in the same context.

linking process and global type for linking sessions are all symmetric. Furthermore, the order of restrictions can be swapped.

$$x^A \to y \equiv y^{A^\perp} \to x$$
$$(\boldsymbol{\nu}\tilde{w}, y, x, \tilde{z} : G)\,\tilde{P} \mid R \mid Q \mid \tilde{S} \equiv (\boldsymbol{\nu}\tilde{w}, x, y, \tilde{z} : G)\,\tilde{P} \mid Q \mid R \mid \tilde{S}$$
$$(\boldsymbol{\nu}z, \tilde{w} : H)\,(\boldsymbol{\nu}x, \tilde{y} : G)\,P \mid \tilde{R} \mid \tilde{Q} \equiv (\boldsymbol{\nu}x, \tilde{y} : G)\,(\boldsymbol{\nu}z, \tilde{w} : H)\,P \mid \tilde{Q} \mid \tilde{R}$$

Properties. We finish the presentation of MCC by establishing the expected meta-theoretic properties of the system. As structural congruence is typing-based, subject congruence is a property holding by construction:

Theorem 1 (Subject Congruence). *$\Sigma \Vdash P \mathrel{⨾} \Psi$ and $P \equiv Q$ implies that $\Sigma \Vdash Q \mathrel{⨾} \Psi$.*

Proof. By induction on the proof that $P \equiv Q$. In [5], it is explained how the rules for structural equivalence were derived, making this proof straightforward.

Moreover, our reductions preserve typing since they are proof transformations.

Theorem 2 (Subject Reduction). *$\Sigma \Vdash P \mathrel{⨾} \Psi$ and $P \longrightarrow Q$ implies $\Sigma \Vdash Q \mathrel{⨾} \Psi$.*

Proof. By induction on the proof that $P \longrightarrow Q$. In [5], it is explained how the semantics of MCC were designed in order to make this proof straightforward.

Finally, we can show that MCC is deadlock-free, since the top-level Scope application can be pushed up the derivation. In case the top-level Scope application is next to an application of Conn, either the choreography can reduce directly or both rules can be pushed up. Proof-theoretically, this procedure can be viewed as MCC's equivalent of the Principal Lemma of Cut Elimination.

Theorem 3 (Deadlock-freedom). *If P begins with a restriction and $\Sigma \Vdash P \mathrel{⨾} \Psi$, then there exists Q such that $P \longrightarrow Q$.*

Proof (Sketch). Our proof idea is similar to that of Theorem 3 in [9]. We apply induction on the size of the proof of $\Sigma \Vdash P \mathrel{⨾} \Psi$. If a rule from Fig. 4 or Fig. 6 is applicable (corresponding to a proof where an application of Conn and an application of Scope meet), then the thesis immediately holds.

Otherwise, we apply commuting conversions from Fig. 3 or Fig. 7, "pushing" the top-level Scope application up in the derivation (and, if it is preceded by an application of Conn, "pushing" also that application). This results in a smaller proof of $\Sigma \Vdash P \mathrel{⨾} \Psi$, to which the induction hypothesis can be applied.

5 Projection and Extraction

As suggested by the previous sections, interactions can be implemented in two ways: as a single choreography term, or as multiple process terms appearing in different behaviours composed in parallel. In this section, we formally show that choreography interactions can be projected to process implementations, and symmetrically, process implementations can be extracted to choreographies. We do this by transforming proofs (derivations in the typing system), similarly to the way we defined equivalences and reductions for MCC.

We start by defining the principal transformations for projection and extraction, a set of equivalences that require proof terms to have a special shape. We report such transformations in Fig. 8: they perform extraction if read from left to right, while they perform projection if read from right to left. The extraction relation requires access to the list of open sessions Σ to ensure that we have all the endpoints participating in the session to extract a choreography from. The first two rules deal with axioms: the parallel composition (rule Conn) of an axiom with a process P can be expressed by rule $\mathsf{C_{Ax}}$ and vice-versa. On the third line, we show how to transform the parallel composition of an output ($\otimes$) and an input ($\parr$) into a $\mathsf{C}_{\otimes\parr}$. Similarly, $\tilde{x}$ closes $y; P$ is the choreographic representation of the term $(\mathsf{close}[x_i])_i \mid \mathsf{wait}[y]; P$. Each branching operation (left, right, non-deterministic) has a representative in both fragments with straightforward transformations. A server $\mathsf{srv}\, y; Q$ can either be used by a client, killed or cloned. In the first two cases, such interactions trivially correspond to the choreographic terms $x\, \mathsf{starts}\, \tilde{y}; (P \mid \tilde{Q})$ and $x\, \mathsf{kills}\, \widetilde{y(Q)}; P$. In the case of cloning, we create the interaction term $x\, \mathsf{clones}\, \tilde{y}(x', \tilde{y}'); (P \mid (\mathsf{srv}\, y_i; Q_i)_i \mid (\mathsf{srv}\, y_i'; Q_i')_i)$, which shows how the choreographic cloning $x\, \mathsf{clones}\, \tilde{y}(x', \tilde{y}')$; must be followed by two instances of the server that is cloned. Note that these transformations are derived by applying similar techniques as those of cut elimination. Concrete derivations, here omitted, are straightforward: an example can be found in [5].

$$
\begin{array}{rcll}
P \mid x^{X} \to y & \rightleftharpoons & x \leftarrow y^{X^\perp} \to w; P & (w, y) \in \mathsf{dom}(\Sigma) \\
P \mid y^{X} \to x & \rightleftharpoons & x \leftarrow y^{X} \to w; P & (w, y) \in \mathsf{dom}(\Sigma) \\
\left(\overline{x_i}(x_i'); (P_i \mid Q_i)\right)_i \mid y(y'); R \mid \tilde{S} & \rightleftharpoons & \tilde{x}(\tilde{x}') \to y(y'); \left(\tilde{P} \mid \tilde{Q} \mid R \mid \tilde{S}\right) & \\
(\mathsf{close}[x_i])_i \mid \mathsf{wait}[y]; P & \rightleftharpoons & \tilde{x}\ \mathsf{closes}\ y; P & \\
x.\mathsf{inl}; P \mid (y_i.\mathsf{case}(Q_i, R_i))_i \mid \tilde{S} & \rightleftharpoons & x \to \tilde{y}.\mathsf{inl}(P \mid \tilde{Q} \mid \tilde{S}; R_1, \ldots, R_n) & \\
x.\mathsf{inr}; P \mid (y_i.\mathsf{case}(Q_i, R_i))_i \mid \tilde{S} & \rightleftharpoons & x \to \tilde{y}.\mathsf{inr}(Q_1, \ldots, Q_n; P \mid \tilde{R} \mid \tilde{S}) & \\
x.(\mathsf{inl}: P, \mathsf{inr}: Q) \mid \left(y_i.\mathsf{case}(R_i, S_i)\right)_i \mid \tilde{T} & \rightleftharpoons & x \to \tilde{y}.(\mathsf{inl}: P \mid \tilde{R} \mid \tilde{T}, \mathsf{inr}: Q \mid \tilde{S} \mid \tilde{T}) & \\
\mathsf{use}\, x; P \mid (\mathsf{srv}\, y_i; Q_i)_i & \rightleftharpoons & x\ \mathsf{starts}\ \tilde{y}; (P \mid \tilde{Q}) & \\
\mathsf{kill}\, x \mid P \mid (\mathsf{srv}\, y_i; Q_i)_i & \rightleftharpoons & x\ \mathsf{kills}\ \widetilde{y(Q)}; P & \\
\mathsf{clone}\, x(x'); P \mid (\mathsf{srv}\, y_i; Q_i)_i & \rightleftharpoons & x\ \mathsf{clones}\ \tilde{y}(x', \tilde{y}'); (P \mid (\mathsf{srv}\, y_i; Q_i)_i \mid (\mathsf{srv}\, y_i'; Q_i')_i) &
\end{array}
$$

Fig. 8. Extraction ($\rightharpoonup$) and projection ($\leftharpoondown$).

Remark 2. In order to project/extract an arbitrary well-typed term, given the strict format required by the transformations in Fig. 8, we will sometimes have to perform rewriting of terms in accordance with the commuting conversions to reach an expected shape. In particular, we note that when projecting, we must first project the subterms (we start from the leaves of a proof), step by step moving down to the main term. In contrast, when extracting, we must proceed from the root of the proof towards the leaves.

Note that our example in Sect. 2 does not provide an exact projection: in order to improve readability, we have removed all parallels that follow output operations, which would be introduced by the translation presented above. This is not problematic, since the outputs in the example are just basic types.

Properties. In the sequel, we write $P \xrightarrow{\tilde{x}}_{\mathsf{extr}} P'$ whenever it is possible to apply one of the transformations in Fig. 8 to (a term equivalent to) term P from left to right, where $\tilde{x}$ are the endpoints involved in the transformation. Similarly, we write $P \xrightarrow{\tilde{x}}_{\mathsf{proj}} P'$ whenever it is possible to apply a transformation from Fig. 8 to (a term equivalent to) term P from right to left. We also write $P \Longrightarrow_{\mathsf{extr}} P'$ ($P \Longrightarrow_{\mathsf{proj}} P'$) if there is a finite sequence of applications of $\longrightarrow_{\mathsf{extr}}$ ($\longrightarrow_{\mathsf{proj}}$) and P' cannot be further transformed. We then have the following results:

Theorem 4 (Type Preservation). *If $P \xrightarrow{\tilde{x}}_{\mathsf{extr}} Q$ and $\Sigma \Vdash P :: \Psi$, then $\Sigma \Vdash Q :: \Psi$, and if $Q \xrightarrow{\tilde{x}}_{\mathsf{proj}} P$ and $\Sigma \Vdash Q :: \Psi$, then $\Sigma \Vdash P :: \Psi$.*

Proof. By induction on the proof that $P \xrightarrow{\tilde{x}}_{\mathsf{extr}} Q$ or $Q \xrightarrow{\tilde{x}}_{\mathsf{proj}} P$. In [5], we explain how the rules for projection and extraction were derived from the typing rules to ensure that the proof of this result is straightforward.

Theorem 5 (Admissibility of Conn and C-rules). *Let P be a proof term such that $\Vdash P :: \vdash \Gamma$. Then,*

- *there exists P' such that $P \Longrightarrow_{\mathsf{extr}} P'$ and P' is* Conn*-free;*
- *there exists P' such that $P \Longrightarrow_{\mathsf{proj}} P'$ and P' is free from* C*-rules.*

Proof (Sketch). The idea is similar to the proof of Theorem 4.4.1 in [17]: by applying commuting conversions we can always rewrite P such that one of the rules in Fig. 8 is applicable, thus eliminating the outermost application of Conn (in the case of extraction) or the innermost application of a C-rule (in the case of projection). See also Remarks 2 and 3.

Remark 3. The theorem above is only applicable to judgments of the form $\Vdash P :: \vdash \Gamma$. This is because of the commuting conversion of the server rule

$$(\boldsymbol{\nu}\tilde{x}x : G)\,(\mathsf{srv}\, y; P \mid \tilde{Q}) \equiv \mathsf{srv}\, y; (\boldsymbol{\nu}\tilde{x}x : G)\,(P \mid \tilde{Q})$$

where we can only permute Conn and Scope together. This conversion is needed to rearrange certain proofs into the format required by the transformations in Fig. 8. Note that any judgement $\Sigma \Vdash P :: \Psi$ can always be transformed into this format, by repeatedly applying rule Scope to all elements in Σ.

As a consequence of the admissibility of Conn, every program can be rewritten into a (non-unique) process containing only process terms by applying the rules in Fig. 8 from right to left until no longer possible. Conversely, because of admissibility of C-rules, every program can be rewritten into a maximal choreographic form by applying the same rules from left to right until no longer possible.

We conclude this section with our main theorem that shows the correspondence between the two fragments with respect to their semantics. In order to do that, we annotate our semantics with the endpoints where the reduction takes place. This is denoted by $P \longrightarrow^{\tilde{x}} Q$ and $P \longrightarrow^{\bullet\tilde{x}} Q$ where the first relation is a reduction in the action fragment, while the second is a reduction in the interaction fragment. The sequence $\mathsf{rev}(\tilde{x})$ is obtained by reversing $\tilde{x}$.

Theorem 6 (Correspondence). *Let P be a proof term such that $\Sigma \Vdash P \,⨾\, \Psi$. Then,*

- *$P \longrightarrow^{\tilde{x}} Q$ implies that there exists P' s.t. $P \xrightarrow{\tilde{x}}_{\mathsf{extr}} P'$ and $P' \longrightarrow^{\bullet\tilde{x}} Q$;*
- *$P \longrightarrow^{\bullet\tilde{x}} Q$ implies that there exists P' s.t. $P \xrightarrow{\mathsf{rev}(\tilde{x})}_{\mathsf{proj}} P'$ and $P' \longrightarrow^{\tilde{x}} Q$.*

Proof. This proof follows the same strategy as that of Theorem 6 in [9].

6 Related Work and Discussion

Related Work. The principle of choreographies as cut reductions was introduced in [9]. As discussed in Sect. 1, that system cannot capture services or multiparty sessions. Another difference is that it is based on intuitionistic linear logic, whereas ours on classical linear logic – in particular, on Classical Processes [22].

Switching to classical linear logic is not a mere change of appearance. It is what allows us to reuse the logical understanding of multiparty sessions in linear logic as *coherence proofs*, introduced in [10] and later extended to polymorphism in [7]. These works did not consider choreographic programs, and thus do not offer a global view on how different sessions are composed, as we do in this paper.

Extracting choreographies from compositions of process code is well-known to be a hard problem. In [15], choreographies that abstract from the exchanged values and computation are extracted from communicating finite-state machines. The authors of [11] present an efficient algorithm for extracting concrete choreographic programs with asynchronous messaging. These works do not consider the composition of multiple sessions, multiparty sessions, and services, as in MCC. However, they can both deal with infinite behaviour (through loops or recursion), which we do not address. An interesting direction for this feature would be to integrate structural recursion for classical linear logic [16].

Our approach can be seen as a principled reconstruction of previous works on choreographic programming. The first work that typed choreographies using multiparty session types is [8]. The idea of mixing choreographies with processes using multiparty session types is from [19]. None of these consider extraction.

Discussion. For the sake of clarity, our presentation of MCC adopts simplifications that may limit the model expressivity. Below, we discuss some key points as well as possible extensions based on certain developments in this research line.

Non-determinism. We introduced non-determinism in a straightforward way, i.e., our non-deterministic rules in both action and interaction fragments require for each branch to have the same type, as done for standard session typing. However, this solution breaks the property of confluence that we commonly have in logics. In order to preserve confluence, we would have to extend MCC with the non-deterministic linear types from [3].

η-expansion. GCP in [7] allows for the axiom to be of any type A. This requires heavily using η-expansions for transforming axioms into processes with communication actions. It is straightforward to do this in the action fragment of MCC. However, given the way choreographies work, we can only define an axiom for binary sessions in the interaction fragment. As a consequence, in order to apply extraction to a process where an axiom is engaged in a multiparty session with several endpoints, we would need to first use η-expansions to transform such axiom into an ordinary process. In the opposite direction, we would never be able to project a process containing an axiom from a choreography, unless it is part of a binary session. We leave further investigation of this as future work.

Annotated Types. The original version of GCP [7] comes with an extension called MCP, where an endpoint type A is annotated with names of endpoints which it will be in a session with. In this way, endpoint types become more expressive, since it is possible to specify with whom each endpoint has to communicate, without having to use a global type (coherence proof) during execution. We claim that this extension is straightforward for our presentation of MCC.

Polymorphism. As in GCP [7], we can easily add polymorphic types to MCC. However, for simplifying the presentation of this work, we have decided to leave it out, even though adding the GCP rules to the action fragment is straightforward. In the case of the interaction fragment, we obtain the following rule:

$$\frac{X \notin \mathsf{fv}(\Psi, \Gamma, (\Gamma_i)_i) \qquad \Sigma, \boxed{(x, \tilde{y}, \tilde{u}) : G\{A/X\}} \Vdash P\{A/X\} \,\mathbin{⨾}\, \Psi \mid \vdash \Gamma, \underline{x : B\{A/X\}} \mid \underline{(\vdash \Gamma_i, y_i : B_i\{A/X\})_i}}{\Sigma, \boxed{(x, \tilde{y}, \tilde{u}) : x \to \tilde{y}.(X)G} \Vdash x[A] \to \tilde{y}(X); P \,\mathbin{⨾}\, \Psi \mid \vdash \Gamma, \underline{x : \exists X.B} \mid \underline{(\vdash \Gamma_i, y_i : \forall X.B_i)_i}} \; \mathsf{C}_{\exists\forall}$$

Above we have added to the syntax of global types the term $x \to \tilde{y}.(X)G$, denoting a session where an endpoint x is supposed to send a type to endpoints $\tilde{y}$. At choreography level, endpoint x realises the abstraction of the global type sending the actual type A. When it comes to extraction and projection, we would have to add the following transformation:

$$x[A]; P \mid (y_i(X); Q_i)_i \mid \tilde{S} \quad \rightleftharpoons \quad x[A] \to \tilde{y}(X); \left(P \mid \tilde{Q} \mid \tilde{S}\right)$$

where $x[A]; P$ and $y_i(X); Q_i$ are action fragment terms (as those of GCP).

Other Extensions. By importing the functional stratification from [21], we could obtain a monadic integration of choreographies with functions. The calculus of classical higher-order processes [18] could be of inspiration for adding code mobility to MCC, by adding higher-order types. Types for manifest sharing in [2] may lead us to global specifications of sharing in choreographies. And the asynchronous interpretation of cut reductions in [12] might give us an asynchronous implementation of choreographies in MCC. We leave an exploration of these extensions to future work. Hopefully, the shared foundations of linear logic will make it possible to build on these pre-existing technical developments following the same idea of choreographies as cut reductions.

References

1. Atkey, R.: Observed communication semantics for classical processes. In: Yang, H. (ed.) ESOP 2017. LNCS, vol. 10201, pp. 56–82. Springer, Heidelberg (2017). https://doi.org/10.1007/978-3-662-54434-1_3
2. Balzer, S., Pfenning, F.: Manifest sharing with session types. PACMPL **1**(ICFP), 37:1–37:29 (2017)
3. Caires, L., Pérez, J.A.: Linearity, control effects, and behavioral types. In: Yang, H. (ed.) ESOP 2017. LNCS, vol. 10201, pp. 229–259. Springer, Heidelberg (2017). https://doi.org/10.1007/978-3-662-54434-1_9
4. Caires, Luís, Pfenning, Frank: Session types as intuitionistic linear propositions. In: Gastin, Paul, Laroussinie, François (eds.) CONCUR 2010. LNCS, vol. 6269, pp. 222–236. Springer, Heidelberg (2010). https://doi.org/10.1007/978-3-642-15375-4_16
5. Carbone, M., Cruz-Filipe, L., Montesi, F., Murawska, A.: Multiparty classical choreographies. CoRR, abs/1808.05088 (2018)
6. Carbone, M., Honda, K., Yoshida, N.: Structured communication-centered programming for web services. ACM TOPLAS **34**(2), 8 (2012)
7. Carbone, M., Lindley, S., Montesi, F., Schürmann, C., Wadler, P.: Coherence generalises duality: a logical explanation of multiparty session types. In: CONCUR, LIPIcs, vol. 59 , pp. 33:1–33:15. Schloss Dagstuhl - Leibniz-Zentrum fuer Informatik (2016)
8. Carbone, M., Montesi, F.: Deadlock-freedom-by-design: multiparty asynchronous global programming. In: POPL, pp. 263–274 (2013)
9. Carbone, M., Montesi, F., Schürmann, C.: Choreographies, logically. Distrib. Comput. **31**(1), 51–67 (2018)
10. Carbone, M., Montesi, F., Schürmann, C., Yoshida, N.: Multiparty session types as coherence proofs. Acta Inf. **54**(3), 243–269 (2017). Also: CONCUR 2015
11. Cruz-Filipe, L., Larsen, K.S., Montesi, F.: The paths to choreography extraction. In: Esparza, J., Murawski, A.S. (eds.) FoSSaCS 2017. LNCS, vol. 10203, pp. 424–440. Springer, Heidelberg (2017). https://doi.org/10.1007/978-3-662-54458-7_25
12. DeYoung, H., Caires, L., Pfenning, F., Toninho, B.: Cut reduction in linear logic as asynchronous session-typed communication. In: CSL, LIPIcs, vol. 16, pp. 228–242. Schloss Dagstuhl - Leibniz-Zentrum fuer Informatik (2012)
13. Honda, K., Yoshida, N., Carbone, M.: Multiparty asynchronous session types. J. ACM **63**(1), 91–967 (2016)
14. JBoss Community and Red Hat. Testable Architecture. http://www.jboss.org/savara/

15. Lange, J., Tuosto, E., Yoshida, N.: From communicating machines to graphical choreographies. In: POPL, pp. 221–232. ACM (2015)
16. Lindley, S., Morris, J.G.: Talking bananas: structural recursion for session types. In: ICFP, pp. 434–447. ACM (2016)
17. Montesi, F.: Choreographic Programming. Ph.D. thesis, IT University of Copenhagen (2013). http://www.itu.dk/people/fabr/papers/phd/thesis.pdf
18. Montesi, F.: Classical higher-order processes. In: Bouajjani, A., Silva, A. (eds.) FORTE 2017. LNCS, vol. 10321, pp. 171–178. Springer, Cham (2017). https://doi.org/10.1007/978-3-319-60225-7_12
19. Montesi, F., Yoshida, N.: Compositional choreographies. In: D'Argenio, P.R., Melgratti, H. (eds.) CONCUR 2013. LNCS, vol. 8052, pp. 425–439. Springer, Heidelberg (2013). https://doi.org/10.1007/978-3-642-40184-8_30
20. OpenID. OpenID specifications. http://openid.net/developers/specs/
21. Toninho, B., Caires, L., Pfenning, F.: Higher-order processes, functions, and sessions: a monadic integration. In: Felleisen, M., Gardner, P. (eds.) ESOP 2013. LNCS, vol. 7792, pp. 350–369. Springer, Heidelberg (2013). https://doi.org/10.1007/978-3-642-37036-6_20
22. Wadler, P.: Propositions as sessions. J. Funct. Program. **24**(2–3), 384–418 (2014)

A Pragmatic, Scalable Approach to Correct-by-Construction Process Composition Using Classical Linear Logic Inference

Petros Papapanagiotou(✉) and Jacques Fleuriot

School of Informatics, University of Edinburgh, 10 Crichton Street, Edinburgh EH8 9AB, UK
{ppapapan,jdf}@inf.ed.ac.uk

Abstract. The need for rigorous process composition is encountered in many situations pertaining to the development and analysis of complex systems. We discuss the use of Classical Linear Logic (CLL) for correct-by-construction resource-based process composition, with guaranteed deadlock freedom, systematic resource accounting, and concurrent execution. We introduce algorithms to automate the necessary inference steps for binary compositions of processes in parallel, conditionally, and in sequence. We combine decision procedures and heuristics to achieve intuitive and practically useful compositions in an applied setting.

Keywords: Process modelling · Composition · Correct by construction · Workflow · Linear logic

1 Introduction

The ideas behind process modelling and composition are common across a variety of domains, including program synthesis, software architecture, multi-agent systems, web services, and business processes. Although the concept of a "process" takes a variety of names – such as agent, role, action, activity, and service – across these domains, in essence, it always captures the idea of an abstract, functional unit. Process composition then involves the combination and connection of these units to create systems that can perform more complex tasks. We typically call the resulting model a (*process*) *workflow*. Viewed from this standpoint, resource-based process composition then captures a structured model of the *resource flow* across the components, focusing on the resources that are created, consumed, or passed from one process to another within the system.

Workflows have proven useful tools for the design and implementation of complex systems by providing a balance between an intuitive **abstract model**, typically in diagrammatic form, and a **concrete implementation** through process automation. Evidence can be found, for example, in the modelling of clinical

F. Mesnard and P. J. Stuckey (Eds.): LOPSTR 2018, LNCS 11408, pp. 77–93, 2019.
https://doi.org/10.1007/978-3-030-13838-7_5

care pathways where workflows can be both understandable by healthcare stakeholders and yet remain amenable to formal analysis [10,15].

A scalable approach towards establishing trust in the correctness of the modelled system is that of *correct-by-construction* engineering [12,26]. In general, this refers to the construction of systems in a way that guarantees correctness properties about them at design time. In this spirit, we have developed the `WorkflowFM` system for correct-by-construction process composition [21]. It relies on Classical Linear Logic (see Sect. 2.1) to rigorously compose abstract process specifications in a way that:

1. systematically accounts for resources and exceptions;
2. prevents deadlocks;
3. results in a concrete workflow where processes are executed concurrently.

From the specific point of view of program synthesis, these benefits can be interpreted as (1) *no memory leaks or missing data*, (2) *no deadlocks, hanging threads, or loops*, and (3) *parallel, asynchronous (non-blocking) execution.*

The inference is performed within the proof assistant HOL Light, which offers systematic guarantees of correctness for every inference step [11]. The logical model can be translated through a process calculus to a concrete workflow implementation in a host programming language.

There are numerous aspects to and components in the `WorkflowFM` system, including, for instance, the diagrammatic interface (as shown in Fig. 1), the code translator, the execution engine, the process calculus correspondence, and the architecture that brings it all together [21]. In this particular paper we focus on the proof procedures that make such resource-based process compositions feasible and accessible. These are essential for creating meaningful workflow models with the correctness-by-construction properties highlighted above, but without the need for tedious manual CLL reasoning. Instead, the user can use high level composition actions triggered by simple, intuitive mouse gestures and without the need to understand the underlying proof, which is guaranteed to be correct thanks to the rigorous environment of HOL Light.

It is worth emphasizing that our work largely aims at tackling pragmatic challenges in real applications as opposed to establishing theoretical facts. We rely on existing formalisms, such as the proofs-as-processes theory described below, in our attempt to exploit its benefits in real world scenarios. As a result, the vast majority of our design decisions are driven by practical experience and the different cases we have encountered in our projects.

Table 1 is a list of some of our case studies in the healthcare and manufacturing domain that have driven the development of `WorkflowFM`. It includes an indication of the size of each case study based on (1) the number of (atomic) component processes, (2) the number of different types of resources involved in the inputs and outputs of the various processes (see Sect. 3), (3) the number of binary composition actions performed to construct the workflows (see Sect. 4), and (4) the total number of composed workflows.

All of these case studies are models of actual workflows, built based on data from real-world scenarios and input from domain experts such as clinical teams

Table 1. Sample case studies and an indication of their size.

Case study theme	Processes	Resource types	Actions	Workflows
Patient handovers	9	16	13	2
Tracheostomy care pathway	33	47	32	3
HIV care pathways	128	129	121	13
Pen manufacturing *(ongoing)*	42	45	60	20
Total	**212**	**237**	**226**	**38**

and managers of manufacturing facilities. The results have been useful towards process improvement in their respective organisations, including a better qualitative understanding based on the abstract model and quantitative analytics obtained from the concrete implementation. As a result, we are confident that the evidence and experience we accumulated from these case studies are representative of the requirements and needs of real applications and that the approach and algorithms presented in this paper can offer significant value.

We note that the presentation accompanying this paper is available online[1].

2 Background

The systematic accounting of resources in our approach can be demonstrated through a hypothetical example from the healthcare domain [21]. Assume a process `DeliverDrug` that corresponds to the delivery of a drug to a patient by a nurse. Such a process requires information about the *Patient*, the *Dosage* of the drug, and some reserved $NurseTime$ for the nurse to deliver the drug. The possible outcomes are that either the patient is *Treated* or that the drug $Failed$. In the latter case, we would like to apply the `Reassess` process, which, given some allocated clinician time ($ClinTime$) results in the patient being *Reassessed*. A graphical representation of these 2 processes, where dashed edges denote the optional outcomes of `DeliverDrug`, is shown at the top of Fig. 1.

If we were to compose the 2 processes in a workflow where the drug failure is always handled by `Reassess`, what would be the specification (or specifically the output) of the composite process?

Given the workflow representation in Fig. 1, one may be inclined to simply connect the $Failed$ edge of `DeliverDrug` to the corresponding edge of `Reassess`, leading to an overall output of either *Treated* or *Reassessed*. However, this would be erroneous, as the input $ClinTime$, is consumed in the composite process even if `Reassess` is never used. Using our CLL-based approach, the workflow output is either *Reassessed* which occurs if the drug failed, or *Treated* coupled with the unused $ClinTime$, as shown at the bottom of Fig. 1 [21].

Systematically accounting for such unused resources is non-trivial, especially considering larger workflows with tens or hundreds of processes and many different outcomes. The CLL inference rules enforce this by default and the proof

[1] https://github.com/PetrosPapapa/Presentations/raw/master/LOPSTR2018.pdf.

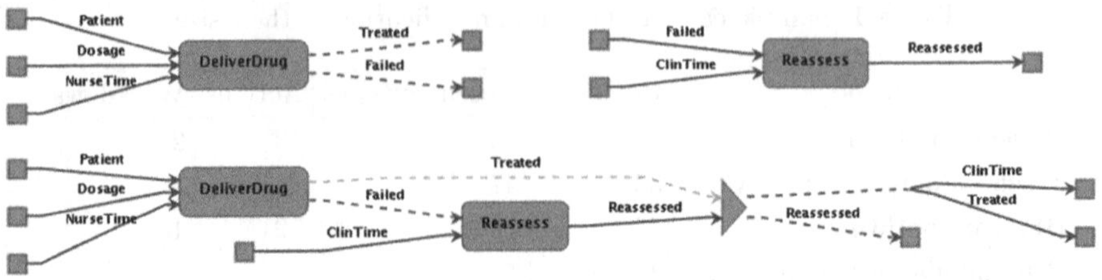

Fig. 1. The visualisation of the `DeliverDrug` and `Reassess` processes (top) and their sequential composition. The auxiliary triangle helps properly display the output.

reflects the level of reasoning required to achieve this. In addition, the process code generated from this synthesis is fully asynchronous and deadlock-free, and relies on the existence of concrete implementations of `DeliverDrug` and `Reassess`.

2.1 Classical Linear Logic

Linear Logic, as proposed by Girard [9], is a refinement to classical logic where the rules of contraction and weakening are limited to the modalities ! and ?. Propositions thus resemble resources that cannot be ignored or copied arbitrarily.

In this work, we use a one-sided sequent calculus version of the multiplicative additive fragment of propositional CLL without units (MALL). Although there exist process translations of full CLL and even first-order CLL, the MALL fragment allows enough expressiveness while keeping the reasoning complexity at a manageable level (MALL is PSPACE-complete whereas full CLL is undecidable [14]). The inference rules for MALL are presented in Fig. 2.

$$\frac{}{\vdash A^{\perp}, A}\ Id \qquad\qquad \frac{\vdash \Gamma, C \quad \vdash \Delta, C^{\perp}}{\vdash \Gamma, \Delta}\ Cut$$

$$\frac{\vdash \Gamma, A \quad \vdash \Delta, B}{\vdash \Gamma, \Delta, A \otimes B}\ \otimes \qquad\qquad \frac{\vdash \Gamma, A^{\perp}, B^{\perp}}{\vdash \Gamma, (A \otimes B)^{\perp}}\ ⅋$$

$$\frac{\vdash \Gamma, A}{\vdash \Gamma, A \oplus B}\ \oplus_L \qquad \frac{\vdash \Gamma, B}{\vdash \Gamma, A \oplus B}\ \oplus_R \qquad \frac{\vdash \Gamma, A^{\perp} \quad \vdash \Gamma, B^{\perp}}{\vdash \Gamma, (A \oplus B)^{\perp}}\ \&$$

Fig. 2. One-sided sequent calculus versions of the CLL inference rules.

In this version of MALL, linear negation $(\cdot^{\perp})$ is defined as a syntactic operator with no inference rules, so that both A and $A^{\perp}$ are considered atomic formulas. The de Morgan style equations in Fig. 3 provide a *syntactic* equivalence of formulas involving negation [27]. This allows us to use syntactically equivalent formulas, such as $A^{\perp} ⅋ B^{\perp}$ and $(A \otimes B)^{\perp}$ interchangeably. In fact, in the proofs presented in this paper we choose to present formulas containing $\otimes$ and $\oplus$ over their counterparts $⅋$ and & due to the polarity restrictions we introduce in Sect. 3.

$$(A^{\perp})^{\perp} \equiv A \qquad (A \otimes B)^{\perp} \equiv A^{\perp} ⅋ B^{\perp} \qquad (A \oplus B)^{\perp} \equiv A^{\perp} \& B^{\perp}$$
$$(A ⅋ B)^{\perp} \equiv A^{\perp} \otimes B^{\perp} \qquad (A \& B)^{\perp} \equiv A^{\perp} \oplus B^{\perp}$$

Fig. 3. The equations used to define linear negation for MALL.

In the 90s, Abramsky, Bellin and Scott developed the so-called proofs-as-processes paradigm [2,4]. It involved a correspondence between CLL inference and concurrent processes in the π-calculus [18]. They proved that cut-elimination in a CLL proof corresponds to reductions in the π-calculus translation, which in turn correspond to communication between concurrent processes. As a result, π-calculus terms constructed via CLL proofs are inherently free of deadlocks.

The implications of the proofs-as-processes correspondence have been the subject of recent research in concurrent programming by Wadler [28], Pfenning et al. [3,5,25], Dardha [7,8] and others. Essentially, each CLL inference step can be translated to an executable workflow, with automatically generated code to appropriately connect the component processes. As a result, the CLL proofs have a direct correspondence to the "piping", so to speak, that realises the appropriate resource flow between the available processes, such that it does not introduce deadlocks, accounts for all resources explicitly, and maximizes run-time concurrency. The current paper examines CLL inference and we take the correspondence to deadlock-free processes for granted.

2.2 Related Work

Diagrammatic languages such as BPMN [20] are commonly used for the description of workflows in different organisations. However, they typically lack rigour and have limited potential for formal verification [23]. Execution languages such as BPEL [19] and process calculi such as Petri Nets [1] are often used for workflow management in a formal way and our CLL approach could potentially be adapted to work with these. Linear logic has been used in the context of web service composition [22], but in a way that diverges significantly from the original theory and compromises the validity of the results. Finally, the way the resource flow is managed through our CLL-based processes is reminiscent of monad-like structures such as Haskell's arrows[2]. One of the key differences is the lack of support for optional resources, which is non-trivial as we show in this paper.

[2] https://www.haskell.org/arrows.

3 Process Specification

Since CLL propositions can naturally represent resources, CLL sequents can be used to represent processes, with each literal representing a type of resource that is involved in that process. These abstract types can have a concrete realisation in the host programming language, from primitive to complicated objects.

Our approach to resource-based composition is to construct CLL specifications of abstract processes based on their inputs (and preconditions) and outputs (and effects), also referred to as IOPEs. This is standard practice in various process formalisms, including WSDL for web services [6], OWL-S for Semantic Web services [16], PDDL for actions in automated planning [17], etc.

The symmetry of linear negation as shown in Fig. 3 can be used to assign a *polarity* to each CLL connective in order to distinctly specify input and output resources. We choose to treat negated literals, $\parr$, and & as **inputs**, and positive literals, $\otimes$, and $\oplus$ as **outputs**, with the following intuitive interpretation:

- Multiplicative conjunction (*tensor* $\otimes$) indicates a pair of parallel outputs.
- Additive disjunction (*plus* $\oplus$) indicates exclusively optional outputs (alternative outputs or exceptions).
- Multiplicative disjunction (*par* $\parr$) indicates a pair of simultaneous inputs.
- Additive conjunction (*with* &) indicates exclusively optional input.

Based on this, a process can be specified as a CLL sequent consisting of a list of input formulas and a **single** output formula. In this, the order of the literals does not matter, so long as they obey the polarity restrictions (all but exactly one are negative). In practice, we treat sequents as multisets of literals and manage them using particular multiset reasoning techniques in HOL Light. The description of these techniques is beyond the scope of this paper.

The polarity restrictions imposed on our process specifications match the specification of Laurent's Polarized Linear Logic (LLP) [13], and has a proven logical equivalence to the full MALL. Moreover, these restrictions match the programming language paradigm of a *function* that can have multiple input arguments and returns a single (possibly composite) result.

4 Process Composition

Using CLL process specifications as assumptions, we can produce a composite process specification using forward inference. Each of the CLL inference rules represent a logically legal way to manipulate and compose such specifications.

The axiom $\vdash A, A^{\perp}$ represents the so-called *axiom buffer*, a process that receives a resource of type A and outputs the same resource unaffected.

Unary inference rules, such as the $\oplus_L$ rule, correspond to manipulations of a single process specification. For example, the $\oplus_L$ rule (see Fig. 2) takes a process P specified by $\vdash \Gamma, A$, i.e. a process with some inputs Γ and an output A, and produces a process $\vdash \Gamma, A \oplus B$, i.e. a process with the same inputs Γ and output either A or B. Note that, in practice, the produced composite process is a transformation of P and thus will always produce A and never B.

Binary inference rules, such as the $\otimes$ rule, correspond to binary process composition. The $\otimes$ rule in particular (see Fig. 2) takes a process P specified by $\vdash \Gamma, A$ and another process Q specified by $\vdash \Delta, B$ and composes them, so that the resulting process $\vdash \Gamma, \Delta, A \otimes B$ has all their inputs Γ and Δ and a simultaneous output $A \otimes B$. Notably, the *Cut* rule corresponds to the composition of 2 processes in sequence, where one consumes a resource A given by the other.

Naturally, these manipulations and compositions are primitive and restricted. Constructing meaningful compositions requires several rule applications and, therefore, doing this manually would be a very tedious and impractical task. Our work focuses on creating high level actions that use CLL inference to automatically produce binary process compositions that are correct-by-construction based on the guarantees described above. More specifically, we introduce actions for parallel (`TENSOR`), conditional (`WITH`), and sequential composition (`JOIN`).

Since we are using forward inference, there are infinitely many ways to apply the CLL rules and therefore infinite possible compositions. We are interested in producing compositions that are intuitive for the user. It is practically impossible to produce a formal definition of what these compositions should be. Instead, as explained earlier, we rely on practical experience and user feedback from the various case studies for workflow modelling (see Table 1).

Based on this, we have introduced a set of what can be viewed as *unit tests* for our composition actions, which describe the expected and logically valid results of example compositions. As we explore increasingly complex examples in practice, we augment our test set and ensure our algorithms satisfy them. *Selected* unit tests for the `WITH` and `JOIN` actions are shown in Tables 2 and 3 respectively. Moreover, as a general principle, our algorithms try to *maximize* resource usage, i.e. involve as many resources as possible, and *minimize* the number of rule applications to keep the corresponding process code more compact.

For example, row 3 of Table 3 indicates that a process with output $A \oplus B$ when composed with a process specified by $\vdash A^{\perp}, B$ should produce a process with output B. As we discuss in Sect. 8.3, a different CLL derivation for the same scenario could lead to a process with output $B \oplus B$. This result is unnecessarily more complicated, and its complexity will propagate to all subsequent compositions which will have to deal with 2 options of a type B output. The unit test therefore ensures that the algorithm always leads to a minimal result.

All our algorithms are implemented within the Higher Order Logic proof tactic system of HOL Light. As a result, the names of some methods have the `_TAC` suffix, which is conventionally used when naming HOL Light tactics.

5 Auxiliary Processes

During composition, we often need to construct auxiliary processes that manipulate the structure of a CLL type in particular ways. We have identified 2 types of such processes: *buffers* and *filters*.

Table 2. Examples of the expected result of the `WITH` action between $X^\perp$ of a process `P` and $Y^\perp$ of a process `Q`.

P	Q	Result
$\vdash X^\perp, Z$	$\vdash Y^\perp, Z$	$\vdash (X \oplus Y)^\perp, Z$
$\vdash X^\perp, Z$	$\vdash Y^\perp, W$	$\vdash (X \oplus Y)^\perp, A^\perp, B^\perp, Z \oplus W$
$\vdash X^\perp, A^\perp, B^\perp, Z$	$\vdash Y^\perp, Z$	$\vdash (X \oplus Y)^\perp, Z \oplus (Z \otimes A \otimes B)$
$\vdash X^\perp, A^\perp, Z$	$\vdash Y^\perp, B^\perp, W$	$\vdash (X \oplus Y)^\perp, A^\perp, B^\perp, (Z \otimes B) \oplus (W \otimes A)$
$\vdash X^\perp, A^\perp, C^\perp, Z$	$\vdash Y^\perp, B^\perp, W$	$\vdash (X \oplus Y)^\perp, A^\perp, B^\perp, C^\perp, (Z \otimes B) \oplus (W \otimes A \otimes C)$
$\vdash X^\perp, A^\perp, C^\perp, Z$	$\vdash Y^\perp, B^\perp, C^\perp, W$	$\vdash (X \oplus Y)^\perp, A^\perp, B^\perp, C^\perp, (Z \otimes B) \oplus (W \otimes A)$
$\vdash X^\perp, A^\perp, C^\perp, C^\perp, Z$	$\vdash Y^\perp, B^\perp, C^\perp, W$	$\vdash (X \oplus Y)^\perp, A^\perp, B^\perp, C^\perp, C^\perp, (Z \otimes B) \oplus (W \otimes A \otimes C)$
$\vdash X^\perp, A \otimes B$	$\vdash Y^\perp, B \otimes A$	$\vdash (X \oplus Y)^\perp, A \otimes B$
$\vdash X^\perp, A^\perp, Z \otimes A$	$\vdash Y^\perp, Z$	$\vdash (X \oplus Y)^\perp, A^\perp, Z \otimes A$
$\vdash X^\perp, A^\perp, A \otimes Z$	$\vdash Y^\perp, Z$	$\vdash (X \oplus Y)^\perp, A^\perp, A \otimes Z$
$\vdash X^\perp, A^\perp, Z \oplus (Z \otimes A)$	$\vdash Y^\perp, Z$	$\vdash (X \oplus Y)^\perp, A^\perp, Z \oplus (Z \otimes A)$

Buffers: Similarly to the axiom buffer introduced in the previous section, *composite buffers* (or simply *buffers*) can carry any composite resource without affecting it. This is useful when a process is unable to handle the entire type on its own, and some resources need to be simply *buffered* through. For example, if a process needs to handle a resource of type $A \otimes B$, but only has an input of type $A^\perp$, then B will be handled by a buffer.

More formally, buffers are processes specified by $\vdash A^\perp, A$, where A is arbitrarily complex. Such lemmas are always provable in CLL for any formula A. We have introduced an automatic procedure `BUFFER_TAC` that can accomplish this, but omit the implementation details in the interest of space and in favour of the more interesting composition procedures that follow.

We also introduce the concept of a *parallel buffer*, defined as a process $\vdash A_1^\perp, A_2^\perp, ..., A_n^\perp, A_1 \otimes A_2 \otimes ... \otimes A_n$. Such buffers are useful when composing processes with an optional output (see Sect. 8.3). Their construction can also be easily automated with a decision procedure we call `PARBUF_TAC`.

Filters: Often during process composition by proof, resources need to match exactly for the proof to proceed. In some cases, composite resources may not match exactly, but may be manipulated using the CLL inference rules so that they end up matching. For example, the term $A \otimes B$ does not directly match $B \otimes A$. However, both terms intuitively represent resources A and B in parallel. This intuition is reflected formally to the commutativity property of $\otimes$, which is easily provable in CLL: $\vdash (A \otimes B)^\perp, B \otimes A$. We can then use the *Cut* rule with this property to convert an output of type $A \otimes B$ to $B \otimes A$ (similarly for inputs).

We call such lemmas that are useful for converting CLL types to logically equivalent ones, *filters*. In essence, a filter is any provable CLL lemma that preserves our polarity restrictions. We prove such lemmas automatically using the proof strategies developed by Tammet [24]. We call such lemmas that are useful for converting CLL types to logically equivalent ones, *filters*. In essence, a filter is any provable CLL lemma that preserves our polarity restrictions. We prove such lemmas automatically using the proof strategies developed by Tammet [24].

We give some examples of how filters are used to match terms as we go through them below. However, as a general rule the reader may assume that, for the remainder of this paper, by "equal" or "matching" terms we refer to terms that are equal modulo the use of filters.

A main consequence of this is that our algorithms often attempt to match literals that do not match. For example, the attempt to compose $\vdash A^\perp, B$ in sequence with $\vdash C^\perp, D^\perp, E$ would generate and try to prove 2 false conjectures $\vdash B^\perp, C$ and $\vdash B^\perp, D$ in an effort to match the output B with any of the 2 inputs $C^\perp$ and $D^\perp$ before failing[3]. This highlights the need for an efficient proof procedure for filters, with an emphasis on early failure.

Table 3. Examples of the expected result of the `JOIN` action between a process `P` and a process `Q`. Column *Pr.* gives the *priority* parameter (see Sect. 8.4).

P	Pr.	Q	Selected input	Result
$\vdash X^\perp, A$		$\vdash A^\perp, Y$	$A^\perp$	$\vdash X^\perp, Y$
$\vdash X^\perp, A \otimes B$	L	$\vdash A^\perp, Y$	$A^\perp$	$\vdash X^\perp, Y \otimes B$
$\vdash X^\perp, A \oplus B$	L	$\vdash A^\perp, B$	$A^\perp$	$\vdash X^\perp, B$
$\vdash X^\perp, A \otimes B \otimes C$	L	$\vdash A^\perp, Y$	$A^\perp$	$\vdash X^\perp, Y \otimes B \otimes C$
$\vdash X^\perp, A \oplus B$	L	$\vdash A^\perp, C^\perp, Y$	$A^\perp$	$\vdash X^\perp, C^\perp, Y \oplus (C \otimes B)$
$\vdash X^\perp, A \oplus B$	R	$\vdash B^\perp, C^\perp, Y$	$B^\perp$	$\vdash X^\perp, C^\perp, (C \otimes A) \oplus Y$
$\vdash X^\perp, A \oplus B$	L	$\vdash (B \oplus A)^\perp, Y$	$(B \oplus A)^\perp$	$\vdash X^\perp, Y$
$\vdash X^\perp, A \oplus (B \otimes C)$	L	$\vdash (B \oplus A)^\perp, Y$	$(B \oplus A)^\perp$	$\vdash X^\perp, Y \oplus (B \otimes C)$
$\vdash X^\perp, A \oplus (B \otimes C)$	RL	$\vdash (B \oplus A)^\perp, Y$	$(B \oplus A)^\perp$	$\vdash X^\perp, A \oplus (Y \otimes C)$
$\vdash X^\perp, A \oplus B$	L	$\vdash (C \oplus A \oplus D)^\perp, Y$	$(C \oplus A \oplus D)^\perp$	$\vdash X^\perp, Y \oplus B$
$\vdash X^\perp, C \oplus (A \otimes B)$	L	$\vdash C^\perp, A \otimes B$	$C^\perp$	$\vdash X^\perp, A \otimes B$
$\vdash X^\perp, C \oplus (A \otimes B)$	L	$\vdash C^\perp, B \otimes A$	$C^\perp$	$\vdash X^\perp, B \otimes A$
$\vdash X^\perp, C \oplus (A \otimes (B \oplus D))$	L	$\vdash C^\perp, (B \oplus D) \otimes A$	$C^\perp$	$\vdash X^\perp, (B \oplus D) \otimes A$
$\vdash X^\perp, C \oplus (A \otimes B)$	L	$\vdash C^\perp, Y \oplus (B \otimes A)$	$C^\perp$	$\vdash X^\perp, Y \oplus (B \otimes A)$
$\vdash X^\perp, C \oplus (A \otimes B)$	L	$\vdash C^\perp, (B \otimes A) \oplus Y$	$C^\perp$	$\vdash X^\perp, (B \otimes A) \oplus Y$
$\vdash X^\perp, (A \otimes B) \oplus C$	R	$\vdash C^\perp, Y \oplus (B \otimes A)$	$C^\perp$	$\vdash X^\perp, Y \oplus (B \otimes A)$
$\vdash X^\perp, (A \otimes B) \oplus C$	R	$\vdash C^\perp, (B \otimes A) \oplus Y$	$C^\perp$	$\vdash X^\perp, (B \otimes A) \oplus Y$
$\vdash X^\perp, C \oplus (A \otimes B)$	L	$\vdash C^\perp, Y \oplus (B \otimes A)$	$C^\perp$	$\vdash X^\perp, Y \oplus (B \otimes A)$

6 Parallel Composition - The `TENSOR` Action

The `TENSOR` action corresponds to the parallel composition of two processes so that their outputs are provided in parallel. It trivially relies on the tensor ($\otimes$)

[3] In practice, the user will have to select a matching input to attempt such a composition (see Sect. 8).

inference rule. Assuming 2 processes, $\vdash A^\perp, C^\perp, D$ and $\vdash B^\perp, E$, the TENSOR action will perform the following composition:

$$\frac{\vdash A^\perp, C^\perp, D \quad \vdash B^\perp, E}{\vdash A^\perp, B^\perp, C^\perp, D \otimes E} \otimes$$

7 Conditional Composition - The WITH Action

The WITH action corresponds to the *conditional* composition of two processes. This type of composition is useful in cases where each of the components of an optional output of a process needs to be handled by a different receiving process.

For example, assume a process S has an optional output $A \oplus C$ where C is an exception. We want A to be handled by some process P, for example specified by $\vdash A^\perp, B^\perp, X$, while another process Q specified by $\vdash C^\perp, Y$ plays the role of the exception handler for exception C. For this to happen, we need to compose P and Q together using the WITH action so that we can cnostruct an input that matches the output type $A \oplus C$ from S. This composition can be viewed as the construction of an *if-then* statement where if A is provided then P will be executed (assuming B is also provided), and if C is provided then Q will be executed in a mutually exclusive choice. The generated proof tree for this particular example is the following:

$$\frac{\dfrac{\overline{\vdash A^\perp, B^\perp, X}\ \mathtt{P}}{\vdash A^\perp, B^\perp, X \oplus (Y \otimes B)} \oplus L \quad \dfrac{\dfrac{\overline{\vdash C^\perp, Y}\ \mathtt{Q} \quad \overline{\vdash B^\perp, B}\ Id}{\vdash C^\perp, B^\perp, Y \otimes B} \otimes}{\vdash C^\perp, B^\perp, X \oplus (Y \otimes B)} \oplus R}{\vdash (A \oplus C)^\perp, B^\perp, X \oplus (Y \otimes B)} \& \quad (1)$$

The WITH action fundamentally relies on the & rule of CLL. The following derivation allows us to compose 2 processes that also have different outputs X and Y:

$$\frac{\dfrac{\vdash \Gamma, A^\perp, X}{\vdash \Gamma, A^\perp, X \oplus Y} \oplus L \quad \dfrac{\vdash \Gamma, C^\perp, Y}{\vdash \Gamma, C^\perp, X \oplus Y} \oplus R}{\vdash \Gamma, (A \oplus C)^\perp, X \oplus Y} \& \quad (2)$$

The particularity of the & rule is that the context Γ, i.e. all the inputs except the ones involved in the WITH action, must be the same for both the involved processes. In practice, this means we need to account for unused inputs. In the example above, P apart from input $A^\perp$ has another input $B^\perp$ which is missing from Q. In the conditional composition of P and Q, if exception C occurs, the provided B will not be consumed since P will not be invoked. In this case, we use a buffer to let B pass through together with the output Y of Q.

More generally, in order to apply the & rule to 2 processes P and Q, we need to minimally adjust their contexts Γ_P and Γ_Q (i.e. their respective multisets of inputs excluding the ones that will be used in the rule) so that they end up being the same $\Gamma = \Gamma_P \cup \Gamma_Q$. By "*minimal*" adjustment we mean that we only add the inputs that are "*missing*" from either side, i.e. the multiset $\Delta_P = \Gamma_Q \setminus \Gamma_P$ for P and $\Delta_Q = \Gamma_P \setminus \Gamma_Q$ for Q, and no more.

In the previous example in (1), exculding the inputs $A^\perp$ and $C^\perp$ used in the rule, we obtain $\Delta_Q = \Gamma_P \setminus \Gamma_Q = \{B^\perp\} \setminus \{\} = \{B^\perp\}$. We then construct a parallel buffer (see Sect. 5) of type $\otimes\Delta_Q^{\perp}$[4] (converting all inputs in Δ_Q to an output; in this example only one input) using `PARBUF_TAC`. In the example, this is an atomic B buffer. The parallel composition between this buffer and Q results in the process $\vdash \Gamma_Q, \Delta_Q, C^\perp, Y \otimes (\otimes\Delta_Q^\perp)$. The same calculation for P yields $\Delta_P = \emptyset$ so no change is required for P.

Since $\Gamma_P \uplus \Delta_P = \Gamma_Q \uplus \Delta_Q = \Gamma$ (where $\uplus$ denotes multiset union), the & rule is now applicable and derivation (2) yields the following process:

$$\vdash \Gamma, (A \oplus C)^\perp, (X \otimes (\otimes\Delta_P^\perp)) \oplus (Y \otimes (\otimes\Delta_Q^\perp)) \tag{3}$$

The output Y of Q has now been paired with the buffered resources Δ_Q.

Finally, we consider the special case where the following holds:

$$(X \otimes (\otimes\Delta_P^\perp)) = (Y \otimes (\otimes\Delta_Q^\perp)) = G \tag{4}$$

In this case, the output of the composition in (3) will be $G \oplus G$. Instead we can apply the & directly without derivation (2), yielding the simpler output G.

Note that, as discussed in Sect. 5, (4) above does not strictly require equality. The special case can also be applied if we can prove and use the filter $\vdash (X \otimes (\otimes\Delta_P^\perp))^\perp, (Y \otimes (\otimes\Delta_P^\perp))$.

These results and the complexity underlying their construction demonstrate the non-trivial effort needed to adhere to CLL's systematic management of resources and, more specifically, its systematic accounting of unused resources. These properties, however, are essential guarantees of correct resource management offered by construction in our process compositions.

8 Sequential Composition - The `JOIN` Action

The `JOIN` action reflects the connection of two processes in sequence, i.e. where (some of) the outputs of a process are connected to (some of) the corresponding inputs of another. More generally, we want to compose a process P with specification $\vdash \Gamma, X$, i.e. with some (multiset of) inputs Γ and output X in sequence with a process Q with specification $\vdash \Delta, C^\perp, Y$, i.e. with an input $C^\perp$, output Y, and (possibly) more inputs in context Δ. We also assume the user selects a subterm A of X in P and a matching subterm A of the input $C^\perp$ in Q.

The strategy of the algorithm behind the `JOIN` action is to construct a new input for Q based on the chosen $C^\perp$ such that it directly matches the output X of P (and prioritizing the output selection A). This will enable the application of the *Cut* rule, which requires the cut literal to match exactly. In what follows, we present how different cases for X are handled.

---

[4] $\otimes\{a_1, ..., a_n\}^\perp = a_1^\perp \otimes ... \otimes a_n^\perp$.

8.1 Atomic or Matching Output

If X is atomic, a straighforward use of the *Cut* rule is sufficient to connect the two processes. For example, the `JOIN` action between $\vdash A^\perp, B^\perp, X$ and $\vdash X^\perp, Z$ results in the following proof:

$$\dfrac{\dfrac{}{\vdash A^\perp, B^\perp,\ X}\,\mathtt{P} \qquad \dfrac{}{\vdash X^\perp, Z}\,\mathtt{Q}}{\vdash A^\perp, B^\perp, Z}\,Cut$$

The same approach can be applied more generally for any non-atomic X as long as a matching input of type $X^\perp$ (including via filtering) is selected in `Q`.

8.2 Parallel Output

If X is a parallel output, such as $B \otimes C$, we need to manipulate process `Q` so that it can receive an input of type $(B \otimes C)^\perp$.

If `Q` has both inputs $B^\perp$ and $C^\perp$, then we can use the $\parr$ rule to combine them. For example, the generated proof tree of the `JOIN` action between $\vdash A^\perp, D^\perp, B \otimes C$ and $\vdash B^\perp, C^\perp, E^\perp, Y$ is the following:

$$\dfrac{\dfrac{}{\vdash A^\perp, D^\perp, B \otimes C}\,\mathtt{P} \qquad \dfrac{\dfrac{}{\vdash B^\perp, C^\perp, E^\perp, Y}\,\mathtt{Q}}{\vdash (B \otimes C)^\perp, E^\perp, Y}\,\parr}{\vdash A^\perp, D^\perp, E^\perp, Y}\,Cut$$

As previously mentioned, the `JOIN` action attempts to connect the output of `P` to `Q` maximally, i.e. both B and C, regardless of the user choice. The user may, however, want to only connect one of the two resources. We have currently implemented this approach as it is the most commonly used in practice, but are investigating ways to enable better control by the user.

If `Q` has only one of the two inputs, for example $B^\perp$, i.e. `Q` is of the form $\vdash \Delta, B^\perp, Y$ and $C^\perp \notin \Delta$, then C must be buffered. In this case, we use the following derivation:

$$\dfrac{\dfrac{\dfrac{}{\vdash \Delta, B^\perp, Y}\,\mathtt{Q} \qquad \begin{array}{c}\mathtt{BUFFER\_TAC}\\ \vdots \\ \vdash C^\perp, C\end{array}}{\vdash \Delta, B^\perp, C^\perp, Y \otimes C}\,\otimes}{\vdash \Delta, (B \otimes C)^\perp, Y \otimes C}\,\parr \tag{5}$$

We use `BUFFER_TAC` from Sect. 5 to prove the buffer of C.

Depending on the use of the $\otimes$ rule in (5), the resulting output could be either $Y \otimes C$ or $C \otimes Y$. We generally try to match the form of `P`'s output, so in this case we would choose $Y \otimes C$ to match $B \otimes C$. Our algorithm keeps track of this orientation through the `orient` parameter (see Sect. 8.4).

8.3 Optional Output

If X is an optional output, such as $B \oplus C$, then we need to manipulate process `Q` to synthesize an input $(B \oplus C)^\perp$. Assume `Q` can handle B (symmetrically for C) and thus has specification $\vdash \Delta, B^\perp, Y$. We construct a parallel buffer (using `PARBUF_TAC`, see Sect. 5) of type $(\otimes\Delta^\perp) \otimes C$ (converting all inputs in Δ to outputs). We then apply derivation (2) as follows:

$$\dfrac{\dfrac{\dfrac{}{\vdash \Delta, B^\perp, Y}\,\texttt{Q}}{\vdash \Delta, B^\perp, Y \oplus ((\otimes\Delta^\perp)\otimes C)}\,\oplus L \qquad \dfrac{\dfrac{\texttt{PARBUF\_TAC}}{\vdash \Delta, C^\perp, (\otimes\Delta^\perp)\otimes C}\,\vdots}{\vdash \Delta, C^\perp, Y \oplus ((\otimes\Delta^\perp)\otimes C)}\,\oplus R}{\vdash \Delta, (B\oplus C)^\perp, Y \oplus ((\otimes\Delta^\perp)\otimes C)}\,\& \tag{6}$$

Similarly to the `WITH` action, the particular structure of the & rule ensures the systematic management of unused resources. In the example above, if C is received then `Q` will never be executed. As a result, any resources in Δ will remain unused and need to be buffered together with C. This is the reason behind the type $(\otimes\Delta^\perp) \otimes C$ of the constructed buffer (as opposed to plainly using type C).

The proof tree of an example of the `JOIN` action between process `P` specified by $\vdash A^\perp, D^\perp, B \oplus C$ and process `Q` specified by $\vdash B^\perp, E^\perp, Y$ is shown below:

$$\dfrac{\dfrac{}{\vdash A^\perp, D^\perp, B\oplus C}\,\texttt{P} \qquad \dfrac{\dfrac{\dfrac{}{\vdash B^\perp, E^\perp, Y}\,\texttt{Q}}{\vdash B^\perp, E^\perp, Y \oplus (C\otimes E)}\,\oplus L \qquad \dfrac{\dfrac{\dfrac{}{\vdash C^\perp, C}\,Id \quad \dfrac{}{\vdash E^\perp, E}\,Id}{\vdash C^\perp, E^\perp, C\otimes E}\,\otimes}{\vdash C^\perp, E^\perp, Y\oplus(C\otimes E)}\,\oplus R}{\vdash (B\oplus C)^\perp, E^\perp, Y\oplus (C\otimes E)}\,\&}{\vdash A^\perp, D^\perp, E^\perp, Y\oplus(C\otimes E)}\,Cut$$

It is interesting to consider a couple of special cases.

Case 1: If $\vdash \Delta, C^\perp, Y$ is a parallel buffer, (6) can be simplified as follows:

$$\dfrac{\dfrac{}{\vdash \Delta, B^\perp, Y}\,\texttt{Q} \qquad \dfrac{\texttt{PARBUF\_TAC}}{\vdash \Delta, C^\perp, Y}\,\vdots}{\vdash \Delta, (B\oplus C)^\perp, Y}\,\& \tag{7}$$

This may occur, for example, if $\Delta = \emptyset$ and $Y = C$. Such cases arise in processes used to recover from an exception. For instance, a recovery process $\vdash \mathit{Exception}^\perp, \mathit{Resource}$ can convert an output $\mathit{Resource} \oplus \mathit{Exception}$ to simply $\mathit{Resource}$ (which either was there in the first place, or was produced through the recovery process).

Case 2: If $Y = D \oplus E$ for some D and E such that $\vdash \Delta, C^\perp, D$ (or symmetrically $\vdash \Delta, C^\perp, E$) is a parallel buffer, then we can apply the following derivation:

$$\dfrac{\dfrac{}{\vdash \Delta, B^\perp, D \oplus E}\,\mathtt{Q} \qquad \dfrac{\dfrac{\mathtt{PARBUF\_TAC}}{\vdash \Delta, C^\perp, D}}{\vdash \Delta, C^\perp, D \oplus E}\,\oplus L}{\vdash \Delta, (B \oplus C)^\perp, D \oplus E}\,\& \tag{8}$$

This may occur, for example, if $\Delta = \emptyset$ and $Y = C \oplus E$. The recovery process above may itself throw an exception: $\vdash Exception^\perp, Resource \oplus Failed$. This will convert output $Resource \oplus Exception$ to $Resource \oplus Failed$ (either we had the *Resource* from the beginning, or we recovered and still got a *Resource*, or the recovery process failed) instead of $(Resource \oplus Failed) \oplus Resource$.

Table 4. Examples of how the `priority` parameter can affect the behaviour of INPUT_TAC. The selected subterms and the output of Q are highlighted in bold.

Target	Priority	Q	Result of INPUT_TAC
$X = \mathbf{A} \otimes (A \oplus B)$	*Left*	$\vdash A^\perp, \mathbf{Y}$	$\vdash X^\perp, \mathbf{Y} \otimes (A \oplus B)$
$X = A \otimes (\mathbf{A} \oplus B)$	*Right*; *Left*	$\vdash A^\perp, \mathbf{Y}$	$\vdash X^\perp, A \otimes (\mathbf{Y} \oplus B)$
$X = \mathbf{A} \oplus (B \otimes C)$	*Left*	$\vdash (B \oplus A)^\perp, \mathbf{Y}$	$\vdash X^\perp, \mathbf{Y} \oplus (B \otimes C)$
$X = A \oplus (\mathbf{B} \otimes C)$	*Right*; *Left*	$\vdash (B \oplus A)^\perp, \mathbf{Y}$	$\vdash X^\perp, A \oplus (\mathbf{Y} \otimes C)$

8.4 Putting It All Together

In the general case, the output X of P can be a complex combination of multiple parallel and optional outputs. For that reason, we apply the above proof strategies in a recursive, bottom-up way, prioritizing the user selections. We call the algorithm that produces the appropriate input $X^\perp$ (or equivalent) from Q "INPUT_TAC" and it has the following arguments (see Algorithm 1):

- **sel**: optional term corresponding to the user selected input $C^\perp$ of Q.
- **priority**: a list representing the path of the user selected subterm A in the syntax tree of the output X of P. For example, if the user selects B in the output $(A \otimes B) \oplus C$, the priority is [*Left*; *Right*].
- **orient**: our latest path (left or right) in the syntax tree of X so that we add the corresponding buffers on the same side (see Sect. 8.2).
- **inputs**: a list of inputs of Q. We remove used inputs from this to avoid reuse.
- **target**: the input term we are trying to construct. This is initially set to X, but may take values that are subterms of X in recursive calls.
- **proc**: the CLL specification of Q as it evolves.

The `priority` parameter is useful when more than one subterms of the output either (a) are the same or (b) have the same matching input in Q. Table 4 shows examples of how different priorities change the result of INPUT_TAC.

Algorithm 1. Derives a new process specification from the given "**proc**" such that it includes an input of type "**target**".

```
 1: function INPUT_TAC(sel, priority, orient, inputs, target, proc)
 2:     Try to match target with sel (if provided) or one of the inputs
 3:     if it matches then return proc

 4:     else if target is atomic then
 5:         if priority ≠ None then fail       ▷ we couldn't match the user selected output
 6:         else Create a target buffer using (5) depending on orient
 7:         end if

 8:     else if target is L ⊗ R then
 9:         if priority = Left then
10:             proc' = INPUT_TAC(sel, tail(priority), orient, inputs, L, proc)
11:             proc = INPUT_TAC(None, None, Right, inputs - {L}, R, proc')
12:         else
13:             proc' = INPUT_TAC(sel, tail(priority), orient, inputs, R, proc)
14:             proc = INPUT_TAC(None, None, Left, inputs - {R}, L, proc')
15:         end if
16:         Use the ⅋ rule to create the (L ⊗ R)⊥ input

17:     else if target is L ⊕ R then
18:         if priority = Left then
19:             proc = INPUT_TAC(sel, tail(priority), orient, inputs, L, proc)
20:             Try derivation (7) orElse Try derivation (8) orElse Use derivation (6)
21:         else if priority = Right then
22:             proc = INPUT_TAC(sel, tail(priority), orient, inputs, R, proc)
23:             Try derivation (7) orElse Try derivation (8) orElse Use derivation (6)
24:         else
25:             Try as if priority = Left orElse Try as if priority = Right
26:                 else Create a target buffer using (5) depending on orient
27:         end if
28:     end if
29:     return proc
30: end function
```

---

9 Conclusion

CLL's inherent properties make it an ideal language to reason about resources. CLL sequents (under polarity restrictions) can be viewed as resource-based specifications of processes. The CLL inference rules then describe the logically legal, but primitive ways to manipulate and compose such processes.

We presented algorithms that allow intuitive composition in parallel, conditionally, and in sequence. We call these composition actions TENSOR, WITH, and JOIN respectively, and they are implemented in HOL Light. We analysed how each action functions in different cases and examples.

As a result of the rigorous usage of CLL inference rules, the constructed compositions have guaranteed resource accounting, so that no resources disappear or are created out of nowhere. The proofs-as-processes paradigm and its recent evolutions allow the extraction of process calculus terms from these proofs, for concurrent and guaranteed deadlock-free execution.

In the future, we intend to work towards relaxing identified limitations along 2 main lines: (a) functionality, by incorporating and dealing with increasingly more complex specifications including those requiring formulation of more complex filters, and (b) expressiveness, by extending the fragment of CLL we are using while keeping a balance in terms of efficiency.

Through this work, it is made obvious that intuitive process compositions in CLL require complex applications of a large number of inference rules. Our algorithms automate the appropriate deductions and alleviate this burden from the user. We have tied these with the diagrammatic interface of `WorkflowFM` [21], so that the user is not required to know or understand CLL or theorem proving, but merely sees inputs and outputs represented graphically. They can then obtain intuitive process compositions with the aforementioned correctness guarantees with a few simple clicks.

Acknowledgements. This work was supported by the "DigiFlow: Digitizing Industrial Workflow, Monitoring and Optimization" Innovation Activity funded by EIT Digital. We would like to thank the attendants of the LOPSTR conference, 4–6 September 2018, in Frankfurt, Germany for their insightful comments that helped improve this paper.

References

1. Van der Aalst, W.M.: The application of petri nets to workflow management. J. Circ. Syst. Comput. **8**(01), 21–66 (1998)
2. Abramsky, S.: Proofs as processes. Theoret. Comput. Sci. **135**(1), 5–9 (1994)
3. Acay, C., Pfenning, F.: Refinements for session typed concurrency (2016)
4. Bellin, G., Scott, P.: On the π-calculus and linear logic. TCS **135**(1), 11–65 (1994)
5. Caires, L., Pfenning, F.: Session types as intuitionistic linear propositions. In: Gastin, P., Laroussinie, F. (eds.) CONCUR 2010. LNCS, vol. 6269, pp. 222–236. Springer, Heidelberg (2010). https://doi.org/10.1007/978-3-642-15375-4_16
6. Christensen, E., Curbera, F., Meredith, G., Weerawarana, S.: Web services description language (WSDL) 1.1 (2001)
7. Dardha, O., Gay, S.J.: A new linear logic for deadlock-free session-typed processes. In: Baier, C., Dal Lago, U. (eds.) FoSSaCS 2018. LNCS, vol. 10803, pp. 91–109. Springer, Cham (2018). https://doi.org/10.1007/978-3-319-89366-2_5
8. Dardha, O., Pérez, J.A.: Comparing deadlock-free session typed processes. In: Proceedings of the 22th International Workshop on Expressiveness in Concurrency EXPRESS/SOS, pp. 1–15 (2015)
9. Girard, J.Y.: Linear logic: its syntax and semantics. In: Girard, J.Y., Lafont, Y., Regnier, L. (eds.) Advances in Linear Logic. No. 222 in London Mathematical Society Lecture Notes. Cambridge University Press, Cambridge (1995)
10. Gooch, P., Roudsari, A.: Computerization of workflows, guidelines and care pathways: a review of implementation challenges for process-oriented health information systems. J. Am. Med. Inform. Assoc. **18**(6), 738–748 (2011)
11. Harrison, J.: HOL light: a tutorial introduction. In: Srivas, M., Camilleri, A. (eds.) FMCAD 1996. LNCS, vol. 1166, pp. 265–269. Springer, Heidelberg (1996). https://doi.org/10.1007/BFb0031814

12. Kezadri Hamiaz, M., Pantel, M., Thirioux, X., Combemale, B.: Correct-by-construction model driven engineering composition operators. Formal Aspects Comput. **28**(3), 409–440 (2016)
13. Laurent, O.: Etude de la polarisation en logique. Ph.D. thesis, Université de la Méditerranée-Aix-Marseille II (2002)
14. Lincoln, P., Mitchell, J., Scedrov, A., Shankar, N.: Decision problems for propositional linear logic. Ann. Pure Appl. Logic **56**(1), 239–311 (1992)
15. Manataki, A., Fleuriot, J., Papapanagiotou, P.: A workflow-driven formal methods approach to the generation of structured checklists for intrahospital patient transfers. J. Biomed. Health Inform. **21**(4), 1156–1162 (2017)
16. Martin, D., et al.: OWL-S: Semantic markup for web services (2004)
17. McDermott, D., et al.: PDDL-the planning domain definition language (1998)
18. Milner, R.: Communicating and Mobile Systems: The π-calculus. Cambridge University Press, Cambridge (1999)
19. OASIS: Web Services Business Process Execution Language, version 2.0, OASIS Standard (2007). http://docs.oasis-open.org/wsbpel/2.0/OS/wsbpel-v2.0-OS.pdf
20. Object Management Group: Business Process Model and Notation (BPMN), version 2.0 (2011). http://www.omg.org/spec/BPMN/2.0/PDF
21. Papapanagiotou, P., Fleuriot, J.: WorkflowFM: a logic-based framework for formal process specification and composition. In: de Moura, L. (ed.) CADE 2017. LNCS (LNAI), vol. 10395, pp. 357–370. Springer, Cham (2017). https://doi.org/10.1007/978-3-319-63046-5_22
22. Rao, J., Küngas, P., Matskin, M.: Composition of semantic web services using linear logic theorem proving. Inf. Syst. **31**(4–5), 340–360 (2006)
23. Szpyrka, M., Nalepa, G.J., Ligęza, A., Kluza, K.: Proposal of formal verification of selected BPMN models with Alvis Modeling Language. In: Brazier, F.M.T., Nieuwenhuis, K., Pavlin, G., Warnier, M., Badica, C. (eds.) Intelligent Distributed Computing V. Studies in Computational Intelligence, vol. 382, pp. 249–255. Springer, Heidelberg (2012). https://doi.org/10.1007/978-3-642-24013-3_26
24. Tammet, T.: Proof strategies in linear logic. J. Autom. Reasoning **12**(3), 273–304 (1994)
25. Toninho, B., Caires, L., Pfenning, F.: Dependent session types via intuitionistic linear type theory. In: 13th International ACM SIGPLAN Symposium on Principles and Practices of Declarative Programming PPDP 2011, pp. 161–172. ACM (2011)
26. Tounsi, I., Hadj Kacem, M., Hadj Kacem, A.: Building correct by construction SOA design patterns: modeling and refinement. In: Drira, K. (ed.) ECSA 2013. LNCS, vol. 7957, pp. 33–44. Springer, Heidelberg (2013). https://doi.org/10.1007/978-3-642-39031-9_4
27. Troelstra, A.S.: Lectures on Linear Logic. CSLI Lecture Notes 29, Stanford (1992)
28. Wadler, P.: Propositions as sessions. In: Proceedings of the 17th ACM SIGPLAN International Conference on Functional Programming, pp. 273–286. ACM (2012)

Confluence of CHR Revisited: Invariants and Modulo Equivalence

Henning Christiansen(✉) and Maja H. Kirkeby(✉)

Computer Science, Roskilde University, Roskilde, Denmark
{henning,majaht}@ruc.dk

Abstract. Abstract simulation of one transition system by another is introduced as a means to simulate a potentially infinite class of similar transition sequences within a single transition sequence. This is useful for proving confluence under invariants of a given system, as it may reduce the number of proof cases to consider from infinity to a finite number. The classical confluence results for Constraint HThe invariant is formalizedandling Rules (CHR) can be explained in this way, using CHR as a simulation of itself. Using an abstract simulation based on a ground representation, we extend these results to include confluence under invariant and modulo equivalence, which have not been done in a satisfactory way before.

Keywords: Constraint Handling Rules · Confluence · Confluence modulo equivalence · Invariants · Observable confluence

1 Introduction

Confluence of a transition system means that any two alternative transition sequences from a given state can be extended to reach a common state. Proving confluence of nondeterministic systems may be important for correctness proofs and it anticipates parallel implementations and application order optimizations. Confluence modulo equivalence generalizes this so that these "common states" need not be identical, but only equivalent according to an equivalence relation. This allows for redundant data representations (e.g., sets as lists) and procedures that search for an optimal solution to a problem, when any of two equally good solutions can be accepted (e.g., the Viterbi algorithm analyzed for confluence modulo equivalence in [8]).

We introduce a notion of abstract simulation of one system, the object system, by another, the meta level system, and show how proofs of confluence (under invariant, modulo equivalence) for an object system may be expressed within a meta level system. This may reduce the number of proof cases to be considered,

This work is supported by The Danish Council for Independent Research, Natural Sciences, grant no. DFF 4181-00442.

F. Mesnard and P. J. Stuckey (Eds.): LOPSTR 2018, LNCS 11408, pp. 94–111, 2019.
https://doi.org/10.1007/978-3-030-13838-7_6

often from infinity to a finite number. We apply this to the programming language of Constraint Handling Rules, CHR [14–16], giving a clearer exposition of existing results and extending them for invariants and modulo equivalence.

By nature, invariants and state equivalences are meta level properties that in general cannot be expressed in its own system: the state itself is implicit and properties such as groundness (or certain arguments restricted to be uninstantiated variables) cannot be expressed in a logic-based semantics for CHR. Using abstract simulation we can add the necessary enhanced expressibility to the meta level, and the ground representation of logic programs, that was studied in-depth in the late 1980s and -90s in the context of meta-programming in logic (e.g., [5,18,19]), comes in readily as a well-suited and natural choice for this. The following minimalist example motivates both invariant and state equivalence for CHR.

Example 1 ([7,8]). The following CHR program, consisting of a single rule, collects a number of separate items into a set represented as a list of items.

```
set(L), item(A) <=> set([A|L]).
```

This rule will apply repeatedly, replacing constraints matched by the left hand side by the one indicated to the right. The query

```
?- item(a), item(b), set([]).
```

may lead to two different final states, {`set([a,b])`} and {`set([b,a])`}, both representing the same set. Thus, the program is not confluent, but it may be confluent modulo an equivalence that disregards the order of the list-elements. Confluence modulo equivalence still requires an invariant that excludes more than one `set/1` constraint, as otherwise, an element may go to an arbitrary of those.

1.1 Related Work

Some applications of our abstract simulations may be seen as special cases of abstract interpretation [10]. This goes for the re-formulation of the classical confluence results for CHR, but when invariants are introduced, this is not obvious; a detailed argument is given in Sect. 5. It is related to symbolic execution and constraint logic programming [22], where reasoning takes place on compact abstract representations parameterized in suitable ways, rather than checking multitudes of concrete instances. Bisimulation [26], which has been applied in many contexts, indicates a tighter relationship between states and transitions of two systems than the abstract simulation: when a state s_0 is simulated by an abstract state s_0' and there is a transition $s_0 \to s_1$, bisimulation would require the existence of an abstract transition $s_0' \to' s_1'$, which may not be case as demonstrated by Example 6.

Previous results on confluence of CHR programs, e.g., [1–3], mainly refer to a logic-based semantics, which is well-suited for showing program properties, but it does not comply with typical implementations [20,28] and applies only for a small subset of CHR programs. Other works [7,8] suggest an alternative operational semantics that lifts these limitations, including the ability to handle Prolog-style built-in predicates such as `var/1`, etc. To compare with earlier work and for simplicity, the present paper refers to the logic-based semantics.

As long as invariants and modulo equivalence are not considered, the logic-based semantics allows for elegant confluence proofs based on Newman's Lemma (Lemma 1, below). A finite set of critical pairs can be defined, whose joinability ensures confluence for terminating programs. Duck et al. [13] proposed a generalization of this approach to confluence under invariant, called observable confluence; no practically relevant methods were suggested, and (as the authors point out) even a simple invariant such as groundness explodes into infinitely many cases.

Confluence modulo equivalence was introduced and motivated for CHR by [7], also arguing that invariants are important for specifying meaningful equivalences. An in-depth theoretical analysis, including the use of a ground representation, is given by [8] in relation the alternative semantics mentioned above. However, it has not been related to abstract simulations, and the proposal for a detailed language of meta level constraints in the present paper is new. Repeating the motivations of [7,8] in the context of the logic-based semantics, [17] suggested to handle confluence modulo equivalence along the lines of [13], thus inheriting the problems of infinitely many proof case pointed out above.

An approach to show confluence of a transition system, by producing a mapping into another confluent system, is described by [11] and extended to confluence modulo equivalence by [23]; the relationship between such two systems is different from the abstract simulations introduced in the present paper. Confluence, including modulo equivalence, has been studied since the first half of the 20th century in a variety of contexts; see, e.g., [8,21] for overview.

1.2 Contributions

We introduce abstract simulation as a setting for proofs of confluence for general transitions systems and demonstrate this specifically for CHR. We recast classical results (without invariant and equivalence), showing that they are essentially based on a simulation of CHR's logic-based semantics by itself, and we can pinpoint, why it does not generalize for invariants (see Example 4, p. 9).

These results are extended for invariants and modulo equivalence, using an abstract simulation; it is based on a ground meta level representation and suitable meta level constraints to reason about it.

1.3 Overview

Sections 2 and 3 introduce basic concepts of confluence plus our notion of abstract simulation. Section 4 gives syntax and semantics of CHR along with a discussion of how much nondeterminism to include in a semantics used when considering confluence. Section 5 re-explains the classical results in terms of abstract simulation. Section 6 extends these results for invariants and modulo equivalence;

proofs can be found in an extended report [6]. The concluding Sect. 7 gives a summary and explains briefly how standard mechanisms, used to prevent loops by CHR's propagation rules, can be added.

2 Basic Concepts, Confluence, Invariants and Equivalences

A *transition system* $D = \langle S, \mapsto \rangle$ consists of a set of *states* S, and a *transition* is an element of $\mapsto : S \times S$, written $s_0 \mapsto s_1$ or, alternatively, $s_1 \leftarrow\!\!\dashv s_0$. A *transition sequence* or *path* is a chain of transitions $s_0 \mapsto s_1 \mapsto \cdots \mapsto s_n$ where $n \geq 0$; if such a path exists, we write $s_0 \overset{*}{\mapsto} s_n$. A state s_0 is *final* (or *normal form*) whenever $\nexists s_1\ s_0 \mapsto s_1$, and D is *terminating* whenever every path is finite. To anticipate the application for logic programming systems, a given transition system may have a special final state called *failure*.

An *invariant* I for $D = \langle S, \mapsto \rangle$ is a subset $I \subseteq S$ such that

$$s_0 \in I \wedge s_0 \mapsto s_1 \quad \Rightarrow \quad s_1 \in I.$$

We write a fact $s \in I$ as $I(s)$ and refer to s as an *I state*. The *restriction of D to I* is the transition system $\langle I, \overset{I}{\mapsto} \rangle$ where $\overset{I}{\mapsto}$ is the restriction of $\mapsto$ to I. A set of *allowed initial states* $S' \subseteq S$ defines an invariant of those states *reachable* from some $s \in S'$, i.e., $\text{reachable}(S') = \{s' \mid s \in S' \wedge s \overset{*}{\mapsto} s'\}$. A *(state) equivalence* is an equivalence relation over S, typically denoted $\approx$. In the context of an invariant I, the relations $\approx$ and $\mapsto$ are understood to be restricted to I.

The following α and β corners[1] were introduced in [7,8], being implicit in [21]. An *α corner* is a structure $s_1 \leftarrow\!\!\dashv s_0 \mapsto s_2$, where $s_0, s_1, s_2 \in S$ and the indicated relationships hold; s_0 is called a *common ancestor* and s_1, s_2 *wing* states. A *β corner* is a structure $s_1 \approx s_0 \mapsto s_2$, where $s_0, s_1, s_2 \in S$ and the indicated relationships hold. In the context of an invariant I, the different types of corners are defined only for I states.

Two states s_1, s_2 are *joinable (modulo $\approx$)* whenever there exist paths $s_1 \overset{*}{\mapsto} s_1'$ and $s_2 \overset{*}{\mapsto} s_2'$ with $s_1' = s_2'$ ($s_1' \approx s_2'$). A corner $s_1 \mathit{Rel}\, s_0 \mapsto s_2$ is *joinable (modulo $\approx$)* when s_1, s_2 are joinable (modulo $\approx$); $\mathit{Rel} \in \{\leftarrow\!\!\dashv, \approx\}$.

A transition system $D = \langle S, \mapsto \rangle$ is *confluent (modulo $\approx$)* whenever

$$s_1 \overset{*}{\leftarrow\!\!\dashv} s_0 \overset{*}{\mapsto} s_2 \quad \Rightarrow \quad s_1 \text{ and } s_2 \text{ are joinable (modulo } \approx).$$

It is *locally confluent* (modulo equivalence $\approx$) whenever all its α (α and β) corners are joinable. The following properties are fundamental.

Lemma 1 (Newman [25]**).** *A terminating transition system (under invariant I) is confluent if and only if it is locally confluent.*

---

[1] In recent literature within term rewriting, the terms peaks and cliffs have been used for α and β corners, respectively.

Lemma 2 (Huet [21]). *A terminating transition system (under invariant I) is confluent modulo $\approx$ if and only if it is locally confluent modulo $\approx$.*

These properties reduce proofs of confluence (mod. equiv.) for terminating systems to proofs of the simpler property of local confluence (mod. equiv.), but still, this may leave an infinite number of corners to be examined.

3 Abstract Simulation

Consider two transition systems, $D_O = \langle S_O, \mapsto_O \rangle$ and $D^M = \langle S^M, \mapsto^M \rangle$, referred to as *object* and *meta level* systems. A *replacement* is a (perhaps partial) function $\rho \colon S^M \to S_O$; the application of ρ to some $s \in S^M$ is written $s\rho$. For any structure $f(s_1, \ldots s_n)$ with states $s_1, \ldots s_n$ of D^M (a transition, a tuple, etc.), replacements apply in a compositional way, $f(s_1, \ldots s_n)\rho = f(s_1\rho, \ldots s_n\rho)$. For a family of replacements $P = \{\rho_i\}_{i \in Inx}$, the *covering* (or *concretization*) of a structure $f(s_1, \ldots s_n)$ is defined as

$$[\![f(s_1, \ldots s_n)]\!]_O^M = \{f(s_1, \ldots s_n)\rho \mid \rho \in P\}.$$

Notice that P is left implicit in this notation, as in the context of given object and meta level systems, there will be one and only one replacement family.

Definition 1. *An* abstract simulation *of D_O by D^M with possible invariants I_O, resp., I^M, and equivalences $\approx_O$, resp., $\approx^M$, is defined by a family of replacements $P = \{\rho_i\}_{i \in Inx}$ which satisfies the following conditions.*

$$\begin{aligned} s_0 \mapsto^M s_1 \quad &\Rightarrow \quad \forall \rho \in P\colon\ s_0\rho \mapsto_O s_1\rho \ \vee\ s_0\rho = s_1\rho \\ I^M(s) \quad &\Rightarrow \quad \forall \rho \in P\colon\ I_O(s\rho) \\ s_0 \approx^M s_1 \quad &\Rightarrow \quad \forall \rho \in P\colon\ s_0\rho \approx_O s_1\rho \end{aligned}$$

Notice that an abstract simulation does not necessarily cover all object level states, transitions, etc.

Example 2. Let $A = \{a_1, a_2, \ldots\}$, $B = \{b_1, b_2, \ldots\}$ and $C = \{c_1, c_2, \ldots\}$ be sets of states, and O and M the following transition systems.

$$\begin{aligned} O \quad &= \quad \langle A \cup B \cup C, \{a_i \mapsto_O b_i \mid i = 1, 2, \ldots\} \cup \{a_i \mapsto_O c_i \mid i = 1, 2, \ldots\}\rangle \\ M \quad &= \quad \langle \{a, b, c\}, \{a \mapsto_M b, a \mapsto_M c\}\rangle \end{aligned}$$

Assume equivalences $b \approx^M c$ and $b_i \approx_O c_i$, for all i. Then the family of replacements $P = \{\rho_i\}_{i=1,2,\ldots}$, where $a\rho_i = a_i$, $b\rho_i = b_i$ and $c\rho_i = c_i$, defines a simulation of O by M. It appears that O and M are not confluent, cf. the non-joinable corners $b_1 \leftarrow_O a_1 \mapsto_O c_1$ and $b \leftarrow_M a \mapsto_M c$, but both are confluent modulo $\approx_O$ ($\approx^M$).

A meta level structure m *covers* an object structure k whenever $k \in [\![m]\!]_O^M$. When $[\![m]\!]_O^M = \emptyset$, m is *inconsistent.* When $[\![m']\!]_O^M \subseteq [\![m]\!]_O^M$, m' is a *sub-state/subcorner*, etc. of m, depending on the inherent type of m. When D_O and D^M both include *failure*, it is required that $[\![failure]\!]_O^M = \{failure\}$. A given meta level state S is *mixed* whenever $[\![S]\!]_O^M$ includes both *failure* and non-*failure* states. Transitions are only allowed from consistent and neither failed nor mixed states.

The following is a consequence of the definitions.

Lemma 3. *An object level corner, which is covered by a joinable (mod. equiv.) meta level corner, is joinable (mod. equiv.).*

When doing confluence proofs, we may search for a small set of *critical* meta level corners,[2] whose joinability guarantees joinability of any object level corner, i.e., any other object level corner not covered by one of these is seen to be joinable in other ways. For term rewriting systems, e.g., [4], and previous work on CHR, such critical sets have been defined by explicit constructions.

We introduce a mechanism for splitting a meta level corner Λ into a set of corners, which together covers the same set of object corners as Λ. This is useful when Λ in itself is not joinable, but each of the new corners are. In some cases, splitting is necessary for proving confluence under an invariant as shown in Sect. 5 and exemplified in Examples 4 and 6.

Definition 2. *Let s be a meta level state (or corner). A set of states (or corners) $\{s_i\}_{i\in Inx}$ is a* splitting *of s whenever $\bigcup_{i\in Inx} [\![s_i]\!]_O^M = [\![s]\!]_O^M$. A corner (set of corners) is* split joinable *(mod. equiv.) if it (each of its corners) is joinable (mod. equiv.), inconsistent, or has a splitting into a set of split joinable (mod. equiv.) corners.*

Corollary 1. *An object level corner, which is covered by a split joinable (mod. equiv.) meta level corner, is joinable (mod. equiv.).*

4 Constraint Handling Rules

Most actual implementations of CHR are fully deterministic, i.e., for a given query, there is at most one answer state (alternatively, the program is non-terminating). In this light, it may be discussed whether confluence is an interesting property, and if so, to what extent the applied semantics should be non-deterministic. Our thesis is the following: choice of next constraints to be tried and which rule to be used should be nondeterministic. Thus a confluent program can be understood by the programmer without considering the detailed control mechanisms in the used implementation; this also anticipates parallel implementations. We see only little interest in considering confluence for the

[2] In the literature, the term *critical pair* is used for the pair of wing states of our critical corners.

so-called refined CHR semantics [12] in which only very little nondeterminism is retained.

Similarly to [7,8], we remove w.l.o.g. two redundancies from the logic-based semantics [1,16]: global variables and the two-component constraint store.

- Global variables are those in the original query. Traditionally they are kept as a separate state-component, such that values bound to them can be reported to the user at the end. The same effect can be obtained by a constraint `global/2` that does not appear in any rule, but may be used in the original query: writing `?- p(X)` as `?- p(X), global('X',X)`, means that the value of the variable named `'X'` can be read out as the second argument of this constraint in a final state.
- We avoid separating the constraint store into query and active parts, as the transition sequences with or without this separation are essentially the same.

4.1 Syntax

Standard first-order notions of variables, terms, predicates atoms, etc. are assumed. Two disjoint sets of *constraint predicates* are assumed, *user constraints* and *built-in constraints*; the actual set of built-ins may vary depending on the application. We use the generalized simpagation form [16] to capture all rules of CHR. A *rule* is a structure of the form

$$H_1 \backslash H_2 \texttt{ <=> } G \,|\, C$$

where $H_1 \backslash H_2$ is the *head* of the rule, H_1 and H_2 being sequences, not both empty, of user constraints; G is the *guard* which is a conjunction of built-in constraints; and C is the *body* which is a sequence of constraints of either sort. When H_2 is empty, the rule is a *simplification*, which may be written H_1 `<=>` $G \,|\, C$; when H_2 is empty, it is a *propagation*, which may be written H_2 `==>` $G \,|\, C$; any other rule is a *simpagation*; when $G = \mathit{true}$, $(G\,|)$ may be left out. The *head variables* of a rule are those appearing in the head, any other variable is *local.* The following notion is convenient when defining the CHR semantics and its meta level simulation.

Definition 3. *A* pre-application *of a rule* $r = (H_1 \backslash H_2 \texttt{<=>} G \,|\, C)$ *is of the form* $(H_1' \backslash H_2' \texttt{<=>} G' \,|\, C')\sigma$ *where* $r' = (H_1' \backslash H_2' \texttt{<=>} G' \,|\, C')$ *is a variant of* r *with fresh variables and* σ *is a substitution to the head variables of* r'*, where, for no variable* x*,* $x\sigma$ *contains a local variable of* r'*.*

The operator $\uplus$ refers to union of multisets, so that, e.g., $\{a, a\} \uplus \{a\} = \{a, a, a\}$; for difference of multisets, we use standard notation for set difference, assuming it takes into account the number of copies, e.g., $\{a, a\} \setminus \{a\} = \{a\}$.

4.2 The Logic-Based Operational Semantics for CHR

The semantics presented here is essentially identical to the one used by [1] and the so-called abstract operational semantics ω_t of [16], taking into account the simplifications explained above. Following [27], we define a state as an equivalence class, abstracting away the specific variables used and the different ways the same logical meaning can be expressed by different conjunctions of built-ins.[3] A logical theory $\mathcal{B}$ is assumed for the built-in predicates.

A *state representation (s.repr.)* is a pair $\langle S, B\rangle$, where the *constraint store* S is a multiset of constraint atoms and the *built-in store* B is a conjunction of built-ins; any s.repr. with an unsatisfiable built-in store is considered identical to *failure*. Two s.repr.s $\langle S, B\rangle$ and $\langle S', B'\rangle$ are *variants* whenever, either[4]

- they are both *failure*, or
- there is a renaming substitution ρ such that
  $\mathcal{B} \models \forall(B\rho \rightarrow \exists(S\rho = S' \wedge B')) \wedge \mathcal{B} \models \forall(B' \rightarrow \exists(S\rho = S' \wedge B\rho))$

A *state* is an equivalence class of s.repr.s under the variant relationship. For simplicity of notation, we typically indicate a state by one of its s.repr.s.

A *rule application* w.r.t. to a non-failure state $\langle S, B\rangle$ is a pre-application $H_1\backslash H_2$ `<=>` $G\,|\,C$ for which $\mathcal{B} \models B \rightarrow \exists_L G$, where L is the list of its local variables. There are two sorts of transitions, *by rule application* and *by built-in*.

$$\langle H_1 \uplus H_2 \uplus S, B\rangle \mapsto_{logic} \langle H_1 \uplus C \uplus S, G \wedge B\rangle$$
when there exists a rule application $H_1\backslash H_2$<=>$G\,|\,C$,
$$\langle \{b\} \uplus S, B\rangle \mapsto_{logic} \langle S, b \wedge B\rangle \qquad \text{for a built-in } b.$$

5 Confluence Under the Logic-Based Semantics Re-Explained, and Why Invariants Are Difficult

Here we explain the results of [1,2], also summarized in [16], using abstract simulation. Object and meta level systems coincide and are given by a CHR program under the logic-based semantics. Two rules give rise to a critical corner if a state can be constructed in which one rule consumes constraints that the other one needs to be applied; in that case, rule applications do not commute and a specific proof of joinability must be considered. We anticipate the re-use of the construction, when invariants are introduced: in a *pre*-corner, the guards are not necessarily satisfied (but may be so in the context of an invariant).

[3] Raiser et al. [27] defined "state" similarly to what we call state representation, and they defined an operational semantics over equivalence classes of such states. We have taken the natural step of promoting such equivalence classes to be our states.

[4] An equation between multisets should be understood as an equation between suitable permutations of their elements.

Definition 4. *Consider two rules* $r\colon H_1\backslash H_2$ `<=>` $G\,|\,C$ *and* $r'\colon H'_1\backslash H'_2$ `<=>` $G'\,|\,C'$ *renamed apart, and let* A *and* A' *be non-empty sets of constraints such that* $A \subseteq H_2$, $A' \subseteq H'_1 \uplus H'_2$ *and* $\mathcal{B} \models \exists(A{=}A')$. *In that case, let*

$$\begin{aligned}\bar{H} &= (H_1 \uplus H_2 \uplus H'_1 \uplus H'_2) \setminus A\\ s_0 &= \langle \bar{H}, (G \wedge G' \wedge A{=}A')\rangle\\ s &= \langle \bar{H}\backslash H_2 \uplus C, (G \wedge G' \wedge A{=}A')\rangle\\ s' &= \langle \bar{H}\backslash H'_2 \uplus C', (G \wedge G' \wedge A{=}A')\rangle\end{aligned}$$

When $s \neq s'$, s_0 *is a* critical, common ancestor state, *and* $s \;\leftarrowtail_{logic}\; s_0 \mapsto_{logic} s'$ *is a* critical α pre-corner; *the constraints* A *(or* A'*) is called the* overlap *of* r *and* r'. *When, furthermore,* $\mathcal{B} \models \exists(G \wedge G' \wedge A{=}A')$, *it is a* critical α *corner.*

The simulation is given by the following cover function.

$$\begin{aligned}[\![\langle S, B\rangle]\!]^{logic}_{logic} &= \{\langle S \uplus S^+, B \wedge B^+\rangle \mid\\ &\qquad S^+ \text{ is a multiset of user and built-in constraints,}\\ &\qquad B^+ \text{ is a conjunction of built-ins}\,\}\\ [\![\langle S, B\rangle \mapsto_{logic} \langle S', B'\rangle]\!]^{logic}_{logic} &= \{(\langle S \uplus S^+, B \wedge B^+\rangle \mapsto_{logic} \langle S' \uplus S^+, B' \wedge B^+\rangle) \mid\\ &\qquad S^+ \text{ is a multiset of user and built-in constraints,}\\ &\qquad B^+ \text{ is a conjunction of built-ins, } \exists(B \wedge B^+) \text{ holds}\}\end{aligned}$$

It is easy to check that this definition satisfies the conditions for being an abstract simulation given in Sect. 3, relying on *monotonicity*: $\mathcal{B} \models B \wedge B^+ \rightarrow \exists_L G$.

It can be shown that any corner not covered by a critical corner (Definition 4) is trivially joinable, see the extended report [6]. Thus, according to Lemmas 1 and 3, the program under investigation is confluent whenever it is terminating and this set of critical corners is joinable. The set of critical corners is finite and that allows for automatic confluence proofs by checking the critical corners, one by one, e.g., [24].

Example 3. Consider the one-rule `set`-program of Example 1, ignoring invariant and state equivalence. There are two critical corners, given by the two ways, the rule can overlap with itself:

$$\begin{array}{cc}\langle\{\texttt{set([X1|L]),item(X2)}\}, \mathit{true}\rangle & \langle\{\texttt{set([X|L1]),set(L2)}\}, \mathit{true}\rangle\\ \uparrow_{logic} & \uparrow_{logic}\\ \langle\{\texttt{item(X1),set(L),item(X2)}\}, \mathit{true}\rangle & \langle\{\texttt{set(L1),item(X),set(L2)}\}, \mathit{true}\rangle\\ \downarrow_{logic} & \downarrow_{logic}\\ \langle\{\texttt{item(X1),set([X2|L])}\}, \mathit{true}\rangle & \langle\{\texttt{set(L1),set([X|L2])}\}, \mathit{true}\rangle\end{array}$$

None of these corners are joinable, so the program is not confluent.

The simulation defined above, relying on monotonicity, do not generalize well for confluence under invariant, referred to as "observable confluence" in [13].

Example 4. Consider the CHR program consisting of the following four rules.

r_1: `p(X) <=> q(X)` r_3: `q(X) <=> X>0 | r(X)`
r_2: `p(X) <=> r(X)` r_4: `r(X) <=> X≤0 | q(X)`

It is not confluent as its single critical corner `q(X)` ↤ `p(X)` ↦ `r(X)` is not joinable (the built-in stores are *true* and thus omitted). However, adding the invariant "reachable from an initial state `p(`n`)` where n is an integer" makes it confluent. We indicate the set of all non-trivial object level corners as follows, with the dashed transitions proving each of them joinable.

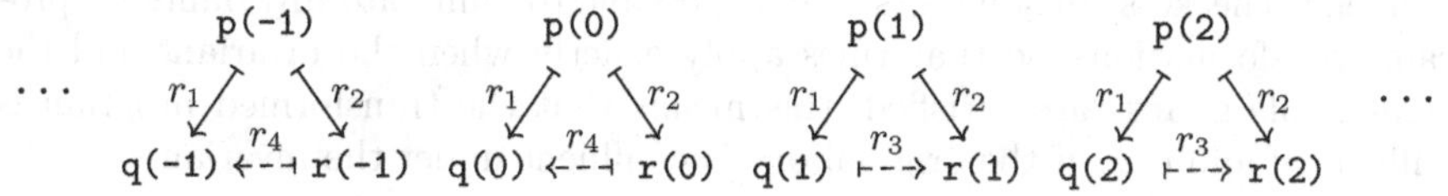

These object corners and their proofs of joinability obviously fall in two groups of similar shapes, but there is no way to construct a finite set (of, say, one or two elements) that covers all object corners. In other words, the smallest set of meta level corners that covers this set is the set itself. This was also noticed in [13] that used a construction that essentially reduces to the abstract simulation shown above.

The abstract simulation given by $[\![-]\!]^{logic}_{logic}$ of Definition 4 above defines an abstract interpretation, whose abstract domain is the complete lattice of CHR states ordered by the substate relationship (Sect. 3). Referring to Example 4, for instance the join of the infinite set of states $\{\langle$`p(`t`)`$, b\rangle \mid t$ is a term, b is a conjunction of built-ins $\}$ is $\langle$`p(X)`$, \mathit{true}\rangle$. When the grounding invariant is introduced, the join operator is not complete; an attempt to join, say, $\langle$`p(0)`$, \mathit{true}\rangle$ and $\langle$`p(1)`$, \mathit{true}\rangle$ would not satisfy the invariant.[5]

6 Invariants and Modulo Equivalence

A program is typically developed with an intended set of queries in mind, giving rise to a state invariant, which may make an otherwise non-confluent program observably confluent (mod. equiv.). We can indicate a few general patterns of invariants and their possible effect on confluence.

- Elimination of non-joinable critical corners that do not cover any object corner satisfying the invariant. This was shown in Example 4 above, and is also demonstrated in the continuation of Example 3 (Example 7, below): "only one `set` constraint allowed".

[5] Such an attempt might be $\langle$`p(X)`$,$ `(X=0` $\vee$ `X=1)`$\rangle$; notice that `X` is a variable, thus breaking the invariant.

- Making it possible to apply a given rule, which otherwise could not apply, e.g., providing a "missing" head constraint or enforcing guard satisfaction:
  1. "if a state contains `p(`*something*`)`, it also contains `q(`*the-same-something*`)`",
  2. "if a state contains `p(`*something*`)`, this *something* is a constant > 1".

An invariant of type 1 ensures confluence mod. equiv. of a version of the Viterbi algorithm [8]; an invariant of type 2 is indicated in Example 4 and formalized in Example 6, below.

As shown in Example 4 above, invariants block for a direct re-use CHR's logical semantics as its own meta-level and, accordingly, existing methods and confluence checkers. In some cases, it is possible to eliminate invariants by program transformations, so that rules apply exactly when the invariant and the original rule guards are satisfied; this means that the transformed program is confluent if and only if the original one is confluent under the invariant.

Example 5. Reconsidering the program of Example 4, the following is an example of such a transformed program; the constants `a` and `b` are introduced as representations of positive, resp., non-positive integers.

```
p(a) <=> q(a).    p(a) <=> r(a).    p(a) <=> r(a).
p(b) <=> q(b).    p(b) <=> r(b).    r(b) <=> q(b).
```

Such program transformations become more complex when the guards describe more involved dependencies between the head variables. More importantly, invariants that exclude certain constraints in a state cannot be expressed in this way, for example "only one `set` constraint allowed" (Examples 3 and 7). Thus we refrain from pursuing a transformational approach. To obtain a maximum degree of generality, we introduce a meta level formalization of CHR's operational semantics that include representations as explicit data objects of states and their components, possibly parameterized by constrained meta variables.

6.1 The Choice of a Ground Representation

Invariants and state equivalences are inherently meta level statements, as they are *about* states, and may refer to notions inexpressible at the object level, e.g., that some part being ground or a variable. Earlier work on meta-interpreters for logic programs, e.g., [5,18,19], offers the desired expressibility in terms of a *ground representation*. Any object term, formula, etc. is named by a ground meta level term. Variables are named by special constants, say `X` by `'X'`, and any other symbol by a function symbol written the same way; e.g., the non-ground object level atom `p(A)` is named by the ground meta level term `p('A')`. For any such ground meta level term mt, we indicate the object it names as $[\![mt]\!]^{Gr}$. For example, $[\![\texttt{p('A')}]\!]^{Gr} = \texttt{p(A)}$ and $[\![\texttt{p('A')} \land \texttt{'A'>2}]\!]^{Gr} = (\texttt{p(A)} \land \texttt{A>2})$.

For a given object entity e, we define its *lifting* to the meta level by (1) selecting a meta level term that names e, and (2) replacing variable names in it consistently by fresh meta level variables. For example, `p(X)` $\land$ `X>2` is lifted to p(x) $\wedge$ x>2, where X and x are object, resp., meta variables. By virtue of this overloaded syntax, we may read such an entity e (implicitly) as its lifting.

A collection of *meta level constraints* is assumed whose meanings are given by a theory $\mathcal{M}$. We start defining meta level states without detailed assumptions about $\mathcal{M}$, that are postponed to Definition 6 below. We assume object level built-in theory $\mathcal{B}$, invariant I_{logic} and state equivalence $\approx_{logic}$.

Definition 5. *A* constrained meta level term *is a structure of the form* (mt WHERE M)*, where* mt *is a meta level term and* M *a conjunction of* $\mathcal{M}$ *constraints. We define*

$$\begin{aligned}[M] &= \{\sigma \mid \mathcal{M} \models M\sigma\},\\ [\![mt \text{ WHERE } M]\!]^{meta}_{logic} &= \{[\![mt\,\sigma]\!]^{Gr} \mid \sigma \in [M]\}.\end{aligned}$$

A meta level state representation (s.repr.) *is a constrained meta level term* st WHERE M *for which* $[\![st \text{ WHERE } M]\!]^{meta}_{logic}$ *is a set of object level states. Two meta level s.repr.s* SR_1*,* SR_2 *are* variants *whenever each object level s.repr. in* $[\![SR_1]\!]^{meta}_{logic}$ *is a variant of some object level s.repr. in* $[\![SR_2]\!]^{meta}_{logic}$ *and vice versa. A* meta level state *is an equivalence class of meta level s.repr.s under the variant relationship. For structures of meta level states (transitions, corners, etc.), we apply the following convention, where* f *may represent any such structure.*

$$\begin{aligned}&[\![f(mt_1 \text{ WHERE } M_1, \ldots, mt_n \text{ WHERE } M_n)]\!]^{meta}_{logic}\\ =\;&[\![f(mt_1, \ldots, mt_n) \text{ WHERE } M_1 \wedge \ldots \wedge M_n]\!]^{meta}_{logic}\end{aligned}$$

Meta level invariant I^{meta}_{logic} *and equivalence* $\approx^{meta}_{logic}$ *are defined as follows.*

- $I^{meta}_{logic}(S)$ *whenever* $I_{logic}(s)$ *for all* $s \in [\![S]\!]^{meta}_{logic}$.
- $S_1 \approx^{meta}_{logic} S_2$ *whenever* $s_1 \approx_{logic} s_2$ *for all* $(s_1, s_2) \in [\![(S_1, S_2)]\!]^{meta}_{logic}$.

As before, we may indicate a meta level state by a representation of it.

Definition 6. *The theory* $\mathcal{M}$ *includes at least the following constraints.*

- =/2 *with its usual meaning of syntactic identity,*
- Type constraints type/2. *For example* type(var,x) *is true in* $\mathcal{M}$ *whenever* x *is the name of an object level variable;* var *is an example of a* type, *and we introduce more types below when we need them.*
- Modal constraints ☺F *and* ☹F *defined to be true in* $\mathcal{M}$ *whenever* $\mathcal{B} \models [\![F]\!]^{Gr}$*, resp.,* $\mathcal{B} \models [\![\neg F]\!]^{Gr}$.
- *We define two constraints* inv *and* equiv *such that* inv(Σ) *is true in* $\mathcal{M}$ *whenever* $[\![\Sigma]\!]^{Gr}$ *is an* I_{logic} *state (representation) of the logical semantics, and* equiv(Σ_1, Σ_2) *whenever* $[\![(\Sigma_1, \Sigma_2)]\!]^{Gr}$ *is a pair of states (representations)* (s_1, s_2) *of the logical semantics such that* $s_1 \approx_{logic} s_2$.
- freshVars(L,T) *is true in* $\mathcal{M}$ *whenever* L *is a list of all different variables names, none of which occur in the term* T*;* freshVars(L_1,L_2,T) *abbreviates* freshVars(L_{12},T)) *where* L_{12} *is the concat. of* L_1 *and* L_2.

Definitions 5 and 6 comprise the first steps towards a simulation of the logic-based semantics, and we continue with the last part, the transition relation.

Definition 7. *Consider a (lifted version of a) pre-application* $H_1 \backslash H_2$ `<=>` $G \,|\, C$ *with local variables* L *and a consistent meta level state* (S WHERE M) *with* $S = \langle H_1 \uplus H_2 \uplus S^+, B^+ \rangle$ *and*

$$\mathcal{M} \;\models\; M \rightarrow \big(\mathtt{inv}(S) \wedge \boxdot B^+ \wedge \boxdot(B^+ \rightarrow \exists_L G) \wedge \mathtt{freshVars}(L, S)\big).$$

Then the following is a meta level transition by rule application.

$$S \text{ WHERE } M \quad \longmapsto^{meta}_{logic} \quad \langle H_1 \uplus C \uplus S^+, G \wedge B^+ \rangle \text{ WHERE } M$$

Consider a (lifted version of a) built-in b *of* $\mathcal{B}$ *and a consistent meta level state* (S WHERE M) *with* $S = \langle \{b\} \uplus S^+, B^+ \rangle$ *and*

$$\mathcal{M} \;\models\; M \;\rightarrow\; \big(\mathtt{inv}(S) \wedge \boxdot B^+\big).$$

Then the following is a meta level transition by built-in.

$$\langle \{b\} \uplus S^+, B^+ \rangle \text{ WHERE } M \quad \longmapsto^{meta}_{logic} \quad \langle S^+, b \wedge B^+ \rangle \text{ WHERE } M$$

Notice that for both sorts of transitions, the implication of $\boxdot B^+$ excludes transitions from failed and mixed states. For built-in transitions, the resulting states may be non-failed, failed or mixed.

Lemma 4. *For a given CHR program with* I_{logic} *and* $\approx_{logic}$*, the definitions of meta level states and transitions* $\longmapsto^{meta}_{logic}$*,* I^{meta}_{logic} *and* $\approx^{meta}_{logic}$*, together with* $[\![-]\!]^{meta}_{logic}$ *comprise an abstract simulation of the logic-based semantics.*

Transitions are not possible from a mixed or failed meta level state, but modal constraints are useful for restricting to the relevant substate, such that transitions are known to exists. This is expressed by the following propositions that are immediate consequences of the definitions.

Proposition 1. *Let* r: $H_1 \backslash H_2$ `<=>` $G \,|\, C$ *be a (lifted version of a) pre-application with local variables* L *and* $\Sigma = (\langle S, B \rangle$ WHERE $M)$ *a meta level state with* $H_1 \uplus H_2 \subseteq S$*. Whenever the meta level state* $\Sigma^{\boxdot} = (\langle S, B \rangle$ WHERE $M \wedge \widehat{M})$ *is consistent, with* $\widehat{M} = \mathtt{inv}(\langle S, B \rangle) \wedge \boxdot B \wedge \boxdot(B \rightarrow \exists_L G) \wedge \mathtt{freshVars}(L, \Sigma)$*, there exists a meta level rule application by* r*,*

$$\Sigma^{\boxdot} \quad \longmapsto^{meta}_{logic} \quad \langle S \backslash H_2 \uplus C, B \wedge G \rangle \text{ WHERE } M \wedge \widehat{M}.$$

Furthermore, $\Sigma^{\boxdot}$ *is the greatest substate of* Σ *to which* r *can apply.*

Proposition 2. *Let* b *be a (lifted version of a) built-in and* $\Sigma = (\langle S, B \rangle$ WHERE $M)$ *a meta level state with* $b \in S$*. When* $\Sigma^{\boxdot} = (\langle S, B \rangle$ WHERE $M \wedge \widehat{M})$ *is consistent, with* $\widehat{M^{\boxdot}} = \mathtt{inv}(\langle S, B \rangle) \wedge \boxdot B \wedge \boxdot(B \rightarrow b)$*, there is a meta level trans.,*

$$\Sigma^{\boxdot} \quad \longmapsto^{meta}_{logic} \quad \langle S \backslash \{b\}, B \wedge b \rangle \text{ WHERE } M \wedge \widehat{M^{\boxdot}}.$$

Whenever $\Sigma^{\text{☹}} = (\langle S, B\rangle\ \text{WHERE}\ M \wedge \widehat{M^{\text{☹}}})$ *is consistent, with* $\widehat{M^{\text{☹}}} = \mathtt{inv}(\langle S, B\rangle) \wedge \text{☺}B \wedge \text{☹}(B \to b)$, *there is a meta level transition by* b,

$$\Sigma^{\text{☹}} \quad \longmapsto^{meta}_{logic} \quad \langle S \backslash \{b\}, B \wedge b\rangle\ \text{WHERE}\ M \wedge \widehat{M^{\text{☹}}}.$$

The state $\Sigma^{\text{☺}}$ *(resp.* $\Sigma^{\text{☹}}$*) is the greatest substate of* Σ *for which the meta level transition by* b *leads to a non-failure and non-mixed (resp. failed) state.*

With Propositions 1 and 2 in mind, we define meta level critical corners from the critical corners of Definition 4.

Definition 8. *Let* $\langle S_1, B_1\rangle \leftarrowtail_{logic} \langle S_0, B_0\rangle \mapsto_{logic} \langle S_2, B_2\rangle$ *be a (lifted version of a) critical* α *pre-corner given by Definition 4, in which the leftmost (rightmost) rule application has local variables* L_1 *(*L_2*) and guard* G_1 *(*G_2*). Assume* S^+ *and* B^+ *are fresh meta level variables and let, for* $i = 0, 1, 2$,

$$\begin{aligned} \Sigma_i &= \langle S_i \uplus S^+, B_i \wedge B^+\rangle \\ M &= \mathtt{inv}(\Sigma_0) \wedge \text{☺}B_0 \wedge \text{☺}(B_0 \wedge B^+ \to \exists_{L_1} G_1) \wedge \text{☺}(B_0 \wedge B^+ \to \exists_{L_2} G_2) \wedge \\ &\quad\ \mathtt{freshVars}(L_1, L_2, \Sigma) \end{aligned}$$

When $(\Sigma_0\ \text{WHERE}\ M)$ *is consistent, the following is* a critical meta level α corner.

$$(\Sigma_1\ \text{WHERE}\ M) \quad \leftarrowtail^{meta}_{logic} \quad (\Sigma_0\ \text{WHERE}\ M) \quad \longmapsto^{meta}_{logic} \quad (\Sigma_2\ \text{WHERE}\ M)$$

Example 6. (Continuing Example 4) The invariant is formalized at the meta level as states of the form $\langle\{\mathit{pred}(n)\}, \mathit{true}\rangle$ WHERE $\mathtt{type(int,}n\mathtt{)}$ where *pred* is one of `p`, `q` and `r`. Below is shown the non-joinable critical meta level corner generated by Definition 8. It is split-joinable as demonstrated by its splitting into two corners; each shown joinable by the indicated dotted transition. Let M stand for the meta-level constraint $\mathtt{type(int,}n\mathtt{)}$, M_1 for $M \wedge \text{☺}n \leq 0$ and M_2 for $M \wedge \text{☺}n > 0$.

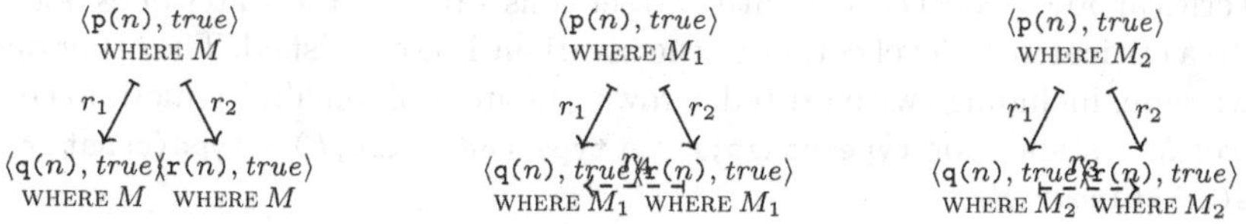

According to Lemma 5 shown below, the program is confluent.

When, furthermore, a state equivalence $\approx_{logic}$ is assumed, we need also show joinability of β corners, i.e., those composed by an equivalence and a transition.

Definition 9. *Let* $H \backslash H'$ `<=>` $G | C$ *be a (lifted version of a) variant of a rule with local variables* L. *Assume* S^+, B^+ *and* Σ_1 *are fresh meta-variables, and let*

$$\begin{aligned} \Sigma_0 &= \langle H \uplus H' \uplus S^+, B^+\rangle \qquad\qquad \Sigma_2 = \langle H \uplus C \uplus S^+, G \wedge B^+\rangle \\ M &= \mathtt{inv}(\Sigma_0) \wedge \text{☺}B \wedge \text{☺}(B \to \exists L G) \wedge \mathtt{freshVars}(L, \Sigma_0) \wedge \mathtt{equiv}(\Sigma_0, \Sigma_1) \end{aligned}$$

When $(\Sigma_0$ WHERE $M)$ *is consistent, the following is* a critical meta level β corner by rule application.

$$(\Sigma_1 \text{ WHERE } M) \approx^{meta}_{logic} (\Sigma_0 \text{ WHERE } M) \longmapsto^{meta}_{logic} (\Sigma_2 \text{ WHERE } M)$$

Let b be a (lifted version of a) built-in atom whose arguments are fresh variables. Assume S^+, B^+ and Σ_1 are fresh meta-variables, and let

$$\Sigma_0 = \langle\{b\}\uplus S^+, B^+\rangle \qquad\qquad \Sigma_2 = \langle S^+, b\wedge B^+\rangle$$
$$M = \mathtt{inv}(\Sigma_0) \wedge \boxdot B \wedge \mathtt{freshVars}(L,\Sigma_0) \wedge \mathtt{equiv}(\Sigma_0,\Sigma_1)$$

When $(\Sigma_0$ WHERE $M)$ *is consistent, the following is* a critical meta level β corner by built-in.

$$(\Sigma_1 \text{ WHERE } M) \approx^{meta}_{logic} (\Sigma_0 \text{ WHERE } M) \longmapsto^{meta}_{logic} (\Sigma_2 \text{ WHERE } M)$$

Lemma 5. *Let a terminating CHR program Π with invariant I_{logic} (and state quivalence $\approx_{logic}$) be given. Then Π is confluent (modulo $\approx_{logic}$) if and only if its set of critical corners (Definitions 8–9) is split-joinable w.r.t. I^{meta}_{logic} (modulo $\approx^{meta}_{logic}$).*

Example 7. (Cont. Example 3; adapted from [8]). The invariant is formalized at the meta level as states of the form

$$\langle\{\mathtt{set}(L)\}\uplus S, true\rangle \text{ WHERE } \mathtt{type(constList},L)\wedge\mathtt{type(constItems},S);$$

we assume types $\mathtt{const}$ for all constants, $\mathtt{constList}$ for all lists of such, and $\mathtt{constItems}$ for sets of constraints of the form $\mathtt{item}(c)$ where c is a constant.

The state equivalence is formalized at the meta level as the relationships of states of the following form, where $\mathtt{perm}(L_1,L_2)$ means that L_1 and L_2 are lists being permutations of each other; and $M^\approx$ stands for $\mathtt{type(constList},L_1)\wedge$ $\mathtt{type(constList},L_1)\wedge\mathtt{perm}(L_1,L_2)\wedge\mathtt{type(constItems},S)$,

$$\langle\{\mathtt{set}(L_1)\}\uplus S, true\rangle \text{ WHERE } M^\approx \quad \approx^{meta}_{logic} \quad \langle\{\mathtt{set}(L_2)\}\uplus S, true\rangle \text{ WHERE } M^\approx$$

The critical object level corner with two set constraints in the states does not give rise to a critical meta level corner as the invariant is not satisfied. The other one is shown here, including (with dotted arrows) its proof of joinability modulo equivalence; M^α stands for $\mathtt{type(const},x_1) \wedge \mathtt{type(constList},L) \wedge \mathtt{type(const},x_2) \wedge \mathtt{type(constItems},S)$.

$$\langle\{\mathtt{item}(x_1),\mathtt{set}(L),\mathtt{item}(x_2)\}\uplus S, true\rangle \text{ WHERE } M^\alpha$$

$\langle\{\mathtt{set}([x_1|L]),\mathtt{item}(x_2)\}\uplus S, true\rangle$ WHERE M^α $\qquad$ $\langle\{\mathtt{item}(x_1),\mathtt{set}([x_2|L]),\}\uplus S, true\rangle$ WHERE M^α

$\langle\{\mathtt{set}([x_2,x_1|L])\}\uplus S, true\rangle$ WHERE M^α $\approx\!\approx\!\approx\!\approx$ $\langle\{\mathtt{set}([x_1,x_2|L])\}\uplus S, true\rangle$ WHERE M^α

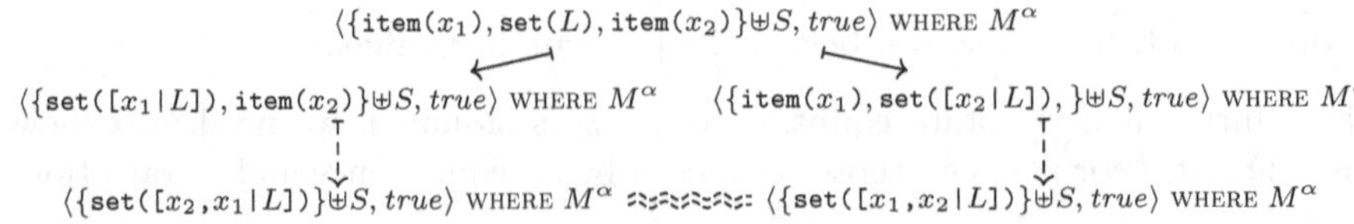

We consider the following critical meta level β corner. M^β stands for $\mathtt{type(const},x)\wedge\mathtt{type(constList},L_1)\wedge\mathtt{type(constList},L_2)\wedge\mathtt{perm}(L_1,L_2)\wedge\mathtt{type}$ $(\mathtt{constItems},S)$.

$\langle \{\texttt{item}(x), \texttt{set}(L_1)\} \uplus S, \mathit{true} \rangle$ WHERE M^β

$\langle \{\texttt{item}(x), \texttt{set}(L_2)\} \uplus S, \mathit{true} \rangle$ WHERE M^β $\quad$ $\langle \{\texttt{set([}x\,|\,L_1\texttt{])}\} \uplus S, \mathit{true} \rangle$ WHERE M^β

$\langle \{\texttt{set([}x\,|\,L_2\texttt{])}\} \uplus S, \mathit{true} \rangle$ WHERE M^β

All critical corners are joinable modulo equivalence, and since the program is obviously terminating, Lemma 5 gives that the program is confluent mod. equiv.

7 Conclusion

We generalized the critical pair approach using a meta level simulation to prove confluence under invariant and modulo equivalence for Constraint Handling Rules. We have demonstrated how this principle makes it possible to express natural invariants and equivalences, that cannot be expressed in CHR itself, in a formal way at the meta level, anticipating machine supported proofs using a meta level constraint solver, based on a ground representation. A constraint solver is currently under development, partly inspired by [5]. Depending on the complexity of the invariants and equivalences – and of the CHR programs under investigation – it may be difficult to obtain a complete solver.

For simplicity of notation, we did not include mechanisms to prevent loops caused by propagation rules; [8] has included this in a meta level representation for the Prolog based semantics, and is easily adapted for the logic based semantics exposed in the present paper. For comparison with earlier work on confluence for CHR, we used here a logic-based CHR semantics, which has nice theoretical properties, but is incompatible with standard implementations of CHR and applies only for a limited set of programs. In [9], we have defined meta level constraints and a simulation for an alternative CHR semantics [7,8] that reflects CHR's Prolog based implementation, including a correct handling of Prolog's non-logical devices (e.g., `var/1`, `nonvar/2`, `is/2`) and runtime errors.

The abstract simulations used for the classical CHR confluence results are special cases of abstract interpretations, but when invariants are introduced – or when considering full CHR including Prolog-style non-logical devices, cf. [9] – this correspondence does not hold. The concept of abstract simulations and their use for proving confluence (mod. equiv.) seem obvious to investigate for a large variety of rewrite based systems, e.g., constrained term rewriting, conditional term rewriting, interactive theorem provers, and rule-based specifications of abstract algorithms.

Acknowledgement. We thank the anonymous reviewers for their insightful comments, suggesting to compare with a transformational approach, cf. Example 5, and helping us to clarify the relationship between abstract simulation and abstract interpretation.

References

1. Abdennadher, S.: Operational semantics and confluence of constraint propagation rules. In: Smolka, G. (ed.) CP 1997. LNCS, vol. 1330, pp. 252–266. Springer, Heidelberg (1997). https://doi.org/10.1007/BFb0017444
2. Abdennadher, S., Frühwirth, T., Meuss, H.: On confluence of constraint handling rules. In: Freuder, E.C. (ed.) CP 1996. LNCS, vol. 1118, pp. 1–15. Springer, Heidelberg (1996). https://doi.org/10.1007/3-540-61551-2_62
3. Abdennadher, S., Frühwirth, T.W., Meuss, H.: Confluence and semantics of constraint simplification rules. Constraints **4**(2), 133–165 (1999)
4. Baader, F., Nipkow, T.: Term rewriting and all that. Cambridge University Press, Cambridge (1999)
5. Christiansen, H.: Automated reasoning with a constraint-based metainterpreter. J. Logic Program. **37**(1–3), 213–254 (1998)
6. Christiansen, H., Kirkeby, M.: Confluence of CHR revisited: invariants and modulo equivalence. [Extended version with proofs], Computer Science Research Report, vol. 153. Roskilde University, October 2018. https://forskning.ruc.dk/files/63000759/ChrKir_LOPSTR2018_ExtReport.pdf
7. Christiansen, H., Kirkeby, M.H.: Confluence modulo equivalence in constraint handling rules. In: Proietti, M., Seki, H. (eds.) LOPSTR 2014. LNCS, vol. 8981, pp. 41–58. Springer, Cham (2015). https://doi.org/10.1007/978-3-319-17822-6_3
8. Christiansen, H., Kirkeby, M.H.: On proving confluence modulo equivalence for constraint handling rules. Formal Aspects Comput. **29**(1), 57–95 (2017)
9. Christiansen, H., Kirkeby, M.H.: Towards a constraint solver for proving confluence with invariant and equivalence of realistic CHR programs. In: WFLP, LNCS, vol. 11285 (2018, to appear)
10. Cousot, P., Cousot, R.: Abstract interpretation: a unified lattice model for static analysis of programs by construction or approximation of fixpoints. POPL **1977**, 238–252 (1977)
11. Curien, P.-L., Ghelli, G.: On confluence for weakly normalizing systems. In: Book, R.V. (ed.) RTA 1991. LNCS, vol. 488, pp. 215–225. Springer, Heidelberg (1991). https://doi.org/10.1007/3-540-53904-2_98
12. Duck, G.J., Stuckey, P.J., de la Banda, M.G., Holzbaur, C.: The refined operational semantics of constraint handling rules. In: Demoen, B., Lifschitz, V. (eds.) ICLP 2004. LNCS, vol. 3132, pp. 90–104. Springer, Heidelberg (2004). https://doi.org/10.1007/978-3-540-27775-0_7
13. Duck, G.J., Stuckey, P.J., Sulzmann, M.: Observable confluence for constraint handling rules. In: Dahl, V., Niemelä, I. (eds.) ICLP 2007. LNCS, vol. 4670, pp. 224–239. Springer, Heidelberg (2007). https://doi.org/10.1007/978-3-540-74610-2_16
14. Frühwirth, T.W.: User-defined constraint handling. In: ICLP 1993, pp. 837–838. MIT Press (1993)
15. Frühwirth, T.W.: Theory and practice of constraint handling rules. J. Logic Program. **37**(1–3), 95–138 (1998)
16. Frühwirth, T.W.: Constraint Handling Rules. Cambridge University Press, New York (2009)
17. Gall, D., Frühwirth, T.: Confluence modulo equivalence with invariants in constraint handling rules. In: Gallagher, J.P., Sulzmann, M. (eds.) FLOPS 2018. LNCS, vol. 10818, pp. 116–131. Springer, Cham (2018). https://doi.org/10.1007/978-3-319-90686-7_8

18. Hill, P., Gallagher, J.: Meta-programming in logic programming. In: Handbook of Logic in Artificial Intelligence and Logic Programming, pp. 421–497. Oxford Science Publications, Oxford University Press (1994)
19. Hill, P.M., Lloyd, J.W.: Analysis of meta-programs. In: Meta-Programming in Logic Programming, pp. 23–51. The MIT Press (1988)
20. Holzbaur, C., Frühwirth, T.W.: A PROLOG constraint handling rules compiler and runtime system. Appl. Artif. Intell. **14**(4), 369–388 (2000)
21. Huet, G.P.: Confluent reductions: abstract properties and applications to term rewriting systems. J. ACM **27**(4), 797–821 (1980)
22. Jaffar, J., Lassez, J.: Constraint logic programming. In: Symposium on Principles of Programming Languages. POPL 1987, pp. 111–119. ACM Press (1987)
23. Kirkeby, M.H., Christiansen, H.: Confluence and convergence modulo equivalence in probabilistically terminating reduction systems. Int. J. Approximate Reasoning **105**, 217–228 (2019)
24. Langbein, J., Raiser, F., Frühwirth, T.W.: A state equivalence and confluence checker for CHRs. In: Proceedings of the International Workshop on Constraint Handling Rules, Report CW 588, pp. 1–8. Katholieke Universiteit Leuven, Belgium (2010)
25. Newman, M.: On theories with a combinatorial definition of "equivalence". Ann. Math. **43**(2), 223–243 (1942)
26. Park, D.M.R.: Concurrency and automata on infinite sequences. In: Proceedings of the Theoretical Computer Science, 5th GI-Conference, pp. 167–183 (1981)
27. Raiser, F., Betz, H., Frühwirth, T.W.: Equivalence of CHR states revisited. In: Proceedings of the International Workshop on Constraint Handling Rules, Report CW 555, pp. 33–48. Katholieke Universiteit Leuven, Belgium (2009)
28. Schrijvers, T., Demoen, B.: The K.U.Leuven CHR system: Implementation and Application. In: Workshop on Constraint Handling Rules: Selected Contributions, pp. 1–5. Ulmer Informatik-Berichte, Nr. 2004–01 (2004)

Analysis of Logic Programming

Compiling Control as Offline Partial Deduction

Vincent Nys(✉) and Danny De Schreye

KU Leuven, Leuven, Belgium
{vincent.nys,danny.deschreye}@kuleuven.be

Abstract. We present a new approach to a technique known as compiling control, whose aim is to compile away special mechanisms for non-standard atom selection in logic programs. It has previously been conjectured that compiling control could be implemented as an instance of the first Futamura projection, in which an interpreter is specialized for an input program. However, the exact nature of such an interpreter and of the required technique for specialization were never specified. In this work, we propose a Prolog meta-interpreter which applies the desired non-standard selection rule and which is amenable to specialization using offline partial deduction. After the initial analysis phase of compiling control, we collect annotations to specialize the interpreter using the Logen system for offline partial deduction. We also show that the result of the specialization is equivalent to the program obtained using the traditional approach to compiling control. In this way, we simplify the synthesis step.

Keywords: Compiling control · Offline partial deduction · Coroutines · First Futamura projection

1 Introduction

Compiling control is a program transformation technique which aims to compile the runtime behavior of pure logic programs executed under a non-standard selection rule to logic programs which are totally equivalent under the standard, left-to-right selection rule of Prolog. It was originally presented in [1,2]. The technique is designed to work in two phases. In a first phase, the computation flow of the program, executed under the non-standard rule, is analyzed, resulting in a symbolic evaluation tree that captures the entire flow. In a second phase, from the symbolic evaluation tree, a new logic program is synthesized. The technique was formalized and proven correct under certain technical conditions, but it possessed certain drawbacks. Most importantly, it was an ad hoc solution. Because of this, showing that the analysis phase of the transformation was complete for a specific program required a manual proof by induction. However, since the original presentation of compiling control, several frameworks have been developed which provide a more formal perspective on the two phases of compiling control and whose general correctness results can be reused. Most notably, abstract interpretation [3] and partial deduction [4,5]. In [6], we showed that the technique could

F. Mesnard and P. J. Stuckey (Eds.): LOPSTR 2018, LNCS 11408, pp. 115–131, 2019.
https://doi.org/10.1007/978-3-030-13838-7_7

in some cases be reformulated and formalized using abstract conjunctive partial deduction, a framework proposed in [7] which integrates the aforementioned frameworks. In addition, we proposed a new abstraction, *multi*, to analyze computations with unboundedly growing goals. This allowed us to analyze a diverse set of well-known programs and to compile these into programs executed under the standard selection rule. Unfortunately, the *multi* abstraction also broke an explicit assumption of the abstract conjunctive partial deduction framework. In the current work, we propose a different perspective. We show that the synthesis obtained using the previously published approach can also be obtained by applying the first Futamura projection, in which program specialization is applied to an interpreter and an input program. Such an approach has been speculated upon in the past, but the current work is the first that demonstrates that this is indeed feasible. It is not an instance of the abstract conjunctive partial deduction framework, but rather a standard offline partial deduction, which implies that no changes to the abstract conjunctive partial deduction framework are necessary to relax the aforementioned assumption which is not met. Based on our experiments, there are no programs which can be compiled using the classical approach but not the approach presented here.

The idea of applying the first Futamura projection to obtain a more structured representation of control flow can also be found in [8], where Java bytecode is decompiled to Prolog. The notion of modelling and analyzing the execution of a (PIC) program as a logic program and partially evaluating that can be found in [9]. This is akin to what we do, though we abstractly analyze the program to be executed itself, which is already a logic program, and partially evaluate the interpreter. Other examples of specialization of logic program interpreters, also using the Logen system, are provided in [10].

We will first give a brief introduction to the first Futamura projection and to offline partial deduction in Sect. 2. Then, we will provide a motivating example. We will explain the notation and operations shown in the motivating example by introducing our abstract domain in Sect. 4. We will use the abstract domain to express the scope of the technique in Sect. 5. Next, in Sect. 6, we will round out the analysis for the first example program. We will also show a simple meta-interpreter which, using information obtained from the analysis, can be configured to implement the desired non-standard selection rule. Once the basic idea has been illustrated, we will show the most interesting parts of the analysis of a more complex program, as well as extensions to the meta-interpreter required to run this program in a satisfactory way in Sect. 8. In Sect. 9, we will show how the meta-interpreter can be specialized using the Logen system for offline partial deduction. Then, in Sect. 10, we will show that the obtained specialization is indeed equivalent to the "classical" synthesis. We wrap up with a discussion and with avenues for future work. A set of example programs along with corresponding analyses and syntheses using both techniques is available as an electronic appendix at https://perswww.kuleuven.be/~u0055408/cc-as-opd.html.

2 Preliminaries

In [11], Futamura showed that partially evaluating an interpreter for a language l_1 (written in language l_2) for a "source program" (in l_1) yields an "object program" (in l_2) with the semantics of the source program, as run by the interpreter. That is, partially evaluating an interpreter for a source program is an act of compiling.

This is expressed by the following equation: $int(s, r) = \alpha(int, s)(r)$. Here, *int* is the function encoded by the interpreter. Its arguments s and r are the "static" and "runtime" inputs, i.e. inputs which remain constant and which may vary between executions, respectively. In the setting of partial evaluation of an interpreter, the "static" input is the program to be interpreted, whereas the "runtime" input is the input to the interpreted program. The function α is the partial evaluation function: it specializes its first argument for the static input. In this setting, this produces a program which takes the runtime inputs, so r, and behaves as the interpreter would when also given s. Therefore $\alpha(int, s)$ is the compiled version of the source program which Futamura calls the "object program". The observation that a compiled program can be obtained through specialization of an interpreter is known as the first Futamura projection [12].

Partial deduction is a technique for logic program specialization originally introduced in [4] and formalized in [13]. The idea behind partial deduction is to compute a set of derivation trees for some top level goal A such that all expected queries instantiate A. The computations represented by the branches of these trees can then be collected into logical implications, referred to as "resultants". These are then encoded as logic program clauses, so that a program is obtained which is equivalent to the original program for all queries which instantiate A, but not necessarily for other queries.

An important notion is "closedness". Under closedness, all atoms in a partial deduction are instances of an atom in the root of a derivation tree. This implies that a goal is never reduced to a goal that has not been specialized and that completeness is ensured. Because the set of all roots of trees is denoted $\mathcal{A}$, this is also referred to as $\mathcal{A}$-closedness.

There are two broad approaches for dealing with the issue of control [14]. In "online partial deduction", control is tackled during the specialization phase itself. That is, the construction of SLDNF-trees is monitored and unfolding continues as long as there is evidence that interesting computations are performed.

Offline partial deduction is different in that control decisions are taken before the specialization phase. These are then cast in the form of program annotations for the specializer. During the specialization phase, unfolding proceeds in a left-to-right fashion. Broadly speaking, depending on the annotation of a call, it may be unfolded, it may be treated as an instance of a specialized atom or it may be kept residual. Given the annotations, specialization is straightforward. Annotations can be written manually, but can also be derived automatically in a separate phase. This phase is referred to as a "binding-time analysis" and is performed before the static input is available.

The above concepts and techniques can be generalized to "conjunctive partial deduction". In conjunctive partial deduction, the roots and leaves of derivation trees need not be atoms, but can also be conjunctions. This adds a layer of complexity: While partial deduction splits up conjunctions into atoms before starting new SLDNF-trees, conjunctive partial deduction has more options for splitting them into subconjunctions.

3 Running Example: Permutation Sort

To introduce the essential components of compiling control, we will use a motivating example. The following is a Prolog implementation of permutation sort, which sorts a list by permuting it and then checking if the permutation is ordered correctly.

```
permsort(X,Y) :- perm(X,Y), ord(Y).
perm([],[]).
perm([X|Y],[U|V]) :- select(U,[X|Y],W), perm(W,V).
ord([]).
ord([X]).
ord([X,Y|Z]) :- X =< Y, ord([Y|Z]).
```

While this sorting program clearly expresses the declarative perspective on sorting as creating an ordered permutation, its naive implementation is problematic. Its efficiency can be improved by using a different selection rule. Informally, such a selection rule interleaves calls which build the permutation with calls which check for the correct ordering of elements. Specifically, as soon as the first two elements of the permutation have been generated, their ordering can be checked. Figures 1 and 2 can be considered as symbolic derivation trees representing a computation under this more efficient selection rule. In these figures, a value a_i, where i is a natural number, stands for any term, whereas a value g_j, where j is also a natural number, stands for a ground term. When an atom is underlined once, we consider the effects of resolving said atom. If it is underlined twice, we treat it as a built-in. The reader is not intended to understand every

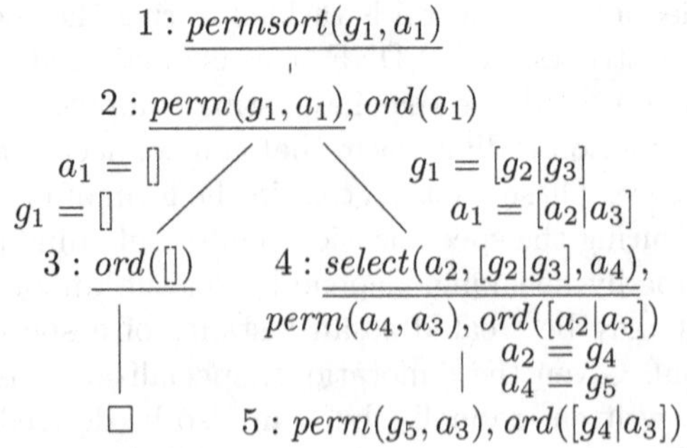

Fig. 1. First analysis tree for permutation sort

aspect of the two trees at this point. They are only intended to give an idea of the type of computation the synthesized program should execute. In the following sections, we will provide formal underpinnings for the data and operations in these symbolic trees and will explain how they can be used to synthesize a program which simulates the program with the desired selection rule.

4 Abstract Domain

The trees shown in Sect. 3 constitute the analysis phase of compiling control, which is a form of abstract interpretation. This abstract interpretation remains entirely the same as in [6]. We reproduce the key points here.

As any abstract interpretation, the analysis phase is based on an abstract domain, whose elements represent *sets* of *concrete* values with specific properties. The fundamental building blocks of the abstract domain are two types of abstract variables, a_i and g_j. An abstract variable a_i represents the set of all concrete values, whereas a variable g_j represents all ground concrete values. The union of these two sets is denoted $AVar_P$.

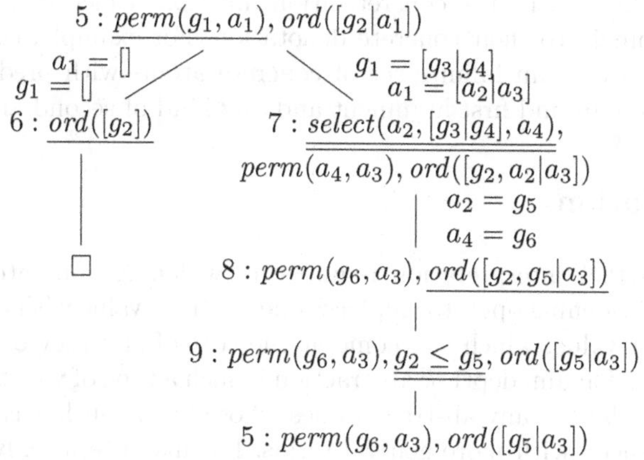

Fig. 2. Second analysis tree for permutation sort

Abstract counterparts to concrete program constants are included in the abstract domain. These represent the singleton sets consisting of the corresponding concrete constants. This is why, in the example in Sect. 3, the empty list [] occurs as an argument. From these abstract variables and abstract constants, abstract terms, abstract atoms and abstract conjunctions are constructed, yielding the sets $ATerm_P$, $AAtom_P$ and $AConAtom_P$. Example members of these sets are $[g_2|g_3]$, $permsort(g_1, a_1)$ and $perm(g_1, a_1), ord(a_1)$, respectively. If an abstract term, atom or conjunction contains some a_i or g_j several times (i.e. the occurrences have the same subscript), then the represented concrete term, atom or conjunction contains the *same* subterm at every position corresponding to the positions of a_i or g_j. For instance, in the second node in the running example, the result of the permutation operation, a_1, must be ordered. Note that two abstract variables a_i and g_j, when $i = j$, are not assumed to be aliased.

Let $ATerm_{P/\approx}$, $AAtom_{P/\approx}$ and $AConAtom_{P/\approx}$ denote the sets of equivalence classes of abstract terms, abstract atoms and abstract conjunctions, respectively. Equivalence of abstract terms (or atoms or conjunctions) is based on abstract substitutions, which are finite sets of ordered pairs in $AVar_P \times ATerm_P$ and whose application instantiates abstract variables in a way that is analogous to how applying substitutions in the concrete domain instantiate concrete variables. Two abstract terms (or atoms or conjunctions) A and B are equivalent, denoted $A \approx B$, if and only if there are abstract substitutions θ_1 and θ_2 such that $A\theta_1 = B$ and $B\theta_2 = A$.

The abstract domain, $ADom_P$, is the union of $AVar_P$, $ATerm_{P/\approx}$ $AAtom_{P/\approx}$ and $AConAtom_{P/\approx}$ (leaving aside the *multi* abstraction until Sect. 8). Note that we will refer to an equivalence class by taking a representative. For instance, we write $permsort(g_1, a_1)$ when we mean "all abstract atoms equivalent to $permsort(g_1, a_1)$" and assume that the intended meaning is clear from the context. Finally, let Dom_P be the concrete domain and let $\gamma : ADom_P \rightarrow 2^{Dom_P}$ be the concretization function, which maps elements of the abstract domain to their concrete denotation. For example, the denotation of $permsort(g_1, a_1)$ is an infinite set of concrete atoms with predicate symbol *permsort*, with a ground first argument and any kind of second argument.

5 Instantiation

In general, abstract interpretation requires a "widening" operator to achieve termination. A widening operator replaces one abstract value with another, more general abstract value, which can come at the cost of accuracy of the analysis. For our abstract domain, depth-k abstraction is such a type of widening. Depth-k abstraction entails that any abstract values whose term depth exceeds a certain limit k are replaced with more general terms. For instance, if only one level of term nesting is allowed and the atom $ord([g_1, g_2|a_1])$ is computed, this term must be generalized. The most specific term which does not exceed the nesting limit is $ord([g_1|a_2])$. If such a widening were applied in the running example, the resulting synthesis would not simulate the desired selection rule. In general, applying depth-k abstraction *may* affect the correctness of the technique, depending on the program and the level of nesting which is allowed. In what follows, we will assume that depth-k abstraction is not required for termination.

The abstract domain is also tied to the selection rule. We assume that the selection rule is an instantiation based selection rule, which is defined as follows:

Definition (*instantiation-based selection rule*). An instantiation-based selection rule for P is a strict partial order $<$ on $AAtom_{P/\approx}$, such that $\gamma(s_1) \subset \gamma(s_2)$ implies $s_2 \nless s_1$, where $\subset$ denotes strict set inclusion.

An instantiation-based selection rule expresses which atom is selected from an abstract conjunction. Our technique requires that an instantiation-based selection rule can completely specify the desired control flow. This is formalized as follows.

Definition (*complete instantiation-based selection rule*). An instantiation-based selection rule for a program P is complete if, for each $A \in ACon_{P/\approx}$, there exists an abstract atom b in A, such that $\forall c \in A : c \not\approx b \Rightarrow b < c$.

Definition (*selection by a complete instantiation-based selection rule*). Let $A \in AConAtom_{P/\approx}$. Then, the abstract atom selected from A by $<$ is the leftmost abstract atom b, such that $\forall c \in A : c \not\approx b \Rightarrow b < c$.

In the running example, a complete instantiation-based selection rule contains a pair $(ord([g_1, g_2|a_1]), perm(g_1, a_1))$. There is no aliasing between the elements. That is, this ordered pair has the same meaning as $(ord([g_1, g_2|a_1]), perm(g_3, a_2))$.

We assume that fully evaluated abstract atoms are dealt with in left-to-right order. We also assume that fully evaluated abstract atoms which can be fully evaluated are selected before those which can be unfolded.[1] Under the assumption that more instantiated atoms are always ordered before less instantiated ones, we will represent $<$ by its generating set, *Preprior*. The selection rule $<$ itself is inferred from *Preprior* using the assumptions about fully evaluated abstract atoms and the fact that $<$ is transitive. For our running example, formally, *Preprior* contains the pairs $perm(g_1, a_1) < ord([g_1|a_1])$ and $ord([g_1, g_2|a_1]) < perm(g_1, a_1)$.

6 The Analysis Phase

The analysis consists of a number of abstract derivation trees whose roots are all in a finite set $\mathcal{A}$ of abstract conjunctions. The first of these conjunctions is the abstract conjunction representing the intended call pattern, e.g. $permsort(g_1, a_1)$. The leaves of these trees are also in $\mathcal{A}$, or they are empty. Atoms underlined once are selected by the non-standard selection rule and an abstraction of resolution is applied to them. Atoms underlined twice represent atoms which, in a concrete computation, are selected, but an abstraction of resolution is not applied to them. Instead, these atoms are considered to be completely executed and the result of this execution is collected in a set of output bindings. That is, the evaluation of such atoms is not interleaved with that of other atoms and we are therefore only interested in the effects they have on the remaining atoms.

[1] Both assumptions pertaining to fully evaluated atoms are strictly for notational convenience.

7 A Suitable Meta-interpreter

If each abstract conjunction in Figs. 1 and 2 is assigned the number in front of the conjunction as an identifier and the empty goal is assigned the atom "empty", a simple meta-interpreter can run permutation sort under the desired selection rule.

```
compute(Gs) :- mi(Gs,1).
mi([],_).
mi([G|Gs],State) :-
  selected_index(State,Idx),
  divide_goals([G|Gs],Idx,Before,Selected,After),
  mi_clause(Selected,Body,RuleIdx),
  state_transition(State,NewState,RuleIdx),
  append(Before,Body,NewGsA),
  append(NewGsA,After,NewGs),
  mi(NewGs,NewState).
mi([G|Gs],State) :-
  selected_index(State,Idx),
  divide_goals([G|Gs],Idx,Before,Selected,After),
  mi_full_eval(Selected,FullAIIdx),
  call(Selected),
  state_transition(State,NewState,FullAIIdx),
  append(Before,After,NewGs),
  mi(NewGs,NewState).
divide_goals(Goals,Idx,Before,Selected,After) :-
  length(Before,Idx),
  append(Before,[Selected|After],Goals).
```

Here, $mi/2$ is the meta-interpretation predicate. It takes a concrete conjunction and a state. The initial call is $compute([permsort(G, A)])$ where G is instantiated to a ground value and A can be any value. The $mi\_clause/3$ predicate encodes clauses as a head, a list of body atoms and a unique identifier for the clause. The $mi\_full\_eval/2$ predicate identifies fully evaluated goals, e.g. $mi\_full\_eval(select(X, Y, Z), fullai1)$ to remove an element X from a list Y, which yields Z. The $selected\_index/2$ predicate supplies the index of the atom to be selected in a particular state. The meta-interpreter itself does not inspect groundness or aliasing characteristics of conjunctions. Such characteristics are derived during the analysis phase. The $state\_transition/3$ predicate expresses which states are directly reachable from which other states and which rules cause the transitions. The full code is in the electronic appendix.

7.1 Instantiation of the First Futamura Projection

Using Logen, the interpreter can be specialized for $mi([permsort(X, Y)], 1)$. We cannot express to Logen that X will be instantiated to a ground value, but the control flow is already encoded in $selected\_index/2$ and $state\_transition/3$.

Therefore, the result of the specialization will still be a compiled program with the desired control flow.

With regard to the equation $int(s, r) = \alpha(int, s)(r)$, the vector s is described in [11] as "a source program and information needed for syntax analysis and semantic analysis". As such, the selection rule is a component of s in addition to the source program, P. Because the program should work for multiple input queries, a program's top-level goal is considered a runtime input. However, a top-level goal instantiated by all runtime top-level goals is a static input. Hence, such a goal is a component of s, even if P is not intended to be run with this goal directly. This is what allows logic programs to be specialized for certain top-level calls. Groundness characteristics of the query pattern can also be considered as static information. This is not done in partial deduction of pure logic programs, but we have to take it into account for our approach.

To this end, the compiling control analysis can be encoded as a component of s. Because it provides all required information about the static inputs to the meta-interpreter, there is no need to provide those as direct inputs to the evaluator as well. However, it does *not* necessarily contain enough information about predicates not involved in the coroutining control flow. That is, certain predicates may be fully evaluated during the analysis phase even if their definition is part of the source program, so the source program is also a component of s. The analysis completely specifies the local and global control for a conjunctive partial deduction of P under the semantics implemented by int. In light of the first Futamura projection, an offline partial evaluation of the interpreter must then produce a program equivalent to that produced by the synthesis step [6].[2] In other words, the "classical" synthesis step can be seen as a problem-specific shortcut to the outcome of the first Futamura projection.

8 Programs Requiring the *multi* Abstraction: Primes

The application of compiling control can be recast as an abstract conjunctive partial deduction [7] in the case of permutation sort. However, this does not hold for every program with an instantiation-based selection rule. This is due to the generation of abstract conjunctions of arbitrary length in some programs. Conjunctive partial deduction can deal with conjunctions of arbitrary length by splitting goals to obtain an $\mathcal{A}$-closed set. In our context, however, this would cause a loss of important information regarding aliasing between subconjunctions. The finite analysis of some coroutining programs therefore requires an addition to the abstract domain, known as the *multi* abstraction.

The formal details of this abstraction are quite elaborate. In brief, the concretization of an abstract conjunction containing a *multi* abstraction contains an infinite number of concrete conjunctions of arbitrary length, but with a structure

[2] We use "partial evaluation" rather than "partial deduction" for impure logic programs.

which follows a constrained pattern, expressed as a conjunction.[3] It is easier to illustrate the *multi* through an example first and to indicate the role each component plays rather than to define it beforehand. Here, we will use the following primes generator as an example:

```
primes(N,Primes) :-
  integers(2,I),sift(I,Primes),length(Primes,N)
integers(N,[]).
integers(N,[N|I]) :- plus(N,1,M),integers(M,I).
sift([N|Ints],[N|Primes]) :-
  filter(N,Ints,F),sift(F,Primes).
sift([],[]).
filter(N,[M|I],F) :- divides(N,M), filter(N,I,F).
filter(N,[M|I],[M|F]) :-
  does_not_divide(N,M), filter(N,I,F).
filter(N,[],[]).
length([],0).
length([H|T],N) :- minus(N,1,M),length(T,M).
```

This program is run with a top-level call $primes(N, P)$, where $N \in \mathbb{N}$.

Rather than list *Preprior* here in full, we will describe it in terms of a set $KA = \{integers(g_1, a_1), sift(a_1, a_2), filter(g_1, a_1, a_2), length(a_1, g_1)\}$. Two rules are sufficient to perform all the comparisons needed to complete the analysis phase: $\forall x \in KA : x \nless integers(g_1, a_1)$ and $\forall x \in AAtom_{P/\approx} : (\exists y \in KA : \gamma(x) \subset \gamma(y)) \Rightarrow \forall y \in KA : x < y$ (where $\subset$ denotes the strict subset relation).

With the resulting order $<$ and without further abstraction, the abstract analysis leads to the introduction of abstract conjunctions with an arbitrary number of $filter/3$ abstract atoms which are aliased in a consistent manner. Given that $\mathcal{A}$ must be finite and that the first argument of $primes/2$ can be an arbitrarily large number, adding a conjunction to $\mathcal{A}$ for every possible number of filters is not an option. Instead, we abstract away the precise number of filters by replacing the $filter/3$ abstract atoms with a *multi* abstraction, which represents any strictly positive natural number of filters. $multi(filter(g_{id,i,1}, a_{id,i,1}, a_{id,i,2}), \{a_{id,1,1} = a_1\}, \{a_{id,i+1,1} = a_{id,i,2}\}, \{a_{id,\mathcal{L},2} = a_2\})$, for example, denotes the following set of abstract conjunctions: $\{filter(g_{f_1}, a_1, a_2), filter(g_{f_1}, a_1, a_{f_1}) \wedge filter(g_{f_2}, a_{f_1}, a_2), filter(g_{f_1}, a_1, a_{f_1}) \wedge filter(g_{f_2}, a_{f_1}, a_{f_2}) \wedge filter(g_{f_3}, a_{f_2}, a_2), \ldots\}$ where every f_N is a unique index which does not occur for that variable type in the conjunction that the set member is part of. The first element of the *multi* abstraction is the conjunctive pattern. In the pattern, *id* represents an identifier unique to this *multi*. This is required as a single abstract conjunction can contain several *multi* abstractions, which need to be distinguished from one another, but whose variables can also be aliased in some cases. The i is symbolic and is not used in the pattern itself, but in the remaining arguments to *multi*, which are sets of constaints. The numeric

[3] In the most recent work on the analysis [6], we have assumed the pattern of a *multi* to be a conjunction. Known examples of other patterns are artificial. One is provided in the appendix.

index plays the same part as a regular abstract variable subscript, i.e. to indicate aliasing within an occurrence of the pattern. The second argument to *multi*, which is called *Init*, is a set of constraints which expresses the aliasing applied to certain variables in the first represented instance of the conjunctive pattern. Here, the symbolic i is replaced with 1 to indicate this. The third argument, *Consecutive*, expresses aliasing between consecutive occurrences of the pattern. The fourth, *Final*, expresses aliasing applied to variables in the last represented instance of the pattern. Here, the symbolic i is replaced with $\mathcal{L}$ (which stands for "last") to indicate this. When an instance of the pattern becomes eligible for abstract resolution, a case split is applied to the *multi* abstraction. The underlying intuition is that it represents either one or multiple occurrences of its pattern. For a more formal and detailed account of the *multi* abstraction, we refer to [6].

A specification of the control flow using *selected_index*/2 is no longer possible if the *multi* abstraction is required for analysis: in two different concrete instances of an abstract conjunction containing *multi*, the concrete atoms selected for resolution can be at different index positions. The solution, then, is to transform the program so that this is no longer the case. Transforming the interpreted program P into a different purely logical program which can be dealt with—at least through a simple transformation—is not an option. It is, however, possible to generalize the SLD-based execution mechanism implemented by the meta-interpreter in a way which still allows the results of partial deduction to be applied. The idea behind this is to introduce an additional operation, *grouping*, which transforms atoms into arguments of an atom with a special predicate symbol, *cmulti*. This operation does not affect the results of the program in any way, but strengthens the correspondence between the abstract analysis and a concrete execution. In this way, the length of *concrete* conjunctions also becomes bounded.

8.1 An Extended Meta-interpreter

The key modification to the meta-interpreter is the addition of the following clauses:

```
mi([G|Gs],State) :-
  selected_index(State,Idx),
  divide_goals([G|Gs],Idx,Before,
               cmulti([building_block(Patt1)]),
               After),
  state_transition(State,NewState,one),
  append(Patt1,After,NewGsA),
  append(Before,NewGsA,NewGs),
  mi(NewGs,NewState).
mi([G|Gs],State) :-
  selected_index(State,Idx),
  divide_goals([G|Gs],Idx,Before,
               cmulti([building_block(Patt1),
```

```
                              building_block(Patt2)|BBs]),
                   After),
  state_transition(State,NewState,many),
  append(Before,Patt1,NewGsA),
  append(NewGsA,[cmulti([building_block(Patt2)|BBs])],NewGsB),
  append(NewGsB,After,NewGs),
  mi(NewGs,NewState).
mi([G|Gs],State) :-
  grouping(State,NextState,Groupings),
  apply_groupings([G|Gs],Groupings,NewGs),
  mi(NewGs,NextState).
```

The first two of these clauses extract atoms from a concrete counterpart to a *multi* abstraction. The third one is the one which introduces the concrete counterpart to the *multi* abstraction during interpretation. It uses *apply_groupings*/3 to group certain concrete conjunctions in a concrete *cmulti* structure. The code for this operation is quite long, but it is sufficient to know that the second argument to *apply_groupings*/3 specifies, for a given state, which subconjunctions of the overall goal should be considered instantiations of a *multi* abstraction. This information is available from the abstract interpretation and is encoded using the *grouping*/3 predicate, which states which atom indices are grouped during the transition from one state to the next. For example, $grouping(54, 55, [[(2,3),(3,4)]])$ expresses that, in a concrete instance of the transition from state 54 to state 55, the atoms at index positions 2 (that is, from index position 2 to right before index 3) and 3 (that is, from index position 3 to right before index position 4) instantiate a *multi* and can be grouped together. Each instance of the pattern of the *multi* is further wrapped inside a *building_block* structure to easily extract a single instance of the pattern from the *cmulti* at a later point in the program. Code for the full meta-interpreter and the encoded primes generator, along with instructions on how to generate the analysis, is in the electronic appendix. In the following sections, we show how a specialization of the meta-interpreter can be obtained using Logen.

9 Specialization Using Logen

Logen is driven by annotations. Specifically, filter declarations and clause annotations. Filter declarations associate arguments of predicates with so-called "binding types". A binding type can be a binding *time*, e.g. "static" or "dynamic", but it can also restrict the structure of the argument. Clause annotations indicate how every call in a clause body should be treated during unfolding. For more detail, we refer to [15,16].

Our filter declarations require the following binding types: "static", "dynamic", "nonvar", "struct" and "list". The first two simply express whether or not an argument will be known at specialization time. The third expresses that an argument has some outermost structure during specialization. The fourth can specify an argument's functor and the binding types of its arguments.

The last binding type is for *closed* lists, i.e. lists whose length is bounded. A binding type can also be a disjunction, in which case an argument is considered to be an instance of the first applicable disjunct. The purpose of binding types is this: before a call to a predicate with certain binding types is specialized, the call is generalized and is used as the root of a partial derivation tree. The binding types determine to which extent the call is generalized. A static argument is not generalized, whereas a dynamic one is replaced with a variable.

All clause annotations for the current work can be written using the following strategies: "unfold", "call", "rescall" and "memo". The first means that an atom should be resolved. The second means that a call should be executed at specialization time, while the third means that it should be executed at runtime. The last one means that it should not be unfolded further, but that it should be used as the root for a new derivation tree.

9.1 Simple Meta-interpreter

For the simple meta-interpreter, we start from the naive program annotation performed by Logen. This annotates every predicate call as "unfold" and every builtin call as "call". We change the recursive call to $mi/2$ from "unfold" to "memo", so that it may be specialized separately. This can be seen as starting a new tree in partial deduction and adding the root of this tree to the set of analyzed conjunctions $\mathcal{A}$. If the default option, "unfold", is used, new derivation trees are not started and the set of analyzed conjunctions $\mathcal{A}$ is not closed. Furthermore, we annotate the call to *call*/1 as "rescall". Calls to *call*/1 apply to atoms which, in the abstract analysis, are underlined twice and which we consider residual. The "rescall" annotation expresses precisely the idea that a call should simply be executed when the program is run. The "call" annotation should not be used, as this executes the call during specialization time instead of during program execution. The most important filters are as follows:

- `compute(struct(permsort,[dynamic,dynamic]))`
  We specify as much information about the top-level call as possible. We cannot specify that the arguments to the call will have certain groundness characteristics, but this is not necessary as the *selected_index*/2 and *state_transition*/3 predicates are based on this information.
- `mi(type(list(nonvar)),static)`
  Neither the goal, which is represented as a list, nor its elements should be abstracted to variables in the root of a derivation tree. We also keep track of the state index and do not generalize it.

The arguments of other filters can be left dynamic: some values *will* be known at specialization time, but if the calls to an annotated predicate are never used as the root of a derivation tree (and they are not, because they never have the "memo" annotation), annotating them as "static" has no impact on the partial deduction.

9.2 Extended Meta-interpreter

For the extended meta-interpreter, the reasoning behind the clause annotations remains mostly the same. However, a crucial change must be applied to deal with the case split on the *multi* abstraction during specialization. During partial evaluation, some information regarding the structure of the *multi* abstraction is necessarily generalized away. To the best of our knowledge, we cannot use filter declarations to preserve info from the abstract analysis about the internal structure of a concrete *multi and* generalize calls so that $\mathcal{A}$ is closed. The problem is that the specialization procedure must generalize over concrete lists of arbitrary length. This can only be done using a variable, which means that information regarding the contents of the list is lost. Specifically, it becomes impossible to use append operations to build a conjunction at specialization time if some of the appended elements are free variables. However, we can re-encode the required information into the call annotations. We modify and annotate the interpreter as follows.

```
logen(mi/2,mi([B|C],A)) :-
        logen(unfold,selected_index(A,D)),
        logen(unfold,extracted_patt_one(A,Patt1)),
        logen(unfold,
          divide_goal(
            [B|C],D,E,
            cmulti([building_block(Patt1)]),F)),
        logen(unfold,state_transition(A,J,one)),
        ...
        logen(memo,mi(L,J)).
logen(mi/2,mi([B|C],A)) :-
        logen(unfold,selected_index(A,D)),
        logen(unfold,
          extracted_patts_many(A,Patt1,
                                      [building_block(Patt2)|BBs])),
        logen(unfold,
          divide_goal(
            [B|C],D,E,
            cmulti([building_block(Patt1),
                    building_block(Patt2)|BBs]),F)),
        logen(unfold,state_transition(A,M,many)),
        ...
        logen(memo,mi(P,M)).
```

Here, *extracted_patt_one*(*State*, *Patt*) defines the structure of the pattern extracted from a *multi* abstraction when a single subconjunction is unfolded. Its counterpart, *extracted_patts_many*(*State*, *Patt*, *Patts*), defines the structure of the extracted pattern and the remaining, non-extracted patterns. Neither predicate affects the correctness of the meta-interpreter. We have included an annotated version of the meta-interpreter without these extra steps in the electronic appendix for comparison.

The filter declarations remain mostly the same. However, goals now consist of program-specific atoms and universal *cmulti*/1 atoms. To reflect this, we use the following filter declaration for *mi*/2:

```
mi(type(
  list(
   (struct(cmulti,
            [struct('.',
                    [struct(building_block,[type(list(nonvar))]),
                     dynamic])]) ;
   nonvar))),
  static)
```

This preserves as much information about each conjunct as possible, as the disjunction (indicated by ;) is not commutative. While this solution is somewhat ad hoc, it can easily be applied to all examples that we are aware of. Furthermore, theoretical work on Logen [16] mentions the possibility of using custom binding types. It is possible that a custom binding type for the multi abstraction could help us avoid the above workaround.

10 Equivalence with the Classical Approach

The programs produced by Logen appear quite different from the syntheses obtained using the classical approach. To bring them together, we applied the ECCE online specializer to both resulting programs, because it can smooth away some differences through several post-processing steps. The resulting programs produce identical answer sets and display identical finite failure behavior.[4] Furthermore, while they retain some surface differences, they produce their answers after a nearly identical number of inferences. This demonstrates that both versions implement the same control flow and have nearly identical runtime performance. For instance, the sum total of the number of inferences required to find all solutions to the 10-queens problem with one approach deviates less than 3.5% from the number of inferences required with the other approach. More exhaustive benchmarks can be found in the electronic appendix. Therefore empirical evidence strongly points to both approaches being equivalent.

The compile-time performance for both approaches can safely be said to be nearly identical. The reason for this is that the analysis phase, which is the most expensive phase, is common to both approaches.

11 Discussion

We have shown that compiling control can be regarded as a specialization of a specific meta-interpreter for logic programs. This is an application of the first

[4] With the exception of the postprocessed classical synthesis of the prime sieve. This suggests a bug in ECCE, but the numbers before postprocessing are still within 16.5%.

Futamura projection, which answers a question which has long remained open. We have also provided a software pipeline which applies this idea in practice. We have restricted ourselves here to programs for which depth-k abstraction is not required, as there is currently no hard-and-fast rule to ascertain whether depth-k abstraction affects the eventual program flow. It would be useful to develop such a rule to further extend the set of programs which can be analyzed correctly in an automated way. It is also possible to apply a counterpart to the *multi* abstraction for terms which contain an arbitrary amount of nesting, but which have a predictable, repeating structure. Finally, we plan to investigate a variant of the *multi* abstraction whose pattern is not a conjunction, but a disjunction of conjunctions.

References

1. Bruynooghe, M., Schreye, D.D., Krekels, B.: Compiling control. In: Proceedings of the 1986 Symposium on Logic Programming, Salt Lake City, 22–25 September 1986, pp. 70–77. IEEE-CS (1986)
2. Bruynooghe, M., Schreye, D.D., Krekels, B.: Compiling control. J. Log. Program. **6**(1&2), 135–162 (1989)
3. Bruynooghe, M.: A practical framework for the abstract interpretation of logic programs. J. Log. Program. **10**(2), 91–124 (1991)
4. Komorowski, H.J.: A specification of an abstract Prolog machine and its application to partial evaluation. Ph.D. thesis, VTT Grafiska (1981)
5. Gallagher, J.P.: Transforming logic programs by specialising interpreters. In: ECAI, vol. I, pp. 313–326 (1986)
6. Nys, V., De Schreye, D.: Abstract conjunctive partial deduction for the analysis and compilation of coroutines. Formal Aspects Comput. **29**(1), 125–153 (2017)
7. Leuschel, M.: A framework for the integration of partial evaluation and abstract interpretation of logic programs. ACM Trans. Program. Lang. Syst. **26**(3), 413–463 (2004)
8. Gómez-Zamalloa, M., Albert, E., Puebla, G.: Decompilation of Java bytecode to prolog by partial evaluation. Inf. Softw. Technol. **51**(10), 1409–1427 (2009)
9. Henriksen, K.S., Gallagher, J.P.: Abstract interpretation of PIC programs through logic programming. In: Sixth IEEE International Workshop on Source Code Analysis and Manipulation (SCAM 2006), 27–29 September 2006, Philadelphia, pp. 184–196. IEEE Computer Society (2006)
10. Leuschel, M., Craig, S.J., Bruynooghe, M., Vanhoof, W.: Specialising interpreters using offline partial deduction. In: Bruynooghe, M., Lau, K.-K. (eds.) Program Development in Computational Logic: A Decade of Research Advances in Logic-Based Program Development. LNCS, vol. 3049, pp. 340–375. Springer, Heidelberg (2004). https://doi.org/10.1007/978-3-540-25951-0_11
11. Futamura, Y.: Partial evaluation of computation process-an approach to a compiler-compiler. Higher-Order Symb. Comput. **12**(4), 381–391 (1999)
12. Jones, N.D., Gomard, C.K., Sestoft, P.: Partial evaluation and automatic program generation. In: Prentice Hall International Series in Computer Science. Prentice Hall (1993)
13. Lloyd, J.W., Shepherdson, J.C.: Partial evaluation in logic programming. J. Log. Program. **11**(3&4), 217–242 (1991)

14. Leuschel, M., Bruynooghe, M.: Logic program specialisation through partial deduction: control issues. TPLP **2**(4–5), 461–515 (2002)
15. Leuschel, M., Jørgensen, J., Vanhoof, W., Bruynooghe, M.: Offline specialisation in prolog using a hand-written compiler generator. CoRR cs.PL/0208009 (2002)
16. Craig, S.-J., Gallagher, J.P., Leuschel, M., Henriksen, K.S.: Fully automatic binding-time analysis for prolog. In: Etalle, S. (ed.) LOPSTR 2004. LNCS, vol. 3573, pp. 53–68. Springer, Heidelberg (2005). https://doi.org/10.1007/11506676_4

Predicate Specialization for Definitional Higher-Order Logic Programs

Antonis Troumpoukis[1] and Angelos Charalambidis[2(✉)]

[1] Department of Informatics and Telecommunications, University of Athens, Athens, Greece
antru@di.uoa.gr

[2] Institute of Informatics and Telecommunications, NCSR "Demokritos", Athens, Greece
acharal@iit.demokritos.gr

Abstract. Higher-order logic programming is an interesting extension of traditional logic programming that allows predicates to appear as arguments and variables to be used where predicates typically occur. Higher-order characteristics are indeed desirable but on the other hand they are also usually more expensive to support. In this paper we propose a program specialization technique based on partial evaluation that can be applied to a modest but useful class of higher-order logic programs and can transform them into first-order programs without introducing additional data structures. The resulting first-order programs can be executed by conventional logic programming interpreters and benefit from other optimizations that might be available. We provide an implementation and experimental results that suggest the efficiency of the transformation.

1 Introduction

Higher-order logic programming has been long studied as an interesting extension of traditional first-order logic programming and various approaches exist with different features and semantics [2,4,12]. Typically, higher-order logic programs are allowed to define predicates that accept other predicates as arguments and variables can appear in places where predicate constants typically occur. Higher-order logic programs enjoy similar merits as their functional counterparts. The support of higher-order features however, usually comes with a price, and the efficient implementation in either logic or functional programming is a non-straightforward task.

The use of higher-order constructs is a standard feature in every functional language in contrast to the logic programming languages. As a result, there exists a plethora of optimizations that target specifically the efficient implementation of such features. A popular direction is to remove higher-order structures altogether by transforming higher-order programs into equivalent first-order ones, with the hope that the execution of the latter will be much more efficient. Reynolds, in his seminal paper [17], proposed a defunctionalization algorithm that is complete,

F. Mesnard and P. J. Stuckey (Eds.): LOPSTR 2018, LNCS 11408, pp. 132–147, 2019.
https://doi.org/10.1007/978-3-030-13838-7_8

i.e. it succeeds to remove all higher-order parameters from an arbitrary functional program. There is however a tradeoff; his algorithm requires the introduction of data structures in order to compensate for the inherent loss of expressivity [7]. Other approaches [5,13,14] have been proposed that do not use data structures, but share the limitation that are not complete.

In the logic programming context there exist many transformation algorithms with the purpose of creating more efficient programs. Partial evaluation algorithms [6,9,11], for example, can be used to obtain a more efficient program by iteratively unfolding logic clauses. Most of the proposals, however, focus on first-order logic programs. Proposals that can be applied to higher-order programs are limited. The prominent technique that targets higher-order logic programs proposed in [4,21] and adopted from Hilog. It employs the Reynolds' defunctionalization adapted for logic programs. As a consequence it naturally suffers from the same shortcomings of the original technique: the resulting programs are not natural and the conventional logic programming interpreters fail to identify potential optimizations without specialized tuning [18].

In this paper, we propose a partial evaluation technique that can be applied to higher-order logic programs. The technique propagates only higher-order arguments and avoids to change the structure of the original program. Moreover, it differs from Reynolds' style defunctionalization approaches as it does not rely on any type of data structures. As a result, the technique will only guarantee to remove the higher-order arguments in a well-defined subset of higher-order logic programs. The main contributions of the present paper are the following:

1. We propose a technique based on the abstract framework of partial evaluation that targets higher-order arguments. We have identified a well-defined fragment of higher-order logic programming that the technique terminates and produces a logic program without higher-order arguments.
2. We provide an implementation of the proposed technique and we experimentally assess its performance. We also compare it with the Reynolds' defunctionalization implemented in Hilog. Moreover, we experiment with the ability of combining this technique with the well-known tabling optimization.

The rest of the paper is organized as follows. In Sect. 2 we give an intuitive overview of our method using a simple example. In Sect. 3 we formally define the fragment of the higher-order logic programs we will use. Section 4 describes the abstract framework of partial evaluation and Sect. 5 introduces the details of our method. Section 6 discusses some implementation issues and Sect. 7 discusses the performance of our transformation on various experiments. Lastly, we compare our method with related approaches in Sect. 8 and we conclude the paper with possible future work.

2 A Simple Example

We start with an introductory example so as to give an informal description of our technique. We borrow an example from the area of knowledge representation which deals with the expression of user preferences [3].

The following program selects the most preferred tuples T out of a given unary relation R, based on a binary preference predicate P. The preference predicate given two tuples it succeeds if the first tuple is more preferred than the second.

```
winnow(P,R,T) :- R(T), not bypassed(P,R,T).
bypassed(P,R,T) :- R(Z), P(Z,T).
```

The program contains *predicate variables* (for example, P and R), that is variables that can occur in places where predicates typically occur.

Assume that we have a unary predicate movie which corresponds to a relation of movies and a binary predicate pref which given two movies succeeds if the first argument has a higher ranking than the second one. Now, suppose that we issue the query:

```
?- winnow(pref,movie,T).
```

We expect as answers the most "preferred" movies, that is all movies with the highest ranking.

In the following, we will show how we can create a first-order version of the original program specialized for this specific query. Notice that the atom winnow(pref,movie,T), that makes up our given query, does not contain any free predicate variables, but on the contrary, all of its predicate variables are substituted with predicate names. Therefore, we can specialize every program clause that defines winnow by substituting its predicate variables with the corresponding predicate names. By doing so, we get a program where our query yields the same results as to those in the original program:

```
winnow(pref,movie,T) :- movie(T), not bypassed(pref,movie,T).
bypassed(P,R,T) :- R(Z), P(Z,T).
```

We can continue this specialization process by observing that in the body of this newly constructed clause there exists the atom bypassed(pref,movie,T), in which all predicate variables are again substituted with predicate names. Therefore, we can specialize the second clause of the program accordingly:

```
winnow(pref,movie,T) :- movie(T), not bypassed(pref,movie,T).
bypassed(pref,movie,T) :- movie(Z), pref(Z,T).
```

There are no more predicate specializations to be performed and the transformation stops. Notice that the resulting program does not contain any predicate variables, but it is not a valid first-order one. Therefore, we have to perform a simple rewriting in order to remove all unnecessary predicate names that appear as arguments.

```
winnow1(T) :- movie(T), not bypassed2(T).
bypassed2(T) :- movie(Z), pref(Z,T).
```

Due to this renaming process, instead of the initial query, the user now has to issue the query ?- winnow1(T). Comparing the final first-order program with the original one it is easy to observe that no additional data structures were introduced during the first-order transformation, a characteristic that leads to performance improvement (ref. Sect. 7).

This technique, however, cannot be applied in every higher-order logic program. Notice that the resulting program of the previous example does not contain any predicate variables. This holds due to the fact that in the original program, every predicate variable that appears in the body of a clause it also appears in the head of this clause. By restricting ourselves to programs that have this property we ensure that the transformation outputs a first-order program. Moreover, the transformation in this example terminates because the set of the *specialization atoms* (i.e. `winnow(pref,movie,T)` and `bypassed(pref,movie,T)`) is finite, which is not the case in every higher-order logic program. To solve this, we need to keep the set specialization atoms finite. This is achieved in two ways. Firstly, we ignore all first-order arguments in every specialization atom, meaning that in a query of the form `?- winnow(pref,movie,m_001)`, we will specialize the program with respect to the atom `winnow(pref,movie,T)`. Secondly, we impose one more program restriction; we focus in programs where the higher-order arguments are either variables or predicate names. Since the set of all predicate names is finite and since we ignore all first-order values, the set of specialization atoms is also finite and as a result the algorithm is ensured to terminate.

3 Higher-Order Logic Programs

In this section we define the higher-order language of our interest. We begin with the syntax of the language $\mathcal{H}$ we use throughout the paper. $\mathcal{H}$ is based on a simple type system with two base types: o, the boolean domain, and ι, the domain of data objects. The composite types are partitioned into three classes: *functional* (assigned to function symbols), *predicate* (assigned to predicate symbols) and *argument* (assigned to parameters of predicates).

Definition 1. *A type can either be functional, argument, or predicate, denoted by σ, ρ and π respectively and defined as:*

$$\sigma := \iota \mid (\iota \to \sigma)$$
$$\pi := o \mid (\rho \to \pi)$$
$$\rho := \iota \mid \pi$$

Definition 2. *The* alphabet *of the language $\mathcal{H}$ consists of the following:*

1. *Predicate variables of every predicate type π (denoted by capital letters such as $\mathsf{P}, \mathsf{Q}, \mathsf{R}, \ldots$).*
2. *Individual variables of type ι (denoted by capital letters such as $\mathsf{X}, \mathsf{Y}, \mathsf{Z}, \ldots$).*
3. *Predicate constants of every predicate type π (denoted by lowercase letters such as $\mathsf{p}, \mathsf{q}, \mathsf{r}, \ldots$).*
4. *Individual constants of type ι (denoted by lowercase letters such as $\mathsf{a}, \mathsf{b}, \mathsf{c}, \ldots$).*
5. *Function symbols of every functional type $\sigma \neq \iota$ (denoted by lowercase letters such as $\mathsf{f}, \mathsf{g}, \mathsf{h}, \ldots$).*

6. *The inverse implication constant* $\leftarrow$, *the negation constant* $\sim$, *the comma, the left and right parentheses, and the equality constant* $\approx$ *for comparing terms of type* ι.

The set consisting of the predicate variables and the individual variables of $\mathcal{H}$ will be called the set of *argument variables* of $\mathcal{H}$. Argument variables will be usually denoted by V and its subscripted versions.

Definition 3. *The set of* expressions *of* $\mathcal{H}$ *is defined as follows:*

- *Every predicate variable (resp. predicate constant) of type* π *is an expression of type* π*; every individual variable (resp. individual constant) of type* ι *is an expression of type* ι*;*
- *if* f *is an* n*-ary function symbol and* $\mathsf{E}_1, \dots, \mathsf{E}_n$ *are expressions of type* ι *then* $(\mathsf{f}\ \mathsf{E}_1 \cdots \mathsf{E}_n)$ *is an expression of type* ι*;*
- *if* E *is an expression of type* $\rho_1 \to \cdots \rho_n \to o$ *and* E_i *an expression of type* ρ_i *for* $i \in \{1, \dots, n\}$ *then* $(\mathsf{E}\ \mathsf{E}_1\ \cdots\ \mathsf{E}_n)$ *is an expression of type* o*.*
- *if* $\mathsf{E}_1, \mathsf{E}_2$ *are expressions of type* ι*, then* $(\mathsf{E}_1 \approx \mathsf{E}_2)$ *is an expression of type* o*.*

We will omit parentheses when no confusion arises. Expressions of type o will often be referred to as *atoms*. We write $vars(\mathsf{E})$ to denote the set of all variables in E. We say that E_i is the i-th argument of an atom $\mathsf{E}\ \mathsf{E}_1\ \cdots\ \mathsf{E}_n$. A *ground expression* E is an expression where $vars(\mathsf{E})$ is the empty set.

Definition 4. *A* clause *is a formula*

$$\mathsf{p}\ \mathsf{V}_1 \cdots \mathsf{V}_n \leftarrow \mathsf{L}_1, \dots, \mathsf{L}_m, \sim \mathsf{L}_{m+1}, \dots, \sim \mathsf{L}_{m+k}$$

where p *is a predicate constant of type* $\rho_1 \to \cdots \to \rho_n \to o$*,* $\mathsf{V}_1, \dots, \mathsf{V}_n$ *are distinct variables of types* $\rho_1, \dots, \rho_n$ *respectively, and* $\mathsf{L}_1, \dots, \mathsf{L}_{m+k}$ *are expressions of type* o*, such that every predicate argument of* L_i *is either variable or ground. A* program P *of the higher-order language* $\mathcal{H}$ *is a finite set of program clauses.*

The syntax of programs given in Definition 4 differs slightly from the usual Prolog-like syntax that we have used in Sect. 2. However, one can easily verify that we can rewrite every program from the former syntax to the latter. For instance, we could use the constant $\approx$ in order to eliminate individual constants that appear in the head of a clause that uses the Prolog-like syntax.

Example 1. Consider the following program in Prolog-like syntax, in which we have three predicate definitions, namely $\mathtt{p} : \iota \to \mathtt{o}$, $\mathtt{q} : \iota \to \iota \to \mathtt{o}$, and $\mathtt{r} : (\iota \to o) \to (\iota \to o) \to (\iota \to \iota) \to o$.

```
p(a).
q(X,X).
r(P,Q,f(X)) :- P(X),Q(Y).
```

In our more formal notation, these clauses can be rewritten as:

```
p X ← (X ≈ a).
q X Y ← (X ≈ Y).
r P Q Z ← (Z ≈ f(X)), (P X), (Q Y).
```

Notice that all clauses are now valid $\mathcal{H}$ clauses.

Notice that in a $\mathcal{H}$ program, all arguments of predicate type are either variables or predicate names, which as discussed in Sect. 2 leads to the termination of our technique. However, in a $\mathcal{H}$ program all head predicate variables to be distinct. That implies that checking for equality between predicates (higher-order unification) is forbidden. In other words, the higher-order parameters can be used in ways similar to functional programming, namely either invoked or passed as arguments. We decided to impose this restriction because equality between predicates is treated differently in various higher-order languages [2,4,12]. Moreover, in Sect. 2, we briefly discussed that the reason why our technique can produce a first-order program is due to the following property:

Definition 5. *A clause will be called* definitional *iff every predicate variable that appears in the body appears also as a formal parameter of the clause. A* definitional program *is a finite set of definitional clauses.*

Example 2. Consider the following program in Prolog-like syntax:

```
p(Q,Q) :- Q(a).
q(X)  :- R(a,X).
```

This program does not belong to our fragment, because the first clause is a non-$\mathcal{H}$ clause and the second clause is a non-definitional clause. Regarding the first clause, the predicate variable Q appears twice in the head, therefore the formal parameters are not distinct. Regarding the second clause, the predicate variable R that appears in the body, does not appear in the head of the clause.

We extend the well-known notion of substitution to apply to $\mathcal{H}$ programs.

Definition 6. *A* substitution *θ is a finite set $\{\mathsf{V}_1/\mathsf{E}_1, \ldots, \mathsf{V}_n/\mathsf{E}_n\}$ where the V_i's are different argument variables and each E_i is a term having the same type as V_i. We write $dom(\theta) = \{\mathsf{V}_1, \ldots, \mathsf{V}_n\}$ to denote the domain of θ.*

Definition 7. *Let θ be a substitution and E be an expression. Then, $\mathsf{E}\theta$ is an expression obtained from E as follows:*

- $\mathsf{E}\theta = \mathsf{E}$ *if* E *is a predicate constant or individual constant;*
- $\mathsf{V}\theta = \theta(\mathsf{V})$ *if* $\mathsf{V} \in dom(\theta)$*; otherwise,* $\mathsf{V}\theta = \mathsf{V}$*;*
- $(\mathsf{f}\ \mathsf{E}_1 \cdots \mathsf{E}_n)\theta = (\mathsf{f}\ \mathsf{E}_1\theta \cdots \mathsf{E}_n\theta)$*;*
- $(\mathsf{E}\ \mathsf{E}_1\ \cdots\ \mathsf{E}_n)\theta = (\mathsf{E}\theta\ \mathsf{E}_1\theta\ \cdots\ \mathsf{E}_n\theta)$*;*
- $(\mathsf{E}_1 \approx \mathsf{E}_2)\theta = (\mathsf{E}_1\theta \approx \mathsf{E}_2\theta)$*;*
- $(\mathsf{L}_1, \ldots, \mathsf{L}_m, \sim \mathsf{L}_{m+1}, \ldots, \sim \mathsf{L}_n)\theta = (\mathsf{L}_1\theta, \ldots, \mathsf{L}_m\theta, \sim (\mathsf{L}_{m+1}\theta), \ldots, \sim (\mathsf{L}_n\theta))$.

Let θ be a substitution and E an expression. Then, $\mathsf{E}\theta$ is called an *instance* of E.

4 Partial Evaluation of Logic Programs

Partial evaluation [8] is a program optimization that specializes a given program according to a specific set of input data, such that the new program is more efficient than the original and both programs behave in the same way according to the given data. In the context of logic programming [6,9,11], a partial evaluation algorithm takes a program P and a goal G and produces a new program P′ such that $P \cup \{G\}$ and $P' \cup \{G\}$ are semantically equivalent. In Fig. 1 we illustrate a basic scheme that aims to describe every partial evaluation algorithm in logic programming, which is based in similar ones in the literature [6,9]. Notice that this general algorithm depends on two operations, namely UNFOLD and ABSTRACT, which can be implemented differently in several partial evaluation systems.

Input: a program P and a goal G
Output: a specialized program P′
$S := \{A : A \text{ is an atom of } G\}$
repeat
  $S' := S$
  $P' :=$ UNFOLD(P, S)
  $S := S \cup \{A : A \text{ is an atom that appears in a body of a clause in } P'\}$
  $S :=$ ABSTRACT(S)
until $S' = S$ (modulo variable renaming)
return P′

Fig. 1. Basic algorithm for partial evaluation.

Firstly, the algorithm uses an *unfolding* rule [19] in order to construct a finite and possibly incomplete proof tree for every atom in the set S and then creates a program P′ such that every clause of it is constructed from all root-to-leaf derivations of these proof trees. This part of the process is referred as the *local control* of partial evaluation. There are many possible unfolding rules, some of which being more useful for a particular application than others. Examples include determinate, leftmost non-determinate, loop-preventing or depth-bound unfolding strategies [6,9]. In some cases though, taking a simple approach which performs no unfolding at all, or in other words by using *one-step unfolding strategy*, may result in useful program optimizations. In such a case, UNFOLD exports a program that is constructed by finding the clauses that unify with each atom in S and then by specializing these clauses accordingly, using simple variable substitutions.

Secondly, the algorithm uses an ABSTRACT operation, which calculates a finite *abstraction* of the set S. We say that S′ is an *abstraction* of S if every atom of S is an instance of some atom in S′, and there does not exist two atoms in S′ that have a common instance in S′. This operation is used to keep the size of the set of atoms S finite, which will ensure the termination of the algorithm. This part of the process is referred as the *global control* of partial evaluation. Examples of abstraction operators include the use of a most specific generalizer and a finite bound in the size of S [9], or by exploiting a distinction between static and dynamic arguments for every atom in S [10].

A partial evaluation algorithm should ensure termination in both levels of control. Firstly, we have the *local termination problem*, which is the problem of the non-termination of the unfolding rule, and the *global termination problem* which is the problem of the non-termination of the iteration process (i.e. the repeat loop in the algorithm). As we stated earlier, the global termination problem is solved by keeping the set S finite through a finite abstraction operation. Regarding the local termination problem, one possible solution is ensuring that all constructed proof trees are finite. The one-step unfolding rule is by definition a strategy that can ensure local termination.

5 Predicate Specialization

In the following, we define our technique using the standard framework of partial evaluation (ref. Sect. 4), by specifying its local and global control strategies (namely UNFOLD and ABSTRACT operations). In particular, we will use a one-step unfolding rule and an abstraction operation which generalizes all individual (i.e. non-predicate) arguments from all atoms of the partial evaluation.

Definition 8. *Let* P *be a program and* S *be a set of atoms. Then,*

$$\textsc{Unfold}(\mathsf{P},\mathsf{S}) = \left\{ \mathsf{p}\ \mathsf{E}_1 \cdots \mathsf{E}_n \leftarrow \mathsf{B}\theta : \begin{array}{r} (\mathsf{p}\ \mathsf{E}_1 \cdots \mathsf{E}_n) \in \mathsf{S}, \\ (\mathsf{p}\ \mathsf{V}_1 \cdots \mathsf{V}_n \leftarrow \mathsf{B}) \in \mathsf{P}, \\ \theta = \{\mathsf{V}_1/\mathsf{E}_1, \ldots, \mathsf{V}_n/\mathsf{E}_n\} \end{array} \right\}$$

Definition 9. *Let* S *be a set of atoms. Then,*

$$\textsc{Abstract}(\mathsf{S}) = \{\mathsf{p}\ \mathsf{E}'_1 \cdots \mathsf{E}'_n : (\mathsf{p}\ \mathsf{E}_1 \cdots \mathsf{E}_n) \in \mathsf{S}\}$$

where $\mathsf{E}'_i = \mathsf{E}_i$ *if* E_i *is of predicate type, otherwise* $\mathsf{E}'_i = \mathsf{V}_i$*, where* V_i *is a fresh variable of the same type as of* E_i*.*

In the following, we will show some properties of our transformation. Firstly we will need the following lemma:

Lemma 1. *Let* P *be a program,* S *be a (possibly infinite) set of atoms. Then:*

1. *If* S *is finite, then* UNFOLD(P, S) *is finite.*
2. ABSTRACT(S) *is a finite abstraction of* S*.*
3. *If every element of* S *does not contain any free predicate variables, then every atom of* UNFOLD(P, S) *does not contain any free predicate variables.*

Proof. 1. Obvious from the construction of UNFOLD(P, S)*.*
2. *Every predicate argument of every atom that appears in* P *is either a variable or a predicate name, therefore* ABSTRACT(S) *is finite.*
3. *Suppose that* UNFOLD(P, S) *contains an atom* A *that contains a free predicate variable* V*. If* A *appears in the head of a clause, then from the construction of* UNFOLD(P, S)*,* S *must contain* A*. If* A *appears in the body of a clause, then since* P *is definitional,* V *also appears in the head of this clause. In any case,* S *must contain an atom that contains the free predicate variable* V*.*

The first part of the lemma ensures local termination and the second part of the lemma ensures global termination. The third part identifies that the transformation to first-order succeeds, provided that the program belongs to our fragment and the initial goal does not contain free higher-order variables. In the following corollaries, by Φ we denote the algorithm of Fig. 1 combined with the operations in Definitions 8 and 9.

Corollary 1. *Let* P *be a* $\mathcal{H}$ *program and* G *an goal. Then, the computation of* $\Phi(\mathsf{P}, \mathsf{G})$ *terminates in a finite number of steps.*

Corollary 2. *Let* P *be a definitional program and* G *an goal that does not contain any free predicate variables. Then, the output of* $\Phi(\mathsf{P}, \mathsf{G})$ *does not contain any free predicate variables.*

The result of Φ is neither a valid $\mathcal{H}$ program since it contains predicate names as arguments in the heads, nor a valid first-order program since some symbols appear both as arguments and as predicate symbols. Therefore, we must apply a simple *renaming* [6, Sect. 3] in order to construct a valid first-order output. In our case, at the end of the partial evaluation algorithm, every atom $\mathsf{p}\ \mathsf{E}_1 \cdots \mathsf{E}_n$ of S is renamed into $\mathsf{p}'\ \mathsf{V}_1 \cdots \mathsf{V}_m$, where p' is a fresh predicate symbol and $\{\mathsf{V}_1 \cdots \mathsf{V}_m\} = vars(\mathsf{p}\ \mathsf{E}_1 \cdots \mathsf{E}_n)$. Moreover, all instances of every atom of S in the resulting program are renamed accordingly.

6 Implementation

We have developed a prototype implementation[1] of our predicate specialization technique. Instead of developing a tailor-made higher-order language only for the purpose of demonstrating the benefits of the transformation, we build upon an existing higher-order logic programming language. The source programs in have to be written in the higher-order language Hilog [4], a mature and well-known language with a stable implementation within the XSB system [20].

A feature that we need and is not supported in Hilog though, is the use of types. Our algorithm needs types not only for deciding whether the input program belongs to our fragment, but also for the abstraction operation in Definition 9. Since the process of extending Hilog with types is outside of the scope of this paper, we assume that the input programs are well-typed and accompanied with type annotations for all predicates that contain predicate arguments.

The fragment that we discussed in Sect. 3 consists of programs that the only elements that can appear as predicate arguments are variables and predicate constants. However, most higher-order languages (and Hilog among them) allow more complex expressions to appear as predicate arguments. One such example is the use of *partial applications*, i.e., the ability to apply a predicate to only some of its arguments. Consider the following simple program.

[1] The implementation of the transformation is open source and can be accessed at http://bitbucket.org/antru/firstify.

```
conj2(P,Q,X) :- P(X),Q(X).
conj3(P,Q,R,X) :- conj2(P,conj2(Q,R),X).
```

In the second clause the expression conj2(Q,R) is a partial application where only the first two arguments are defined. A partial application effectively produces a new relation and therefore typically occur in higher-order arguments.

In the implementation we are able to handle programs that make a limited use of complex predicate expressions, as a syntactic sugar for our initial fragment. In particular, we allow non-variable and non-constant predicate arguments in an expression of the form $\mathsf{p}\ \mathsf{E}_1 \cdots \mathsf{E}_n$ that appears in the body of a clause $\mathsf{q}\ \mathsf{V}_1 \cdots \mathsf{V}_m \leftarrow \mathsf{B}$ only if p and q do not belong in the same cycle in the *predicate dependency graph*.[2] The transformation in this case is also ensured to terminate (because due to the form of the program all predicate variables of a predicate that depends on itself have to be specialized only with predicate names and therefore the set of all possible specialization atoms will remain finite). As we mentioned earlier, this class of programs has the same expressive power as our initial fragment. For example, the aforementioned logic program is equivalent to the following program that does not use any partial applications.

```
conj2(P,Q,X) :- P(X),Q(X).
conj31(P,Q,R,X) :- conj22(P,Q,R,X).
conj22(P,Q,R,X) :- P(X),conj2(Q,R,X).
```

Interestingly, we can use our algorithm to convert a program of the extended fragment into its equivalent $\mathcal{H}$ program. This can be done by initializing the transformation process with the top predicate (here conj3(P,Q,R,X)).

7 Experiments

In this section we present some experiments to illustrate that our technique can lead to the improvement of the execution runtime of higher-order logic programs.

We have tested our method with a set of benchmarks that include the computation of the transitive closure of a chain of elements, a k-ary disjunction and k-ary conjunction of k relations (for $k = 5, 10$), the computation of the shortest path programs of a directed acyclic graph and a set of programs that deal with preference representation [3]. The higher-order program is expressed in Hilog and executed using the Hilog module of XSB. XSB essentially transforms Hilog programs into first-order programs using the techniques and optimizations described in [18], and it also uses an optimized WAM instruction set to efficiently execute Hilog. The measurements obtained include these optimizations. We compare them with the execution of the Prolog programs produced by the our predicate specialization technique. Apart from XSB[3], we also consider for the execution

[2] An edge from the predicate p to predicate q in the predicate dependency graph means that there exists a clause that p appears in the head and p appears in the body of the same clause.

[3] version 3.7, cf. http://xsb.sourceforge.net/.

of the specialized program in other Prolog engines. The Prolog engines that we use are SWI-Prolog[4], and YAP[5]. Every program is executed several times, each time with a predefined set of facts. All data has been artificially generated.

In addition to the standard execution for Hilog and Prolog code, we also perform a *tabled execution* of both the higher-order and the first-order programs in XSB. Tabling is a standard optimization technique that is widely used in Prolog systems. In this optimization, a re-evaluation of a *tabled predicate* is avoided by memorizing (i.e. remembering) its answers. The XSB system is known for its elaborate and efficient implementation of tabling for first-order logic programs. For higher-order Hilog programs however, XSB's tabling mechanism may not be as effective as it is for first-order ones. The reason is that in order to table any Hilog predicate one has to table all Hilog code. This may lead to high memory consumption, and can be problematic for large-scale program development. We decided to table all predicates of the first-order programs as well, despite the fact that it might have been possible to make a more efficient use of tabling in this case. The idea behind this decision is to enable us to draw a fair comparison between tabled Hilog and tabled Prolog.

Table 1. Experiment results. All execution times are in seconds.

Program	Hilog	Prolog			Hilog	Prolog	Program size		
	xsb	xsb	swi	yap	xsb+tab.	xsb+tab.	h.o.	f.o.	Facts
closure	1744.829	17.426	15.813	8.782	16.980	17.067	3	3	1000–8000
closure_1000	12.132	0.801	0.609	0.372	0.872	0.672	3	3	1000
closure_2000	91.284	2.884	2.644	1.332	2.944	3.004	3	3	2000
closure_4000	709.356	11.336	10.918	5.464	10.812	11.076	3	3	4000
closure_6000	2365.728	25.536	23.459	13.532	25.236	25.548	3	3	6000
closure_8000	5545.644	46.576	41.433	23.208	45.036	45.036	3	3	8000
conj5	9.887	1.090	0.026	0.010	2.918	0.571	3	6	1000–8000
genconj(5)	9.921	1.101	0.028	0.011	2.031	0.573	4	4	1000–8000
conj10	21.676	2.414	0.023	0.015	11.741	1.276	3	11	1000–8000
genconj(10)	21.580	2.415	0.039	0.013	9.618	1.275	4	4	1000–8000
union5	0.035	0.028	0.030	0.023	0.037	0.038	4	10	1000–8000
genunion(5)	0.034	0.030	0.025	0.021	0.050	0.042	5	5	1000–8000
union10	0.063	0.062	0.046	0.036	0.075	0.065	4	20	1000–8000
genunion(10)	0.062	0.079	0.054	0.035	0.091	0.104	5	5	1000–8000
path_dag	971.326	679.557	975.027	54.156	0.001	0.001	6	6	10–80
path_naive	5.725	4.248	6.661	0.407	0.021	0.016	6	6	10–80
winnow	0.147	0.130	0.117	0.039	1.107	1.115	3	3	1000–10000
w(2)	3.920	3.257	3.844	0.527	0.168	0.213	10	12	100–2000
w(3)	129.457	107.183	122.556	21.103	0.119	0.123	10	12	100–2000
wt(2)	4.146	3.288	3.857	0.530	0.144	0.219	11	13	100–2000
wt(3)	130.540	108.048	126.876	21.360	0.100	0.119	11	13	100–2000

[4] version 7.2.3, cf. http://www.swi-prolog.org/.
[5] version 6.2.2, cf. http://www.dcc.fc.up.pt/~vsc/Yap/.

Table 1 summarizes the experimental results. The average execution time is depicted in seconds for each program and for each engine. The execution time is measured using the standard `time/1` predicate. Apart from the execution time, the table also contains the number of the (non-fact) clauses of the original higher-order program, the number of the (non-fact) clauses of the resulting first-order program after the transformation, and the ranges of the number of the corresponding facts. We do not show the runtime of each transformation from the higher-order to first-order since the execution of process was negligible (e.g. less than 0.01 s in all cases).

Firstly, we observe that the first-order programs are in general much faster than the higher-order ones. Even in the context of XSB which offers a native support of Hilog, the Prolog code is in almost all cases faster than the Hilog code. Especially in the transitive closure and the k-ary conjunction, we have an improvement by one or more of orders of magnitude. In most programs in our experiment, we noticed that the ratio between the execution time of Prolog code and the execution time of Hilog code does not change much if we increase the number of facts, with the exception of the transitive closure benchmark, in which the more we increase the number of facts, the more this ratio decreases. The most important advantage of executing standard Prolog though, is that it allows us to choose from a wide range of available Prolog engines. From the three Prolog engines that we used, YAP is the most performant one. Therefore, we can get a further decrease in execution times by simply choosing a different Prolog engine, a fact that is not possible if we want to execute Hilog code directly.

As we stated earlier, tabling is another standard optimization technique that is widely used in Prolog systems. Tabling was very effective in many cases in the experiment, especially in the preference operations (winnow, w and wt) and in the path programs (notice the dramatic decrease in the execution times for the path_dag benchmark). It seems that the performance of this optimization offers the same performance gain for both Hilog and Prolog code, since the execution times are in most cases similar. A notable exception is that of the k-ary conjunction benchmark, in which the tabled Prolog code is 5 to 10 times faster than that of the tabled Hilog code. Also, the fact that we table all Hilog and Prolog code did not have much negative effect in our experiment after all, because (with the sole exception of the winnow benchmark) the tabled executions are not slower than their non-tabled counterparts.

Finally, consider the programs that deal with the k-ary conjunction and disjunction, i.e. the pairs conj5 – genconj(5), conj10 – genconj(10), union5 – genunion(5) and union10 – genunion(10). Both programs of each of these pairs are making the same computation, with the former expressed in a non-recursive way and the latter in a recursive way. These programs differ also in the size of their first order counterparts. The first-order form of the non-recursive version has more clauses than the first-order form of the recursive version. We observe that both the higher-order and the first-order versions of the same computation have similar execution times, even though the first-order versions have different numbers of clauses. As a result, an increase on the size of the first-order program did not produce any overhead in the overall program execution time.

8 Related Work

The proposed predicate specialization is closely connected with related work on *partial evaluation* of logic programs [6,9,11]. More specifically, the proposed technique is a special form of partial evaluation which targets higher-order arguments and uses a simple one-step unfolding rule to propagate the constant higher-order arguments without changing the structure of the original program. Consequently, first-order programs remain unchanged. To the extend of our knowledge, partial evaluation techniques have not been previously applied directly to higher-order logic programming with the purpose to produce a simpler first-order program.

Other techniques, however, have been proposed that focus on the removal of higher-order parameters in logic programs. Warren, in one of the early papers that tackle similar issues [21], proposed that simple higher-order structures are non-essential and can be easily encoded as first-order logic programs. The key idea is that every higher-order argument in the program can be encoded as a symbol utilizing its name and a special `apply` predicate should be introduced to distinguish between different higher-order calls. A very similar approach has been employed in Hilog [4]; a language that offers a *higher-order syntax* with first-order semantics. A Hilog program is transformed into an equivalent first-order one using a transformation similar to Warren's technique [21]. Actually, these techniques are closely related to Reynolds' *defunctionalization* [17] that has been originally proposed to remove higher-order arguments in functional programs. These techniques are designed to be applied in arbitrary programs in comparison to our approach. In order to achieve this they require data structures in the resulting program. However, on a theoretical view this imposes the requirement that the target language should support data structures even if the source language does not support that. This is apparent when considering Datalog; transforming a higher-order Datalog program will result into a first-order Prolog program. On a more practical point, the generic data structures introduced during the defunctionalization render the efficient implementation of these programs challenging. The wrapping of the higher-order calls with the generic apply predicate makes it cumbersome to utilize the optimizations in first-order programs such as indexing and tabling. In comparison, our technique produce more natural programs that do not suffer for this phenomenon. Moreover, it does not introduce any data structures and as a result a higher-order Datalog program will be transformed into a first-order one amenable to more efficient implementation.

In order to remedy the shortcomings of defunctionalization there have been proposed some techniques to improve the performance of the transformed programs. [18] proposed a compile-time optimization of the classical Hilog encoding that eliminates some partial applications using a family of apply predicates thus increasing the number of the predicates in the encoded program, which leads to a more efficient execution. The original first-order encoding of Hilog as well as this optimization are included in the XSB system [20]. In the context of functional-logic programming, there exist some mixed approaches that consider defunctionalization together with partial evaluation for functional-logic programs [1,16], where a partial evaluation process is applied in a defunctionalized functional-logic program. Even though these approaches can usually offer a substantial performance improvement, the resulting programs still use a Reynolds' style encoding; for instance, the performance gain of the optimizations offered by XSB is not sufficient when compared to the technique presented in this paper, as presented in Sect. 7.

The process of eliminating higher-order functions is being studied extensively in the functional programming domain. Apart from defunctionalization, there exist some approaches that do not introduce additional data structures while removing higher-order functions. These techniques include the *higher-order removal* method of [5], the *firstification* technique of [14] and the *firstify* algorithm of [13]. The removal of higher-order values here is achieved without introducing additional data structures, so the practical outcome is that the resulting programs can be executed in a more efficient way than the original ones. The basic operation of these transformation methods is *function specialization*, which involves generating a new function in which the function-type arguments of the original definition are eliminated. A predicate specialization operation is also the core operation in our approach, so in this point these approaches are similar to ours. The remaining operations that can be found in those approaches (e.g. simplification rules, inlining, eta-abstractions etc.), are either inapplicable to our domain or not needed for our program transformation. Contrary to Reynolds' defunctionalization, these higher-order removal techniques [5,13,14] are not complete, meaning that they do not remove all higher-order values from a functional program, and therefore the resulting programs are not always first order. This phenomenon would happen in our case as well if we considered the full power of higher-order programming. However, because of the fact that we focus on a smaller but still useful class of higher-order logic programs, we are sure that the output of our transformation technique will produce a valid first-order program for every program that belongs to our fragment.

9 Conclusions and Future Work

In this paper we presented a program transformation technique that reduces higher-order programs into first-order ones through argument specialization. The transformation does not introduce additional data structures and therefore the resulting programs can be executed efficiently in any standard Prolog system. We do not consider the full power of higher-order logic programming, but we focus on a modest but useful class of programs; in these programs we do not allow partial applications or existential predicate variables in the body of a clause.

In our actual implementation we considered a slightly broader class than the fragment discussed before; we allowed a limited use of partial applications in the case of predicates that do not belong to the same cycle in the predicate dependency graph. This extension however does not increase the expressive power of the language. An interesting open question that arises is whether this technique can be used as a first-order reduction method only for programs that belong to our fragment (or a fragment that have the same expressive power as ours) or if it can be used for a wider class of programs that are more expressive than our fragment. Moreover, any expansion of the supported class would be desirable, even if it has the same expressivity as our current fragment.

Until now, we have used and evaluated our transformation technique only as an optimization method for performance improvement. However, in the functional programming domain, such techniques have been used in additional applications, such as program analysis [13] and implementation of debuggers [15]. Therefore, an interesting aspect for future investigation would be the search of similar or completely new applications of our higher-order removal technique in the logic programming domain.

Acknowledgements. We would like to thank the anonymous reviewers for providing constructive comments on our original submission.

References

1. Albert, E., Hanus, M., Vidal, G.: A practical partial evaluation scheme for multi-paradigm declarative languages. J. Funct. Logic Program. **2002** (2002)
2. Charalambidis, A., Handjopoulos, K., Rondogiannis, P., Wadge, W.W.: Extensional higher-order logic programming. ACM Trans. Comput. Logic **14**(3), 21 (2013)
3. Charalambidis, A., Rondogiannis, P., Troumpoukis, A.: Higher-order logic programming: an expressive language for representing qualitative preferences. Sci. Comput. Program. **155**, 173–197 (2018)
4. Chen, W., Kifer, M., Warren, D.S.: HiLog: a foundation for higher-order logic programming. J. Logic Program. **15**(3), 187–230 (1993)
5. Chin, W., Darlington, J.: A higher-order removal method. Lisp Symbolic Comput. **9**(4), 287–322 (1996)
6. Gallagher, J.P.: Tutorial on specialisation of logic programs. In: Proceedings of the ACM SIGPLAN Symposium on Partial Evaluation and Semantics-Based Program Manipulation, PEPM 1993, Copenhagen, Denmark, 14–16 June 1993, pp. 88–98 (1993)
7. Jones, N.D.: The expressive power of higher-order types or, life without CONS. J. Funct. Program. **11**(1), 5–94 (2001)
8. Jones, N.D., Gomard, C.K., Sestoft, P.: Partial Evaluation and Automatic Program Generation. Prentice Hall, Upper Saddle River (1993)
9. Leuschel, M.: Logic program specialisation. In: Partial Evaluation - Practice and Theory, DIKU 1998 International Summer School, Copenhagen, Denmark, June 29–July 10 1998, pp. 155–188 (1998)
10. Leuschel, M., Vidal, G.: Fast offline partial evaluation of logic programs. Inf. Comput. **235**, 70–97 (2014)
11. Lloyd, J.W., Shepherdson, J.C.: Partial evaluation in logic programming. J. Log. Program. **11**(3&4), 217–242 (1991)
12. Miller, D., Nadathur, G.: Programming with Higher-Order Logic, 1st edn. Cambridge University Press, New York (2012)
13. Mitchell, N., Runciman, C.: Losing functions without gaining data: another look at defunctionalisation. In: Proceedings of the 2nd ACM SIGPLAN Symposium on Haskell, Haskell 2009, Edinburgh, Scotland, UK, 3 September 2009, pp. 13–24 (2009)

14. Nelan, G.: Firstification. Ph.D. thesis, Arizona State University (1991)
15. Pope, B.J., Naish, L.: Specialisation of higher-order functions for debugging. Electr. Notes Theor. Comput. Sci. **64**, 277–291 (2002)
16. Ramos, J.G., Silva, J., Vidal, G.: Fast narrowing-driven partial evaluation for inductively sequential programs. In: Proceedings of the 10th ACM SIGPLAN International Conference on Functional Programming, ICFP 2005, Tallinn, Estonia, 26–28 September 2005, pp. 228–239 (2005)
17. Reynolds, J.C.: Definitional interpreters for higher-order programming languages. In: Proceedings of the 25th ACM National Conference, pp. 717–740. ACM (1972)
18. Sagonas, K., Warren, D.S.: Efficient execution of HiLog in WAM-based prolog implementations. In: Proceedings of the 12th International Conference on Logic Programming, Tokyo, Japan, 13–16 June 1995, pp. 349–363 (1995)
19. Shepherdson, J.C.: Unfold/fold transformations of logic programs. Math. Struct. Comput. Sci. **2**(2), 143–157 (1992)
20. Swift, T., Warren, D.S.: XSB: extending prolog with tabled logic programming. TPLP **12**(1–2), 157–187 (2012)
21. Warren, D.H.: Higher-order extensions to prolog-are they needed. Machine Intell. **10**, 441–454 (1982)

An Assertion Language for Slicing Constraint Logic Languages

Moreno Falaschi[1(✉)] and Carlos Olarte[2]

[1] Department of Information Engineering and Mathematics, Università di Siena, Siena, Italy
moreno.falaschi@unisi.it
[2] ECT, Universidade Federal do Rio Grande do Norte, Natal, Brazil
carlos.olarte@gmail.com

Abstract. Constraint Logic Programming (CLP) is a language scheme for combining two declarative paradigms: constraint solving and logic programming. Concurrent Constraint Programming (CCP) is a declarative model for concurrency where agents interact by telling and asking constraints in a shared store. In a previous paper, we developed a framework for dynamic slicing of CCP where the user first identifies that a (partial) computation is wrong. Then, she marks (selects) some parts of the final state corresponding to the data (constraints) and processes that she wants to study more deeply. An automatic process of slicing begins, and the partial computation is "depurated" by removing irrelevant information. In this paper we give two major contributions. First, we extend the framework to CLP, thus generalizing the previous work. Second, we provide an assertion language suitable for both, CCP and CLP, which allows the user to specify some properties of the computations in her program. If a state in a computation does not satisfy an assertion then some "wrong" information is identified and an automatic slicing process can start. We thus make one step further towards automatizing the slicing process. We show that our framework can be integrated with the previous semi-automatic one, giving the user more choices and flexibility. We show by means of examples and experiments the usefulness of our approach.

Keywords: Concurrent Constraint Programming · Constraint Logic Programming · Dynamic slicing · Debugging · Assertion language

1 Introduction

Constraint Logic Programming (CLP) is a language scheme [20] for combining two declarative paradigms: constraint solving and logic programming (see an overview in [19]). Concurrent Constraint Programming (CCP) [28] (see a survey in [25]) combines concurrency primitives with the ability to deal with constraints, and hence, with partial information. The notion of concurrency is based upon the

F. Mesnard and P. J. Stuckey (Eds.): LOPSTR 2018, LNCS 11408, pp. 148–165, 2019.
https://doi.org/10.1007/978-3-030-13838-7_9

shared-variables communication model. CCP is intended for reasoning, modeling and programming concurrent agents (or processes) that interact with each other and their environment by posting and asking information in a medium, a so-called *store*. CCP is a very flexible model and has been applied to an increasing number of different fields such as probabilistic and stochastic, timed and mobile systems [9,26], and more recently to social networks with spatial and epistemic behaviors [25], as well as modeling of biological systems [6,10,11,24].

One crucial problem with constraint logic languages is to define appropriate debugging tools. Various techniques and several frameworks have been proposed for debugging these languages. Abstract interpretation techniques have been considered (e.g. in [12,13,16,17]) as well as (abstract) declarative debuggers following the seminal work of Shapiro [30]. However, these techniques are approximated (case of abstract interpretation) or it can be difficult to apply them when dealing with complex programs (case of declarative debugging) as the user should answer to too many questions.

In this paper we follow a technique inspired by slicing. Slicing was introduced in some pioneer works by Weiser [33]. It was originally defined as a static technique, independent of any particular input of the program. Then, the technique was extended by introducing the so called dynamic program slicing [22]. This technique is useful for simplifying the debugging process, by selecting a portion of the program containing the faulty code. Dynamic program slicing has been applied to several programming paradigms (see [21] for a survey). In the context of constraint logic languages, we defined a tool [15] able to interact with the user and filter, in a given computation, the information which is relevant to a particular observation or result. In other words, the programmer could mark (select) the information (constraints, agents or atoms) that she is interested to check in a particular computation that she suspects to be wrong. Then, a corresponding depurated partial computation is obtained automatically, where only the information relevant to the marked parts is present.

In a previous paper [15] we presented the first formal framework for debugging CCP via dynamic slicing. In this paper we give two major contributions. First, we extend our framework to CLP. Second, we introduce an assertion language which is integrated within the slicing process for automatizing it further. The extension to CLP is not immediate, as while for CCP programs non-deterministic choices give rise to one single computation, in CLP all computations corresponding to different non-deterministic choices can be followed and can lead to different solutions. Hence, some rethinking of the framework is necessary. We show that it is possible to define a transformation from CLP programs to CCP programs, which allows us to show that the set of observables of a CLP program and of its translation to a CCP program correspond. This result also shows that the computations in the two languages are pretty similar and the framework for CCP can be extended to deal with CLP programs.

Our framework [15] consists of three main steps. First the standard operational semantics of the sliced language is extended to an enriched semantics that adds to the standard semantics the needed meta-information for the slicer.

Second, we consider several analyses of the faulty situation based on the program wrong behavior, including causality, variable dependencies, unexpected behaviors and store inconsistencies. This second step was left to the user's responsibility: the user had to examine the final state of the faulty computation and manually mark/select a subset of constraints that she wants to study further. The third step is an automatic marking algorithm that removes the information not relevant to derive the constraints selected in the second step. This algorithm is flexible and applicable to timed extensions of CCP [27]. Here, for CLP programs we introduce also the possibility to mark atoms, besides constraints.

We believe that the second step above, namely identifying the right state and the relevant information to be marked, can be difficult for the user and we believe that it is possible to improve automatization of this step. Hence, one major contribution of this paper is to introduce a specialized assertion language which allows the user to state properties of the computations in her program. If a state in a computation does not satisfy an assertion then some "wrong" information is identified and an automatic slicing process can start. We show that assertions can be integrated in our previous semi-automatic framework [15], giving the user more choices and flexibility. The assertion language is a good companion to the already implemented tool for the slicing of CCP programs to automatically detect (possibly) wrong behaviors and stop the computation when needed. The framework can also be applied to timed variants of CCP.

Organization and Contributions. Section 2 describes CCP and CLP and their operational semantics. We introduce a translation from CLP to CCP programs and prove a correspondence theorem between successful computations. In Sect. 3 we recall the slicing technique for CCP [15] and extend it to CLP. The extension of our framework to CLP is our first contribution. As a second major contribution, in Sect. 4 we present our specialized assertion language and describe its main operators and functionalities. In Sect. 4.2 we show some examples to illustrate the expressiveness of our extension, and the integration into the former tool. Within our examples we show how to automatically debug a biochemical system specified in timed CCP and one classical search problem in CLP. Finally, Sect. 5 discusses some related work and concludes.

2 Constraint Logic Languages

In this section we define an operational semantics suitable for both, CLP [19] and CCP programs [28]. We start by defining CCP programs and then we obtain CLP by restricting the set of CCP operators.

Processes in CCP *interact* with each other by *telling* and *asking* constraints (pieces of information) in a common store of partial information. The type of constraints is not fixed but parametric in a constraint system (CS), a central notion for both CCP and CLP. Intuitively, a CS provides a signature from which constraints can be built from basic tokens (e.g., predicate symbols), and two basic operations: conjunction $\sqcup$ (e.g., $x \neq y \sqcup x > 5$) and variable hiding $\exists$ (e.g., $\exists x.y = f(x)$). As usual, $\exists x.c$ binds x in c. The CS defines also an *entailment* relation ($\models$) specifying inter-dependencies between constraints: $c \models d$ means that the information d can be deduced from the information c (e.g., $x > 42 \models x > 37$). We shall use $\mathcal{C}$ to denote the set of constraints with typical elements c, c', d, d'.... We assume that there exist $\mathtt{t}, \mathtt{f} \in \mathcal{C}$, such that for any $c \in \mathcal{C}$, $c \models \mathtt{t}$ and $\mathtt{f} \models \mathcal{C}$. The reader may refer to [25] for different formalizations and examples of constraint systems.

The Language of CCP Processes. In process calculi, the language of processes in CCP is given by a small number of primitive operators or combinators. Processes are built from constraints in the underlying constraint and:

$$P, Q ::= \mathbf{skip} \mid \mathbf{tell}(c) \mid \sum_{i \in I} \mathbf{ask}\ (c_i)\ \mathbf{then}\ P_i \mid P \parallel Q \mid (\mathbf{local}\, x)\, P \mid p(\overline{x})$$

The process **skip** represents inaction. The process **tell**(c) adds c to the current store d producing the new store $c \sqcup d$. Given a non-empty finite set of indexes I, the process $\sum_{i \in I} \mathbf{ask}\ (c_i)\ \mathbf{then}\ P_i$ non-deterministically chooses P_k for execution if the store entails c_k. The chosen alternative, if any, precludes the others. This provides a powerful synchronization mechanism based on constraint entailment. When I is a singleton, we shall omit the "$\sum$" and we simply write **ask** (c) **then** P.

The process $P \parallel Q$ represents the parallel (interleaved) execution of P and Q and $(\mathbf{local}\, x)\, P$ behaves as P and binds the variable x to be local to it.

Given a process definition $p(\overline{y}) \triangleq P$, where all free variables of P are in the set of pairwise distinct variables $\overline{y}$, the process $p(\overline{x})$ evolves into $P[\overline{x}/\overline{y}]$. A CCP program takes the form $\mathcal{D}.P$ where $\mathcal{D}$ is a set of process definitions and P is a process.

The Structural Operational Semantics (SOS) of CCP is given by the transition relation $\gamma \longrightarrow \gamma'$ satisfying the rules in Fig. 1. Here we follow the formulation in [14] where the local variables created by the program appear explicitly in the transition system and parallel composition of agents is identified by a multiset of agents. More precisely, a *configuration* γ is a triple of the form $(X; \Gamma; c)$, where c is a constraint representing the store, Γ is a multiset of processes, and X is a set of hidden (local) variables of c and Γ. The multiset $\Gamma = P_1, P_2, \ldots, P_n$ represents the process $P_1 \parallel P_2 \parallel \cdots \parallel P_n$. We shall indistinguishably use both notations to denote parallel composition. Moreover, processes are quotiented by a structural congruence relation $\cong$ satisfying: (STR1) $P \cong Q$ if P and Q differ only by a renaming of bound variables (alpha conversion); (STR2) $P \parallel Q \cong Q \parallel P$; (STR3) $P \parallel (Q \parallel R) \cong (P \parallel Q) \parallel R$; (STR4) $P \parallel \mathbf{skip} \cong P$. We denote by $\longrightarrow^*$ the reflexive and transitive closure of a binary relation $\longrightarrow$.

Definition 1 (Observables and traces). *A trace $\gamma_1\gamma_2\gamma_3\cdots$ is a sequence of configurations s.t. $\gamma_1 \longrightarrow \gamma_2 \longrightarrow \gamma_3 \cdots$. We shall use π, π' to denote traces and $\pi(i)$ to denote the i-th element in π. If $(X; \Gamma; d) \longrightarrow^* (X'; \Gamma'; d')$ and $\exists X'.d' \models c$ we write $(X; \Gamma; d) \Downarrow_c$. If $X = \emptyset$ and $d = \mathtt{t}$ we simply write $\Gamma \Downarrow_c$.*

Intuitively, if P is a process then $P \Downarrow_c$ says that P can reach a store d strong enough to entail c, *i.e.*, c is an output of P. Note that the variables in X' above are hidden from d' since the information about them is not observable.

$$\frac{}{(X;\mathbf{tell}(c),\Gamma;d) \longrightarrow (X;\mathbf{skip},\Gamma;c \sqcup d)}\ \mathrm{R_{TELL}} \qquad \frac{d \models c_k \quad k \in I}{(X;\sum_{i\in I}\mathbf{ask}\ (c_i)\ \mathbf{then}\ P_i,\Gamma;d) \longrightarrow (X;P_k,\Gamma;d)}\ \mathrm{R_{SUM}}$$

$$\frac{x \notin X \cup fv(d) \cup fv(\Gamma)}{(X;(\mathbf{local}\,x)\,P,\Gamma;d) \longrightarrow (X \cup \{x\};P,\Gamma;d)}\ \mathrm{R_{LOC}} \qquad \frac{p(\overline{y}) \triangleq P \in \mathcal{D}}{(X;p(\overline{x}),\Gamma;d) \longrightarrow (X;P[\overline{x}/\overline{y}],\Gamma;d)}\ \mathrm{R_{CALL}}$$

$$\frac{(X;\Gamma;c) \cong (X';\Gamma';c') \longrightarrow (Y';\Delta';d') \cong (Y;\Delta;d)}{(X;\Gamma;c) \longrightarrow (Y;\Delta;d)}\ \mathrm{R_{EQUIV}}$$

Fig. 1. Operational semantics for CCP calculi

2.1 The Language of CLP

A CLP program [20] is a finite set of rules of the form

$$p(\overline{x}) \leftarrow A_1, \ldots, A_n$$

where $A_1, \ldots A_n$, with $n \geq 0$, are literals, i.e. either atoms or constraints in the underlying constraint system $\mathcal{C}$, and $p(\overline{x})$ is an atom. An atom has the form $p(t_1, \ldots, t_m)$, where p is a user defined predicate symbol and the t_i are terms from the constraint domain.

The top-down operational semantics is given by derivations from goals [20]. A configuration takes the form $(\Gamma; c)$ where Γ (a goal) is a multiset of literals and c is a constraint (the current store). The reduction relation is as follows.

Definition 2 (Semantics of CLP [20]**).** *Let $\mathcal{H}$ be a CLP program. A configuration $\gamma = (L_1, ..., L_i, ...L_n; c)$ reduces to ψ, notation $\gamma \longrightarrow_{CLP(\mathcal{H})} \psi$, by selecting and removing a literal L_i and then:*

1. *If L_i is a constraint d and $d \sqcup c \neq f$, then $\gamma \longrightarrow_{CLP(\mathcal{H})} (L_1, ..., L_n; c \sqcup d)$.*
2. *If L_i is a constraint d and $d \sqcup c = f$ (i.e., the conjunction of c and d is inconsistent), then $\gamma \longrightarrow_{CLP(\mathcal{H})} (\square; f)$ where $\square$ represents the empty multiset.*
3. *If L_i is an atom $p(t_1, ..., t_k)$, then $\gamma \longrightarrow_{CLP(\mathcal{H})} (L_1, ..., L_{i-1}, \Delta, L_{i+1} ..., L_n; c)$ where one of the definitions for p, $p(s_1, ..., s_k) \leftarrow A_1, \ldots, A_n$, is selected and $\Delta = A_1, \ldots, A_n, s_1 = t_1, ..., s_k = t_k$.*

A computation from a goal G is a (possibly infinite) sequence $\gamma_1 = (G; \mathtt{t}) \longrightarrow_{CLP(\mathcal{H})} \gamma_2 \longrightarrow_{CLP(\mathcal{H})} \cdots$. We say that a computation finishes if the last configuration γ_n cannot be reduced, i.e., $\gamma_n = (\square; c)$. In this case, if $c = f$ then the derivation fails otherwise we say that it succeeds.

Given a goal with free variables $\overline{x} = var(G)$, we shall also use the notation $G \Downarrow_c^{\mathcal{H}}$ to denote that there is a successful computation $(G; \mathtt{t}) \longrightarrow^*_{CLP(\mathcal{H})} (\square; d)$ s.t. $\exists \overline{x}.d \models c$. We note that the free variables of a goal are progressively "instantiated" during computations by adding new constraints. Finally, the answers of a goal G, notation $G \Downarrow^{\mathcal{H}}$ is the set $\{\exists_{var(c) \setminus var(G)}(c) \mid (G; \mathtt{t}) \longrightarrow^*_{CLP(\mathcal{H})} (\square; c), c \neq \mathtt{f}\}$ where "\" denotes set difference.

From CLP to CCP. CCP is a very general paradigm that extends both Concurrent Logic Programming and Constraint Logic Programming [23]. However, in CLP, we have to consider non-determinism of the type "don't know" [29], which means that each predicate call can be reduced by using each rule which defines such a predicate. This is different from the kind of non-determinism in CCP, where the choice operator selects randomly one of the choices whose ask guard is entailed by the constraints in the current store (see $\mathrm{R_{SUM}}$ in Fig. 1).

It turns out that by restricting the syntax of CCP and giving an alternative interpretation to non-deterministic choices, we can have an encoding of CLP programs as CCP agents. More precisely, we shall remove the synchronization operator and we shall consider only blind choices of the form $Q = \sum_{i \in I} \textbf{ask}\,(\texttt{t})\,\textbf{then}\,P_i$. Note that $c \models \texttt{t}$ for any c and then, the choices in Q are not guarded/constrained. Hence, any of the P_i can be executed regardless of the current store. This mimics the behavior of CLP predicates (see (3) in Definition 2), but with a different kind of non-determinism. The next definition formalizes this idea.

Definition 3 (Translation). *Let $\mathcal{C}$ be a const. system, $\mathcal{H}$ be a CLP program and G be a goal. We define the set of CCP process definitions $[\![\mathcal{H}]\!] = \mathcal{D}$ as follows. For each user defined predicate symbol p of arity j and $1..m$ defined rules of the form $p(t_1^i, ..., t_j^i) \leftarrow A_1^i, \ldots, A_{n_i}^i$, we add to $\mathcal{D}$ the following process definition*

$$p(x_1, ..., x_j) \overset{\Delta}{=} \textbf{ask}\,(t)\,\textbf{then}\,((\textbf{local}\ \overline{z_1})\ \textstyle\prod D_1 \parallel [\![A_1^1]\!] \parallel \cdots \parallel [\![A_{n_1}^1]\!]) \\ +... + \textbf{ask}\,(t)\,\textbf{then}\,((\textbf{local}\,\overline{z_m})\ \textstyle\prod D_m \parallel [\![A_1^m]\!] \parallel \cdots \parallel [\![A_{n_m}^m]\!])$$

where $\overline{z_i} = var(t_1^i, ..., t_j^i) \cup var(A_1^i, ..., A_{n_i}^i)$, D_i is the set of constraints $\{x_1 = t_1^i, ..., x_j = t_j^i\}$, $\prod D_i$ means $\textbf{tell}(x_1 = t_1^i) \parallel \cdots \parallel \textbf{tell}(x_j = t_j^i)$ and literals are translated as $[\![A(\bar{t})]\!] = A(\bar{t})$ (case of atoms) and $[\![c]\!] = \textbf{tell}(c)$ (case of constraints). Moreover, we translate the goal $[\![A_1, ..., A_n]\!]$ as $[\![A_1]\!] \parallel \cdots \parallel [\![A_n]\!]$.

The head $p(\overline{x})$ of a definition $p(\overline{x}) \overset{\Delta}{=} P$ in CCP can only have variables while a head of a CLP rule $p(\overline{t}) \leftarrow B$ may have arbitrary terms with (free) variables. Moreover, in CLP, each call to a predicate returns a variant with distinct new variables (renaming the parameters of the predicate) [20]. These two features of CLP can be encoded in CCP by first introducing local variables ((**local** z_i) in the above definition) and then, using constraints (D_i) to establish the connection between the formal and the actual parameters of the process definition.

Consider for instance this simple CLP program dealing with lists:

```
p([] , []) .
p([H1 | L1] , [H2 | L2]) :- c(H1,H2), p(L1,L2) .
```

and its translation

$$p(x, y) \overset{\Delta}{=} \textbf{ask}\,(\texttt{t})\,\textbf{then}\,(\textbf{tell}(x = []) \parallel \textbf{tell}(y = [])) \\ + \textbf{ask}\,(\texttt{t})\,\textbf{then}\,(\textbf{local}\,X)\,(\textstyle\prod D \parallel c(H1, H2) \parallel p(L1, L2))$$

where $D = \{x = [H1|L1], y = [H2|L2]\}$ and $X = \{H1, H2, L1, L2\}$. Note that the CCP process $p(l_a, l_b)$ can lead to 2 possible outcomes:

- Using the first branch, the store becomes $l_a = [] \sqcup l_b = []$.

- In the second branch, due to rule $\mathrm{R_{LOC}}$, four local distinct variables are created (say $h1, h2, l1, l2$), the store becomes $l_a = [h1|l1] \sqcup l_b = [h2|l2] \sqcup c(h1, h2)$ and the process $p(l1, l2)$ is executed on this new store.

These CCP executions match exactly the behavior of the CLP goal `p(LA, LB)`.

We emphasize that one execution of a CCP program will give rise to a single computation (due to the kind of non-determinism in CCP) while the CLP computation model characterizes the set of all possible successful derivations and corresponding answers. In other terms, for a given initial goal G, the CLP model defines the full set of answer constraints for G, while the CCP translation will compute only one of them, as only one possible derivation will be followed.

Theorem 1 (Adequacy). *Let $\mathcal{C}$ be a constraint system, $c \in \mathcal{C}$, $\mathcal{H}$ be a CLP program and G be a goal. Then, $G \Downarrow_c^{\mathcal{H}}$ iff $[\![G]\!] \Downarrow_c$.*

3 Slicing CCP and CLP Programs

Dynamic slicing is a technique that helps the user to debug her program by simplifying a partial execution trace, thus depurating it from parts which are irrelevant to find the bug. It can also help to highlight parts of the programs which have been wrongly ignored by the execution of a wrong piece of code. In [15] we defined a slicing technique for CCP programs that consisted of three main steps:

S1 *Generating a (finite) trace* of the program. For that, a new semantics is needed in order to generate the (meta) information needed for the slicer.
S2 *Marking the final store*, to select some of the constraints that, according to the wrong behavior detected, should or should not be in the final store.
S3 *Computing the trace slice*, to select the processes and constraints that were relevant to produce the (marked) final store.

We shall briefly recall the step **S1** in [15] which remains the same here. Steps **S2** and **S3** need further adjustments to deal with CLP programs. In particular, we shall allow the user to select processes (literals in the CLP terminology) in order to start the slicing. Moreover, in Sect. 4, we provide further tools to automatize the slicing process.

Enriched Semantics (Step S1). The slicing process requires some extra information from the execution of the processes. More precisely, (1) in each operational step $\gamma \rightarrow \gamma'$, we need to highlight the process that was reduced; and (2) the constraints accumulated in the store must reflect, exactly, the contribution of each process to the store. In order to solve (1) and (2), we introduced in [15] the enriched semantics that extracts the needed meta information for the slicer. Roughly, we identify the parallel composition $Q = P_1 \parallel \cdots \parallel P_n$ with the *sequence* $\Gamma_Q = P_1 : i_1, \cdots, P_n : i_n$ where $i_j \in \mathbb{N}$ is a unique identifier for P_j. The use of indexes allow us to distinguish, e.g., the three different occurrences of P in "$\Gamma_1, P : i, \Gamma_2, P : j, (\textbf{ask}\ (c)\ \textbf{then}\ P) : k$". The enriched semantics uses transitions with labels of the form $\xrightarrow{[i]_k}$ where i is the identifier of the reduced process and k can be either $\perp$ (undefined) or a natural number indicating the branch chosen in a non-deterministic choice (Rule $\mathrm{R}'_{\mathrm{SUM}}$). This allows us to identify, unequivocally, the selected alternative in an execution. Finally, the store in the enriched semantics is not a constraint (as in Fig. 1) but a set of (atomic) constraints where $\{d_1, \cdots, d_n\}$ represents the store $d_1 \sqcup \cdots \sqcup d_n$. For that, the rule of **tell**(c) first decomposes c in its atomic components before adding them to the store.

Marking the Store (Step S2). In [15] we identified several alternatives for marking the final store in order to indicate the information that is relevant to the slice that the programmer wants to recompute. Let us suppose that the final configuration in a partial computation is $(X; \Gamma; S)$. The user has to select a subset S_{sliced} of the final store S that may explain the (wrong) behavior of the program. S_{sliced} can be chosen based on the following criteria:

1. *Causality:* the user identifies, according to her knowledge, a subset $S' \subseteq S$ that needs to be explained (i.e., we need to identify the processes that produced S').
2. *Variable Dependencies:* The user may identify a set of relevant variables $V \subseteq freeVars(S)$ and then, we mark $S_{sliced} = \{c \in S \mid vars(c) \cap V \neq \emptyset\}$.
3. *Unexpected behaviors*: there is a constraint c entailed from the final store that is not expected from the intended behavior of the program. Then, one would be interested in the following marking $S_{sliced} = \bigcup\{S' \subseteq S \mid \bigsqcup S' \models c \text{ and } S' \text{ is set minimal}\}$, where "$S'$ is set minimal" means that for any $S'' \subset S'$, $S'' \not\models c$.
4. *Inconsistent output*: The final store should be consistent with respect to a given specification (constraint) c, i.e., S in conjunction with c must not be inconsistent. In this case, we have $S_{sliced} = \bigcup\{S' \subseteq S \mid \bigsqcup S' \sqcup c \models \mathtt{f} \text{ and } S' \text{ is set minimal}\}$.

For the analysis of CLP programs, it is important also to mark literals (i.e., calls to procedures in CCP). In particular, the programmer may find that a particular goal $p(x)$ is not correct if the parameter x does not satisfy certain conditions/constraints. Hence, we shall consider also markings on the set of processes, i.e., the marking can be also a subset $\Gamma_{sliced} \subseteq \Gamma$.

Trace Slice (Step S3). Starting from the pair $\gamma_{sliced} = (S_{sliced}, \Gamma_{sliced})$ denoting the user's marking, we define a backward slicing step. Roughly, this step allows us to eliminate from the execution trace all the information not related to γ_{sliced}. For that, the fresh constant symbol $\bullet$ is used to denote an "irrelevant" constraint or process. Then, for instance, "$c \sqcup \bullet$" results from a constraint $c \sqcup d$ where d is irrelevant. Similarly in processes as, e.g., **ask** (c) **then** $(P \parallel \bullet) + \bullet$. A replacement is either a pair of the shape $[T/i]$ or $[T/c]$. In the first (resp. second) case, the process with identifier i (resp. constraint c) is replaced with T. We shall use θ to denote a set of replacements and we call these sets as "replacing substitutions". The composition of replacing substitutions θ_1 and θ_2 is given by the set union of θ_1 and θ_2, and is denoted as $\theta_1 \circ \theta_2$.

Input: - a trace $\gamma_0 \xrightarrow{[i_1]_{k_1}} \cdots \xrightarrow{[i_n]_{k_n}} \gamma_n$ where $\gamma_i = (X_i; \Gamma_i; S_i)$
    - a marking $(S_{sliced}, \Gamma_{sliced})$ s.t. $S_{sliced} \subseteq S_n$ and $\Gamma_{sliced} \subseteq \Gamma_n$
Output: a sliced trace $\gamma_0' \longrightarrow \cdots \longrightarrow \gamma_n'$

```
 1 begin
 2      let θ = {[•/i] | P:i ∈ Γₙ \ Γₛ} in
 3      γ'ₙ ← (Xₙ ∩ vars(S_sliced, Γ_sliced); Γₙθ; S_sliced);
 4      for l= n − 1 to 0 do
 5          let⟨θ', c⟩ = sliceProcess(γₗ, γₗ₊₁, iₗ₊₁, kₗ₊₁, θ, Sₗ)  in
 6          S_sliced ← S_sliced ∪ S_minimal(Sₗ, c)
 7          θ ← θ' ∘ θ
 8          γ'ₗ ← (Xₗ ∩ vars(S_sliced, Γ_sliced) ; Γₗθ ; Sₗ ∩ S_sliced)
 9      end
10 end
```

Algorithm 1. Trace Slicer. $S_{minimal}(S, c) = \emptyset$ if $c = \mathsf{t}$; otherwise, $S_{minimal}(S, c) = \bigcup \{S' \subseteq S \mid \bigsqcup S' \models c$ and S' is set minimal$\}$.

Algorithm 1 extends the one in [15] to deal with the marking on processes (Γ_{sliced}). The last configuration (γ_n' in line 3) means that we only observe the local variables of interest, i.e., those in $vars(S_{sliced}, \Gamma_{sliced})$ as well as the relevant processes (Γ_{sliced}) and constraints (S_{sliced}). The algorithm backwardly computes the slicing by accumulating replacing pairs in θ (line 7). The new replacing substitutions are computed by the function $sliceProcess$ that returns both, a replacement substitution and a constraint needed in the case of ask agents as explained below.

```
 1 Function sliceProcess(γ, ψ, i, k, θ, S)
 2      let γ = (X_γ; Γ, P:i, Γ'; S_γ) and ψ = (X_ψ; Γ, Γ_Q, Γ'; S_ψ) in
 3      match P with
 4          case tell(c) do
 5              let c' = sliceConstraints(X_γ, X_ψ, S_γ, S_ψ, S) in
 6              if c' = • or c' = ∃x̄.• then return  ⟨[•/i], t⟩ else return  ⟨[tell(c')/i], t⟩;
 7          case ∑ ask (cₗ) then Qₗ do
 8              if Γ_Qθ = • then return  ⟨[•/i], t⟩ else return
                  ⟨[ask (cₖ) then (Γ_Qθ) + • / i], cₖ⟩;
 9          case (local x) Q do
10              let {x'} = X_ψ \ X_γ in
11              if Γ_Q[x'/x]θ = • then return  ⟨[•/i], t⟩ else return
                  ⟨[(local x') Γ_Q[x'/x]θ/i], t⟩;
12          case p(ȳ) do
13              | if Γ_Qθ = • then return  ⟨[•/i], t⟩ else return  ⟨∅, t⟩;
14      end
15 end
16 Function sliceConstraints(X_γ, X_ψ, S_γ, S_ψ, S)
17      let S_c = S_ψ \ S_γ and θ = ∅ in
18      foreach cₐ ∈ S_c \ S do  θ ← θ ∘ [•/cₐ] ;
19      return ∃_{X_ψ\X_γ}.⨆ S_cθ
20 end
```

Algorithm 2. Slicing processes and constraints

Marking Algorithms. Let us explain how the function $sliceProcess$ works. Consider for instance the process $Q = (\mathbf{ask}\ (c')\ \mathbf{then}\ P) + (\mathbf{ask}\ (c)\ \mathbf{then}\ \mathbf{tell}(d \sqcup e))$ and assume that we are backwardly slicing the trace $\cdots \gamma \xrightarrow{[i]_2} \cdots \psi \xrightarrow{[j]} \rho \cdots$

where Q (identified with i) is reduced in γ by choosing the second branch and, in ψ, the tell agent $\mathbf{tell}(d \sqcup e)$ (identified by j) is executed. Assume that the configuration ρ has already been sliced and d was considered irrelevant and removed (see $S_l \cap S_{sliced}$ in line 8 of Algorithm 1). The procedure *sliceProcess* is applied to ψ and it determines that only e is relevant in $\mathbf{tell}(d \sqcup e)$. Hence, the replacement $[\mathbf{tell}(\bullet \sqcup e)/j]$ is returned (see line 7 in Algorithm 1). The procedure is then applied to γ. We already know that the ask agent Q is (partially) relevant since $\mathbf{tell}(d \sqcup e)\theta \neq \bullet$ (i.e., the selected branch does contribute to the final result). Thus, the replacement $[\bullet + \mathbf{ask}\ (c)\ \mathbf{then}\ \mathbf{tell}(\bullet \sqcup e)/i]$ is accumulated in order to show that the first branch is irrelevant. Moreover, since the entailment of c was necessary for the reduction, the procedure returns also the constraint c (line 5 of Algorithm 1) and the constraints needed to entail c are added to the set of relevant constraints (line 6 of Algorithm 1).

Example 1. Consider the following (wrong) CLP program:

```
length([],0).
length([A | L],M) :- M = N, length(L, N).
```

The translation to CCP is similar to the example in Sect. 2.1. An excerpt of a possible trace for the execution of the goal `length([10,20], Ans).` is

```
[0 ; length([10,20],Ans) ; t] -->
[0 ; ask() ... + ask() ... ; t] ->
[0 ; local ... ; t] ->
[H1 L1 N1 M1 ; [10,20]= [H1|L1] || Ans=N1 || N1=M1 || length(L1, M1) ; t] ->
...
[... H2 L2 N2 M2 ; [20]=[H2 | L2] || M1=N2 || N2=M2 || length(L2, M2) ; [10,20]= [H1|L1], Ans=N1, N1=M1] ->
[... H2 L2 N2 M2 ; M1=N2 || N2=M2 || length(L2, M2) ; [10,20]= [H1|L1], Ans=N1, N1=M1, [20]=[H2 | L2]] ->
...
[... H2 L2 N2 M2 ; M2=0 ; [10,20]= [H1|L1], Ans=N1, N1=M1, [20]=[H2 | L2], M1=N2, N2=M2, L2=[]] ->
[... H2 L2 N2 M2 ; [10,20]= [H1|L1], Ans=N1, N1=M1, [20]=[H2 | L2], M1=N2, N2=M2, L2=[], M2=0 ]
```

Here, we can see how the calls to the process definition `length` are unfolded and, in each state, new constraints are added. Those constraint relate, e.g., the variable `Ans` and the local variables created in each invocation (e.g., `M1` and `M2`).

In the last configuration, it is possible to mark only the equalities dealing with numerical expressions (i.e., `Ans=N1,N1=M1,M1=N2,N2=M2,M2=0`) and the resulting trace will abstract away from all the constraints and processes dealing with equalities on lists:

```
[0 ; length([10,20],Ans) ; t] -->
[0 ; * + ask() ... ; t] ->
[0 ; local ... ; t] ->
[N1 M1 ; * || Ans=N1 || N1=M1 || length(L1, M1) ; t] ->
[N1 M1 ; Ans=N1 || N1=M1 || length(L1, M1) ; ] ->
[N1 M1 ; N1=M1 || length(L1, M1) ;   Ans=N1] ->
[N1 M1 ; length(L1, M1) ;  Ans=N1, N1=M1] ->
...
```

The fourth line should be useful to discover that `Ans` cannot be equal to `M1` (the parameter used in the second invocation to `length`).

4 An Assertion Language for Logic Programs

The declarative flavor of programming with constraints in CCP and CLP allows the user to reason about (partial) invariants that must hold during the execution of her programs. In this section we give a simple yet powerful language of assertion to state such invariants. Then, we give a step further in automatizing the process of debugging.

Definition 4 (Assertion Language). *Assertions are built from:*
$F ::= \texttt{pos}(c) \mid \texttt{neg}(c) \mid \texttt{cons}(c) \mid \texttt{icons}(c) \mid F \oplus F \mid p(\overline{x})[F] \mid p(\overline{x})\langle F \rangle$
where c is a constraint ($c \in \mathcal{C}$), $p(\cdot)$ is a process name and $\oplus \in \{\wedge, \vee, \rightarrow\}$.

The first four constructs deal with partial assertions about the current store. These constructs check, respectively, whether the constraint c: (1) is entailed, (2) is not entailed, (3) is consistent wrt the current store or (4) leads to an inconsistency when added to the current store. Assertions of the form $F \oplus F$ have the usual meaning. The assertions $p(\overline{x})[F]$ states that all instances of the form $p(\overline{t})$ in the current configuration must satisfy the assertion F. The assertions $p(\overline{x})\langle F \rangle$ is similar to the previous one but it checks for the existence of an instance $p(\overline{t})$ that satisfies the assertion F.

Let $\pi(i) = (X_i; \Gamma_i; S_i)$. We shall use $store(\pi(i))$ to denote the constraint $\exists X_i. \bigsqcup S_i$ and $procs(\pi(i))$ to denote the sequence of processes Γ_i. The semantics for assertions is formalized next.

Definition 5 (Semantics). *Let π be a sequence of configurations and F be an assertion. We inductively define $\pi, i \models_{\mathcal{F}} F$ (read as π satisfies the formula F at position i) as:*

- $\pi, i \models_{\mathcal{F}} \texttt{pos}(c)$ *if* $store(\pi(i)) \models c$.
- $\pi, i \models_{\mathcal{F}} \texttt{neg}(c)$ *if* $store(\pi(i)) \not\models c$.
- $\pi, i \models_{\mathcal{F}} \texttt{cons}(c)$ *if* $store(\pi(i)) \sqcup c \not\models f$.
- $\pi, i \models_{\mathcal{F}} \texttt{icons}(c)$ *if* $store(\pi(i)) \sqcup c \models f$.
- $\pi, i \models_{\mathcal{F}} F \wedge G$ *if* $\pi, i \models_{\mathcal{F}} F$ *and* $\pi, i \models_{\mathcal{F}} G$.
- $\pi, i \models_{\mathcal{F}} F \vee G$ *if* $\pi, i \models_{\mathcal{F}} F$ *or* $\pi, i \models_{\mathcal{F}} G$.
- $\pi, i \models_{\mathcal{F}} F \rightarrow G$ *if* $\pi, i \models_{\mathcal{F}} F$ *implies* $\pi, i \models_{\mathcal{F}} G$.
- $\pi, i \models_{\mathcal{F}} p(\overline{x})[F]$ *if for all* $p(\overline{t}) \in procs(\pi(i))$, $\pi, i \models_{\mathcal{F}} F[\overline{t}/\overline{x}]$.
- $\pi, i \models_{\mathcal{F}} p(\overline{x})\langle F \rangle$ *if there exists* $p(\overline{t}) \in procs(\pi(i))$, $\pi, i \models_{\mathcal{F}} F[\overline{t}/\overline{x}]$.

If it is not the case that $\pi, i \models_{\mathcal{F}} F$, then we say that F does not hold at $\pi(i)$ and we write $\pi(i) \not\models_{\mathcal{F}} F$.

The above definition is quite standard and reflects the intuitions given above. Moreover, let us define $\sim F$ as $\sim \texttt{pos}(c) = \texttt{neg}(c)$ (and vice-versa), $\sim \texttt{cons}(c) = \texttt{icons}(c)$ (and vice-versa), $\sim (F \oplus F)$ as usual and $\sim p(\overline{x})[F(\overline{x})] = p(\overline{x})\langle \sim F(\overline{x}) \rangle$ (and vice-versa). Note that, $\pi(i) \models_{\mathcal{F}} F$ iff $\pi(i) \not\models_{\mathcal{F}} \sim F$.

Example 2. Assume that the store in $\pi(1)$ is $S = x \in 0..10$. Then,

- $\pi, 1 \models_{\mathcal{F}} \texttt{cons}(x = 5)$, i.e., the store is consistent wrt the specification $x = 5$.
- $\pi, 1 \not\models_{\mathcal{F}} \texttt{icons}(x = 5)$, i.e., the store is not inconsistent wrt the specification $x = 5$.
- $\pi, 1 \not\models_{\mathcal{F}} \texttt{pos}(x = 5)$, i.e., the store is not "strong enough" in order to satisfy the specification $x = 5$.

- $\pi, 1 \models_{\mathcal{F}} \texttt{neg}(x = 5)$, i.e., store is "consistent enough" to guarantee that it is not the case that $x = 5$.

Note that $\pi, i \models_{\mathcal{F}} \texttt{pos}(c)$ implies $\pi, i \models_{\mathcal{F}} \texttt{cons}(c)$. However, the other direction is in general not true (as shown above). We note that CCP and CLP are monotonic in the sense that when the store c evolves into d, it must be the case that $d \models c$ (i.e., information is monotonically accumulated). Hence, $\pi, i \models \texttt{pos}(c)$ implies $\pi, i{+}j \models \texttt{pos}(c)$. Finally, if the store becomes inconsistent, $\texttt{cons}(c)$ does not hold for any c. Temporal [23] and linear [14] variants of CCP remove such restriction on monotonicity.

Checking assertions amounts, roughly, to testing the entailment relation in the underlying constraint system. Checking entailments is the basic operation CCP agents perform. Hence, from the implementation point of view, verification of assertions does not introduce a significant extra computational cost.

Example 3 (Conditional assertions). Let us introduce some patterns of assertions useful for verification.

- *Conditional constraints*: The assertion $\texttt{pos}(c) \to F$ checks for F only if c can be deduced from the store. For instance, the assertion $\texttt{pos}(c) \to \texttt{neg}(d)$ says that d must not be deduced when the store implies c.
- *Conditional predicates*: Let $G = p(\overline{x})\langle\texttt{cons(t)}\rangle$. The assertion $G \to F$ states that F must be verified whenever there is a call/goal of the form $p(\overline{t})$ in the context. Moreover, $(\sim G) \to F$ verifies F when there are no calls of the form $p(\overline{t})$ in the context.

4.1 Dynamic Slicing with Assertions

Assertions allow the user to specify conditions that her program must satisfy during execution. If this is not the case, the program should stop and start the debugging process. In fact, the assertions may help to give a suitable marking pair $(S_{sliced}, \Gamma_{sliced})$ for the step **S2** of our algorithm as follows.

Definition 6. *Let F be an assertion, π be a partial computation, $n > 0$ and assume that $\pi, n \not\models_{\mathcal{F}} F$, i.e., $\pi(n)$ fails to establish the assertion F. Let $\pi(n) = (X; \Gamma; S)$. As testing hypotheses, we define $symp(\pi, F, n) = (S_{sl}, \Gamma_{sl})$ where*

1. *If $F = \textbf{\textit{pos}}(c)$ then $S_{sl} = \{d \in S \mid vars(d) \cap vars(c) \neq \emptyset\}$, $\Gamma_{sl} = \emptyset$.*
2. *If $F = \textbf{\textit{neg}}(c)$ then $S_{sl} = \bigcup\{S' \subseteq S \mid \bigsqcup S' \models c$ and S' is set min.$\}$, $\Gamma_{sl} = \emptyset$*
3. *If $F = \textbf{\textit{cons}}(c)$ then $S_{sl} = \bigcup\{S' \subseteq S \mid \bigsqcup S' \sqcup c \models f$ and S' is set minimal$\}$, $\Gamma_{sl} = \emptyset$.*
4. *If $F = \textbf{\textit{icons}}(c)$ $S_{sl} = \{d \in S \mid vars(d) \cap vars(c) \neq \emptyset\}$ and $\Gamma_{sl} = \emptyset$.*
5. *If $F = F_1 \wedge F_2$ then $symp(\pi, F_1, n) \cup symp(\pi, F_2, n)$.*
6. *If $F = F_1 \vee F_2$ then $symp(\pi, F_1, n) \cap symp(\pi, F_2, n)$.*
7. *If $F = F_1 \to F_2$ then $symp(\pi, \sim F_1, n) \cup symp(\pi, F_2, n)$.*
8. *If $F = p(\overline{x})[F_1]$ then $S_{sl} = \emptyset$ and $\Gamma_{sl} = \{p(\overline{t}) \in \Gamma \mid \pi, n \not\models_{\mathcal{F}} F_1[\overline{t}/\overline{x}]\}$.*
9. *If $F = p(\overline{x})\langle F_1\rangle$ then $S_{sl} = \{d \in S \mid vars(d) \cap vars(F_1) \neq \emptyset\}$, $\Gamma_{sl} = \{p(\overline{t}) \in \Gamma\}$*

Let us give some intuitions about the above definition. Consider a (partial) computation π of length n where $\pi(n) \not\models_{\mathcal{F}} F$. In the case (1) above, c must be entailed but the current store is not strong enough to do it. A good guess is to start examining the processes that added constraints using the same variables as in c. It may be the case that such processes should have added more information to entail c as expected in the specification F. Similarly for the case (4): c in conjunction with the current store should be inconsistent but it is not. Then, more information on the common variables should have been added. In the case (2), c should not be entailed but the store indeed entails c. In this case, we mark the set of constraints that entails c. The case (3) is similar. In cases (5) to (7) we use $\cup$ and $\cap$ respectively for point-wise union and intersection in the pair (S_{sl}, Γ_{sl}). These cases are self-explanatory (e.g., if $F_1 \wedge F_2$ fails, we collect the failure information of either F_1 or F_2). In (8), we mark all the calls that do not satisfy the expected assertion $F(\overline{x})$. In (9), if F fails, it means that either (a) there are no calls of the shape $p(\overline{t})$ in the context or (b) none of the calls $p(\overline{t})$ satisfy F_1. For (a), similarly to the case (1), a good guess is to examine the processes that added constraints with common variables to F_1 and see which one should have added more information to entail F_1. As for (b), we also select all the calls of the form $p(\overline{t})$ from the context. The reader may compare these definitions with the information selected in Step **S2** in Sect. 3, regarding possibly wrong behavior.

Classification of Assertions. As we explained in Sect. 2.1, computations in CLP can succeed or fail and the answers to a goal is the set of constraints obtained from successful computations. Hence, according to the kind of assertion, it is important to determine when the assertions in Definition 4 must stop or not the computation to start the debugging process. For that, we introduce the following classification:

- **post-conditions, post(F) assertions**: assertions that are meant to be verified only when an answer is found. This kind of assertions are used to test the "quality" of the answers wrt the specification. In this case, the slicing process begins only when an answer is computed and it does not satisfy one of the assertions. Note that assertions of the form $p(\overline{x})[F(\overline{x})]$ and $p(\overline{x})\langle F(\overline{x})\rangle$ are irrelevant as post-conditions since the set of goals in an answer must be empty.
- **path invariants, inv(F) assertions**: assertions that are meant to hold along the whole computation. Then, not satisfying an invariant must be understood as a symptom of an error and the computation must stop. We note that due to monotonicity, only assertions of the form neg(c) and cons(c) can be used to stop the computation (note that if the current configuration fails to satisfy neg(c), then any successor state will also fail to satisfy that assertion). Constraints of the form pos(c), icons(c) can be only checked when the answer is found since, not satisfying those conditions in the partial computation, does not imply that the final state will not satisfy them.

4.2 Experiments

We conclude this section with a series of examples showing the use of assertions. Examples 4 and 5 deal with CLP programs while Examples 6 and 7 with CCP programs.

Example 4. The debugger can automatically start and produce the same marking in Example 1 with the following (invariant) assertion:

```
length([A | L],M) :- M = N, length(L, N), inv(pos(M>0)).
```

Example 5. Consider the following CLP program (written in GNU-Prolog with integer finite domains) for solving the well known problem of posing N queens on a $N \times N$ chessboard in such a way that they do not attack each other.

```
queens(N, Queens) :- length(Queens, N), fd_domain(Queens,1,N),
                     constrain(Queens), fd_labeling(Queens,[]).
constrain(Queens) :-fd_all_different(Queens), diagonal(Queens).
diagonal([]).
diagonal([Q|Queens]):-secure(Q, 1, Queens), diagonal(Queens).
secure(_,_,[]).
secure(X,D,[Q|Queens]) :- doesnotattack(X,Q,D),D1 is D+1, secure(X,D1,Queens).
doesnotattack(X,Y,D) :- X + D #\= Y,Y + X #\= D.
```

The program contains one mistake, which causes the introduction of a few additional and not correct solutions, e.g., `[1,5,4,3,2]` for the goal `queens(5,X)`. The user now has two possible strategies: either she lets the interpreter compute the solutions, one by one and then, when she sees a wrong solution she uses the slicer for marking manually the final store to get the sliced computation; or she can define an assertion to be verified. In this particular case, any solution must satisfy that the difference between two consecutive positions in the list must be greater than 1. Hence, the user can introduce the following post-condition assertion:

```
secure(X,D,[Q|Queens]) :- doesnotattack(X,Q,D),D1 is D+1, secure(X,D1,Queens),
                          post(cons(Q #\= X+1)).
```

Now the slicer stops as soon as the constraint `X #\= Q+1` becomes inconsistent with the store in a successful computation (e.g., the assertion fails on the –partial– assignment "5,4") and an automatic slicing is performed.

Example 6. In [15] we presented a compelling example of slicing for a timed CCP program modeling the synchronization of events in musical rhythmic patterns. As shown in Example 2 at http://subsell.logic.at/slicer/, the slicer for CCP was able to sufficiently abstract away from irrelevant processes and constraints to highlight the problem in a faulty program. However, the process of stopping the computation to start the debugging was left to the user. The property that failed in the program can be naturally expressed as an assertion. Namely, in the whole computation, if the constraint `beat` is present (representing a sound in the musical rhythm), the constraint `stop` cannot be present (representing the end of the rhythm). This can be written as the conditional assertion `pos(beat)` → `neg(stop)`. Following Definition 6, the constraints marked in the wrong computation are the same we considered in [15], thus automatizing completely the process of identifying the wrong computation.

Example 7. Example 3 in the URL above illustrates the use of timed CCP for the specification of biochemical systems (we invite the reader to compare in the website the sliced and non-sliced traces). Roughly, in that model, constraints of the form `Mdm2` (resp. `Mdm2A`) state that the protein `Mdm2` is present (resp. absent). The model includes activation (and inhibition) of biological rules modeled as processes (omitting some details) of the form **ask** (`Mdm2A`) **then next tell**(`Mdm2`) modeling that "if `Mdm2` is absent now, then it must be present in the next time-unit". The interaction of many of these rules makes the model trickier since rules may "compete" for resources and then, we can wrongly observe at the same time-unit that `Mdm2` is both present and absent. An assertion of the form $(\mathtt{pos}(\mathtt{Mdm2A}) \rightarrow \mathtt{neg}(\mathtt{Mdm2})) \wedge (\mathtt{pos}(\mathtt{Mdm2}) \rightarrow \mathtt{neg}(\mathtt{Mdm2A}))$ will automatically stop the computation and produce the same marking we used to depurate the program in the website.

5 Related Work and Conclusions

Related Work. Assertions for automatizing a slicing process have been previously introduced in [4] for the functional logic language Maude. The language they consider as well as the type of assertions are completely different from ours. They do not have constraints, and deal with functional and equational computations. Another previous work [31] introduced static and dynamic slicing for CLP programs. However, [31] essentially aims at identifying the parts of a goal which do not share variables, to divide the program in slices which do not interact. Our approach considers more situations, not only variable dependencies, but also other kinds of wrong behaviors. Moreover we have assertions, and hence an automatic slicing mechanism not considered in [31]. The well known debugging box model of Prolog [32] introduces a tool for observing the evolution of atoms during their reduction in the search tree. We believe that our methodology might be integrated with the box model and may extend some of its features. For instance, the box model makes basic simplifications by asking the user to specify which predicates she wants to observe. In our case, one entire computational path is simplified automatically by considering the marked information and identifying the constraints and the atoms which are relevant for such information.

Conclusions and Future Work. In this paper we have first extended a previous framework for dynamic slicing of (timed) CCP programs to the case of CLP programs. We considered a slightly different marking mechanism, extended to atoms besides constraints. Don't know non-determinism in CLP requires a different identification of the computations of interest wrt CCP. We considered different modalities specified by the user for selecting successful computations rather than all possible partial computations. As another contribution of this paper, in order to automatize the slicing process, we have introduced an assertion language. This language is rather flexible and allows one to specify different types of assertions that can be applied to successful computations or to all possible partial computations. When assertions are not satisfied by a state of a selected computation then an automatic slicing of such computation can start.

We implemented a prototype of the slicer in Maude and showed its use in debugging several programs. We are currently extending the tool to deal with CLP don't know non-determinism. Being CLP a generalization of logic programming, our extended implementation could be also eventually used to analyze Prolog programs. Integrating the kind of assertions proposed here with already implemented debugging mechanisms in Prolog is an interesting future direction. We also plan to add more advanced graphical tools to our prototype, as well as to study the integration of our framework with other debugging techniques such as the box model and declarative or approximated debuggers [2,18]. We also want to investigate the relation of our technique with dynamic testing (e.g. concolic techniques) and extend the assertion language with temporal operators, e.g. the past operator ($\ominus$) for expressing the relation between two consecutive states. Another future topic of investigation is a static version of our framework in order to try to compare and possibly integrate it with analyses and semi automatic corrections based on different formal techniques, and other programming paradigms [1,3,5,7,8].

Acknowledgments. We thank the anonymous reviewers for their detailed and very useful criticisms and recommendations that helped us to improve our paper. The work of Olarte was supported by CNPq and by CAPES, Colciencias, and INRIA via the STIC AmSud project EPIC (Proc. No 88881.117603/2016-01), and the project CLASSIC.

References

1. Alpuente, M., Ballis, D., Baggi, M., Falaschi, M.: A fold/unfold transformation framework for rewrite theories extended to CCT. In: Proceedings of PEPM 2010, pp. 43–52. ACM (2010)
2. Alpuente, M., Ballis, D., Correa, F., Falaschi, M.: An integrated framework for the diagnosis and correction of rule-based programs. Theor. Comput. Sci. **411**(47), 4055–4101 (2010)
3. Alpuente, M., Ballis, D., Falaschi, M., Romero, D.: A semi-automatic methodology for repairing faulty web sites. In: Proceedings of SEFM 2006, pp. 31–40. IEEE (2006)
4. Alpuente, M., Ballis, D., Frechina, F., Sapiña, J.: Debugging maude programs via runtime assertion checking and trace slicing. J. Log. Algebr. Meth. Program. **85**, 707–736 (2016)
5. Alpuente, M., Falaschi, M., Moreno, G., Vidal, G.: A transformation system for lazy functional logic programs. In: Middeldorp, A., Sato, T. (eds.) FLOPS 1999. LNCS, vol. 1722, pp. 147–162. Springer, Heidelberg (1999). https://doi.org/10.1007/10705424_10
6. Bernini, A., Brodo, L., Degano, P., Falaschi, M., Hermith, D.: Process calculi for biological processes. Nat. Comput. **17**(2), 345–373 (2018)
7. Bodei, C., Brodo, L., Bruni, R.: Static detection of logic flaws in service-oriented applications. In: Degano, P., Viganò, L. (eds.) ARSPA-WITS 2009. LNCS, vol. 5511, pp. 70–87. Springer, Heidelberg (2009). https://doi.org/10.1007/978-3-642-03459-6_5

8. Bodei, C., Brodo, L., Bruni, R., Chiarugi, D.: A flat process calculus for nested membrane interactions. Sci. Ann. Comp. Sci. **24**(1), 91–136 (2014)
9. Brodo, L.: On the expressiveness of the π-calculus and the mobile ambients. In: Johnson, M., Pavlovic, D. (eds.) AMAST 2010. LNCS, vol. 6486, pp. 44–59. Springer, Heidelberg (2011). https://doi.org/10.1007/978-3-642-17796-5_3
10. Chiarugi, D., Falaschi, M., Hermith, D., Olarte, C., Torella, L.: Modelling non-Markovian dynamics in biochemical reactions. BMC Syst. Biol. **9**(S–3), S8 (2015)
11. Chiarugi, D., Falaschi, M., Olarte, C., Palamidessi, C.: Compositional modelling of signalling pathways in timed concurrent constraint programming. In: Proceedings of ACM BCB 2010, pp. 414–417. ACM, New York (2010)
12. Codish, M., Falaschi, M., Marriott, K.: Suspension analyses for concurrent logic programs. TOPLAS **16**(3), 649–686 (1994)
13. Comini, M., Titolo, L., Villanueva, A.: Abstract diagnosis for timed concurrent constraint programs. TPLP **11**(4–5), 487–502 (2011)
14. Fages, F., Ruet, P., Soliman, S.: Linear concurrent constraint programming: operational and phase semantics. Inf. Comput. **165**(1), 14–41 (2001)
15. Falaschi, M., Gabbrielli, M., Olarte, C., Palamidessi, C.: Slicing concurrent constraint programs. In: Hermenegildo, M.V., Lopez-Garcia, P. (eds.) LOPSTR 2016. LNCS, vol. 10184, pp. 76–93. Springer, Cham (2017). https://doi.org/10.1007/978-3-319-63139-4_5
16. Falaschi, M., Olarte, C., Palamidessi, C.: A framework for abstract interpretation of timed concurrent constraint programs. In: Proceedings of PPDP 2009, pp. 207–218. ACM (2009)
17. Falaschi, M., Olarte, C., Palamidessi, C.: Abstract interpretation of temporal concurrent constraint programs. TPLP **15**(3), 312–357 (2015)
18. Falaschi, M., Olarte, C., Palamidessi, C., Valencia, F.: Declarative diagnosis of temporal concurrent constraint programs. In: Dahl, V., Niemelä, I. (eds.) ICLP 2007. LNCS, vol. 4670, pp. 271–285. Springer, Heidelberg (2007). https://doi.org/10.1007/978-3-540-74610-2_19
19. Jaffar, J., Maher, M.: Constraint logic programming: a survey. J. Log. Program. **19–20**(Supplement 1), 503–581 (1994)
20. Jaffar, J., Maher, M.J., Marriott, K., Stuckey, P.J.: The semantics of constraint logic programs. J. Log. Program. **37**(1–3), 1–46 (1998)
21. Josep, S.: A vocabulary of program slicing-based techniques. ACM Comput. Surv. **44**(3), 12:1–12:41 (2012)
22. Korel, B., Laski, J.: Dynamic program slicing. Inf. Process. Lett. **29**(3), 155–163 (1988)
23. Nielsen, M., Palamidessi, C., Valencia, F.D.: Temporal concurrent constraint programming: denotation, logic and applications. Nord. J. Comput. **9**(1), 145–188 (2002)
24. Olarte, C., Chiarugi, D., Falaschi, M., Hermith, D.: A proof theoretic view of spatial and temporal dependencies in biochemical systems. Theor. Comput. Sci. **641**, 25–42 (2016)
25. Olarte, C., Rueda, C., Valencia, F.D.: Models and emerging trends of concurrent constraint programming. Constraints **18**(4), 535–578 (2013)
26. Olarte, C., Valencia, F.D.: Universal concurrent constraint programing: symbolic semantics and applications to security. In: Proceedings of SAC 2008, pp. 145–150. ACM (2008)
27. Saraswat, V.A., Jagadeesan, R., Gupta, V.: Timed default concurrent constraint programming. J. Symb. Comput. **22**(5/6), 475–520 (1996)

28. Saraswat, V.A., Rinard, M.C., Panangaden, P.: Semantic foundations of concurrent constraint programming. In: Wise, D.S. (ed.) POPL, pp. 333–352. ACM Press, New York (1991)
29. Shapiro, E.: The family of concurrent logic programming languages. ACM Comput. Surv. **21**(3), 413–510 (1989)
30. Shapiro, E.Y.: Algorithmic Program DeBugging. MIT Press, Cambridge (1983)
31. Szilágyi, G., Gyimóthy, T., Maluszyński, J.: Static and dynamic slicing of constraint logic programs. Autom. Softw. Eng. **9**(1), 41–65 (2002)
32. Clocksin, W.F., Mellish, C.S.: Programming in Prolog. Springer, Heidelberg (1981). https://doi.org/10.1007/978-3-642-96661-3
33. Weiser, M.: Program slicing. IEEE Trans. Soft. Eng. **10**(4), 352–357 (1984)

Program Analysis

Eliminating Unstable Tests in Floating-Point Programs

Laura Titolo[1(✉)], César A. Muñoz[2(✉)], Marco A. Feliú[1], and Mariano M. Moscato[1]

[1] National Institute of Aerospace, Hampton, USA
{laura.titolo,marco.feliu,mariano.moscato}@nianet.org
[2] NASA Langley Research Center, Hampton, USA
cesar.a.munoz@nasa.gov

Abstract. Round-off errors arising from the difference between real numbers and their floating-point representation cause the control flow of conditional floating-point statements to deviate from the ideal flow of the real-number computation. This problem, which is called test instability, may result in a significant difference between the computation of a floating-point program and the expected output in real arithmetic. In this paper, a formally proven program transformation is proposed to detect and correct the effects of unstable tests. The output of this transformation is a floating-point program that is guaranteed to return either the result of the original floating-point program when it can be assured that both its real and its floating-point flows agree or a warning when these flows may diverge. The proposed approach is illustrated with the transformation of the core computation of a polygon containment algorithm developed at NASA that is used in a geofencing system for unmanned aircraft systems.

Keywords: Floating-point numbers · Round-off error · Program transformation · Test instability · Formal verification

1 Introduction

Floating-point numbers are widely used to represent real numbers in computer programs since they offer a good trade-off between efficiency and precision. The round-off error of a floating-point expression is the difference between the ideal computation in real arithmetic and the actual floating-point computation. These round-off errors accumulate during numerical computations. Besides having a direct effect on the result of mathematical operations, round-off errors may significantly impact the control flow of a program. This happens when the guard of a conditional statement contains a floating-point expression whose round-off

Research by the first, the third, and the fourth authors was supported by the National Aeronautics and Space Administration under NASA/NIA Cooperative Agreement NNL09AA00A.

F. Mesnard and P. J. Stuckey (Eds.): LOPSTR 2018, LNCS 11408, pp. 169–183, 2019.
https://doi.org/10.1007/978-3-030-13838-7_10

error makes the actual Boolean value of the guard differ from the value that would be obtained assuming real arithmetic. In this case, the conditional statement is called an *unstable test*. Unstable tests are an inherent feature of floating-point programs. In general, it is not possible to completely avoid them. However, it is possible to mitigate their effect by transforming the original program into another program that conservatively (and soundly) detects and corrects unstable tests.

This paper presents a program transformation technique to transform a given program into a new one that returns either the same result of the original program or a warning when the real and floating-point flows may diverge. This transformation is parametric with respect to two Boolean abstractions that take into consideration the round-off error in the expressions occurring in the guard. The transformation replaces the unstable conditions with more restrictive conditions that are guaranteed to preserve the control flow of stable tests. The correctness of the proposed transformation is formally verified in the Prototype Verification System (PVS) [16].

The remainder of the paper is organized as follows. Section 2 provides technical background on floating-point numbers and round-off errors. The proposed program transformation technique is presented in Sect. 3. Section 4 illustrates this technique by transforming the core logic of an algorithm for polygon containment that is part of a geofencing system developed by NASA. Section 5 discusses related work and Sect. 6 concludes the paper.

2 Round-Off Errors and Unstable Tests

A floating-point number can be formalized as a pair of integers $(m, e) \in \mathbb{Z}^2$, where m is called the *significand* and e the *exponent* of the float [1,10]. A floating-point *format* f is defined as a pair of integers (p, e_{min}), where p is called the *precision* and e_{min} is called the *minimal exponent*. For instance, IEEE single and double precision floating-point numbers are specified by the formats $(24, 149)$ and $(53, 1074)$, respectively. A *canonical* float is a float such that is either a normal or subnormal. A *normal* float is a float such that the significand cannot be multiplied by the radix and still fit in the format. A *subnormal* float is a float having the minimal exponent such that its significand can be multiplied by the radix and still fit in the format. Henceforth, $\mathbb{F}$ will denote the set of floating-point numbers in canonical form and the expression $\tilde{v}$ will denote a floating-point number (m, e) in $\mathbb{F}$. A conversion function $R : \mathbb{F} \to \mathbb{R}$ is defined to refer to the real number represented by a given float, i.e., $R((m, e)) = m \cdot \beta^e$.

The expression $F_f(r)$ denotes the floating-point number in format f *closest* to r. The format f will be omitted when clear from the context. Let $\tilde{v}$ be a floating-point number that represents a real number r, the difference $|R(\tilde{v}) - r|$ is called the *round-off error* (or *rounding error*) of $\tilde{v}$ with respect to r.

2.1 Unstable Tests

Given a set $\widetilde{\Omega}$ of pre-defined floating-point operations, the corresponding set Ω of operations over real numbers, a finite set $\mathbb{V}$ of variables representing real values, and a finite set $\widetilde{\mathbb{V}}$ of variables representing floating-point values, where $\mathbb{V}$ and $\widetilde{\mathbb{V}}$ are disjoint, the sets $\mathbb{A}$ and $\widetilde{\mathbb{A}}$ of arithmetic expressions over real numbers and over floating-point numbers, respectively, are defined by the following grammar.

$$A ::= d \mid x \mid op(A, \ldots, A), \qquad \widetilde{A} ::= \tilde{d} \mid \tilde{x} \mid \widetilde{op}(\widetilde{A}, \ldots, \widetilde{A}),$$

where $A \in \mathbb{A}$, $d \in \mathbb{R}$, $x \in \mathbb{V}$, $op \in \Omega$, $\widetilde{A} \in \widetilde{\mathbb{A}}$, $\tilde{d} \in \mathbb{F}$, $\tilde{x} \in \widetilde{\mathbb{V}}$, $\widetilde{op} \in \widetilde{\Omega}$. It is assumed that there is a function $\chi_r : \widetilde{\mathbb{V}} \to \mathbb{V}$ that associates to each floating-point variable $\tilde{x}$ a variable $x \in \mathbb{V}$ representing the real value of $\tilde{x}$. The function $R_{\mathbb{A}} : \widetilde{\mathbb{A}} \to \mathbb{A}$ converts an arithmetic expression on floating-point numbers to an arithmetic expression on real numbers. It is defined by simply replacing each floating-point operation with the corresponding one on real numbers and by applying R and χ_r to floating-point values and variables, respectively.

Boolean expressions are defined by the following grammar.

$$B ::= true \mid false \mid B \wedge B \mid B \vee B \mid \neg B \mid A < A \mid A = A \mid \widetilde{A} < \widetilde{A} \mid \widetilde{A} = \widetilde{A},$$

where $A \in \mathbb{A}$ and $\widetilde{A} \in \widetilde{\mathbb{A}}$. The conjunction $\wedge$, disjunction $\vee$, negation $\neg$, *true*, and *false* have the usual classical logic meaning. The symbols $\mathbb{B}$ and $\widetilde{\mathbb{B}}$ denote the domain of Boolean expressions over real and floating-point numbers, respectively. The function $R_{\mathbb{B}} : \widetilde{\mathbb{B}} \to \mathbb{B}$ converts a Boolean expression on floating-point numbers to a Boolean expression on real numbers. Given a variable assignment $\sigma : \mathbb{V} \to \mathbb{R}$, $eval_{\mathbb{B}}(\sigma, B) \in \{true, false\}$ denotes the evaluation of the real Boolean expression B. Similarly, given $\widetilde{B} \in \widetilde{\mathbb{B}}$ and $\tilde{\sigma} : \widetilde{\mathbb{V}} \to \mathbb{F}$, $\widetilde{eval}_{\widetilde{\mathbb{B}}}(\tilde{\sigma}, \widetilde{B}) \in \{true, false\}$ denotes the evaluation of the floating-point Boolean expression $\widetilde{B}$.

The expression language considered in this paper contains binary and n-ary conditionals, let expressions, arithmetic expressions, and a warning exceptional statement. Given a set Σ of function symbols, the syntax of program expressions in $\mathbb{S}$ is given by the following grammar.

$$\begin{aligned} S ::= \widetilde{A} \mid & \; if\ \widetilde{B}\ then\ S\ else\ S \mid if\ \widetilde{B}\ then\ S\ [elsif\ \widetilde{B}\ then\ S]_{i=1}^{n}\ else\ S \\ \mid & \; let\ \tilde{x} = \widetilde{A}\ in\ S \mid warning, \end{aligned} \tag{2.1}$$

where $\widetilde{A} \in \widetilde{\mathbb{A}}$, $\widetilde{B} \in \widetilde{\mathbb{B}}$, $\tilde{x} \in \widetilde{\mathbb{V}}$, and $n \in \mathbb{N}^{>0}$. The notation $[elsif\ \widetilde{B}\ then\ S]_{i=1}^{n}$ denotes a list of n *elsif* branches.

A program is a *function declaration* of the form $\tilde{f}(\tilde{x}_1, \ldots, \tilde{x}_m) = S$, where $\tilde{x}_1, \ldots, \tilde{x}_m$ are pairwise distinct variables in $\widetilde{\mathbb{V}}$ and all free variables appearing in S are in $\{\tilde{x}_1, \ldots, \tilde{x}_m\}$. The natural number m is called the *arity* of $\tilde{f}$. The set of programs is denoted as $\mathbb{P}$.

When if-then-else guards contain floating-point expressions, the output of the considered program is not only directly influenced by rounding errors, but also by the error of taking the incorrect branch in the case of unstable tests.

Definition 1 (Conditional Instability). *A function declaration* $\tilde{f}(\tilde{x}_1,\ldots,\tilde{x}_n) = S$ *is said to have an* unstable conditional *when its body contains a conditional statement of the form if* $\tilde{\phi}$ *then* S_1 *else* S_2 *and there exist two assignments* $\tilde{\sigma} : \{\tilde{x}_1,\ldots,\tilde{x}_n\} \to \mathbb{F}$ *and* $\sigma : \{\chi_r(\tilde{x}_1),\ldots,\chi_r(\tilde{x}_n)\} \to \mathbb{R}$ *such that for all* $i \in \{1,\ldots,n\}$, $\sigma(\chi_r(\tilde{x}_i)) = R(\tilde{\sigma}(\tilde{x}_i))$ *and* $eval_{\mathbb{B}}(\sigma, R_{\mathbb{B}}(\tilde{\phi})) \neq \widetilde{eval}_{\widetilde{\mathbb{B}}}(\tilde{\sigma},\tilde{\phi})$. *Otherwise, the conditional expression is said to be* stable.

In other words, a conditional statement (or test) $\tilde{\phi}$ is unstable when there exists an assignment from the free variables $\tilde{x}_i$ in $\tilde{\phi}$ to $\mathbb{F}$ such that $\tilde{\phi}$ evaluates to a different Boolean value with respect to its real valued counterpart $R_{\mathbb{B}}(\tilde{\phi})$. In these cases, the program is said to follow an *unstable path*, otherwise, when the flows coincide, it is said to follow a *stable path*.

2.2 Floating-Point Denotational Semantics

This section presents a compositional denotational semantics for the expression language of Formula (2.1) that models both real and floating-point path conditions and outputs. This semantics is a modification of the one introduced in [13,21]. The proposed semantics collects for each combination of real and floating-point program paths: the real and floating-point path conditions, two symbolic expressions representing the value of the output assuming the use of real and floating-point arithmetic, respectively, and a flag indicating if the element refers to either a stable or an unstable path. This information is stored in a *conditional tuple*.

Definition 2 (Conditional Tuple). *A* conditional tuple *is an expression of the form* $\langle \eta, \tilde{\eta} \rangle_t \twoheadrightarrow (r, \tilde{r})$, *where* $\eta \in \mathbb{B}$, $\tilde{\eta} \in \widetilde{\mathbb{B}}$, $r \in \mathbb{A} \cup \{\bot_{\mathbf{u}}\}$, $\tilde{r} \in \widetilde{\mathbb{A}} \cup \{\bot_{\mathbf{u}}\}$, *and* $t \in \{\mathbf{s}, \mathbf{u}\}$.

Intuitively, $\langle \eta, \tilde{\eta} \rangle_t \twoheadrightarrow (r, \tilde{r})$ indicates that if the condition $\eta \wedge \tilde{\eta}$ is satisfied, the output of the ideal real-valued implementation of the program is r and the output of the floating-point execution is $\tilde{r}$. The sub-index t is used to mark by construction whether a conditional tuple corresponds to an unstable path, when $t = \mathbf{u}$, or to a stable path, when $t = \mathbf{s}$. The element $\bot_{\mathbf{u}}$ represents the output of the warning construct. Let $\mathbf{C}$ be the set of all conditional error bounds, and $\mathbb{C} := \wp(\mathbf{C})$ be the domain formed by sets of conditional error bounds.

An *environment* is defined as a function mapping a variable to a set of conditional tuples, i.e., $Env : \widetilde{\mathbb{V}} \to \mathbb{C}$. The empty environment is denoted as $\bot_{Env}$ and maps every variable to the empty set $\varnothing$.

Given $\nu \in Env$, the semantics of program expressions is defined in Fig. 1 as a function $\mathcal{E} : \mathbb{S} \times Env \to \mathbb{C}$ that returns the set of conditional tuples representing the possible real and floating-point computations and their corresponding path conditions. The operator $\sqcup$ denotes the least upper bound of the domain of conditional error bounds.

The semantics of a variable $\tilde{x} \in \widetilde{\mathbb{V}}$ consists of two cases. If $\tilde{x}$ belongs to the environment, then the variable has been previously bound to a program expression S through a let-expression. In this case, the semantics of $\tilde{x}$ is exactly the

$$\mathcal{E}[\![\tilde{d}]\!]_\nu := \{\langle true, true\rangle_{\mathrm{s}} \twoheadrightarrow (R(\tilde{d}), \tilde{d})\}$$

$$\mathcal{E}[\![warning]\!]_\nu := \{\langle true, true\rangle_{\mathrm{s}} \twoheadrightarrow (\bot_{\mathrm{u}}, \bot_{\mathrm{u}})\}$$

$$\mathcal{E}[\![\tilde{x}]\!]_\nu := \begin{cases} \{\langle true, true\rangle_{\mathrm{s}} \twoheadrightarrow (\chi_r(\tilde{x}), \tilde{x})\} & \text{if } \nu(\tilde{x}) = \varnothing \\ \nu(\tilde{x}) & \text{otherwise} \end{cases}$$

$$\mathcal{E}[\![\widetilde{op}(\widetilde{A}_i)_{i=1}^n]\!]_\nu := \bigsqcup\{\langle \bigwedge_{i=1}^n \phi_i, \bigwedge_{i=1}^n \tilde{\phi}_i\rangle_{\mathrm{s}} \twoheadrightarrow (op(r_i)_{i=1}^n, \widetilde{op}(\tilde{r}_i)_{i=1}^n) \mid \forall 1 \le i \le n\colon$$
$$\langle \phi_i, \tilde{\phi}_i\rangle_{\mathrm{s}} \twoheadrightarrow (r_i, \tilde{r}_i) \in \mathcal{E}[\![\widetilde{A}_i]\!]_\nu, \bigwedge_{i=1}^n \phi_i \not\twoheadrightarrow false, \bigwedge_{i=1}^n \tilde{\phi}_i \not\twoheadrightarrow false\}$$

$$\mathcal{E}[\![let\ \tilde{x} = \widetilde{A}\ in\ S]\!]_\nu := \mathcal{E}[\![S]\!]_{\nu[\tilde{x} \mapsto \mathcal{E}[\![\widetilde{A}]\!]_\nu]}$$

$$\mathcal{E}[\![if\ \widetilde{B}\ then\ S_1\ else\ S_2]\!]_\nu := \mathcal{E}[\![S_1]\!]_\nu \Downarrow_{(R_{\mathbb{B}}(\widetilde{B}), \widetilde{B})} \sqcup \mathcal{E}[\![S_2]\!]_\nu \Downarrow_{(\neg R_{\mathbb{B}}(\widetilde{B}), \neg\widetilde{B})} \sqcup$$
$$\bigsqcup\{\langle \phi_2, \tilde{\phi}_1\rangle_{\mathrm{u}} \twoheadrightarrow (r_2, \tilde{r}_1) \mid \langle \phi_1, \tilde{\phi}_1\rangle_{\mathrm{s}} \twoheadrightarrow (r_1, \tilde{r}_1) \in \mathcal{E}[\![S_1]\!]_\nu,$$
$$\langle \phi_2, \tilde{\phi}_2\rangle_{\mathrm{s}} \twoheadrightarrow (r_2, \tilde{r}_2) \in \mathcal{E}[\![S_2]\!]_\nu\} \Downarrow_{(\neg R_{\mathbb{B}}(\widetilde{B}), \widetilde{B})} \sqcup$$
$$\bigsqcup\{\langle \phi_1, \tilde{\phi}_2\rangle_{\mathrm{u}} \twoheadrightarrow (r_1, \tilde{r}_2) \mid \langle \phi_1, \tilde{\phi}_1\rangle_{\mathrm{s}} \twoheadrightarrow (r_1, \tilde{r}_1) \in \mathcal{E}[\![S_1]\!]_\nu,$$
$$\langle \phi_2, \tilde{\phi}_2\rangle_{\mathrm{s}} \twoheadrightarrow (r_2, \tilde{r}_2) \in \mathcal{E}[\![S_2]\!]_\nu\} \Downarrow_{(R_{\mathbb{B}}(\widetilde{B}), \neg\widetilde{B})}$$

$$\mathcal{E}[\![if\ \widetilde{B}_1\ then\ S_1\ [elsif\ \widetilde{B}_i\ then\ S_i]_{i=2}^{n-1}\ else\ S_n]\!]_\nu :=$$
$$\bigsqcup_{i=1}^{n-1} \mathcal{E}[\![S_i]\!]_\nu \Downarrow_{(\widetilde{B}_i \wedge \bigwedge_{j=1}^{i-1} \neg\widetilde{B}_j, R(\widetilde{B}_i) \wedge \bigwedge_{j=1}^{i-1} \neg R(\widetilde{B}_j))}$$
$$\sqcup\, \mathcal{E}[\![S_n]\!]_\nu \Downarrow_{(\bigwedge_{j=1}^{n-1} \neg\widetilde{B}_j, \bigwedge_{j=1}^{n-1} \neg R(\widetilde{B}_j))} \sqcup$$
$$\bigsqcup\{\langle \eta_i, \tilde{\eta}_j\rangle_{\mathrm{u}} \twoheadrightarrow (r_i, \tilde{r}_j) \mid i, j \in \{1, \ldots, n-1\}, i \neq j,\ \langle \eta_i, \tilde{\eta}_i\rangle_{\mathrm{s}} \twoheadrightarrow (r_i, \tilde{r}_i) \in \mathcal{E}[\![S_i]\!]_\nu,$$
$$\langle \eta_j, \tilde{\eta}_j\rangle_{\mathrm{s}} \twoheadrightarrow (r_j, \tilde{r}_j) \in \mathcal{E}[\![S_j]\!]_\nu\} \Downarrow_{(\widetilde{B}_j \wedge \bigwedge_{k=1}^{j-1} \neg\widetilde{B}_k, R(\widetilde{B}_i) \wedge \bigwedge_{k=1}^{i-1} \neg R(\widetilde{B}_k))} \sqcup$$
$$\bigsqcup\{\langle \eta_i, \tilde{\eta}_n\rangle_{\mathrm{u}} \twoheadrightarrow (r_i, \tilde{r}_n) \mid i \in \{1, \ldots, n-1\},\ \langle \eta_i, \tilde{\eta}_i\rangle_{\mathrm{s}} \twoheadrightarrow (r_i, \tilde{r}_i) \in \mathcal{E}[\![S_i]\!]_\nu,$$
$$\langle \eta_n, \tilde{\eta}_n\rangle_{\mathrm{s}} \twoheadrightarrow (r_n, \tilde{r}_n) \in \mathcal{E}[\![S_n]\!]_\nu\} \Downarrow_{(\bigwedge_{k=1}^{n-1} \neg\widetilde{B}_k, R(\widetilde{B}_i) \wedge \bigwedge_{k=1}^{i-1} \neg R(\widetilde{B}_k))} \sqcup$$
$$\bigsqcup\{\langle \eta_n, \tilde{\eta}_i\rangle_{\mathrm{u}} \twoheadrightarrow (r_n, \tilde{r}_i) \mid i \in \{1, \ldots, n-1\},\ \langle \eta_i, \tilde{\eta}_i\rangle_{\mathrm{s}} \twoheadrightarrow (r_i, \tilde{r}_i) \in \mathcal{E}[\![S_i]\!]_\nu,$$
$$\langle \eta_n, \tilde{\eta}_n\rangle_{\mathrm{s}} \twoheadrightarrow (r_n, \tilde{r}_n) \in \mathcal{E}[\![S_n]\!]_\nu\} \Downarrow_{(\widetilde{B}_i \wedge \bigwedge_{k=1}^{i-1} \neg\widetilde{B}_k, \bigwedge_{k=1}^{n-1} \neg R(\widetilde{B}_k))}$$

Fig. 1. Semantics of a program expression.

semantics of S. If $\tilde{x}$ does not belong to the environment, then $\tilde{x}$ is a parameter of the function. Here, a new conditional error bound is added with a placeholder $\chi_r(\tilde{x})$ representing the real value of $\tilde{x}$. The semantics of a floating-point arithmetic operation $\widetilde{op}$ is computed by composing the semantics of its operands. The real and floating-point values are obtained by applying the corresponding arithmetic operation to the values of the operands. The new conditions are obtained as the combination of the conditions of the operands. The semantics of the expression $let\ \tilde{x} = \widetilde{A}\ in\ S$ updates the current environment by associating with variable $\tilde{x}$ the semantics of expression $\widetilde{A}$.

The semantics of the conditional *if* $\widetilde{B}$ *then* S_1 *else* S_2 uses an auxiliary operator $\Downarrow$.

Definition 3 (Condition propagation operator). *Given* $b \in \mathbb{B}$ *and* $\tilde{b} \in \widetilde{\mathbb{B}}$, $\langle \phi, \tilde{\phi} \rangle_t \twoheadrightarrow (r, \tilde{r}) \Downarrow_{(b,\tilde{b})} = \langle \phi \wedge b, \tilde{\phi} \wedge \tilde{b} \rangle_t \twoheadrightarrow (r, \tilde{r})$ *if* $\phi \wedge b \wedge \tilde{\phi} \wedge \tilde{b} \not\Rightarrow$ *false, otherwise it is undefined. The definition of* $\Downarrow$ *naturally extends to sets of conditional tuples: given* $C \in \mathbb{C}$, $C \Downarrow_{(b,\tilde{b})} = \bigcup_{c \in C} c \Downarrow_{(b,\tilde{b})}$.

The semantics of S_1 and S_2 are enriched with the information about the fact that real and floating-point control flows match, i.e., both $\widetilde{B}$ and $R_{\mathbb{B}}(\widetilde{B})$ have the same value. In addition, new conditional tuples are built to model the unstable cases when real and floating-point control flows do not coincide and, therefore, real and floating-point computations diverge. For example, if $\widetilde{B}$ is satisfied but $R_{\mathbb{B}}(\widetilde{B})$ is not, the *then* branch is taken in the floating-point computation, but the *else* would have been taken in the real one. In this case, the real condition and its corresponding output are taken from the semantics of S_2, while the floating-point condition and its corresponding output are taken from the semantics of S_1. The condition $(\neg R_{\mathbb{B}}(\widetilde{B}), \widetilde{B})$ is propagated in order to model that $\widetilde{B}$ holds but $R_{\mathbb{B}}(\widetilde{B})$ does not. The conditional tuples representing this case are marked with **u**.

Similarly, the semantics of an n-ary conditional is composed of stable and unstable cases. The stable cases are built from the semantics of all the program sub-expressions S_i by enriching them with the information stating that the correspondent guard and its real counter-part hold and all the previous guards and their real counterparts do not hold. All the unstable combinations are built by combining the real parts of the semantics of a program expression S_i and the floating-point contributions of a different program expression S_j. In addition, the operator $\Downarrow$ is used to propagate the information that the real guard of S_i and the floating-point guard of S_j hold, while the guards of the previous branches do not hold.

3 Program Transformation

In this section, a program transformation is proposed for detecting when round-off errors affect the evaluation of floating-point conditionals and for ensuring that when the floating-point control flow diverges from the real one a warning is issued. The proposed transformation takes into account round-off errors by abstracting the Boolean expressions in the guards of the original program. This is done by means of two Boolean abstractions $\beta^+, \beta^- : \widetilde{\mathbb{B}} \to \widetilde{\mathbb{B}}$.

Given $\tilde{\phi} \in \widetilde{B}$, let $fv(\tilde{\phi})$ be the set of free variables in $\tilde{\phi}$. For all $\sigma : \{\chi_r(\tilde{x}) \mid \tilde{x} \in fv(\tilde{\phi})\} \to \mathbb{R}$, $\tilde{\sigma} : fv(\tilde{\phi}) \to \mathbb{F}$, and $\tilde{x} \in fv(\tilde{\phi})$ such that $R(\tilde{\sigma}(\tilde{x})) = \sigma(\chi_r(\tilde{x}))$, β^+ and β^- satisfy the following properties.

1. $\widetilde{eval}_{\widetilde{\mathbb{B}}}(\tilde{\sigma}, \beta^+(\tilde{\phi})) \Rightarrow \widetilde{eval}_{\widetilde{\mathbb{B}}}(\tilde{\sigma}, \tilde{\phi}) \wedge eval_{\mathbb{B}}(\sigma, R_{\mathbb{B}}(\tilde{\phi}))$.
2. $\widetilde{eval}_{\widetilde{\mathbb{B}}}(\tilde{\sigma}, \beta^-(\tilde{\phi})) \Rightarrow \widetilde{eval}_{\widetilde{\mathbb{B}}}(\tilde{\sigma}, \neg\, \tilde{\phi}) \wedge eval_{\mathbb{B}}(\sigma, \neg\, R_{\mathbb{B}}(\tilde{\phi}))$.

Property 1 states that for all floating-point Boolean expressions $\tilde{\phi}$, $\beta^+(\tilde{\phi})$ implies both $\tilde{\phi}$ and its real counterpart. Symmetrically, Property 2 ensures that $\beta^-(\tilde{\phi})$ implies both the negation of $\tilde{\phi}$ and the negation of its real counterpart.

Example 1. The Boolean abstractions β^+ and β^- can be instantiated as follows for conjunctions and disjunction of sign tests. Properties 1 and 2 are formally proven in PVS to hold for the following definitions of β^+ and β^-. Let $\widetilde{expr} \in \tilde{\mathbb{A}}$ and $\epsilon \in \mathbb{F}$ such that $|\widetilde{expr} - R_{\mathbb{A}}(\widetilde{expr})| \leq \epsilon$.

$$
\begin{aligned}
&\beta^+(\widetilde{expr} \leq 0) = \widetilde{expr} \leq -\epsilon && \beta^-(\widetilde{expr} \leq 0) = \widetilde{expr} > \epsilon\\
&\beta^+(\widetilde{expr} \geq 0) = \widetilde{expr} \geq \epsilon && \beta^-(\widetilde{expr} \geq 0) = \widetilde{expr} < -\epsilon\\
&\beta^+(\widetilde{expr} < 0) = \widetilde{expr} < -\epsilon && \beta^-(\widetilde{expr} < 0) = \widetilde{expr} \geq \epsilon\\
&\beta^+(\widetilde{expr} > 0) = \widetilde{expr} > \epsilon && \beta^-(\widetilde{expr} > 0) = \widetilde{expr} \leq -\epsilon\\
&\beta^+(\tilde{\phi}_1 \wedge \tilde{\phi}_2) = \beta^+(\tilde{\phi}_1) \wedge \beta^+(\tilde{\phi}_2) && \beta^-(\tilde{\phi}_1 \wedge \tilde{\phi}_2) = \beta^-(\tilde{\phi}_1) \vee \beta^-(\tilde{\phi}_2)\\
&\beta^+(\tilde{\phi}_1 \vee \tilde{\phi}_2) = \beta^+(\tilde{\phi}_1) \vee \beta^+(\tilde{\phi}_2) && \beta^-(\tilde{\phi}_1 \vee \tilde{\phi}_2) = \beta^-(\tilde{\phi}_1) \wedge \beta^-(\tilde{\phi}_2)\\
&\beta^+(\neg\, \tilde{\phi}) = \beta^-(\tilde{\phi}) && \beta^-(\neg\, \tilde{\phi}) = \beta^+(\tilde{\phi})
\end{aligned}
$$

The abstractions performed for sign tests are not correct for generic inequalities of the form $a \leq b$. In this case, to compensate for the round-off errors of both expressions, additional floating-point operations must be performed. Thus, the round-off error generated by such operations needs to be considered as well to obtain a sound approximation. The naive application of this strategy leads to a non-terminating transformation. The design of an effective approximation for these generic inequalities is left as future work.

The program transformation is defined as follows.

Definition 4 (Program Transformation). *Let $\tilde{f}(\tilde{x}_1, \ldots, \tilde{x}_n) = S \in \mathbb{P}$ be a floating-point program that does not contain any warning statements, the transformed program is defined as $\tilde{f}(\tilde{x}_1, \ldots, \tilde{x}_n) = \tau(S)$ where τ is defined as follows.*

$\tau(\tilde{A}) = \tilde{A}$

$\tau(\textit{if } \tilde{\phi} \textit{ then } S_1 \textit{ else } S_2) =$

  $\textit{if } \beta^+(\tilde{\phi}) \textit{ then } \tau(S_1) \textit{ elseif } \beta^-(\tilde{\phi}) \textit{ then } \tau(S_2) \textit{ else warning}$

$\tau(\textit{if } \tilde{\phi}_1 \textit{ then } S_1 \ [\textit{elsif } \tilde{\phi}_i \textit{ then } S_i]_{i=2}^{n-1} \textit{ else } S_n) =$

  $\textit{if } \beta^+(\tilde{\phi}_1) \textit{ then } \tau(S_1) \ [\textit{elsif } \beta^+(\tilde{\phi}_i) \wedge \bigwedge_{j=1}^{i-1} \beta^-(\tilde{\phi}_j) \textit{ then } \tau(S_i)]_{i=2}^{n-1}$

  $\textit{elsif } \bigwedge_{j=1}^{n-1} \beta^-(\tilde{\phi}_j) \textit{ then } \tau(S_n)$

  else warning

$\tau(\textit{let } \tilde{x} = \tilde{A} \textit{ in } S) = \textit{let } \tilde{x} = \tilde{A} \textit{ in } \tau(S)$

In the case of the binary conditional statement, the *then* branch of the transformed program is taken when $\beta^+(\tilde{\phi})$ is satisfied. By Property 1, this means that in the original program both $\tilde{\phi}$ and $R(\tilde{\phi})$ hold and, thus, the *then* branch is taken in both real and floating-point control flows. Similarly, the *else* branch of the transformed program is taken when $\beta^-(\tilde{\phi})$ holds. This means, by Property 2, that in the original program the else branch is taken in both real and floating-point control flows. In the case real and floating-flows diverge, neither $\beta^+(\tilde{\phi})$ nor $\beta^-(\tilde{\phi})$ is satisfied and a warning is returned.

In the case of the n-ary conditional statements, the guard $\tilde{\phi}_i$ of the i-th branch is replaced by the conjunction of $\beta^+(\tilde{\phi}_i)$ and $\beta^-(\tilde{\phi}_j)$ for all the previous branches $j < i$. By properties 1 and 2, it follows that the transformed program takes the i-th branch only when the same branch is taken in both real and floating-point control flows of the original program. Additionally, a warning is issued by the transformed program when real and floating-point control flows of the original program differ.

The following theorem states the correctness of the program transformation τ. If the transformed program $\tau(P)$ returns an output $\tilde{r}$ different from *warning*, then the original program follows a stable path and returns the floating-point output $\tilde{r}$. Furthermore, in the case the original program presents an unstable behavior, the transformed program returns *warning*.

Theorem 1 (Program Transformation Correctness). *Given* $\tilde{f}(\tilde{x}_1,\ldots,\tilde{x}_n) = S \in \mathbb{P}$, $\sigma : \{\chi_r(\tilde{x}_1)\ldots\chi_r(\tilde{x}_n)\} \to \mathbb{R}$, *and* $\tilde{\sigma} : \{\tilde{x}_1\ldots\tilde{x}_n\} \to \mathbb{F}$, *such that for all* $i \in \{1,\ldots,n\}$, $R(\tilde{\sigma}(\tilde{x}_i)) = \sigma(\chi_r(\tilde{x}_i))$*:*

1. *for all* $\langle\eta',\tilde{\eta}'\rangle_{t'} \twoheadrightarrow (r',\tilde{r}') \in \mathcal{E}[\![\tau(S)]\!]_{\perp_{Env}}$ *such that* $\tilde{r} \neq \perp_{\mathbf{u}}$*, there exists* $\langle\eta,\tilde{\eta}\rangle_{\mathbf{s}} \twoheadrightarrow (r,\tilde{r}) \in \mathcal{E}[\![S]\!]_{\perp_{Env}}$ *such that* $\widetilde{eval_{\mathbb{B}}}(\tilde{\sigma},\tilde{\eta}') \Rightarrow eval_{\mathbb{B}}(\sigma,\eta) \wedge \widetilde{eval_{\mathbb{B}}}(\tilde{\sigma},\tilde{\eta})$ *and* $\tilde{r} = \tilde{r}'$*;*
2. *for all* $\langle\eta,\tilde{\eta}\rangle_{\mathbf{u}} \twoheadrightarrow (r,\tilde{r}) \in \mathcal{E}[\![S]\!]_{\perp_{Env}}$*, there exists* $\langle\eta',\tilde{\eta}'\rangle_{t'} \twoheadrightarrow (r',\perp_{\mathbf{u}}) \in \mathcal{E}[\![\tau(S)]\!]_{\perp_{Env}}$ *such that* $eval_{\mathbb{B}}(\sigma,\eta) \wedge \widetilde{eval_{\mathbb{B}}}(\tilde{\sigma},\tilde{\eta}) \Rightarrow \widetilde{eval_{\mathbb{B}}}(\tilde{\sigma},\tilde{\eta}')$*.*

The program transformation defined in Definition 4 has been formalized and Theorem 1 has been proven correct in PVS.[1]

It is important to remark that the intended semantics of the floating-point transformed program is the real-valued semantics of the original one, i.e., the real-valued semantics of the transformed program is irrelevant. Therefore, even if the transformed program presents unstable tests, Theorem 1 ensures that its floating-point control flow preserves the control flow of stable tests in the original program.

Example 2. Consider the program *eps_line*, which is part of the ACCoRD conflict detection and resolution algorithm [11]. This function is used to compute an implicitly coordinated horizontal resolution direction for the aircraft involved in a pair-wise conflict.

$$eps\_line(\tilde{v}_x,\tilde{v}_y,\tilde{s}_x,\tilde{s}_y) = \mathit{if}\ \widetilde{expr} > 0\ \mathit{then}\ 1\ \ \mathit{elsif}\ \widetilde{expr} < 0\ \mathit{then}\ -1\ \ \mathit{else}\ 0,$$

[1] This formalization is available at https://shemesh.larc.nasa.gov/fm/PRECiSA.

where $\widetilde{expr} = (\tilde{s}_x * \tilde{v}_y) - (\tilde{s}_y * \tilde{v}_x)$ and $\tilde{v}_x, \tilde{v}_y, \tilde{s}_x, \tilde{s}_y$ are floating-point variables. For example, if the values of such variables are assumed to lie in the range $[-100, 100]$, the tool PRECiSA [13,21] can be used to compute the round-off error estimation $\epsilon = 6.4801497501321145 \times 10^{-12}$ for $\widetilde{expr}$. PRECiSA is a tool that over-approximates the round-off error of floating-point programs. It is fully automatic and generates PVS proof certificates that guarantee the correctness of the error estimations with respect to the floating-point IEEE-754 standard. The following program is obtained by using the transformation τ with the Boolean approximations of Example 1.

$$\tau(eps\_line(\tilde{v}_x, \tilde{v}_y, \tilde{s}_x, \tilde{s}_y)) = \mathit{if}\ \widetilde{expr} > \epsilon\ \mathit{then}\ 1\ \ \mathit{elsif}\ \widetilde{expr} < -\epsilon\ \mathit{then}\ -1$$
$$\mathit{elsif}\ \widetilde{expr} \geq \epsilon \wedge \widetilde{expr} \leq -\epsilon\ \mathit{then}\ 0\ \ \mathit{else\ warning}$$

The condition $\widetilde{expr} \geq \epsilon \wedge \widetilde{expr} \leq -\epsilon$ never holds since ϵ is a positive number. Therefore, the transformed program never returns 0. Indeed, when $\widetilde{expr}$ is close to 0, the test is unstable. The transformed program detects these unstable cases and returns a warning.

4 Case Study: PolyCARP Algorithm

PolyCARP[2] (Algorithms for Computations with Polygons) [14,15] is a suite of algorithms for geo-containment applications. One of the main applications of PolyCARP is to provide geofencing capabilities to unmanned aerial systems (UAS), i.e., detecting whether a UAS is inside or outside a given geographical region, which is modeled using a 2D polygon with a minimum and a maximum altitude. Another application of PolyCARP is the detection of weather cells, modeled as moving polygons, along an aircraft trajectory.

A core piece of logic in PolyCARP is the polygon containment algorithm, i.e., the algorithm that checks whether or not a point lies in the interior of a polygon. Algorithms for polygon containment have to be carefully implemented since numerical errors may lead to wrong answers, even in cases where the point is far from the boundaries of the polygon. PolyCARP uses several techniques to detect if a point is contained in a polygon. One of these techniques relies on the computation of the *winding number*. This number corresponds to the number of times the polygon winds around a point p.

Consider two consecutive vertices v and v' of the polygon in the Cartesian plane with the point p as the origin. The function *winding_number_edge* checks in which quadrants v and v' are located and counts how many axes are crossed by the edge (v, v'). If v and v' belong to the same quadrant, the contribution of the edge to the winding number is 0 since no axis is crossed. If v and v' lie in adjacent quadrants, the contribution is 1 (respectively -1) if moving from v to v' along the edge is in counterclockwise (respectively clockwise) direction. In the case v and v' are in opposite quadrants, the determinant is computed for checking the direction of the edge. If it is counterclockwise the contribution is 2, otherwise

[2] PolyCARP is available at https://github.com/nasa/polycarp.

it is −2. The winding number is obtained as the sum of the contributions of all the edges of the polygon. If the result is 0 or 4, the point is inside the polygon, otherwise, it is outside.

$$
\begin{aligned}
&\mathit{winding\_number\_edge}(v_x, v_y, v'_x, v'_y, p_x, p_y) = \\
&\quad \mathit{let}\ t_x = v_x - p_x\ \mathit{in}\ \mathit{let}\ t_y = v_y - p_y\ \mathit{in}\ \mathit{let}\ n_x = v'_x - p_x\ \mathit{in}\ \mathit{let}\ n_y = v'_y - p_y\ \mathit{in} \\
&\qquad \mathit{if}\ \mathit{same\_quad}\ \mathit{then}\ 0 \\
&\qquad \mathit{elsif}\ \ \mathit{adj\_quad\_ctrclock}\ \mathit{then}\ 1 \\
&\qquad \mathit{elsif}\ \ \mathit{adj\_quad\_clock}\ \mathit{then}\ {-1} \\
&\qquad \mathit{elsif}\ \ \mathit{det\_pos}\ \mathit{then}\ 2 \\
&\qquad \mathit{else}\ \ {-2}
\end{aligned}
$$

where

$$
\begin{aligned}
&\mathit{same\_quad} = \\
&\quad (t_x \geq 0 \wedge t_y \geq 0 \wedge n_x \geq 0 \wedge n_y \geq 0) \vee (t_x \leq 0 \wedge t_y \geq 0 \wedge n_x \leq 0 \wedge n_y \geq 0)\ \vee \\
&\quad (t_x \geq 0 \wedge t_y \leq 0 \wedge n_x \geq 0 \wedge n_y \leq 0) \vee (t_x \leq 0 \wedge t_y \leq 0 \wedge n_x \leq 0 \wedge n_y \leq 0) \\
&\mathit{adj\_quad\_ctrclock} = \\
&\quad (t_x \geq 0 \wedge t_y \leq 0 \wedge n_x \geq 0 \wedge n_y \geq 0) \vee (t_x \geq 0 \wedge t_y \geq 0 \wedge n_x \leq 0 \wedge n_y \geq 0)\ \vee \\
&\quad (t_x \leq 0 \wedge t_y \geq 0 \wedge n_x \leq 0 \wedge n_y \leq 0) \vee (t_x \leq 0 \wedge t_y \leq 0 \wedge n_x \geq 0 \wedge n_y \leq 0), \\
&\mathit{adj\_quad\_clock} = \\
&\quad (t_x \geq 0 \wedge t_y \geq 0 \wedge n_x \geq 0 \wedge n_y \leq 0) \vee (t_x \leq 0 \wedge t_y \geq 0 \wedge n_x \leq 0 \wedge n_y \geq 0)\ \vee \\
&\quad (t_x \leq 0 \wedge t_y \leq 0 \wedge n_x \leq 0 \wedge n_y \geq 0) \vee (t_x \geq 0 \wedge t_y \leq 0 \wedge n_x \leq 0 \wedge n_y \leq 0), \\
&\mathit{det\_pos} = (n_x - t_x) * t_y - (n_y - t_y) * t_x \leq 0.
\end{aligned}
$$

The function *winding_number_edge* has been verified in PVS using real arithmetic. However, due to floating-point errors, taking the incorrect branch for one of the edges in the computation of the winding number may result in an incorrect conclusion about the position of the point with respect to the polygon. In order to overcome this problem, the transformation τ of Definition 4 is applied to the function *winding_number_edge* resulting in the following function. Given initial bounds for the input variables, PRECiSA [13,21] can be used to compute the round-off error estimations for n_x, n_y, t_x, t_y and the determinant, which are denoted ϵ_{t_x}, ϵ_{t_y}, ϵ_{n_x}, ϵ_{n_y}, and ϵ_{det}, respectively.

$$
\begin{aligned}
&\tau(\mathit{winding\_number\_edge}(v_x, v_y, v'_x, v'_y, p_x, p_y)) = \\
&\quad \mathit{let}\ t_x = v_x - p_x\ \mathit{in}\ \mathit{let}\ t_y = v_y - p_y\ \mathit{in}\ \mathit{let}\ n_x = v'_x - p_x\ \mathit{in}\ \mathit{let}\ n_y = v'_y - p_y\ \mathit{in} \\
&\qquad \mathit{if}\ \ \mathit{same\_quad}^{\beta}\ \mathit{then}\ 0 \\
&\qquad \mathit{elsif}\ \ \mathit{adj\_quad\_ctrclock}^{\beta}\ \mathit{then}\ 1 \\
&\qquad \mathit{elsif}\ \ \mathit{adj\_quad\_clock}^{\beta}\ \mathit{then}\ {-1} \\
&\qquad \mathit{elsif}\ \ \mathit{det\_pos}^{\beta}\ \mathit{then}\ 2
\end{aligned}
$$

elsif original_else$^\beta$ *else* -2
else warning,

where

$$same\_quad^\beta = \beta^+(same\_quad) = (t_x \geq \epsilon_{t_x} \wedge t_y \geq \epsilon_{t_y} \wedge n_x \geq \epsilon_{n_x} \wedge n_y \geq \epsilon_{n_y}) \vee (t_x \leq -\epsilon_{t_x} \wedge t_y \geq \epsilon_{t_y} \wedge n_x \leq -\epsilon_{n_x} \wedge n_y \geq \epsilon_{n_y}) \vee (t_x \geq \epsilon_{t_x} \wedge t_y \leq -\epsilon_{t_y} \wedge n_x \geq \epsilon_{n_x} \wedge n_y \leq -\epsilon_{n_y}) \vee (t_x \leq -\epsilon_{t_x} \wedge t_y \leq -\epsilon_{t_y} \wedge n_x \leq -\epsilon_{n_x} \wedge n_y \leq -\epsilon_{n_y}),$$

$$adj\_quad\_ctrclock^\beta = \beta^+(adj\_quad\_counterclock) \wedge \beta^-(same\_quad),$$

$$adj\_quad\_clock^\beta = \beta^+(adj\_quad\_clock) \wedge \beta^-(adj\_quad\_ctrclock) \wedge \beta^-(same\_quad),$$

$$det\_pos^\beta = (n_x - t_x) * t_y - (n_y - t_y) * t_x \leq -\epsilon_{det} \wedge \beta^-(adj\_quad\_clock) \wedge \beta^-(adj\_quad\_ctrclock) \wedge \beta^-(same\_quad),$$

$$original\_else^\beta = (n_x - t_x) * t_y - (n_y - t_y) * t_x > \epsilon_{det} \wedge \beta^-(adj\_quad\_clock) \wedge \beta^-(adj\_quad\_ctrclock) \wedge \beta^-(same\_quad),$$

$$\beta^-(same\_quad) = (t_x < -\epsilon_{t_x} \vee t_y < -\epsilon_{t_y} \vee n_x < -\epsilon_{n_x} \vee n_y < -\epsilon_{n_y}) \wedge (t_x > \epsilon_{t_x} \vee t_y < -\epsilon_{t_y} \vee n_x > \epsilon_{n_x} \vee n_y < -\epsilon_{n_y}) \wedge (t_x < -\epsilon_{t_x} \vee t_y > \epsilon_{t_y} \vee n_x < -\epsilon_{n_x} \vee n_y > \epsilon_{n_y}) \wedge (t_x > \epsilon_{t_x} \vee t_y > \epsilon_{t_y} \vee n_x > \epsilon_{n_x} \vee n_y > \epsilon_{n_y}),$$

$$\beta^+(adj\_quad\_ctrclock) = (t_x \geq \epsilon_{t_x} \wedge t_y \leq -\epsilon_{t_y} \wedge n_x \geq \epsilon_{n_x} \wedge n_y \geq \epsilon_{n_y}) \vee (t_x \geq \epsilon_{t_x} \wedge t_y \geq \epsilon_{t_y} \wedge n_x \leq -\epsilon_{n_x} \wedge n_y \geq \epsilon_{n_y}) \vee (t_x \leq -\epsilon_{t_x} \wedge t_y \geq \epsilon_{t_y} \wedge n_x \leq -\epsilon_{n_x} \wedge n_y \leq -\epsilon_{n_y}) \vee (t_x \leq -\epsilon_{t_x} \wedge t_y \leq -\epsilon_{t_y} \wedge n_x \geq \epsilon_{n_x} \wedge n_y \leq -\epsilon_{n_y}),$$

$$\beta^-(adj\_quad\_ctrclock) = (t_x < -\epsilon_{t_x} \vee t_y > \epsilon_{t_y} \vee n_x < -\epsilon_{n_x} \vee n_y < -\epsilon_{n_y}) \wedge (t_x < -\epsilon_{t_x} \vee t_y < -\epsilon_{t_y} \vee n_x > \epsilon_{n_x} \vee n_y < -\epsilon_{n_y}) \wedge (t_x > \epsilon_{t_x} \vee t_y < -\epsilon_{t_y} \vee n_x > \epsilon_{n_x} \vee n_y > \epsilon_{n_y}) \wedge (t_x > \epsilon_{t_x} \vee t_y > \epsilon_{t_y} \vee n_x < -\epsilon_{n_x} \vee n_y > \epsilon_{n_y}),$$

$$\beta^+(adj\_quad\_clock) = (t_x \geq \epsilon_{t_x} \wedge t_y \geq \epsilon_{t_y} \wedge n_x \geq \epsilon_{n_x} \wedge n_y \leq -\epsilon_{n_y}) \vee (t_x \leq -\epsilon_{t_x} \wedge t_y \geq \epsilon_{t_y} \wedge n_x \leq -\epsilon_{n_x} \wedge n_y \geq \epsilon_{n_y}) \vee (t_x \leq -\epsilon_{t_x} \wedge t_y \leq -\epsilon_{t_y} \wedge n_x \leq -\epsilon_{n_x} \wedge n_y \geq \epsilon_{n_y}) \vee (t_x \geq \epsilon_{t_x} \wedge t_y \leq -\epsilon_{t_y} \wedge n_x \leq -\epsilon_{n_x} \wedge n_y \leq -\epsilon_{n_y}),$$

$$\begin{aligned}\beta^{-}(adj\_quad\_clock) = \; & (t_x < -\epsilon_{t_x} \lor t_y < -\epsilon_{t_y} \lor n_x < -\epsilon_{n_x} \lor n_y > \epsilon_{n_y}) \;\land \\ & (t_x > \epsilon_{t_x} \lor t_y < -\epsilon_{t_y} \lor n_x > \epsilon_{n_x} \lor n_y < -\epsilon_{n_y}) \;\land \\ & (t_x > \epsilon_{t_x} \lor t_y > \epsilon_{t_y} \lor n_x > \epsilon_{n_x} \lor n_y < -\epsilon_{n_y}) \;\land \\ & (t_x < -\epsilon_{t_x} \lor t_y > \epsilon_{t_y} \lor n_x > \epsilon_{n_x} \lor n_y > \epsilon_{n_y}).\end{aligned}$$

Consider a polygonal geofence and a set of randomly generated points in the square that circumscribes it. For each edge of the polygon and each generated point, the original function *winding_number_edge* is executed by using both exact real arithmetic and double-precision floating-point arithmetic. Additionally, the transformed function $\tau(winding\_number\_edge)$ is executed with double-precision floating-point arithmetic. For these randomly generated points, both the original and the transformed program return the same result. However, the closer the generated point is to the border of the polygon, the more likely is for the original program to take an unstable path. By considering a set of randomly generated points very close to the edges of the polygon, the transformed program always returns a warning, showing that these are the cases for which the floating-point computation may diverge from the real one. Since an over-approximation of the round-off error is used, not all the generated warnings reflect an actual problem. In fact, false warnings occur when the compensated error computed by the abstraction is larger than the round-off error that actually occurs in the computation. The amount of false warnings converges to the 50% of the number of total warnings as the distance to the edge decreases.

5 Related Work

Recently, several program transformations have been proposed with the aim of improving accuracy and efficiency of floating-point computations. It is possible to distinguish two kinds of approaches: precision allocation tools and program optimization ones. Precision allocation (or tuning) tools aim at selecting the lowest floating-point precision that is necessary to achieve a desired accuracy. This approach avoids using more precision than needed and improves the performance of the program. Rosa [8,9] uses a compilation algorithm that, from an ideal real-valued implementation, produces a finite-precision version (if it exists) that is guaranteed to meet the desired overall precision. Rosa soundly deals with unstable tests and with bounded loops. Similarly, FPTuner [3] implements a rigorous approach to precision allocation of mixed-precision arithmetic expressions. Precimonius [18] is a dynamic tool able to identify parts of a program that can be performed at a lower precision. It generates a transformed program where each floating-point variable is typed to the lowest precision necessary to meet a set of given accuracy and performance constraints. Hence, the transformed program uses variables of lower precision and performs better than the original program.

Program optimization tools aim at improving the accuracy of floating-point programs by rewriting arithmetic expressions in equivalent ones with a lower accumulated round-off error. Herbie [17] is a tool that automatically improves the accuracy of floating-point programs though a heuristic search. Herbie detects the expressions where rounding-errors occur and it applies a series of rewriting and simplification rules. It generates a set of transformed programs that are equivalent to the original one but potentially more accurate. The rewriting and simplification process is then applied recursively to the generated transformed programs until the most accurate program is obtained. CoHD [19] is a source-to-source transformer for C code that automatically compensates for the round-off errors of some basic floating-point operations. SyHD [20] is a C code optimizer that explores a set of programs generated by CoDH and selects the one with the best accuracy and computation-time trade-off. The tool Sardana [12], given a Lustre [2] program, produces a set of equivalent programs with simplified arithmetic expressions. Then, it selects the ones for which a better accuracy bound can be proved. Salsa [4] combines Sardana with techniques for intra-procedure [5] and inter-procedure [6,7] program transformation in order to improve the accuracy of a target variable in larger pieces of code containing assignments and control structures. To the best of the authors' knowledge, the program transformation proposed in this work is the only approach that addresses the problem of conditional instability for floating-point programs.

6 Conclusion

This paper presents a formally verified program transformation to detect instability in floating-point programs. The transformed program is guaranteed to return a warning when real and floating-point flows may diverge. Otherwise, it behaves as the original program when real and floating-point control flows coincide. The proposed approach is parametric with respect to two Boolean expression abstractions that return more restrictive Boolean conditions using an over-approximation of the round-off error occurring in the guard. These abstractions cause a loss of precision since the guards occurring in the transformed program are more restrictive and, therefore, some stable original traces may be lost in the transformed program. This leads to the possibility of having false instability warnings. However, it is ensured that all the unstable paths of the original program are detected.

This transformation has been formalized and formally proven correct in the interactive theorem prover PVS. The PVS tool PVSio can be used to execute the program transformation. However, a full integration with PRECiSA is the missing step to compute the round-off error approximations and to make the presented approach fully automatic.

The program transformation presented in this paper is the first step towards the much broader goal of improving the quality and reliability of floating-point programs. Future work includes the extension of the formalization to a more expressive language where conditionals are allowed inside Boolean expressions and function calls and loops are supported. This extension is not straightforward since it involves several changes in the formalization. In fact, in such setting, the evaluation of the expressions in the guards can also present unstable behaviors. Additionally, an extensive experimental evaluation is needed in order to assess the quality of the approach and its applicability to real-world applications. Another interesting future direction is the integration of the proposed approach with tools such as Salsa [4] and Herbie [17]. This integration will improve the accuracy of the mathematical expressions used inside a program and, at the same time, prevent unstable tests that may cause unexpected behaviors.

References

1. Boldo, S., Muñoz, C.: A high-level formalization of floating-point numbers in PVS. Technical report CR-2006-214298, NASA (2006)
2. Caspi, P., Pilaud, D., Halbwachs, N., Plaice, J.A.: LUSTRE: a declarative language for real-time programming. In: Conference Record of the 14th ACM Symposium on Principles of Programming Languages, POPL 1987, pp. 178–188. ACM (1987)
3. Chiang, W., Baranowski, M., Briggs, I., Solovyev, A., Gopalakrishnan, G., Rakamarić, Z.: Rigorous floating-point mixed-precision tuning. In: Proceedings of the 44th ACM SIGPLAN Symposium on Principles of Programming Languages, POPL 2017, pp. 300–315. ACM (2017)
4. Damouche, N., Martel, M.: Salsa: an automatic tool to improve the numerical accuracy of programs. In: 6th Workshop on Automated Formal Methods, AFM 2017 (2017)
5. Damouche, N., Martel, M., Chapoutot, A.: Optimizing the accuracy of a rocket trajectory simulation by program transformation. In: Proceedings of the 12th ACM International Conference on Computing Frontiers (CF 2015), pp. 40:1–40:2. ACM (2015)
6. Damouche, N., Martel, M., Chapoutot, A.: Improving the numerical accuracy of programs by automatic transformation. Int. J. Softw. Tools Technol. Transf. **19**(4), 427–448 (2017)
7. Damouche, N., Martel, M., Chapoutot, A.: Numerical accuracy improvement by interprocedural program transformation. In: Proceedings of the 20th International Workshop on Software and Compilers for Embedded Systems, SCOPES 2017, pp. 1–10. ACM (2017)
8. Darulova, E., Kuncak, V.: Sound compilation of reals. In: Proceedings of the 41st Annual ACM SIGPLAN-SIGACT Symposium on Principles of Programming Languages, POPL 2014, pp. 235–248. ACM (2014)
9. Darulova, E., Kuncak, V.: Towards a compiler for reals. ACM Trans. Program. Lang. Syst. **39**(2), 8:1–8:28 (2017)
10. Daumas, M., Rideau, L., Théry, L.: A generic library for floating-point numbers and its application to exact computing. In: Boulton, R.J., Jackson, P.B. (eds.) TPHOLs 2001. LNCS, vol. 2152, pp. 169–184. Springer, Heidelberg (2001). https://doi.org/10.1007/3-540-44755-5_13
11. Dowek, G., Muñoz, C., Carreño, V.: Provably safe coordinated strategy for distributed conflict resolution. In: Proceedings of the AIAA Guidance Navigation, and Control Conference and Exhibit 2005, AIAA-2005-6047 (2005)
12. Ioualalen, A., Martel, M.: Synthesizing accurate floating-point formulas. In: 24th International Conference on Application-Specific Systems, Architectures and Processors, ASAP 2013, pp. 113–116. IEEE Computer Society (2013)
13. Moscato, M., Titolo, L., Dutle, A., Muñoz, C.A.: Automatic estimation of verified floating-point round-off errors via static analysis. In: Tonetta, S., Schoitsch, E., Bitsch, F. (eds.) SAFECOMP 2017. LNCS, vol. 10488, pp. 213–229. Springer, Cham (2017). https://doi.org/10.1007/978-3-319-66266-4_14

14. Narkawicz, A., Hagen, G.: Algorithms for collision detection between a point and a moving polygon, with applications to aircraft weather avoidance. In: Proceedings of the AIAA Aviation Conference (2016)
15. Narkawicz, A., Muñoz, C., Dutle, A.: The MINERVA software development process. In: 6th Workshop on Automated Formal Methods, AFM 2017 (2017)
16. Owre, S., Rushby, J.M., Shankar, N.: PVS: a prototype verification system. In: Kapur, D. (ed.) CADE 1992. LNCS, vol. 607, pp. 748–752. Springer, Heidelberg (1992). https://doi.org/10.1007/3-540-55602-8_217
17. Panchekha, P., Sanchez-Stern, A., Wilcox, J.R., Tatlock, Z.: Automatically improving accuracy for floating point expressions. In: Proceedings of the 36th ACM SIGPLAN Conference on Programming Language Design and Implementation, PLDI 2015, pp. 1–11. ACM (2015)
18. Rubio-González, C., et al.: Precimonious: tuning assistant for floating-point precision. In: International Conference for High Performance Computing, Networking, Storage and Analysis, SC 2013, p. 27. ACM (2013)
19. Thévenoux, L., Langlois, P., Martel, M.: Automatic source-to-source error compensation of floating-point programs. In: 18th IEEE International Conference on Computational Science and Engineering, CSE 2015, pp. 9–16. IEEE Computer Society (2015)
20. Thévenoux, L., Langlois, P., Martel, M.: Automatic source-to-source error compensation of floating-point programs: code synthesis to optimize accuracy and time. Concurr. Comput. Pract. Exp. **29**(7), e3953 (2017)
21. Titolo, L., Feliú, M.A., Moscato, M., Muñoz, C.A.: An abstract interpretation framework for the round-off error analysis of floating-point programs. In: Dillig, I., Palsberg, J. (eds.) VMCAI 2018. LNCS, vol. 10747, pp. 516–537. Springer, Cham (2018). https://doi.org/10.1007/978-3-319-73721-8_24

Multivariant Assertion-Based Guidance in Abstract Interpretation

Isabel Garcia-Contreras[1,2(✉)], Jose F. Morales[1(✉)], and Manuel V. Hermenegildo[1,2(✉)]

[1] IMDEA Software Institute, Madrid, Spain
{isabel.garcia,josef.morales,manuel.hermenegildo}@imdea.org
[2] Universidad Politécnica de Madrid (UPM), Madrid, Spain

Abstract. Approximations during program analysis are a necessary evil, as they ensure essential properties, such as soundness and termination of the analysis, but they also imply not always producing useful results. Automatic techniques have been studied to prevent precision loss, typically at the expense of larger resource consumption. In both cases (i.e., when analysis produces inaccurate results and when resource consumption is too high), it is necessary to have some means for users to provide information to guide analysis and thus improve precision and/or performance. We present techniques for supporting within an abstract interpretation framework a rich set of assertions that can deal with multivariance/context-sensitivity, and can handle different run-time semantics for those assertions that cannot be discharged at compile time. We show how the proposed approach can be applied to both improving precision and accelerating analysis. We also provide some formal results on the effects of such assertions on the analysis results.

Keywords: Program analysis · Multivariance · Context sensitivity · Abstract interpretation · Assertions · Static analysis · User guidance

1 Introduction

Abstract Interpretation [6] is a well-established technique for performing static analyses to determine properties of programs. It allows inferring at compile-time and in finite time information that is guaranteed to hold for all program executions corresponding to all possible sets of inputs to the program. Reasoning about these generally infinite sets of inputs and program paths requires *(safe) approximations* –computing over *abstract domains*– to ensure termination and soundness. If such approximations are not carefully designed, the information reported by the analyzer may not be accurate enough to be useful for the

Research partially funded by Spanish MINECO grant TIN2015-67522-C3-1-R *TRACES*, the Madrid M141047003 *N-GREENS* program, and Spanish MECD grant FPU16/04811. We thank the anonymous reviewers for their useful comments.

F. Mesnard and P. J. Stuckey (Eds.): LOPSTR 2018, LNCS 11408, pp. 184–201, 2019.
https://doi.org/10.1007/978-3-030-13838-7_11

intended application, such as, e.g., performing optimizations or verifying properties. Similarly, although abstract interpretation-based analyzers are guaranteed to terminate, this does not necessarily imply that they do so in acceptable time or space, i.e., their resource usage may be higher than desirable.

Much work has been done towards improving both the accuracy and efficiency of analyzers through the design of automatic analysis techniques that include clever abstract domains, widening and narrowing techniques [1,28,29], and sophisticated fixpoint algorithms [3,15,21,26]. Despite these advances, there are still cases where it is necessary for the user to provide input to the analyzer to guide the process in order to regain accuracy, prevent imprecision from propagating, and improve analyzer performance [5,8]. Interestingly, there is comparatively little information on these aspects of analyzers, perhaps because they are perceived as internal or analyzer implementation-specific.

In this paper we focus on techniques that provide a means for the programmer to be able to optionally annotate program parts in which precision needs to be recovered. Examples are the *entry* and *trust* declarations of CiaoPP [5,24] and the *known facts* of Astrée [7,8] (see Sect. 6 for more related work). Such user annotations allow dealing with program constructs for which the analysis is not complete or the source is only partially available. However, as mentioned before, there is little information in the literature on these assertions beyond a sentence or two in the user manuals or some examples of use in demo sessions. In particular, no precise descriptions exist on how these assertions affect the analysis process and its results.

We clarify these points by proposing a user-guided multivariant fixpoint algorithm that makes use of information contained in different kinds of assertions, and provide formal results on the influence of such assertions on the analysis. We also extend the semantics of the assertions to control if precision can be relaxed, and also to deal with both the cases in which the program execution will and will not incorporate run-time tests for unverified assertions. Note that almost all current abstract interpretation systems assume in their semantics that the run-time checks will be run. However, due to efficiency considerations, assertion checking in often turned off in production code, specially for complex properties [16]. To the best of our knowledge this is the first precise description of how such annotations are processed within a standard parametric and multivariant fixpoint algorithm, and of their effects on analysis results.

2 Preliminaries

Program Analysis with Abstract Interpretation. Our approach is based on *abstract interpretation* [6], a technique in which execution of the program is simulated on an *abstract domain* (D_α) which is simpler than the actual, *concrete domain* (D). Although not strictly required, we assume that D_α has a lattice structure with meet ($\sqcap$), join ($\sqcup$), and less than ($\sqsubseteq$) operators. Abstract values and sets of concrete values are related via a pair of monotonic mappings $\langle\alpha, \gamma\rangle$: *abstraction* $\alpha : D \rightarrow D_\alpha$, and *concretization* $\gamma : D_\alpha \rightarrow D$, which form a Galois connection. A description (or abstract value) $d \in D_\alpha$ *approximates* a concrete value $c \in D$ if $\alpha(c) \sqsubseteq d$ where $\sqsubseteq$ is the partial ordering on D_α. Concrete operations on D values are (over-)approximated by corresponding abstract operations on D_α values. The key result for abstract interpretation is that it guarantees that the analysis terminates, provided that D_α meets some conditions (such as finite ascending chains) and that the results are safe approximations of the concrete semantics (provided D_α safely approximates the concrete values and operations).

Intermediate Representation. For generality, we formulate our analysis to work on a block-level intermediate representation of the program, encoded using Constrained Horn clauses (CHC). A *definite CHC program*, or *program*, is a finite sequence of clauses. A *clause* is of the form H:-$B_1, \ldots, B_n$ where H, the *head*, is an atom, and $B_1, \ldots, B_n$ is the *body*, a possibly empty finite conjunction of atoms. Atoms are also called *literals*. We will refer to the head and the body of a clause cl with cl.head and cl.body respectively. An *atom* is of the form $p(V_1, \ldots, V_n)$. It is *normalized* if the $V_1, \ldots, V_n$ are all distinct variables. Normalized atoms are also called *predicate descriptors*. Each maximal set of clauses in the program with the same descriptor as head (modulo variable renaming) defines a *predicate* (or *procedure*). Body literals can be predicate descriptors, which represent *calls* to the corresponding predicates, or *constraints*. A *constraint* is a finite conjunction of built-in relations for some background theory. We assume that all non-builtin atoms are normalized. This is not restrictive since programs can always be put in this form, and it simplifies the presentation of the algorithm. However, in the examples we use non-normalized programs. The encoding of program semantics in CHC depends on the source language and is beyond the scope of the paper. It is trivial for (C)LP programs, and also well studied for several types of imperative programs and compilation levels (e.g., bytecode, llvm-IR, or ISA – see [2,9,11,12,17,20,23]).

Concrete Semantics. The concrete semantics that we abstract is that of Constraint Logic Programs – (C)LP [19]. In particular, we use the constraint extension of top-down, left-to-right SLD-resolution, which, given a *query* (*initial state*), returns the answers (*exit states*) computed for it by the program. A *query* is a pair $G:\theta$ with G a (non-empty) conjunction of atoms and θ a constraint. Executing (answering) a query with respect to a CHC program consists on determining whether the query is a logical consequence of the program and for which constraints (answers). However, since we are interested in abstracting the calls and answers (states) that occur at different points in the program, we base our semantics on the well-known notion of generalized AND trees [4]. The concrete semantics of a program P for a given set of queries $\mathcal{Q}$, $[\![P]\!]_{\mathcal{Q}}$, is then the set of generalized AND trees that result from the execution of the queries in $\mathcal{Q}$ for P. Each node $\langle G, \theta^c, \theta^s \rangle$ in the generalized AND tree represents a call to a predicate G (an atom), with the constraint (state) for that call, θ^c, and the corresponding success constraint θ^s (answer). The *calling_context*$(G, P, \mathcal{Q})$ of a predicate given by the predicate descriptor G defined in P for a set of queries $\mathcal{Q}$ is the set $\{\theta^c \mid \exists T \in [\![P]\!]_{\mathcal{Q}}\ s.t.\ \exists \langle G', \theta'^c, \theta'^s \rangle\ in\ T \wedge \exists \sigma, \sigma(G') = G, \sigma(\theta'^c) = \theta^c\}$, where σ

is a *renaming* substitution, i.e., a substitution that replaces each variable in the term it is applied to with distinct, fresh variables. We use $\sigma(X)$ to denote the application of σ to X. We denote by $answers(P, \mathcal{Q})$ the set of success constraints computed by P for queries $\mathcal{Q}$.

Goal-Dependent Abstract Interpretation. We use goal-dependent abstract interpretation, in particular a simplified version (PLAI-simp) of the PLAI algorithm [21,22], which is essentially an efficient abstraction of the generalized AND trees semantics, parametric on the abstract domain. It takes as input a program P, an abstract domain D_α, and a set of abstract initial queries $\mathcal{Q}_\alpha = \{G_i{:}\lambda_i\}$, where G_i is a normalized atom, and $\lambda_i \in D_\alpha$ is abstract constraint. The algorithm computes a set of triples $A = \{\langle G_1, \lambda_1^c, \lambda_1^s\rangle, \ldots, \langle G_n, \lambda_n^c, \lambda_n^s\rangle\}$. In each $\langle G_i, \lambda_i^c, \lambda_i^s\rangle$ triple, G_i is a normalized atom, and λ_i^c and λ_i^s, elements of D_α, are, respectively, abstract call and success constraints. The set of triples for a predicate cover all the concrete call and success constraints that appear during execution of the initial queries from $\gamma(\mathcal{Q}_\alpha)$, see Definition 2.

As usual, $\bot$ denotes the abstract constraint such that $\gamma(\bot) = \emptyset$. A tuple $\langle G_j, \lambda_j^c, \bot\rangle$ indicates that all calls to predicate G_j with any constraint $\theta \in \gamma(\lambda_j^c)$ either fail or loop, i.e., they do not produce any success constraints. A represents the (possibly infinite) set of nodes of the generalized AND trees for the queries represented in $\mathcal{Q}_\alpha$ to P. In addition, A is multivariant on calls, namely, it may contain more than one triple for the same predicate descriptor G with different abstract call constraints. The PLAI algorithm provides guarantees on termination and correctness (see Theorem 1 for a more precise formulation).

Assertions. Assertions allow stating conditions on the state (current constraint store) that hold or must hold at certain points of program execution. We use for concreteness a subset of the syntax of the `pred` assertions of [5,14,24], which allow describing sets of *preconditions* and *conditional postconditions* on the state for a given predicate. These assertions are instrumental for many purposes, e.g. expressing the results of analysis, providing specifications, and documenting [13, 14,25]. A `pred` assertion is of the form:

`:- [`*Status*`] pred` *Head* `[:` *Pre*`] [=>` *Post*`].`

where *Head* is a predicate descriptor (i.e., a normalized atom) that denotes the predicate that the assertion applies to, and *Pre* and *Post* are conjunctions of *property literals*, i.e., literals corresponding to predicates meeting certain conditions which make them amenable to checking, such as being decidable for any input [24]. *Pre* expresses properties that hold when *Head* is called, namely, at least one *Pre* must hold for each call to *Head*. *Post* states properties that hold if *Head* is called in a state compatible with *Pre* and the call succeeds. Both *Pre* and *Post* can be empty conjunctions (meaning true), and in that case they can be omitted. *Status* is a qualifier of the meaning of the assertion. Here we consider: `trust`, the assertion represents an actual behavior of the predicate that the analyzer will assume to be correct; `check`, the assertion expresses properties that must hold at run-time, i.e., that the analyzer should prove or else generate run-time checks for (we will return to this in Sect. 4). `check` is the default status of assertions.

Example 1. The following assertions describe different behaviors of the pow predicate that computes $P = X^N$: (1) is stating that if the exponent of a power is an even number, the result (P) is non-negative, (2) states that if the base is a non-negative number and the exponent is a natural number the result P also is non-negative:

```
:- pred pow(X,N,P) : (int(X), even(N)) => P ≥ 0.  % (1)
:- pred pow(X,N,P) : (X ≥ 0, nat(N))   => P ≥ 0.  % (2)
pow(_, 0, 1).
pow(X, N, P) :- N > 0,
    N1 is N - 1, pow(X, N1, P0), P is X * P0.
```

Here, for simplicity we assume that the properties even/1, int/1, nat/1, and $\geq$ are *built-in properties* handled natively by the abstract domain.

In addition to predicate assertions we also consider *program-point assertions*. They can appear in the places in a program in which a literal (statement) can be added and are expressed using literals corresponding to their *Status*, i.e., trust(*Cond*) and check(*Cond*). They imply that whenever the execution reaches a state originated at the program point in which the assertion appears, *Cond* (should) hold. Example 2 illustrates their use. Program-point assertions can be translated to pred assertions,[1] so without loss of generality we will limit the discussion to pred assertions.

Definition 1 (Meaning of a Set of Assertions for a Predicate). *Given a predicate represented by a normalized atom Head, and a corresponding set of assertions $\{a_1 \ldots a_n\}$, with a_i = ":- pred Head : Pre_i => $Post_i$." the set of* assertion conditions *for Head is $\{C_0, C_1, \ldots, C_n\}$, with:*

$$C_i = \begin{cases} \texttt{calls}(Head, \bigvee_{j=1}^{n} Pre_j) & i = 0 \\ \texttt{success}(Head, Pre_i, Post_i) & i = 1..n \end{cases}$$

where $\texttt{calls}(Head, Pre)$[2] states conditions on all concrete calls to the predicate described by *Head*, and $\texttt{success}(Head, Pre_j, Post_j)$ describes conditions on the success constraints produced by calls to *Head* if Pre_j is satisfied.

The assertion conditions for the assertions in Example 1 are:

$$\left\{ \begin{array}{ll} \texttt{calls(} \; pow(X,N,P), ((int(X), even(N)) \vee (X \geq 0, nat(N)))), & \\ \texttt{success(} pow(X,N,P), (int(X), even(N)), & (P \geq 0)), \\ \texttt{success(} pow(X,N,P), (X \geq 0, nat(N)), & (P \geq 0)) \end{array} \right\}$$

Uses of Assertions. We show examples of the use assertions to guide analysis.

Example 2. Regaining precision during analysis. If we analyze the following program with a simple (non-relational) intervals domain, the information inferred

[1] E.g., we can replace line 4 in Example 2, by "assrt_aux(Z),", and add a predicate to the program, assrt_aux(_)., with an assertion ":- pred assrt_aux(Z) : Z = 2.".

[2] We denote the calling conditions with calls (plural) for historic reasons, and to avoid confusion with the higher order predicate in Prolog call/2.

for `Z` would be "any integer" (line 3), whereas it can be seen that it is $Z = 2$ for any `X` and `Y`. We provide the information to the analyzer with an assertion (line 4). The analyzer will *trust* this information even if it cannot be inferred with this domain (because it cannot represent relations between variables).

```
1 p(Y) :-                  % (Y > 0)
2     X is Y + 2,          % (X > 2, Y > 0)
3     Z is X - Y,          % (int(Z), X > 2, Y > 0)
4     trust(Z = 2), % (Z = 2, X > 2, Y > 0)
5     % implementation continues
```

Example 3. Speeding up analysis. Very precise domains suffer less from loss of precision and are useful for proving complex properties, but can be very costly. In some cases less precise information in enough, e.g., this code extracted from LPdoc, the Ciao documentation generator, `html_escape` is a predicate that takes a string of characters and transforms it to html:

```
:- trust pred html_escape(S0, S) => (string(S0), string(S)).
html_escape("‘‘"||S0, "&ldquo;"||S) :- !, html_escape(S0, S).
html_escape("’’"||S0, "&rdquo;"||S) :- !, html_escape(S0, S).
html_escape([34|S0],  "&quot;"||S)  :- !, html_escape(S0, S).
html_escape([39|S0],  "&apos;"||S)  :- !, html_escape(S0, S).
% ...
html_escape([X|S0], [X|S])          :- !, character_code(X), html_escape(S0,
    S).
html_escape([],[]).

% string(Str) :- list(Str, int).
```

Analyses based on regular term languages, as, e.g. `eterms` [28] infer precise regular types with subtyping, which is often costly. In this example it would be equivalent to computing an accurate regular language that over-approximates the HTML text encoding. The `trust` assertion provides a general invariant that the analyzer will take instead of inferring a more complex type.

Example 4. Defining abstract usage or specifications of libraries or dynamic predicates. When sources are not available, or cannot be analyzed, assertions can provide the missing abstract semantics. The following code illustrate the use of an assertion to describe the behavior of predicate `receive` in a `sockets` library that is written in C. The assertion in this case transcribes what is stated in natural language in the documentation of the library. Note that if no annotations were made, the analyzer would have to assume the most general abstraction ($\top$) for the library arguments.

```
:- module(sockets, []).

:- export(receive/2).
:- pred receive(S, M) : (socket(S), var(M)) => list(M, utf8).
% receive is written in C
```

Example 5. (Re)defining the language semantics for abstract domains. **trust** assertions are also a useful tool for defining the meaning (transfer function) of the basic operations of the language. In this example we define some basic properties of the product predicate in a simple types-style abstract domain:

```
:- trust pred '*'(A, B, C) : (int(A), int(B)) => int(C).
:- trust pred '*'(A, B, C) : (flt(A), int(B)) => flt(C).
:- trust pred '*'(A, B, C) : (int(A), flt(B)) => flt(C).
:- trust pred '*'(A, B, C) : (flt(A), flt(B)) => flt(C).
```

The semantics of bytecodes or machine instructions can be specified for each domain after transformation into CHCs. Assertions allow representing behaviors for the same predicate for different call descriptions (multivariance).

3 Basic Fixpoint Algorithm

We first present a basic, non-guided algorithm to be used as starting point –see Fig. 1. PLAI-simp is essentially the PLAI algorithm [22], but omitting some optimizations that are independent from the issues related with the guidance. The algorithm is parametric on the abstract domain D_α, given by implementing the domain-dependent operations $\sqsubseteq, \sqcap, \sqcup$, `abs_call`, `abs_proceed`, `abs_generalize`, `abs_project`, and `abs_extend` (which will be described later), and transfer functions for program built-ins, that abstract the meaning of the basic operations of the language. These operations are assumed to be monotonic and to correctly over-approximate their correspondent concrete version. As stated before, the goal of the analyzer is to capture the behavior of each procedure (function or predicate) in the program with a set A of triples $\langle G, \lambda^c, \lambda^s \rangle$, where G is a normalized atom and λ^c and λ^s are, respectively, the abstract call and success constraints, elements of D_α. For conciseness, we denote looking up in A with a partial function $a : Atom * D_\alpha \mapsto D_\alpha$, where $\lambda^s = a[G, \lambda^c]$ *iff* $\langle G, \lambda^c, \lambda^s \rangle \in A$, and modify the value of a for (G, λ^c), denoted with $a[G, \lambda^c] \leftarrow \lambda^{s'}$ by removing $\langle G, \lambda^c, \_ \rangle$ from A and inserting $\langle G, \lambda^c, \lambda^{s'} \rangle$. In A there may be more than one triple with the same G, capturing multivariance, but only one for each λ^c during the algorithm's execution or in the final results.

Operation of the Algorithm. Analysis proceeds from the initial abstract queries $\mathcal{Q}_\alpha$ assuming $\bot$ as under-approximation of their success constraint. The algorithm iterates over possibly incomplete results (in A), recomputing them with any newly inferred information, until a global fixpoint is reached (controlled by flag *changes*). First, the set of captured call patterns and the clauses whose head applies (i.e., there exists a renaming σ s.t. $G = \sigma(\mathsf{cl.head})$) is stored in W. Then, each clause is solved with the following process. An "abstract unification" (`abs_call`) is made, which performs the abstract parameter passing. It includes *renaming* the variables, abstracting the parameter values (via function α), and *extending* the abstract constraint to all variables present in the head and the body of the clause. To abstractly execute a clause the function `solve_body` abstractly executes each of the literals of the body. This implies, for each literal, *projecting* the abstract constraint onto the variables of the literal (`abs_project`)

Algorithm **Analyze**($P, \mathcal{Q}_\alpha$)
input: $P, \mathcal{Q}_\alpha$ **output global:** $A \leftarrow \emptyset$
$a[L_i, \lambda_i] \leftarrow \bot$ **for all** $L_i : \lambda_i \in \mathcal{Q}_\alpha$, *changes* $\leftarrow$ true ▷ Initial queries
while *changes* **do**
    changes $\leftarrow$ false
    $W \leftarrow \{(G, \lambda^c, \mathsf{cl}) \mid a[G, \lambda^c]$ is defined $\wedge\ \mathsf{cl} \in P\ \wedge \exists\sigma$ s.t. $G = \sigma(\mathsf{cl.head})\}$
    for each $(G, \lambda^c, \mathsf{cl}) \in W$ **do**
        $\lambda^t \leftarrow$ `abs_call`$(G, \lambda^c, \mathsf{cl.head})$
        $\lambda^t \leftarrow$ `solve_body`$(\mathsf{cl.body}, \lambda^t)$
        $\lambda^{so} \leftarrow$ `abs_proceed`$(G, \mathsf{cl.head}, \lambda^t)$
        $\lambda^{s'} \leftarrow$ `abs_generalize`$(\lambda^{so}, \{a[G, \lambda^c]\})$
        if $\lambda^{s'} \neq \lambda^s$ **then**
            $a[G, \lambda^c] \leftarrow \lambda^{s'}$, *changes* $\leftarrow$ true ▷ Fixpoint not reached yet
function `solve_body`(B, λ^t)
    for each $L \in B$ **do**
        $\lambda^c \leftarrow$ `abs_project`(L, λ^t)
        $Call = \{\lambda \mid a[H, \lambda']$ is defined $\wedge \exists\sigma$ s.t. $\sigma(H) = L \wedge \lambda = \sigma(\lambda')\}$
        $\lambda^{c'} \leftarrow$ `abs_generalize`$(\lambda^c, Call)$
        $\lambda^s \leftarrow$ `solve`$(L, \lambda^{c'})$
        $\lambda^t \leftarrow$ `abs_extend`$(L, \lambda^s, \lambda^t)$
    return λ^t

Fig. 1. Baseline fixpoint analysis algorithm (PLAI-simp).

Global: A
function `solve`(L, λ)
    if L is a *built-in* **then**
        return $f^\alpha(L, \lambda)$ ▷ apply transfer function
    else if $a[G, \lambda^c]$ is defined and $\exists\sigma$ s.t. $\sigma(G) = L$ **then**
        return $\sigma(a[G, \lambda^c])$
    else
        $a[L, \lambda] \leftarrow \bot$
        return $\bot$

Fig. 2. Pseudocode for solving a literal.

and *generalizing* it if necessary (`abs_generalize`) before calling `solve`. Generalization is necessary to ensure termination since we support multivariance and infinite domains. Lastly, after returning from `solve` (returning from the literal call), `abs_extend` propagates the information given by λ^s (success abstract constraint over the variables of L) to the constraint of the variables of the clause λ^t. The `solve` function executes abstractly a literal (Fig. 2). Depending on the nature of the literal, different actions will be performed. For *built-in operations*, the corresponding transfer function (f^α) is applied. For *predicates defined in the program*, the answer is first looked up in A. If there is already a computed tuple that matches the abstract call, the previously inferred result is taken. Else (no stored tuple matches the abstract call), an entry with that call pattern and $\bot$ as success value is added. This will trigger the analysis of this call in the next

```
fact(0,1).
fact(N,R) :-
    N > 0,
    N1 is N - 1,
    fact(N1, R1),
    R is N * R1.
```

$$A = \{ \langle fact(X,R), (X/\top, R/\top), \ (X/int, R/+) \rangle \ \langle fact(X,R), (X/int, R/\top), (X/int, R/+) \rangle \}$$

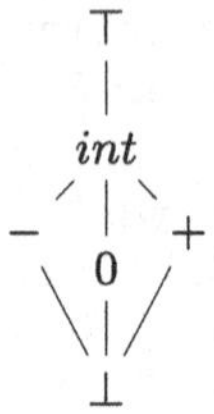

Fig. 3. Factorial program and a possible analysis result.

iteration of the loop. Once a body is processed, the actions of `abs_call` have to be undone in `abs_proceed`, which performs the "abstract return" from the clause. It *projects* the temporary abstract constraint (used to solve the body) back to the variables in the head of the clause and *renames* the resulting abstract constraint back to the variables of the analyzed head. The result is then abstractly *generalized* with the previous results (either from other clauses that also unify or from previous results of the processed clause), and it is compared with the previous result to check whether the fixpoint was reached. Termination is ensured even in the case of domains with infinite ascending chains because `abs_generalize` includes performing a widening if needed, in addition to the join operation $\sqcup$. This process is repeated for all the tuples of the analysis until the analysis results are the same in two consecutive iterations.

Figure 3 shows a factorial program and an analysis result A for $\mathcal{Q}_\alpha = \{\texttt{fact}(X,R) : \top\}$ with an abstract domain that keeps information about signs for each of the program variables with values of the lattice shown. For example, the first tuple in A states that `fact(X,R)` may be called with any possible input and, if it succeeds, X will be an integer and R will be a positive number.

We define analysis results to be correct if the abstract call constraints cover all the call constraints (and, respectively, the abstract success constraints cover all the success constraints) which appear during the concrete execution of the initial queries in $\mathcal{Q}$. Formally:

Definition 2 (Correct analysis). *Given a program P and initial queries $\mathcal{Q}$, an analysis result A is correct for $P, \mathcal{Q}$ if:*

- $\forall G, \theta^c \in calling\_context(G, P, \mathcal{Q})\ \exists \langle G, \lambda^c, \lambda^s \rangle \in A$ *s.t.* $\theta^c \in \gamma(\lambda^c)$.
- $\forall \langle G, \lambda^c, \lambda^s \rangle \in A, \forall \theta^c \in \gamma(\lambda^c)$ *if* $\theta^s \in answers(P, \{G : \theta^c\})$ *then* $\theta^s \in \gamma(\lambda^s)$.

We recall the result from [22], adapted to the notation used in this paper.

Theorem 1. Correctness of PLAI. *Consider a program P and a set of initial abstract queries $\mathcal{Q}_\alpha$. Let $\mathcal{Q}$ be the set of concrete queries: $\mathcal{Q} = \{G : \theta \mid \theta \in \gamma(\lambda) \wedge G : \lambda \in \mathcal{Q}_\alpha\}$. The analysis result $A = \{\langle G_1, \lambda_1^c, \lambda_1^s \rangle, \ldots, \langle G_n, \lambda_n^c, \lambda_n^s \rangle\}$ for P with $\mathcal{Q}_\alpha$ is* correct *for $P, \mathcal{Q}$.*

4 Adding Assertion-Based Guidance to the Algorithm

We now address how to apply the guidance provided by the user in the analysis algorithm. But before that we make some observations related to the run-time behavior of assertions.

Run-Time Semantics of Assertions. Most systems make assumptions during analysis with respect to the run-time semantics of assertions: for example, Astrée assumes that they are always run, while CiaoPP assumes conservatively that they may not be (because in general they may in fact be disabled by the user). In order to offer the user the flexibility of expressing these different situations we introduce a new status for assertions, `sample-check`, as well as a corresponding program-point assertion, `sample-check(`*Cond*`)`. This `sample-check` status indicates that the properties in these assertions may or may not be checked during execution, i.e., run-time checking can be turned on or off (or done intermittently) for them. In contrast, for `check` assertions (provided that they have not been discharged statically) run-time checks must always be performed. Table 1 summarizes this behavior with respect to whether run-time testing will be performed and whether the analysis can "trust" the information in the assertion, depending on its status. The information in `trust` assertions is used by the analyzer but they are never checked at run time. `check` assertions are also checked at run time and the execution will not pass beyond that point if the conditions are not met.[3] This means that `check` assertions can also be "trusted," in a similar way to `trust` assertions, because execution only proceeds beyond them if they hold. Finally, `sample-check` assertions may or may not be checked at run-time (e.g., for efficiency reasons) and thus they cannot be used as `trusts` during analysis.

Table 1. Usage of assertions during analysis.

Status	Use in analyzer	Run-time test (if not discharged at compile-time)
`trust`	Yes	No
`check`	Yes	Yes
`sample-check`	No	Optional

Correctly Applying Guidance. We recall some definitions (adapted from [25]) which are instrumental to correctly approximate the properties of the assertions during the guidance.

Definition 3 (Set of Calls for which a Property Formula Trivially Succeeds (Trivial Success Set)). *Given a conjunction L of property literals and the definitions for each of these properties in P, we define the* trivial success set *of L in P as:*

$$TS(L,P) = \{\theta | Var(L) \ s.t. \ \exists \theta' \in answers(P, \{L:\theta\}), \theta \models \theta'\}$$

[3] This strict run-time semantics for `check` assertions was used in [27].

where $\theta|Var(L)$ above denotes the projection of θ onto the variables of L, and $\models$ denotes that θ' is a more general constraint than θ (entailment). Intuitively, $TS(L, P)$ is the set of constraints θ for which the literal L succeeds without adding new constraints to θ (i.e., without constraining it further). For example, given the following program P:

```
list([]).
list([_|T]) :- list(T).
```

and $L = list(X)$, both $\theta_1 = \{X = [1, 2]\}$ and $\theta_2 = \{X = [1, A]\}$ are in the trivial success set of L in P, since calling $(X = [1, 2], list(X))$ returns $X = [1, 2]$ and calling $(X = [1, A], list(X))$ returns $X = [1, A]$. However, $\theta_3 = \{X = [1|\_]\}$ is not, since a call to $(X = [1|Y], list(X))$ will further constrain the term $[1|Y]$, returning $X = [1|Y], Y = []$. We define abstract counterparts for Definition 3:

Definition 4 (Abstract Trivial Success Subset of a Property Formula). *Under the same conditions of Definition 3, given an abstract domain D_α, $\lambda^-_{TS(L,P)} \in D_\alpha$ is an* abstract trivial success subset *of L in P iff $\gamma(\lambda^-_{TS(L,P)}) \subseteq TS(L, P)$.*

Definition 5 (Abstract Trivial Success Superset of a Property Formula). *Under the same conditions of Definition 4, an abstract constraint $\lambda^+_{TS(L,P)}$ is an* abstract trivial success superset *of L in P iff $\gamma(\lambda^+_{TS(L,P)}) \supseteq TS(L, P)$.*

I.e., $\lambda^-_{TS(L,P)}$ and $\lambda^+_{TS(L,P)}$ are, respectively, safe under- and over-approximations of $TS(L, P)$. These abstractions come useful when the properties expressed in the assertions cannot be represented exactly in the abstract domain. Note that they are always computable by choosing the closest element in the abstract domain, and at the limit $\bot$ is a trivial success subset of any property formula and $\top$ is a trivial success superset of any property formula.

4.1 Including Guidance in the Fixpoint Algorithm

In Fig. 4 we present a version of PLAI-simp (from Fig. 1) that includes our proposed modifications to apply assertions during analysis. The additions to the algorithm are calls to functions `apply_succ` and `apply_call`, that guide analysis results with the information of the assertion conditions, and E, an analysis-like set of triples representing inferred states before applying the assertions that will be used to check whether the assertions provided by the user could be proved by the analyzer (see Sect. 5). Success conditions are applied (`apply_succ`) after the body of the clause has been abstractly executed. It receives an atom G and λ^c as parameters to decide correctly which success conditions have to be applied. Call conditions are applied (`apply_call`) before calling function `solve`. Otherwise, a less precise call pattern will be captured during the procedure (it adds new entries to the table). The last addition, E, collects tuples to be used later to check that the assertions were correct (see Sect. 5). We collect all success constraints before applying any success conditions (line 11 of Fig. 4) and all call constraints before applying any call condition (line 20 of Fig. 4).

ALGORITHM **Guided_analyze**$(P, \mathcal{Q}_\alpha)$
input: $P, \mathcal{Q}_\alpha$ **global output:** $A \leftarrow \emptyset, E \leftarrow \emptyset$
1: $a[G_i, \lambda_i] \leftarrow \bot$ **for all** $G_i : \lambda_i \in \{G : \lambda^t | \lambda^t = \texttt{apply\_call}(G, \lambda), G : \lambda \in \mathcal{Q}_\alpha\}$
2: $changes \leftarrow$ true
3: **while** $changes$ **do**
4:     $changes \leftarrow$ false
5:     $W \leftarrow \{(G, \lambda^c, \mathsf{cl}) \mid a[G, \lambda^c]$ is defined $\wedge$ $\mathsf{cl} \in P \wedge \exists \sigma$ s.t. $G = \sigma(\mathsf{cl.head})\}$
6:     **for each** $(G, \lambda^c, \mathsf{cl}) \in W$ **do**
7:         $\lambda^t \leftarrow \texttt{abs\_call}(G, \lambda^c, \mathsf{cl.head})$
8:         $\lambda^t \leftarrow \texttt{solve\_body}(\mathsf{cl.body}, \lambda^t)$
9:         $\lambda^{s0} \leftarrow \texttt{abs\_proceed}(G, \mathsf{cl.head}, \lambda^t)$
10:        $\lambda^{s1} \leftarrow \texttt{abs\_generalize}(\lambda^{s0}, \{a[G, \lambda^c]\})$
11:        $E \leftarrow E \cup \{\langle G, \lambda^c, \lambda^{s1}\rangle\}$
12:        $\lambda^s \leftarrow \texttt{apply\_succ}(G, \lambda^c, \lambda^{s1})$
13:        **if** $\lambda^s \neq a[G, \lambda^c]$ **then**
14:            $a[G, \lambda^c] \leftarrow \lambda^s, changes \leftarrow$ true   ▷ Fixpoint not reached yet
15: **function** **solve_body**(B, λ^t)
16:    **for each** $L \in B$ **do**
17:        $\lambda^c \leftarrow \texttt{abs\_project}(L, \lambda^t)$
18:        $Call = \{\lambda \mid a[H, \lambda']$ is defined $\wedge \exists \sigma$ s.t. $\sigma(H) = L \wedge \lambda = \sigma(\lambda')\}$
19:        $\lambda^{c'} \leftarrow \texttt{abs\_generalize}(\lambda^c, Call)$
20:        $E \leftarrow E \cup \{\langle L, \lambda^{c'}, \_\rangle\}$
21:        $\lambda^{c'} \leftarrow \texttt{apply\_call}(L, \lambda^c)$
22:        $\lambda^s \leftarrow \texttt{solve}(L, \lambda^{c'})$
23:        $\lambda^t \leftarrow \texttt{abs\_extend}(L, \lambda^s, \lambda^t)$
24:    **return** λ^t

Fig. 4. Fixpoint analysis algorithm using assertion conditions.

global flag: speed-up
1: **function** **apply_call**(L, λ^c)
2:     **if** $\exists \sigma, \lambda^t = \lambda^+_{TS(\sigma(Pre), P)}$ s.t. **calls**$(H, Pre) \in C, \sigma(H) = L$ **then**
3:         **if** **speed-up** **return** λ^t **else return** $\lambda^c \sqcap \lambda^t$
4:     **else return** λ^c
5: **function** **apply_succ**$(G, \lambda^c, \lambda^{s0})$
6:     $app = \{\lambda \mid \exists \sigma, \textbf{success}(H, Pre, Post) \in C, \sigma(H) = G,$
7:         $\lambda = \lambda^+_{TS(\sigma(Post), P)}, \lambda^-_{TS(\sigma(Pre), P)} \sqsupseteq \lambda^c\}$
8:     **if** $app \neq \emptyset$ **then**
9:         $\lambda^t = \bigsqcap app$
10:        **if** **speed-up** **return** λ^t **else return** $\lambda^t \sqcap \lambda^{s0}$
11:    **else return** λ^{s0}

Fig. 5. Applying assertions.

Assuming that we are analyzing program P and the applicable assertion conditions are stored in C, the correct application of assertions is described in Fig. 5. Flag **speed-up** controls if assertions are used to recover accuracy or to (possibly) speed up fixpoint computation.

Applying Call Conditions. Given an atom G and an abstract call constraint λ^c, if there is a call assertion condition for G, if `speed-up` is true, $\lambda^+_{TS(Pre,P)}$ is used directly, otherwise the operation $\lambda^+_{TS(Pre,P)} \sqcap \lambda^c$ will prune from the analysis result the (abstracted) states that are outside the precondition. An over-approximation has to be made, otherwise we may remove calling states that the user did not specify.

Applying Success Conditions. Given an atom G, an abstract call constraint λ^c and its corresponding abstract success constraint λ^s, all success conditions whose precondition applies ($\lambda^c \sqsubseteq \lambda^-_{TS(Pre,P)}$) are collected in *app*. Making an under-approximation of *Pre* is necessary to consider the application of the assertion condition only if it would be applied in the concrete executions of the program. An over-approximation of *Post* needs to be performed since otherwise success states that actually happen in the concrete execution of the program may be removed. If no conditions are applicable (i.e., *app* is empty), the result is kept as it was. Otherwise, if the flag `speed-up` is true $\lambda^+_{TS(Post,P)}$ is used, as it is; otherwise, it is used to refine the value of the computed answer λ^s.

Applying assertion conditions bounds the extrapolation (widening) performed by `abs_generalize`, avoiding unnecessary precision losses. Note that the existence of guidance assertions for a predicate does not save having to analyze the code of the corresponding predicate if it is available, since otherwise any calls generated within that predicate would be omitted and not analyzed for, resulting in an incorrect analysis result.

4.2 Fundamental Properties of Analysis Guided by Assertions

We claim the following properties for analysis of a program P applying assertions as described in the previous sections. The inferred abstract execution states are covered by the call and (applicable) success assertion conditions.

Lemma 1. ***Applied call conditions.*** *Let* `calls`(H, Pre) *be an assertion condition from program* P, *and let* $\langle G, \lambda^c, \lambda^s \rangle$ *be a triple derived for* P *and initial queries* $\mathcal{Q}_\alpha$ *by* GUIDED_ANALYZE$(P, \mathcal{Q}_\alpha)$. *If* $G = \sigma(H)$ *for some renaming* σ *then* $\lambda^c \sqsubseteq \lambda^+_{TS(\sigma(Pre),P)}$.

Proof. Function `apply_call` obtains in λ^t the trusted value for the call. It restricts the encountered call λ^c or uses it as is, in any case $\lambda^c \sqsubseteq \lambda^t = \lambda^+_{TS(Pre,P)}$. Hence if this function is applied whenever inferred call patterns are introduced in the analysis results, the lemma will hold.

The lemma holds after initialization, since the function is applied before inserting the tuples in A. Now we reason about how the algorithm changes the results. The two spots in which analysis results are updated are in function `solve` (line 7 of Fig. 2) and in the body of the loop of the algorithm (line 14 of Fig. 4). Function `solve` adds tuples to the analysis whenever new encountered call patterns are found, it is called right after `apply_call`, therefore it only inserts call patterns taking into account calls conditions. The analysis updates made in the body of the loop do not insert new call patterns, only the recomputed success abstractions for those already present (previously collected in W), therefore all call patterns encountered are added taking into account the call conditions and the lemma holds. □

Lemma 2. ***Applied success conditions.*** *Let* success$(H, Pre, Post)$ *be an assertion condition from program P and let $\langle G, \lambda^c, \lambda^s\rangle$ be a triple derived for P with $\mathcal{Q}_\alpha$ initial queries by* GUIDED_ANALYZE$(P, \mathcal{Q}_\alpha)$. *If $G = \sigma(H)$ for some renaming σ then $\lambda^c \sqsubseteq \lambda^-_{TS(\sigma(Pre),P)} \Rightarrow \lambda^s \sqsubseteq \lambda^+_{TS(\sigma(Post),P)}$.*

Proof. Function `apply_succ` computes the $\sqcap$ of all applicable assertion conditions (checking $\lambda^c \sqsubseteq \lambda^-_{TS(Pre,P)}$), if existing. Since we make the $\sqcap$ of all applied conditions, $\lambda^s \sqsubseteq \bigsqcap \lambda^+_{TS(Post_i,P)} \sqsubseteq \lambda^+_{TS(Post,P)}$ for any *Post*. Hence if all results inserted in the analysis result have been previously processed by `apply_succ` the lemma holds. The lemma holds for the initialized results, because $\lambda^s = \bot \sqsubseteq \lambda^+_{TS(Post,P)}$ for any *Post*. Now we reason about how the algorithm changes the results. We have the same points in the algorithm that change the analysis result as in the proof of Lemma 1. The `solve` function initializes λ^s of the newly encountered calls with $\bot$, so it is the same situation as when initializing. In the body of the loop `apply_succ` is always called before updating the value in the result and the lemma holds. □

5 Checking Correctness in a Guided Analysis

We discuss how assertions may introduce errors in the analysis, depending on their status. `sample-check` assertions are not used by the analyzer. Any part of the execution stopped by them will conservatively be considered to continue, keeping the analysis safe. `check` assertions stop the execution of the program if the properties of the conditions are not met. Hence it is safe to narrow the analysis results using their information. Last, `trust` assertions are not considered during the concrete executions, so they may introduce errors. Such assertion conditions express correct properties if they comply with the following definitions:

Definition 6 (Correct call condition). *Let P be a program with an assertion condition $C =$* calls(H, Pre). *C is correct for a query $\mathcal{Q}$ to P if for any predicate descriptor G, s.t. $G = \sigma(H)$ for some renaming σ, $\forall \theta^c \in$ calling_context$(G, P, \mathcal{Q})$, $\theta^c \in \gamma(\lambda^+_{TS(\sigma(Pre),P)})$.*

Definition 7 (Correct success condition). *Let P be a program with an assertion condition $C =$* success$(H, Pre, Post)$. *C is correct for P if for any predicate descriptor G, s.t. $G = \sigma(H)$ for some renaming σ, $\theta^c \in \gamma(\lambda^-_{TS(\sigma(Pre),P)})$, $\theta^s \in answers(P, \{G : \theta^c\}) \Rightarrow \theta^s \in \gamma(\lambda^+_{TS(\sigma(Post),P)})$.*

Theorem 2. Correctness modulo assertions. *Let P be a program with* correct *assertion conditions C and $\mathcal{Q}_\alpha$ a set of initial abstract queries. Let $\mathcal{Q}$ be the set of concrete queries: $\mathcal{Q} = \{G:\theta \mid \theta \in \gamma(\lambda) \wedge G:\lambda \in \mathcal{Q}_\alpha\}$.*
The analysis result $A = \{\langle G_1, \lambda_1^c, \lambda_1^s\rangle, \ldots, \langle G_n, \lambda_n^c, \lambda_n^s\rangle\}$ computed with GUIDED_ANALYZE$(P, \mathcal{Q}_\alpha)$ *is* correct *(Definition 2) for $P, \mathcal{Q}$.*

Proof. For conciseness in the proof we omit the renaming part. Fixed program P, given an abstract description d from an assertion (*Pre* or *Post*), let $\lambda_d^- = \lambda_{TS(d,P)}^-, \lambda_d^+ = \lambda_{TS(d,P)}^+$. If there are no assertion conditions, the theorem trivially holds (Theorem 1). If assertion conditions are used to generalize, the theorem also holds because $\lambda^c = \lambda_{Pre}^+$ and $\lambda^s = \lambda_{Post}^+$ are by definition (Definition 6, Definition 7, respectively) correct over-approximations. If assertion conditions are used to regain precision:
Call: We want to prove that
$\forall G, \theta^c \in \mathit{calling\_context}(G, P, \mathcal{Q})\ \exists \langle G, \lambda^c, \lambda^s\rangle \in A$ s.t. $\theta^c \in \gamma(\lambda^c)$ (Definition 2).

We applied: $\texttt{calls}(G, \mathit{Pre})$

$$\theta^c \in \gamma(\lambda_{Pre}^+) \qquad \text{(by Definition 6)}$$
$$\text{In } E: \exists \langle G, \lambda_E^c, \lambda_E^s\rangle \in E, \theta^c \in \gamma(\lambda_E^c) \qquad \text{(by algorithm (Fig. 4 line 20))}$$
$$\text{Then: } \theta^c \in \gamma(\lambda_E^c) \cap \gamma(\lambda_{Pre}^+) \subseteq \gamma(\alpha(\gamma(\lambda_E^c) \cap \gamma(\lambda_{Pre}^+))) \subseteq \gamma(\lambda_E^c \sqcap \lambda_{Pre}^+)$$
$$\theta^c \in \gamma(\lambda_E^c \sqcap \lambda_{Pre}^+) = \gamma(\lambda^c) \qquad \text{(by algorithm (Fig. 5 line 3))}$$

Success: We want to prove that
$\forall \langle G, \lambda^c, \lambda^s\rangle \in A, \forall \theta^c \in \gamma(\lambda^c)$ if $\theta^s \in \mathit{answers}(P, \{G:\theta^c\})$ then $\theta^s \in \gamma(\lambda^s)$.

We applied: $\texttt{success}(G, \mathit{Pre}_i, \mathit{Post}_i)$

$$\lambda^c \sqsubseteq \lambda_{TS(Pre_i)}^- \implies \lambda^s \sqsubseteq \lambda_{Post_i}^+ \qquad \text{(by Lemma 2)}$$
$$\theta^c \in \gamma(\lambda_{Pre_i}^-), \theta^s \in \mathit{answers}(P, \{G:\theta^c\}) \implies \theta^s \in \lambda_{Post_i}^+$$
$$\text{(by Definition 7)}$$
$$\lambda^p = \bigsqcap \{\lambda_{Post}^+ \mid \texttt{success}(G, \mathit{Pre}, \mathit{Post}), \forall \theta^c \in \lambda^c, \theta^c \in \gamma(\lambda_{Pre}^-)\}$$
$$\theta^c \in \gamma(\lambda^c), \theta^s \in \mathit{answers}(P, \{G:\theta^c\}) \implies \theta^s \in \lambda^p$$
$$\exists \langle G, \lambda_E^c, \lambda_E^s\rangle \in E, \text{ s.t. } \lambda^c \sqsupseteq \gamma(\lambda_E^c) \qquad \text{(unrefined abstractions)}$$
$$\text{We have: } \theta^s \in \gamma(\lambda_E^s), \theta^s \in \gamma(\lambda^p)$$
$$\theta^s \in \gamma(\lambda_E^s) \cap \gamma(\lambda^p) \subseteq \gamma(\alpha(\gamma(\lambda_E^s) \cap \gamma(\lambda^p))) \subseteq \gamma(\lambda_E^s \sqcap \lambda^p)$$
$$\theta^s \in \gamma(\lambda_E^s \sqcap \lambda^p) = \gamma(\lambda^s)$$
□

In other words, Theorem 2 and Lemmas 1 and 2 ensure that correct assertion conditions bound imprecision in the result, without affecting correctness. By applying the assertion conditions no actual concrete states are removed from the abstractions.

We can identify suspicious pruning during analysis. Let λ^a be the correct approximation of a condition and λ be an inferred abstract state, typically a value in the tuples of E. If $\lambda \sqcap \lambda^a = \bot$ the inferred information is incompatible with that in the condition, therefore it is likely that the assertion is *erroneous*. $\lambda \not\sqsubseteq \lambda^a$ indicates that the algorithm inferred more concrete constraint states than described in the assertion and the analysis results may be wrong. These checks can be performed while the algorithm is run or off-line, by comparing the properties of the assertion conditions against the triples stored in E, which, as mentioned earlier, stores partial analysis results with no assertions applied. A full description of this checking procedure is described in [25,27].

6 Related Work

The inference of arbitrary semantic properties of programs is known to be both undecidable and expensive, requiring user interaction in many realistic settings. Abstract interpreters allow the **selection of different domains and parameters for such domains** (e.g., polyhedra, octagons, regtypes with depth-k, etc.), as well as their widening operations (e.g., type shortening, structural widening, etc.). Other parameters include policies for partial evaluation and other transformations (loop unrolling, inlining, slicing, etc.). These parameters are orthogonal or complementary to the issues discussed in this paper. To the extent of our knowledge the use of **program-level annotations** (such as assertions) to guide abstract interpretation has not been widely studied in the literature, contrary to their (necessary) use in verification and theorem proving approaches. The **Cibai** [18] system includes *trust-style* annotations while sources are processed to encode some predefined runtime semantics. In [10] analysis is guided by modifying the analyzed program to restrict some of its behaviors. However, this guidance affects the *order of program state exploration*, rather the analysis results, as in our case. As mentioned in the introduction, the closest to our approach is **Astrée**, that allows *assert*-like statements, where correctness of the analysis is ensured by the presence of compulsory runtime checks, and trusted (*known facts*) asserts. These refine and guide analysis operations at program points. Like in CiaoPP, the analyzer shows errors if a known fact can be falsified statically. However, as with the corresponding Ciao assertions, while there has been some examples of use [8], there has been no detailed description of how such assertions are handled in the fixpoint algorithm. We argue that this paper contributes in this direction.

7 Conclusions

We have proposed a user-guided multivariant fixpoint algorithm that makes use of check and trust assertion information, and we have provided formal results on the influence of such assertions on correctness and efficiency. We have extended the semantics of the guidance (and all) assertions to deal with both the cases in which the program execution will and will not incorporate run-time tests for unverified assertions, as well as the cases in which the assertions are intended for refining the information or instead to lose precision in order to gain efficiency.

We show that these annotations are not only useful when dealing with incomplete code but also provide the analyzer with recursion/loop invariants for speeding up global convergence.

References

1. Bagnara, R., Hill, P.M., Zaffanella, E.: Widening operators for powerset domains. In: Steffen, B., Levi, G. (eds.) VMCAI 2004. LNCS, vol. 2937, pp. 135–148. Springer, Heidelberg (2004). https://doi.org/10.1007/978-3-540-24622-0_13
2. Bjørner, N., Gurfinkel, A., McMillan, K., Rybalchenko, A.: Horn clause solvers for program verification. In: Beklemishev, L.D., Blass, A., Dershowitz, N., Finkbeiner, B., Schulte, W. (eds.) Fields of Logic and Computation II. LNCS, vol. 9300, pp. 24–51. Springer, Cham (2015). https://doi.org/10.1007/978-3-319-23534-9_2
3. Bourdoncle, F.: Interprocedural abstract interpretation of block structured languages with nested procedures, aliasing and recursivity. In: Deransart, P., Maluszyński, J. (eds.) PLILP 1990. LNCS, vol. 456, pp. 307–323. Springer, Heidelberg (1990). https://doi.org/10.1007/BFb0024192
4. Bruynooghe, M.: A practical framework for the abstract interpretation of logic programs. J. Logic Program. **10**, 91–124 (1991)
5. Bueno, F., Cabeza, D., Hermenegildo, M., Puebla, G.: Global analysis of standard Prolog programs. In: Nielson, H.R. (ed.) ESOP 1996. LNCS, vol. 1058, pp. 108–124. Springer, Heidelberg (1996). https://doi.org/10.1007/3-540-61055-3_32
6. Cousot, P., Cousot, R.: Abstract interpretation: a unified lattice model for static analysis of programs by construction or approximation of fixpoints. In: Proceedings of POPL 1977, pp. 238–252. ACM Press (1977)
7. Cousot, P., Cousot, R., Feret, J., Mauborgne, L., Miné, A., Monniaux, D., Rival, X.: The ASTREÉ analyzer. In: Sagiv, M. (ed.) ESOP 2005. LNCS, vol. 3444, pp. 21–30. Springer, Heidelberg (2005). https://doi.org/10.1007/978-3-540-31987-0_3
8. Delmas, D., Souyris, J.: Astrée: from research to industry. In: Nielson, H.R., Filé, G. (eds.) SAS 2007. LNCS, vol. 4634, pp. 437–451. Springer, Heidelberg (2007). https://doi.org/10.1007/978-3-540-74061-2_27
9. Gómez-Zamalloa, M., Albert, E., Puebla, G.: Modular decompilation of low-level code by partial evaluation. In: SCAM, pp. 239–248. IEEE Computer Society (2008)
10. Gopan, D., Reps, T.: Guided static analysis. In: Nielson, H.R., Filé, G. (eds.) SAS 2007. LNCS, vol. 4634, pp. 349–365. Springer, Heidelberg (2007). https://doi.org/10.1007/978-3-540-74061-2_22
11. Gurfinkel, A., Kahsai, T., Komuravelli, A., Navas, J.A.: The SeaHorn verification framework. In: Kroening, D., Păsăreanu, C.S. (eds.) CAV 2015. LNCS, vol. 9206, pp. 343–361. Springer, Cham (2015). https://doi.org/10.1007/978-3-319-21690-4_20
12. Henriksen, K.S., Gallagher, J.P.: Abstract interpretation of PIC programs through logic programming. In: SCAM, pp. 184–196. IEEE Computer Society (2006)
13. Hermenegildo, M., Puebla, G., Bueno, F., García, P.L.: Integrated program debugging, verification, and optimization using abstract interpretation (and the Ciao system preprocessor). Sci. Comp. Progr. **58**(1–2), 115–140 (2005)
14. Hermenegildo, M., Puebla, G., Bueno, F.: Using global analysis, partial specifications, and an extensible assertion language for program validation and debugging. In: Apt, K.R., Marek, V.W., Truszczynski, M., Warren, D.S. (eds.) The Logic Programming Paradigm. Artificial Intelligence, pp. 161–192. Springer, Heidelberg (1999). https://doi.org/10.1007/978-3-642-60085-2_7

15. Kelly, A., Marriott, K., Søndergaard, H., Stuckey, P.: A generic object oriented incremental analyser for constraint logic programs. In: ACSC, pp. 92–101 (1997)
16. Klemen, M., Stulova, N., Lopez-Garcia, P., Morales, J.F., Hermenegildo, M.V.: Static performance guarantees for programs with run-time checks. In: PPDP. ACM Press (2018)
17. Liqat, U., et al.: Energy consumption analysis of programs based on XMOS ISA-level models. In: Gupta, G., Peña, R. (eds.) LOPSTR 2013. LNCS, vol. 8901, pp. 72–90. Springer, Cham (2014). https://doi.org/10.1007/978-3-319-14125-1_5
18. Logozzo, F.: Cibai: an abstract interpretation-based static analyzer for modular analysis and verification of Java classes. In: Cook, B., Podelski, A. (eds.) VMCAI 2007. LNCS, vol. 4349, pp. 283–298. Springer, Heidelberg (2007). https://doi.org/10.1007/978-3-540-69738-1_21
19. Marriott, K., Stuckey, P.J.: Programming with Constraints: An Introduction. MIT Press, Cambridge (1998)
20. Méndez-Lojo, M., Navas, J., Hermenegildo, M.V.: A flexible, (C)LP-based approach to the analysis of object-oriented programs. In: King, A. (ed.) LOPSTR 2007. LNCS, vol. 4915, pp. 154–168. Springer, Heidelberg (2008). https://doi.org/10.1007/978-3-540-78769-3_11
21. Muthukumar, K., Hermenegildo, M.: Determination of variable dependence information at compile-time through abstract interpretation. In: NACLP 1989, pp. 166–189. MIT Press, October 1989
22. Muthukumar, K., Hermenegildo, M.: Compile-time derivation of variable dependency using abstract interpretation. JLP **13**(2/3), 315–347 (1992)
23. Navas, J., Méndez-Lojo, M., Hermenegildo, M.V.: User-definable resource usage bounds analysis for Java bytecode. In: BYTECODE 2009. ENTCS, vol. 253, pp. 6–86. Elsevier, March 2009
24. Puebla, G., Bueno, F., Hermenegildo, M.: An assertion language for constraint logic programs. In: Deransart, P., Hermenegildo, M.V., Małuszynski, J. (eds.) Analysis and Visualization Tools for Constraint Programming. LNCS, vol. 1870, pp. 23–61. Springer, Heidelberg (2000). https://doi.org/10.1007/10722311_2
25. Puebla, G., Bueno, F., Hermenegildo, M.: Combined static and dynamic assertion-based debugging of constraint logic programs. In: Bossi, A. (ed.) LOPSTR 1999. LNCS, vol. 1817, pp. 273–292. Springer, Heidelberg (2000). https://doi.org/10.1007/10720327_16
26. Puebla, G., Hermenegildo, M.: Optimized algorithms for incremental analysis of logic programs. In: Cousot, R., Schmidt, D.A. (eds.) SAS 1996. LNCS, vol. 1145, pp. 270–284. Springer, Heidelberg (1996). https://doi.org/10.1007/3-540-61739-6_47
27. Stulova, N., Morales, J.F., Hermenegildo, M.V.: Some trade-offs in reducing the overhead of assertion run-time checks via static analysis. Sci. Comput. Program. **155**, 3–26 (2018)
28. Vaucheret, C., Bueno, F.: More precise yet efficient type inference for logic programs. In: Hermenegildo, M.V., Puebla, G. (eds.) SAS 2002. LNCS, vol. 2477, pp. 102–116. Springer, Heidelberg (2002). https://doi.org/10.1007/3-540-45789-5_10
29. Zaffanella, E., Bagnara, R., Hill, P.M.: Widening sharing. In: Nadathur, G. (ed.) PPDP 1999. LNCS, vol. 1702, pp. 414–431. Springer, Heidelberg (1999). https://doi.org/10.1007/10704567_25

Author Index

Printed in the United States
By Bookmasters